Sport Management

Now available in a fully revised and updated fourth edition, *Sport Management: Principles and applications* introduces the sport industry and examines the role of the state, non-profit and professional sectors in sport. It focuses on core management principles and their application in a sporting context, highlighting the unique challenges faced in a career in sport management.

Written in an engaging and accessible style, each chapter has a clear structure designed to make key information and concepts simple to find and to utilize. Chapters contain a conceptual overview, references, further reading, links to important websites, study questions and up-to-date case studies from around the world to show how theory works in the real world, and a companion website offers additional activities for students and guidance notes and slides for instructors. The book covers every core functional area of management, including:

- strategic planning
- organizational culture
- organizational structures
- human resource management
- leadership
- governance
- financial management
- marketing
- performance management.

This fourth edition also includes expanded coverage of sport media, change management and other contemporary management issues, providing a comprehensive introduction to the practical application of management principles within sport organizations. It is ideal for first and second year students on sport management-related courses, as well as those studying business-focussed or human movement courses seeking an overview of applied sport management principles.

Russell Hoye is Professor of Sport Management and Director, Centre for Sport and Social Impact at La Trobe University, Australia. He is the editor of the Sport Management Series published by Routledge, a member of the editorial board for *Sport Management Review* and the *International Journal of Sport Policy and Politics*, past President of the

Sport Management Association of Australia and New Zealand (SMAANZ), and a graduate of the Australian Institute of Company Directors.

Aaron C.T. Smith is Professor in the Graduate School of Business and Law at RMIT University, Melbourne, Australia. Aaron has research interests in the management of psychological, organizational and policy change in business, and sport and health. In recent times he has focussed on the impact of commercial and global sport policy, the ways in which internal cultures shape organizational conduct, the role of social forces in managing change, and the management of social policy change such as those associated with health and drug use.

Matthew Nicholson is an Associate Professor in the Centre for Sport and Social Impact at La Trobe University, Australia. His research interests focus on sport policy and development, the contribution of sport to social capital and the relationship between sport and the media.

Bob Stewart is Associate Professor of Sport Studies at Victoria University, Australia. Bob has been teaching and researching the field of sport management and sport policy for 15 years, and is currently working with the University's College of Sport and Exercise Science, and Institute of Sport, Exercise and Active Living. Bob has a special interest in cartel structures, social control, and player regulation in elite sports, and the ways in which neo-liberal ideologies shape sport's governance and management practices.

http://www.routledge.com/cw/hoye/

Sport Management Series

Series Editor: Russell Hoye, La Trobe University, Australia

This **Sport Management Series** has been providing a range of texts for core subjects in undergraduate sport business and management courses around the world for more than 10 years. These textbooks are considered essential resources for academics, students and managers seeking an international perspective on the management of the complex world of sport.

Many millions of people around the globe are employed in sport organizations in areas as diverse as event management, broadcasting, venue management, marketing, professional sport, community and collegiate sport, and coaching, as well as in allied industries such as sporting equipment manufacturing, sporting footwear and apparel, and retail.

At the elite level, sport has moved from being an amateur pastime to one of the world's most significant industries. The growth and professionalization of sport has driven changes in the consumption and production of sport and in the management of sporting organizations at all levels.

Managing sport organizations at the start of the twenty-first century involves the application of techniques and strategies evident in leading business, government and nonprofit organizations. This series explains these concepts and applies them to the diverse global sport industry.

To support their use by academics, each text is supported by current case studies, targeted study questions, further reading lists, links to relevant web-based resources, and supplementary online materials such as case study questions and classroom presentation aids.

Available in this series:

Sport and Policy
Russell Hoye, Matthew Nicholson and Barrie Houlihan

Sports Economics
Paul Downward, Alistair Dawson and Trudo Dejonghe

Sport and the Media
Matthew Nicholson

Sport Governance
Russell Hoye and Graham Cuskelly

Sport Funding and Finance (Second edition)
Bob Stewart

Managing People in Sport Organizations
A strategic human resource management perspective (Second edition)
Tracy Taylor, Alison Doherty and Peter McGraw

Introduction to Sport Marketing (Second edition)
Aaron C.T. Smith and Bob Stewart

Sport Management
Principles and applications (Fourth edition)
Russell Hoye, Aaron C.T. Smith, Matthew Nicholson and Bob Stewart

Sport Management
Principles and applications

FOURTH EDITION

**Russell Hoye, Aaron C.T. Smith,
Matthew Nicholson and
Bob Stewart**

Routledge
Taylor & Francis Group

LONDON AND NEW YORK

First published 2005
by Butterworth-Heinemann, an imprint of Elsevier

This edition published 2015
by Routledge
2 Park Square, Milton Park, Abingdon, Oxon OX14 4RN

and by Routledge
711 Third Avenue, New York, NY 10017

Routledge is an imprint of the Taylor & Francis Group, an informa business

British Library Cataloguing-in-Publication Data
A catalogue record for this book is available from the British Library

Library of Congress Cataloging in Publication Data
A catalog record has been requested for this book

ISBN: 978-1-138-83959-5 (hbk)
ISBN: 978-1-138-83960-1 (pbk)
ISBN: 978-1-315-73337-1 (ebk)

Typeset in Berling and Futura
by Saxon Graphics Ltd, Derby

Contents

Part II: Sport management principles   **85**

Preface

This fourth edition of *Sport Management: Principles and applications* continues to fill the gap for an introductory text in sport management that provides an appropriate balance between management theory and contextual analysis of the sport industry. The success of the first three editions, as illustrated by its adoption in many educational institutions across Australia, Canada, New Zealand, the United Kingdom and Europe, and being reprinted in five other languages, shows that we have the balance right. As with the original text, our intention with this edition is not to replace the many very good introductory texts on management theory, or to ignore the increasing volume of books that examine the international sport industry. Our aim is to provide a textbook that includes sufficient conceptual detail for students to grasp the essentials of management, while highlighting the unique aspects of sport management across the globe.

The book provides a comprehensive introduction to the principles of management and their practical application to sport organizations operating at the community, state/ provincial, national and professional levels. The book is primarily written for first and second year university students studying sport management courses and students who wish to research the nonprofit, government and commercial dimensions of sport. It is especially suitable for students studying sport management within business-focussed courses, as well as students seeking an overview of sport management principles within human movement, sport science or physical education courses.

As with the first three editions, the book is divided into two parts. Part I provides a concise analysis of the evolution of sport, the unique features of sport and sport management, the current drivers of change in the sport industry, and the role of the state, nonprofit and professional sectors of sport. Part II covers core management principles and their application in sport, highlighting the unique features of how sport is managed compared to other industrial sectors with chapters on strategic management, organizational structure, human resource management, leadership, organizational culture, financial management, marketing, sport and the media, governance, and performance management.

To assist lecturers and instructors, all chapters include an overview, a set of objectives, a summary of core principles, a set of review questions, suggestions for further reading, and a list of relevant websites for further information. In addition, Chapters 2 to 14 each contain three or four substantial examples we have dubbed 'In Practice' that help illustrate concepts and accepted practice at the community, state/provincial, national and international levels of sport. The majority of these have been completely rewritten with new examples, and the remainder extensively revised with up-to-date information.

We have also written thirteen entirely new Case Studies for Chapters 2 to 14, in addition to revising and updating the cases from the third edition, which can be used by lecturers and instructors for classroom discussion or assessment. For those academics who prescribe the book as essential reading for students, a comprehensive website is available that contains:

- an updated set of PowerPoint slides that summarize each chapter;
- teaching notes to accompany each of the case studies to guide instructors in their use for in-class activities or assessment tasks;
- updated tutorial activities to accompany each chapter; and
- a testbank of questions for use in online learning environments.

We would like to thank our colleagues and students for their valuable comments on the first three editions of the book and the valuable anonymous reviews provided on those editions. It would be remiss of us not to mention the great assistance of Simon Whitmore, our editor, and Will Bailey for his patience during the production process. As always we acknowledge and thank our respective partners and families for understanding our need to devote our time and energy to this fourth edition.

Russell Hoye
Aaron Smith
Matthew Nicholson
Bob Stewart

Figures and tables

FIGURES

TABLES

In Practice examples and Case Studies

IN PRACTICE EXAMPLES

CASE STUDIES

PART I

The sport management environment

CHAPTER 1

Sport management

OVERVIEW

This chapter provides a brief review of the development of sport into a major sector of economic and social activity and outlines the importance of sport management as a field of study. It discusses the unique nature of sport and the drivers of change that affect how sport is produced and consumed. A model that explains the public, nonprofit and professional elements of sport is presented, along with a brief description of the salient aspects of the management context for sport organizations. The chapter also serves as an introduction to the remaining sections of the book, highlighting the importance of each of the topics.

After completing this chapter the reader should be able to:

- describe the unique features of sport;
- understand the environment in which sport organizations operate;
- describe the three sectors of the sport industry; and
- explain how sport management is different to other fields of management study.

WHAT IS SPORT MANAGEMENT?

Sport employs many millions of people around the globe, is played or watched by the majority of the world's population, and, at the elite or professional level, has moved from being an amateur pastime to a significant industry. The growth and professionalization of sport has driven changes in the consumption, production and management of sporting events and organizations at all levels of sport. Countries with emerging economies such as Brazil, hosts of the 2014 World Cup for football and the 2016 Olympic Games, increasingly see sport as a vehicle for driving investment in infrastructure, for promoting their country to the world to stimulate trade, tourism and investment, and for stimulating national pride amongst their citizens.

Managing sport organizations at the start of the twenty-first century involves the application of techniques and strategies evident in the majority of modern business, government and nonprofit organizations. Sport managers engage in strategic planning, manage large numbers of paid and voluntary human resources, deal with broadcasting contracts worth billions of dollars, manage the welfare of elite athletes who sometimes earn 100 times the average working wage, and work within highly integrated global networks of international sports federations, national sport organizations, government agencies, media corporations, sponsors and community organizations.

Students seeking a career as a sport manager need to develop an understanding of the special features of sport and its allied industries, the environment in which sport organizations operate, and the types of sport organizations that operate in the public, nonprofit and professional sectors of the sport industry. The remainder of the chapter is devoted to a discussion of these points and highlights the unique aspects of sport organization management.

UNIQUE FEATURES OF SPORT

Smith and Stewart (2010) provide a list of ten unique features of sport which can assist us to understand why the management of sport organizations requires the application of specific management techniques. A unique feature of sport is the phenomenon of people developing irrational passions for sporting teams, competitions, or athletes. Sport has a symbolic significance in relation to performance outcomes, success and celebrating achievement that does not occur in other areas of economic and social activity. Sport managers must learn to harness these passions by appealing to people's desire to buy tickets for events, become a member of a club, donate time to help run a voluntary association, or purchase sporting merchandise. They must also learn to apply clear business logic and management techniques to the maintenance of traditions and connections to the nostalgic aspects of sport consumption and engagement.

There are also marked differences between sport organizations and other businesses in how they evaluate performance. Private or publicly listed companies exist to make profits and increase the wealth of shareholders or owners, whereas in sport, other imperatives such as winning championships, delivering services to stakeholders and members, or meeting community service obligations may take precedence over financial outcomes. Sport managers need to be cognizant of these multiple organizational outcomes, while at the same time being responsible financial managers to ensure they have the requisite resources to support their organization's strategic objectives.

Competitive balance is also a unique feature of the interdependent nature of relationships between sporting organizations that compete on the field but cooperate off the field to ensure the long-term viability of both clubs and their league. In most business environments the aim is to secure the largest market share, defeat all competitors and secure a monopoly. In sport leagues, clubs and teams need the opposition to remain in business, so they must cooperate to share revenues and playing talent, and regulate themselves to maximize the level of uncertainty in the outcome of games between them, so that fans' interest will be maintained. In some ways such behaviour could be construed as anti-competitive but governments support such actions due to the unique aspects of sport.

The sport product, when it takes the form of a game or contest, is also of variable quality. Game outcomes are generally uncertain, one team might dominate, which will diminish the attractiveness of the game. The perception of those watching the game might be that the quality has also diminished as a result, particularly if it is your team that loses! The variable quality of sport therefore makes it hard to guarantee quality in the marketplace relative to providers of other consumer products such as mobile phones, cars or other general household goods.

Sport also enjoys a high degree of product or brand loyalty, with fans unlikely to change the team or club they support or to switch sporting codes because of a poor match result, or the standard of officiating. Consumers of household products have a huge range to choose from and will readily switch brands for reasons of price or quality, whereas sporting competitions are hard to substitute. This advantage is also a negative, as sporting codes that wish to expand market share find it difficult to attract new fans from other codes due to their familiarity with the customs and traditions of their existing sport affiliation.

Sport engenders unique behaviours in people, such as emulating their sporting heroes in play, wearing the uniform of their favourite player, or purchasing the products that sporting celebrities endorse. This vicarious identification with the skills, abilities and lifestyles of sports people can be used by sport managers and allied industries to influence the purchasing decisions of individuals who follow sport.

Sport fans also exhibit a high degree of optimism, at times insisting that their team, despite a string of bad losses, is only a week, game or lucky break away from winning the next championship. It could also be argued that the owners or managers of sport franchises exhibit a high degree of optimism by toting their star recruits or new coach as the path to delivering them on-field success.

Sporting organizations, argue Smith and Stewart (2010), are relatively reluctant to adopt new technologies unless they are related to sports science, where on-field performance improvements are possible. In this regard sport organizations can be considered conservative, and tied to traditions and behaviours more than other organizations.

The final unique aspect of sport is its limited availability. In other industries, organizations can increase production to meet demand, but in sport, clubs are limited by season length and the number of scheduled games. This constrains their ability to maximize revenue through ticket sales and associated income. The implication for sport managers is that they must understand the nature of their business, the level of demand for their product and services (whatever form that may take), and the appropriate time to deliver them.

Collectively, these unique features of sport create some challenges for managers of sport organizations and events. It is important to understand the effects of these features on the management approaches and strategies used by sport managers; the next section explains how these unique features of sport influence the operating environment for sport organizations and their managers.

SPORT MANAGEMENT ENVIRONMENT

Globalization has been a major force in driving change in the ways sport is produced and consumed. The enhanced integration of the world's economies has enabled communication to occur between producers and consumers at greater speed and variety, and sport has been one sector to reap the benefits. Consumers of elite sport events and competitions such as the Olympic Games, World Cups for rugby, cricket and football, English Premier League Football, the National Basketball Association (NBA), and Grand Slam tournaments for tennis and golf enjoy unprecedented access through mainstream and social media. Aside from actually attending the events live at a stadium or venue, fans can view these events through free-to-air and pay or cable television; listen to them on radio and the internet; read about game analyses, their favourite players and teams through newspapers and magazines in both print and digital editions; receive progress scores, commentary or vision on their mobile phones or tablets through websites or social media platforms such as Twitter; and sign up for special deals and information through online subscriptions using their email address or preferred social media platform. The global sport marketplace has become very crowded and sport managers seeking to carve out a niche need to understand the global environment in which they must operate. Thus, one of the themes of this book is the impact of globalization on the ways sport is produced, consumed and managed.

Most national governments view sport as a vehicle for nationalism, economic development, or social development. As such, they consider it their role to enact policies and legislation to support, control or regulate the activities of sport organizations. Most national governments support elite training institutes to assist in developing athletes for national and international competition, provide funding to national sporting organizations to deliver high performance and community level programs, support sport organizations to bid for major events, and facilitate the building of major stadiums. In return for this support, governments can influence sports to recruit more mass participants, provide services to discrete sectors of the community, or have sports enact policies on alcohol and drug use, gambling, and general health promotion messages. Governments also regulate the activities of sport organizations through legislation or licensing in areas such as industrial relations, anti-discrimination, taxation and corporate governance. A further theme in the book is the impact that government policy, funding and regulation can have on the way sport is produced, consumed and managed.

The management of sport organizations has undergone a relatively rapid period of professionalization since the 1980s. The general expansion of the global sports industry and commercialization of sport events and competitions, combined with the introduction of paid staff into voluntary governance structures and the growing number of people who now earn a living managing sport organizations or playing sport, has forced sport organizations and their managers to become more professional. This is reflected in the increased number of university sport management courses, the requirement to have business skills as well as industry specific knowledge or experience to be successful in sport management, the growth of professional and academic associations devoted to sport management, and the variety of professionals and specialists that sport managers must deal with in the course of their careers. Sport managers will work with accountants, lawyers, human resource managers, taxation specialists, government policy advisors, project management personnel, architects, market researchers and media specialists, not to mention sports agents, sports scientists, coaches, officials and volunteers. The ensuing chapters of the book will highlight the ongoing professionalization of sport management as an academic discipline and a career.

The final theme of the book is the notion that changes in sport management frequently result from developments in technology. Changes in telecommunications have already been highlighted, but further changes in technology are evident in areas such as performance enhancing drugs, information technology, coaching and high performance techniques, sports venues, sport betting and wagering, and sporting equipment. These changes have forced sport managers to develop policies about their use, to protect intellectual property with a marketable value, and generally adapt their operations to incorporate their use for achieving organizational objectives. Sport managers need to understand the potential of technological development but also the likely impact on future operations.

THREE SECTORS OF SPORT

In order to make sense of the many organizations that are involved in sport management, and how these organizations may form partnerships, influence each others' operations and conduct business, it is useful to see sport as comprising three distinct sectors. The first is the state or public sector, which includes national, state/provincial, regional and local governments, and specialist agencies that develop sport policy, provide funding to other sectors, and support specialist roles such as elite athlete development or drug control. The second is the nonprofit or voluntary sector, made up of community based clubs, governing associations and international sport organizations that provide competition and participation opportunities, regulate and manage sporting codes, and organize major championship events. The third sector is professional or commercial sport organizations, comprising professional leagues and their member teams, as well as allied organizations such as sporting apparel and equipment manufacturers, media companies, major stadium operators and event managers.

These three sectors do not operate in isolation, and in many cases there is significant overlap. For example, the state is intimately involved in providing funding to nonprofit sport organizations for sport development and elite athlete programs, and in return nonprofit sport organizations provide the general community with sporting opportunities and as well as developing athletes, coaches, officials and administrators to sustain sporting participation. The state is also involved in commercial sport, supporting the building of major stadiums and other sporting venues to provide spaces for professional sport to be played, providing a regulatory and legal framework for professional sport to take place and supporting manufacturing and event organizations to do business. The nonprofit sport sector supports professional sport by providing playing talent for leagues, as well as developing the coaches, officials and administrators to facilitate elite competitions. Indeed, in some cases the sport league itself will consist of member teams which are technically nonprofit entities, even though they support a pool of professional managers and players. In return, the professional sport sector markets sport for spectators and participants and in some cases provides substantial funds from TV broadcast rights revenue. Figure 1.1 illustrates the three sectors and the intersections where these relationships take place.

WHAT IS DIFFERENT ABOUT SPORT MANAGEMENT?

Sport managers utilize management techniques and theories that are similar to managers of other organizations, such as hospitals, government departments, banks, mining companies, car manufacturers, and welfare agencies. However, there are some aspects of strategic management, organizational structure, human resource management, leadership, organizational culture, financial management, marketing, governance and performance management that are unique to the management of sport organizations.

Strategic management

Strategic management involves the analysis of an organization's position in the competitive environment, the determination of its direction and goals, the selection of an appropriate strategy and the leveraging of its distinctive assets. The success of any sport organization may largely depend on the quality of their strategic decisions. It could be argued that nonprofit sport organizations have been slow to embrace the concepts associated with strategic management because sport is inherently turbulent, with on-field performance and tactics tending to dominate and distract sport managers from the choices they need to make in the office and boardroom. In a competitive market, sport managers must drive their own futures by undertaking meaningful market analyses, establishing a clear

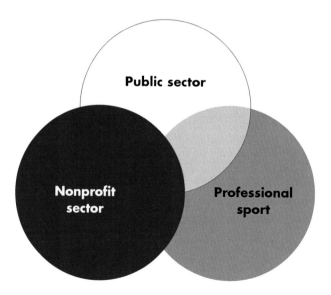

FIGURE 1.1 Three sector model of sport

direction and crafting strategy that matches opportunities. An understanding of strategic management principles and how these can be applied in the specific industry context of sport are essential for future sport managers.

Organizational structure

An organization's structure is important because it defines where staff and volunteers 'fit in' with each other in terms of work tasks, decision-making procedures, the need for collaboration, levels of responsibility and reporting mechanisms. Finding the right structure for a sport organization involves balancing the need to formalize procedures while fostering innovation and creativity, and ensuring adequate control of employee and volunteer activities without unduly affecting people's motivation and attitudes to work. In the complex world of sport, clarifying reporting and communication lines between multiple groups of internal and external stakeholders while trying to reduce unnecessary and costly layers of management, is also an important aspect of managing an organization's structure. The relatively unique mix of paid staff and volunteers in the sport industry adds a layer of complexity to managing the structure of many sport organizations.

Human resource management

Human resource management, in mainstream business or sport organizations, is essentially about ensuring an effective and satisfied workforce. However, the sheer size of some sport organizations, as well as the difficulties in managing a mix of volunteers and paid staff in the sport industry, make human resource management a complex issue for sport managers. Successful sport leagues, clubs, associations, retailers and venues rely on good human resources, both on and off the field. Human resource management cannot be divorced from other key management tools, such as strategic planning or managing organizational culture and structure, and is a further element that students of sport management need to understand to be effective practitioners.

Leadership

Managers at the helm of sport organizations need to be able to influence others to follow their visions, empower individuals to feel part of a team working for a common goal, and be adept at working with leaders of other sport organizations to forge alliances, deal with conflicts or coordinate common business or development projects. The sport industry thrives on organizations having leaders who are able to collaborate effectively with other organizations to run a professional league, work with governing bodies of sport, and coordinate the efforts of government agencies, international and national sport organizations, and other groups to deliver large-scale sport events. Sport management students wishing to work in leadership roles need to understand the ways in which leadership skills can be developed and how these principles can be applied.

Organizational culture

Organizational culture consists of the assumptions, norms and values held by individuals and groups within an organization, which impact upon the activities and goals in the workplace and in many ways influences how employees work. Organizational culture is related to organizational performance, excellence, employee commitment, cooperation, efficiency, job performance and decision-making. However, how organizational culture can be defined, diagnosed and changed is subject to much debate in the business and academic world. Due to the strong traditions of sporting endeavour and behaviour, managers of sport organizations, particularly those such as professional sport franchises or traditional sports, must be cognizant of the power of organizational culture as both an inhibitor and driver of performance. Understanding how to identify, describe, analyse and ultimately influence the culture of a sport organization is an important element in the education of sport managers.

Financial management

Financial management in sport involves the application of accounting and financial decision-making processes to the relatively unique revenue streams and costs associated with sport organizations. It is important for sport managers to understand the financial management principles associated with membership income, ticketing and merchandise sales, sports betting income, sponsorship, broadcast rights fees, and government grants and subsidies. Sport managers also need to understand the history of the commercial development of sport and the ways in which sport is likely to be funded and financed in the future, in particular the move to private ownership of sport teams and leagues, sport clubs being listed on the stock exchange, greater reliance on debt finance, and public–private partnerships.

Sport marketing

Sport marketing is the application of marketing concepts to sport products and services, and the marketing of non-sports products through an association with sport. Like other forms of marketing, sport marketing seeks to fulfil the needs and wants of consumers. It achieves this by providing sport services and sport-related products to consumers. However, sport marketing is unlike conventional marketing in that it also has the ability to encourage the consumption of non-sport products and services by association. It is important to understand that sport marketing means the marketing of sport as well as the use of sport as a tool to market other products and services.

Sport and the media

The relationship between sport and the media is the defining commercial connection for both industries at the beginning of the twenty-first century and at the elite and professional levels sport is becoming increasingly dependent on the media for its commercial success. Managers of professional or commercial sport organizations and events need an understanding of the structure of the sport broadcast industry, the implications of media diversity and convergence, the valuation of media rights, and the restrictions that government policy and regulation has in some cases. The explosion in the use of social media platforms by consumers demands that sport managers know how to use these platforms to communicate, engage and ultimately influence consumer decisions in relation to their product, service or brand.

Governance

Organizational governance involves the exercise of decision-making power within organizations and provides the system by which the elements of organizations are controlled and directed. Governance is a particularly important element of managing sport organizations, many of whom are controlled by elected groups of volunteers, as it deals with issues of policy and direction for the enhancement of organizational performance rather than day-to-day operational management decision-making. Appropriate governance systems help ensure that elected decision-makers and paid staff seek to deliver outcomes for the benefit of the organization and its members and that the means used to attain these outcomes are effectively monitored. As many sport managers work in an environment where they must report to a governing board, it is important that they understand the principles of good governance and how these are applied in sport organizations.

Performance management

Sport organizations over the last 30 years have undergone an evolution to become more professionally structured and managed. Sport organizations have applied business principles to marketing their products, planning their operations, managing their human resource and other aspects of organizational activity. The unique nature of sport organizations and the variation in missions and purposes has led to the development of a variety of criteria with which to assess the performance of sport organizations. Sport management students need to understand the ways in which organizational performance can be conceptualized, analysed and reported and how these principles can be applied in the sport industry.

SUMMARY

Sport has a number of unique features:

- people develop irrational passions;
- differences in judging performance;
- the interdependent nature of relationships between sporting organizations;
- anti-competitive behaviour;
- sport product (a game or contest) is of variable quality;
- it enjoys a high degree of product or brand loyalty;
- it engenders vicarious identification;

- sport fans exhibit a high degree of optimism;
- sport organizations are relatively reluctant adopt new technology; and
- sport often has a limited supply.

Several environmental factors influence the way sport organizations operate, namely globalization, government policy, professionalization, and technological developments.

The sport industry can be defined as comprising three distinct but interrelated industries: The state or public sector, the nonprofit or voluntary sector, and the professional or commercial sector. These sectors do not operate in isolation and often engage in a range of collaborative projects, funding arrangements, joint commercial ventures and other business relationships.

There are some aspects of strategic management, organizational structure, human resource management, leadership, organizational culture, financial management, marketing, the relationship between sport and the media, governance and performance management that are unique to the management of sport organizations. The remainder of the book explores the three sectors of the sport industry and examines each of these core management issues in more detail.

REVIEW QUESTIONS

1 Define sport management.

2 What are the unique features of sport?

3 Describe the main elements of the environment that affect sport organizations.

4 What sort of relationships might develop between sport organizations in the public and nonprofit sectors?

5 What sort of relationships might develop between sport organizations in the public and professional sport sectors?

6 What sort of relationships might develop between sport organizations in the professional and nonprofit sectors?

7 Explain the major differences between managing a sport organization and a commercial manufacturing firm.

8 Why does the sport industry need specialist managers with tertiary sport management qualifications?

9 Identify one organization from each of the public, nonprofit and professional sport sectors. Compare how the environmental factors discussed in this chapter can affect their operation.

10 Discuss whether the special features of sport discussed in this chapter apply to all levels of sport by comparing the operation of a professional sports league, an elite government sport institute and a community sport club.

FURTHER READING

Fort, R. (2011). *Sport Economics.* 3rd Edition. Upper Saddle River, NJ: Prentice Hall/
Pearson.
Hoye, R., Nicholson, M. & Houlihan, B. (2010). *Sport and Policy: Issues and Analysis.*
Oxford, UK: Elsevier/Butterworth Heinemann.
Hoye, R., Nicholson, M. & Smith, A. (2008). Unique aspects of managing sport
organizations. In C. Wankel (ed.), *21st Century Management: A Reference Handbook.*
Thousand Oaks, CA: Sage, pp. 499–507.
Jarvie, G. (2013). *Sport Culture and Society: An Introduction.* 2nd edn. Routledge,
London.
Quirk, J. & Fort, R. (1999). *Hard Ball: The Abuse of Power in Pro-Team Sports.* New
Jersey: Princeton University Press.
Sandy, R., Sloane, P. & Rosentraub, M. (2004). *The Economics of Sport: An International
Perspective.* New York: Palgrave Macmillan.
Slack, T. & Parent, M. (2006). *Understanding Sport Organizations: The Application of
Organization Theory.* 2nd edn. Champaign, IL: Human Kinetics.
Smith, A., Stewart, B. & Haimes, G. (2011). *The Performance Identity: Building High-
Performance Organizational Cultures in Sport.* New York: Nova Science Publishers.

RELEVANT WEBSITES

The following websites are useful starting points for general information on the
management of sport:

- African Sport Management Association at www.asma-online.org/
- Asian Association for Sport management at http://aasm.ntsu.edu.tw/
- European Association for Sport Management at www.easm.net
- Latin American Association for Sport Management (ALGEDE) at http://algede.com/
  homees.html
- North American Society for Sport Management at www.nassm.com
- Sport Management Association of Australia and New Zealand at www.smaanz.org

CHAPTER 2

The role of the state in sport development

OVERVIEW

This chapter examines the different ways in which the state – which, in practical terms means government – can influence the development of sport systems and practices. Particular attention is paid to the reasons why the state seeks to intervene in the operation of sport and the different forms such intervention can take. A distinction is made between interventions that assist and promote sport on the one hand, and interventions that control and regulate sport on the other. A distinction is also made between state initiatives that aim to increase levels of community participation, and those aimed at improving levels of elite athlete performance. Throughout the chapter, incidents and cases are used to illustrate both the concepts and theories that underpin state intervention in sport, and the management implications that arise from this intervention.

After completing this chapter the reader should be able to:

* explain the role and purpose of the state;
* understand how and why the state may want to intervene in a nation's economic, social and cultural landscape;
* distinguish between states that operate from different ideological perspectives, which are, first, socialist, second, reformist, third, neo-liberal and, finally, conservative;
* explain how each of these ideologies impact on the way the state goes about assisting sport on one hand, and regulating it on the other; and
* critically compare and contrast strategies that aim to improve elite sport systems and standards with those that aim to build the participation base of sport.

DEFINING THE STATE

The state, by which we mean the structures that govern and rule societies, has always played an important role in the provision of sport experiences to people. The ancient Olympic Games and other sport festivals were funded and organized by the various city states that made up ancient Greece, and ruling monarchs in Europe during the Middle Ages organized an array of tournaments and combat games to hone the skills of their warrior classes (Mechikoff & Estes 1993). As the world became industrialized and modernized the state expanded its provision of sport activities. In the USA, for example, many government-funded schools and colleges established sport facilities ranging from manicured playing fields and small indoor arenas to large stadiums seating anywhere from 10,000 to 80,000 spectators (Fort 2011).

Today, the state, through its government agencies, provides a complex array of sport facilities and services. Many sport stadiums throughout the world were initially financed by government funds, and while subsequently controlled and operated by independent operators, are now subject to government legislation and policy guidelines (John & Sheard 1997). In most western nations the central government has funded both the establishment of training centres for elite athletes, and their ongoing operation. As a result, many thousands of coaches, sport scientists and sport facility managers are now on the government payroll.

WHY SHOULD THE STATE ENGAGE WITH SPORT?

Sport, especially in western nations, is highly valued by the state, even though many people – and even those with significant political clout – consider it to be a frivolous use of valuable time. It is often seen to be superficial, fleeting, anti-intellectual and trivial (Stebbins 2007). Sport was summarized by the 1960s US sport broadcaster, Howard Cossell, as the 'toy department of life'. Be that as it may, millions of people around the world use sport to satisfy a number of drives and motives. One critic argued that 'sport{...} is life{...}and the rest a shadow.{...}To play sport, or watch others play, and to read and talk about it was to uphold the nation and build its character' (Horne 1964). So, is there really a place for the state in sport, or is it there only because it feels obliged to be?

This idea that sport can be used to build the nation is something to which the state has a strong affinity. The state has responsibility for creating the commercial and cultural space where people can not only build strong families, neighbourhoods, communities and workplaces, but also healthy ones. The fact of the matter is that nearly all modern states allocate a special space for sport, since sport is seen to be a practice that delivers a multitude of individual and social benefits. This is the case in Cuba, North Korea and China as much as it is in the USA, Great Britain and Germany. This is why, from a global perspective, the state has constructed so much infrastructure to service sport's needs, and has given so much money to assist sport organizations deliver services to members. So, what are these 'things' that sport delivers, and that the state values so much? It is not all that difficult to identify the benefits and social utility that the state believes arises from the sport experience.

First, sport is supposed to contribute to the well-being of society by providing the context in which appropriate values, attitudes and behaviours are learnt and perpetuated. It is claimed that sport participation allows young people to better fit into mainstream cultural and behavioural patterns of society. In this way it contributes to the stability, maintenance and perpetuation of established society.

Second, sport is seen as character building, a principle that was the cornerstone of the British public school education system during the Victorian and Edwardian era. The popular nineteenth century novel, *Tom Brown's Schooldays*, provided the most idealized and romanticized descriptions of the deep and culturally significant experiences that were supposed to come from playing sports. But not only does sport build 'character', it inculcates values which support and reinforce the central beliefs of modern industrial societies. These beliefs and attitudes are the ones that industrial societies holds so dear to their hearts, and the ones that drive the progress of these societies (Coakley et al. 2011; Rigauer 1981).

So, what exactly are these values? First and foremost, they include a strong belief in the idea that success comes through hard work, self-discipline and lots of initiative. They also include a respect for authority, and adherence to rules and laws. Finally, they include those traits and disposition that make for a compliant and diligent workforce, which include leadership, hierarchy, cooperative behaviour, and the desire for success and goal achievement. These are exactly the sort of traits a twenty-first century state wants from its citizens, since they enable a fully functioning commercial system, and a strong sense of civic pride, to flourish. Moreover, these are the exact same values that characterized the newly industrialized nineteenth century societies, and strengthened their commitment to the 'Protestant work ethic', which is precisely what enabled them to progress out of feudalism. And sport is seen to be the ideal practice for building these values (Rigauer 1981).

But it doesn't end there for the state in the twenty-first century. It also increasingly recognizes that sport has many other functions that can strengthen the bonds between disparate communities, and build a healthier and stronger society. For instance, it is seen to be a mechanism for the dissipation and management of tension. For some, sport is seen as a socially approved outlet for otherwise unacceptable behaviour and attitudes. For example, mass spectator sports can channel otherwise unpeaceable emotions into socially useful activities. Aggression is therefore cathartically released by crowds of spectators cheering the players and jeering the umpires. Sport can also increase levels of excitement, which means participants use sport to increase tension and stress as an antidote to the routines of their work life (Coakley et al. 2011).

The state also understands that discipline and compliance are just one side of a productive collective psyche, and that in order to sustain a reasonable level of mental health, there needs to be a means of escape from the restricted and bureaucratic world of contemporary work. Recreational sport is the perfect release, and wilderness sports like bushwalking, snow skiing and bicycle touring reflect this urge to escape the automated banality of urban life. It is also a means of providing peak experiences, since sport can be a vehicle for 'realizing' oneself, and removing oneself from the safe realities of everyday life. Sport consequently becomes a 'sacred' time, full of excitement, exhilaration and peace (Stebbins 2007).

The state also recognizes the capacity of sport to deliver a sense of deep spirituality, since it emanates from a natural impulse for freedom, symbolic meaning, and the pursuit of perfection. In this sense, sport is a 'natural' religion. It involves asceticism, a sense of awe and fate, a quest for community, a desire for participation in the rhythms of nature, and a respect for the mystery and power of one's own being. Sport is also a religion in the liturgical aspect of sport spectacles, where the vestments, rituals and pageantry indicate a sacred type of celebration involving a tremor of anticipation and reverence.

With the recognition that sport also delivers healthy bodies and fresh minds, the state is left with no doubt about sport's capacity to build better societies. As a result, a state that does not invest in sport is actually denying its citizens the opportunities to not only find their ideal sport's space, but to also find themselves. So, when faced with the demand to explain itself, and its apparent obsession with sport, the state can, with confidence, say that it has a duty to properly resource sport, since to deny sport any assistance is to undermine the nation's capacity to grow and prosper commercially, socially and spiritually (Mannell & Kleiber 2013).

So, how does all of this discussion sound to you? Are you convinced that the state has a major role in sports planning, and delivering sport to all member of society?

In Practice 2.1 The problem of boxing

In some sports there are very few rules that govern the conduct of its activities. The relatively gentle sport of lawn bowls is a case in point. Apart from having to abide by the laws of the land, lawn bowlers are not externally regulated in any additional ways by the state. At the same time it has to be said that players in lawn bowls clubs are sometimes highly regulated internally, particularly when it comes to dress codes for the playing rink.

At the other extreme, combat sports like boxing are highly regulated, particularly at the professional level (Hoye et al. 2010). Many countries have legislation which sets up government-controlled agencies that both issue licences to promoters and participants, and monitors the conduct of the sport. While the degree of control varies from country to country, the most severe controls are in Norway, where professional boxing is banned. Any Norwegian boxer who wants to enter the professional ranks must relocate to another country.

The basic reason why boxing has such problematic status is because it not only provides community benefits, but also imposes community costs. The community benefits include an opportunity to engage in a vigorous sport that requires both extreme physical fitness and mental toughness. There is also some evidence that boxing is an effective means of channelling the energies of disadvantaged youth into socially constructive activities, and subjecting them to a valuable form of personal discipline. On the other hand, boxing is highly combative, and has high injury rates. In particular there is a high risk of brain damage, which brings with it enormous personal and social costs. Therefore, in order to minimize the risk of physical damage to the participants, strict regulation is required (Hoye et al. 2010). More generally, boxing is seen as a brutal sport that has little relevance to a civilized society where there are rules against physical assault in everyday life. There are a number of medical associations and groups whose aim is to ban competitive boxing on the grounds that it has a net social cost to the community, and that as a result we would all be better off without it. However, most national governments do not agree, and at the amateur level in particular, it is supported and funded. In addition, it is still an integral part of the Olympic Games schedule. And, in recent times women's boxing has been added to the list of Olympic sports. This initiative may be good for women's rights but not so good for their long-term health.

As a result there is a broad array of arrangements by which the state can fund, develop and deliver sport facilities and programs. At one extreme, the state can distance itself from sport development by claiming that sport is a private matter for individuals and communities, and is therefore best left to the market and voluntary sectors to run. This arrangement was the primary feature of Australian sport until the 1970s when the national government resolved to fund sport facilities and programs (Stewart et al. 2004). In the USA the national government has also adopted an arms-length approach to sport, and has left the funding and development of sport to the market, and the school and university sectors (Chalip et al. 1996).

REASONS FOR STATE INTERVENTION

The state has always intervened in the affairs of its society for the fundamental reason that it enables it to set the nation's economic and political direction. More specifically, the state believes that by its various interventions it can improve the well-being of society (Braithwaite & Drahos 2000). For example, by providing rail and road infrastructure it can improve transport systems and thereby increase the levels of overall efficiency in industry and commerce. Similarly, by funding the establishment of schools, universities and hospitals it can go a long way to not only improving the educational abilities of its citizens, but also enhancing their capacity to work more productively, and more vigorously participate in the cultural and commercial affairs of the nation. The same sort of logic underpins the state's goal of having a fit and healthy people that can defend the nation's sovereignty in times of war, and generate international kudos and prestige through the success of its elite athletes.

At the same time the state may wish to more directly control the behaviour if its citizens by establishing laws that prohibit things like industry pollution and anti-competitive behaviour by businesses, and various forms of discrimination and anti-social behaviour of individuals. The aim here is to reduce the negative 'market externalities' (Braithwaite 2008, p. 27). In this context the state has a history of regulating sport to ensure the safety of it participants. One of the best examples is boxing, where the risk of injury is very high, and rules are essential to ensure a lower chance of sustaining acute injury and long-term brain damage.

Because of sport's potential to deliver significant social benefits, there are a number of sound reasons for the state wanting to invest in it. However, government resources and taxpayer funds are always scarce, and sport is one of many institutions that want to claim part of the government budget. As a result, sport assistance cannot always be guaranteed, and it must compete with defence, health, policing, social welfare and education. Additionally, in capitalist economies, sport has also traditionally been seen as outside the scope of government responsibility on the grounds that it is far removed from commerce, and more in the territory of volunteer amateurs. However, it is not that difficult to mount a case for state intervention in sport. For example, a case can be made to support the view that not only will society be better off with more sport facilities and services, but that without state support, the resources invested in sport will be far less than optimal.

Market failure and the supply of sport services

In capitalist nations like Australia, Canada, Great Britain, New Zealand and the USA, resources are in the main allocated in markets through the interaction of demand, supply and prices. However, there are often cases where markets do not operate in the best interests of the community or nation. This is known as market failure (Gratton & Taylor 2000). Market failure can occur when the full benefits of markets are not realized because of an under-supply of socially desirable products, or alternatively, an over-supply of less desirable products. Market failure and under-supply arises in situations where there are significant external or social benefits in addition to private benefits. Private benefits are the value consumers obtain from the immediate purchase of a good or service and are measured by the prices people are prepared to pay for the experience. In sport, private benefits arise from a number of activities and practices. They include attending a major sport event, working out at a gymnasium, playing indoor cricket or spending time at a snow resort. Social benefits, on the other hand, comprise the additional value communities obtain from the production of a good or service. These social benefits are over and above the private benefits. In those cases where social benefits can be identified, society would be better served by allocating additional resources into those activities. However, private investors will not usually do this because of the lack of a profit incentive. Consequently, it will be left to government to fill the breach, and use taxpayers' money to fund additional sporting infrastructure and services.

In other words, since sport provides significant social benefits, it deserves state support to ensure that the welfare of the whole community is maximized. According to the proponents of sport assistance, social benefits can arise from both active participation and spectator sport. In the case of active participation, the benefits include improved community health, a fall in medical costs, a reduction in the crime rate, the inculcation of discipline and character, the development of ethical standards through the emulation of sporting heroes, greater civic engagement, and the building of social capital. Research into social capital building suggests that sport not only expands social networks, but also produces safer neighbourhoods and stronger communities (Productivity Commission 2003). Moreover, the social benefits linked to social capital are extended when sport groups and clubs look outward and encompass people across diverse social cleavages. This bridging or inclusive social capital can be contrasted with bonding social capital, which characterizes sport groups and clubs with a narrow ethnic, social, or occupational base (Putnam 2000, p. 22). Either way, sport is seen to be a great builder of social capital.

In the case of elite and spectator sports, the social benefits include tribal identification with a team or club, social cohesion, a sense of civic and national pride, international recognition and prestige, economic development, and the attraction of out-of-town visitors and tourist dollars (Gratton & Taylor 1991). When these social benefits are aggregated the results are quite extensive, as can be seen in Table 2.1. At the same time, they are often difficult to quantify, and in some cases the evidence to support the claimed benefit is soft and flimsy.

TABLE 2.1 Social benefits of sport development

Arising from active participation	Arising from elite athlete successes
Improvement in community health and productivity	Tribal identification and belonging
Fall in medical costs	Social cohesion
Reduction in juvenile crime rate	Civic and national pride
Development of 'character' and sense of 'fair play'	International recognition and prestige
Building of social capital, social cohesion, and civic engagement	Economic development and tourism

Source: Adapted from Stewart et al. (2004)

Sport as a public good

A case can also be made for the state's involvement in sport on the grounds that sport is often a public or collective good (Li et al. 2001). Public goods are those goods where one person's consumption does not prevent another person's consumption of the same good. For example, a decision to visit a beach, or identify with a winning team or athlete, will not prevent others from doing the same. Indeed, the experience may be enhanced by others being in proximity. This is the non-rival feature of the good. Public goods are also goods where, in their purest form, no one can be prevented from consuming the good. Again, a visit to the beach and identifying with a winning team meet this criterion. This is the non-excludable feature of the good. Public goods can provide substantial benefits throughout the whole of society, and are usually not rationed through high prices. However, they are not attractive to private investors since there is no assurance that all users will pay the cost of providing the benefit. As the number of so-called free-riders increase there is a shrinking incentive for private operators to enter the public good market. In this instance it is argued that the state should provide for this higher demand by increasing its funding to ensure an appropriate infrastructure and level of service.

Sport equity and inclusiveness

Finally, it can be argued that the state should be funding sport on equity grounds. For example, it might be argued that the whole community benefits from being fit and healthy, and therefore no one should be excluded because of low income or lack of facilities. In these cases, the optimal community benefit can only be realized if everyone has access to appropriate sport and recreation services to help them to improve their health and fitness, enhance their self-image, and build the community's social capital. In order to improve accessibility, and ensure equality of opportunity, the state can establish its own low-cost sport facilities, subsidize existing sport activity providers, and design targeted programs for disadvantaged groups.

In Practice 2.2 State-controlled sport: Communist style

There are many good reasons to let the private sector and free market decide on what sports people play, when they play, and what they should pay for the experience. There are sound reasons for moving in the opposite direction and allowing the state to set the sport agenda by both establishing sport facilities across the nation, and funding the management of their operations. This approach was exemplified in the sport development programs of most communist nations during the 1970s and 1980s. In the Soviet Union (USSR) and the German Democratic Republic (GDR), a national sport program was integrated into the school curricula, and sport schools were used to identify and nurture talented young athletes. In addition, sports that had a strong civil defence and para-military flavour were conducted in factory and trade union facilities (Grix & Dennis 2012). Cuba had a similar sport development model in which the state through its government bureaucracy managed the whole sport experience for both the sport-for-all participant and the Olympic athlete. While Cuba banned professionalism in sport, it handsomely rewarded its national sporting heroes by giving them government jobs or enrolling them in college and university courses that they could complete at their convenience. In Cuba, like the USSR and GDR, sport success was not just a sporting victory but a 'psychological, patriotic and revolutionary' one as well (Riordan 1978, p. 147).

EXTENT AND FORM OF STATE INTERVENTION

The state can intervene in sport in all sorts of ways. The extent of the intervention, and the form it takes, is strongly influenced by the ideology, values and overall philosophy of the state and its governing institutions (Gardiner et al. 2009).

The first ideology is conservatism. A conservative ideology values tradition, and customary ways of doing things. Conservative governments have a tendency to regulate the social lives of people, and therefore want to censor works of art and literature they find offensive. They also want to control the distribution of legal drugs like alcohol, and generally act to protect people from themselves. On the other hand, they believe that business should be left to its own devices, where the combination of individual self-interest, the profit motive, and market forces, will ensure a favourable outcome. However, because conservative governments believe a strong private sector is the key to progress, they are prepared to assist and protect industry when the need arises. While on one hand they recognize sport as an integral part of the social life of most people, they do not want to assist or protect it since it is not part of the world of business. Indeed, for many conservatives, it is another world altogether that should be best kept at a distance from business. This sport world is underpinned by the belief that sport fulfils its function best when it is done for its own sake, played by amateurs, managed by volunteers, and generally left to look after its own affairs.

The second ideology is reformism, or as it is also known, welfare statism, or social democracy. Reformism is primarily concerned with social justice and equity. While reformists recognize the necessity of a strong private sector they believe it cannot be trusted to deliver fair and equitable outcomes. It therefore needs to be strictly managed. This could take the form of additional state-owned enterprises, or tight regulations on business behaviour. Reformists share the conservative view that assistance and protection may be necessary in the public interest. Unlike conservatives, though, reformists believe primarily in social development, which not only means legislating for social freedom, but also for social justice. Income redistribution to disadvantaged groups is important, and is done by ensuring that wealthy individuals and corporations are taxed most heavily. State spending is also crucial to reformists, since it is used to stimulate the economy when demand and spending is low. Reformist governments tend to be more centralist, and aim to use this centralized power to engineer positive social outcomes. Reformists consequently see sport as a tool for social development, and aim to make sport more accessible to the whole community. In these cases programs are established to cater for the needs of minority groups like the indigenous, the disabled, migrants who speak another language, and women. In short, reformist government policy focuses more on community, and less on elite sport development.

The third ideology is neo-liberalism. Neo-liberals believe that society is at its most healthy when people can run their daily lives without the chronic intrusion of the state. The rule of law is important, but beyond that, people should be free to choose how they organize their social lives, and businesses should be free to organize their commercial lives as they see fit. Neo-liberals see little value in state-owned enterprises, and argue that the privatization of government services produces greater efficiency and higher quality outcomes. Moreover, deregulated industries are seen to run better than tightly controlled ones. In short, neo-liberals believe government should not engage directly in most economic activity, but rather provide only base level infrastructure, and legislative guidelines within which private business can thrive. Sport is valued as an important social institution, but should not be strictly controlled. However, neo-liberals also believe sport can be used as a vehicle for nation building and economic development, and should be supported in these instances. This produces a sport policy that tends to focus on elite sport at the expense of community sport.

The final ideology is socialism. Socialists believe that a combination of privately owned and unregulated markets will produce severe levels of inequality and alienation. As a result, capitalist modes of production and distribution need to be replaced by a strong state where resource allocation is centrally controlled. Like neo-liberals, socialists agree that sport is an important social institution, but, unlike neo-liberals, go on to assert that sport should be controlled from the centre to ensure a fair spread of clubs and facilities throughout society. To this end, a socialist system of sport development will be driven by a central bureaucracy that sets the sport agenda. The state also provides most of the funds and resources by which to develop sport at both the community and elite levels.

Each ideology not only contains quite different assumptions about the proper role of the state, but also different ideas about what sport can do to improve the welfare of society. As a result each ideology will produce different sport development outcomes, and the ideology often overrides the claims of interest groups like sport scientists, coaches and officials. The four ideologies described provide a simplified typology, and in practice, the state will often take bits and pieces of each ideology when forming its position on a particular sport issue or problem. At the same time, most states will be characterized by more of one, and less of another ideology. Table 2.2 outlines the different ideologies and indicates how they can shape the state's views on sport development.

TABLE 2.2 Links between political ideology and sport development		
Ideological type	*Features*	*Implications for sport development*
Conservatism	Private ownership of business Regulation of social practices	Arms-length association with sport. Sport is seen as a private activity that grows out of the community, and is managed by the volunteer sector.
Reformism	Mixed economy Regulation of both social and economic affairs	Direct involvement in sport facility construction and community sport participation.
Neo-liberalism	Emphasis on the market De-regulation of industry	Most resources go to the elite end of sport development and its commercial outcomes.
Socialism	Limited scope for the market Central planning Bureaucratic control over resource allocation	Direct involvement in all aspects of sport development. Often tightly regulated. Both community and elite sport are resourced.

REGULATION AND CONTROL

There are also many situations where the state may want to regulate and control the provision of sport activities, and limit the resources devoted to some activities (Baldwin et al. 2012). For example it may be necessary to enact laws and rules that safeguard public order when a large number of people are spectators of, or are playing in a sport event. In most countries there are laws that clearly define the parameters within which sport grounds are to be constructed. These laws will cover things like design specifications, the provision for seating, the number of entry and exits points, and fire prevention facilities (Frosdick & Walley 1997). There may also be rules that govern the behaviour of spectators. Most commonly these laws will relate to the consumption of alcohol and disorderly and violent behaviour (Greenfield & Osborn 2001).

One of the most highly regulated activities is horse-racing. It is not just a case of ensuring the animals are treated humanely, but of also making sure the gaming and gambling practices that surround the sport are tightly controlled so that corrupt practices are minimized. There are many cases around the world where horses have not been allowed to run on their merits. This can involve doping activities where stimulants will be given to horses to make them run quicker, and depressants administered to make them go slower. In both instances the aim is to undermine the betting market, and through the use of inside information to back the horse that has been advantaged, and avoid the horse that has been slowed. Similar incidents are now happening more frequently in a number of professional team sports around the world (Muller et al. 2012). Crime syndicates and bookmakers have bribed sport officials, players and even referees to provide confidential information on the game, deliberately play poorly, and make decisions that favour one team and not another. Two recent cases involved Italy's premier football competition and the Pakistan cricket team. In each instance government action was immediately taken to more strictly regulate the competitions.

Another form of regulation involves the media in general and TV in particular. In both Australia and England there are anti-siphoning rules that effectively give free-to-air television stations privileged access to major sport events at the expense of pay and cable television providers (Brown & Walsh 1999). This means that a major sport event like the Australian Football League (AFL) Grand Final must initially be offered to free-to-air stations before being offered to pay TV stations. This is done on the grounds that a sport of national significance should be made as widely available as possible. In Australia the pay TV subscriptions cover less than 50 per cent of all households, and it would therefore be inequitable to give rights to a pay TV station only.

In Practice 2.3 Government assistance to sport: The case of 'active living' promotion

Most developed nations around the world see themselves as a sports-loving nation, and use sport as a means of generating civic pride, national identity and international recognition (Stewart et al. 2004). This is why so many nations are prepared to spend a lot of money on facilities and programs that take talented young athletes and transform them into elite level champions (McDonald 2011). However, sport development is about much more than just winning medals at international sport events. The state has a responsibility to provide the community with rewarding sport experiences, and to make sure disadvantaged groups especially have open and easy access to facilities (Houlihan 1997). The problem of low participation is being addressed in many and varied ways.

England

In the 2013 document titled 'Creating a sporting habit for life: A new youth sport strategy', Sport England expressed concern that when people leave school they often stop playing sports, and thus neither fulfil their sporting potential, nor ensure a healthy lifestyle. As a result the goal is to get more people playing sport regularly and safely throughout their life, no matter what their economic or social background.

These concerns led to the development of a 'Youth Sport Strategy' that aims to increase the number of young people developing sport as a 'habit for life' by undertaking the following initiatives:

- Sport England will invest £1 billion to assist young people to more regularly play sport, and help break down barriers that make participation difficult at the moment.
- Sport England will work with schools, colleges and universities, as well as local county sports partnerships, the national governing bodies for sport, local authorities and the voluntary sector to improve the sporting 'offer'.
- Sport England will seek a consistent increase in the proportion of people regularly playing sport, and especially the 14–25 year-old age group.
- Sport England will work to build links between schools and community sports clubs and work with sports such as Football, Cricket, Rugby Union, Rugby League and Tennis to establish at least 6,000 partnerships between schools and local sports clubs by 2017.
- Sport England will invest £160 million on new and upgraded sports facilities, on top of the 90 million already invested via Sport England's Places, People, Play program.

Ireland

Like many nations around the world, Ireland has dealt with an ageing population. Research shows that a physically active older population is a healthy population. As a result the Irish government has resolved to assist older age groups to engage more strongly with sports and physical activity. This has many benefits. The benefit to the individual is a more productive and vigorous lifestyle. The benefit to the community and society, in general, is a healthier population that contributes to the community, engages productively with local neighbourhoods, spends less time under medical care, and spends less money on prescription medicines.

The Irish Sports Council also introduced a Go for Life program that aims to increase participation among older people in recreational sport activities. The program is administered by the Age and Opportunity agency, and is guided by a steering group comprising representatives of the Irish Sports Council, Age and Opportunity, the Federation of Active Retirement Associations, the Irish Senior Citizens Parliament and the National Council on Ageing and Older People.

In 2007, the Irish Sports Council provided €700,000 to drive the program, and more than 620 community groups nationwide shared the initial allocation of €350,000 under phase seven of the Go for Life National Grant Scheme for Sport and Physical Activity for Older People. The national grant scheme comprises one important element of the Go for Life program, and complements the other main strands in the program, which are 1) the Active Living program and 2) the Sports Participation program.

SUMMARY

The state has the capacity to significantly shape the structure and scope of sport through a number of mechanisms. First, it can construct sport facilities, second, it can fund the day-to-day operations of sporting associations and clubs, third, it can deliver sport programs to the community directly, fourth, it can establish training facilities for elite athletes to assist their ongoing development, and finally, it can control the operation of sport by introducing various laws, regulations and rules that shapes the delivery of sport events, programs and services (Hylton et al. 2001). However, the scale of state support, and the form it takes, will vary between nations depending on the dominant political ideology, and the overall cultural importance of sport to society. In some cases the state will directly control and manage sport, while at the other end of the political spectrum the state will step back from the sport system and encourage the commercial and volunteer sectors to take up the slack.

The evidence suggests that governments have a pivotal role to play in supporting both the community participation and elite sport ends of the sport development continuum. Through the establishment of sports infrastructure and facilities, and the funding of sport programs, it enables greater levels of community participation, creates all sorts of health and social benefits, improves international sport performance, and enhances a country's international status and prestige.

REVIEW QUESTIONS

1 What comprises the state, and what is its role?
2 How does the state go about shaping the political and economic landscape of a nation?
3 Apart from the state, what other social forces contribute to national development?
4 Explain how the state may contribute to sport development.
5 What can the state do to increase the level of sport participation and sport club membership?
6 What can the state do to increase the level of elite sport performance?
7 Why should the state want to intervene in sport?
8 Would sport development be best left to the voluntary and commercial sectors?
9 Is there any evidence that a centralized model of elite sport development is any more effective than a market-based sport development model?
10 How might the state go about increasing the scale of sport participation at the community or 'grassroots' level?

FURTHER READING

For a thorough analysis of the ways in which government can go about regulating a nation's economic, social and cultural affairs, see Baldwin et al. (2012) and Braithwaite and Drahos (2000). There are now a number of publications that examine the ways in which the state has intervened in a nation's sport development. To get a detailed picture of the Australian experience you should read Bloomfield (2003) and Stewart et al. (2004). The British experience is nicely reviewed in Green and Houlihan (2005), Houlihan and White (2002) and Hylton et al. (2001). For a comparative analysis of state involvement in sport, the most comprehensive treatment is contained in Chalip et al. (1996). Houlihan (1997) provides an excellent comparative study of Australia, Canada, Ireland and the United Kingdom (UK). The most definitive account of sport in socialist Cuba, although now a little dated, is Pattavino and Pye (1994).

See also:
Coakley, J. et al. (2011). *Sport in Society*. Sydney: McGraw Hill.
Horne, D. (1964). *The Lucky Country*. Ringwood: Penguin Books.
Rigauer, B. (1981). *Sport and Work*. New York: Columbia University Press.
Stebbins, R. (2007). *Serious Leisure*. New Brunswick; Transactions Publications.

RELEVANT WEBSITES

- To find out more about the state and Australian sport go to the Australian Sports Commission site at www.ausport.gov.au
- To get more details of the English experience go to the Sport England site at www.sportengland.org
- For a comprehensive review of the state's involvement in NZ sport go to the New Zealand Government Sport and Recreation site at www.sparc.org.nz
- For more details on the Irish experience go to www.irishsportscouncil.ie/Participation/Go_for_Life/#sthash.ORQFNbu5.dpuf

CASE STUDY 2.1

Creating order out of chaos: The regulation of mixed martial arts in the USA

ORIGINS
Mixed martial arts (MMA) has taken the sports world by storm over recent years. It has its origins in the Ultimate Fighting Championship (UFC) which was initially staged in Denver, Colorado, USA in 1993. Its laissez-faire – that is, anything goes – brutality attracted lots of people, but it also offended others. Despite regular criticism, it became an overnight sensation, and quickly established itself as one of the most popular combat sports on television. However, its lack of external regulation and the apparent enthusiasm for caged bouts where a lot of blood flowed, led to the show being taken off cable television. UFC marketed its events with the tagline 'There are no rules'.

However, in 2001 UFC reinvented itself as MMA. It had a new controlling body and reshaped what was often seen as a freak show into a sport that was close to being legitimate. MMA was rebranded, and remarketed is an interdisciplinary combat sport where highly-skilled participants combine a variety of fighting disciplines – and especially kickboxing, wrestling, karate, jiu-jitsu and judo – within one match. This means mixed martial artists can no longer rely on a few threatening tattoos and a lot of experience as a bar-room brawler to make their way in the sport.

SETTING THE REGULATORY SCENE

In the USA, where MMA is most popular, the sport is regulated by the Athletic Commission (AC) of the relevant state in which an event is being promoted. These ACs have a strong history in regulating boxing. Most American states have adopted the rules designed for New Jersey and Nevada in 2001. These rules cover both professional and amateur MMA, and include a number of important issues, including:

- weight divisions;
- fighting area safety features;
- specifications for hand-wrapping;
- protective equipment including mouthpieces;
- length of round and length of bout;
- reasons for stopping contests;
- fouls and related penalties.

The AC directly oversees events, and also administers the weigh-ins, officiating and judging. The AC can refuse to license fighters if they fail to pass a pre-fight medical which may include blood tests to confirm a fighter's HIV status, an eye assessment and a physical examination. They can also impose limitations on fighters engaging in contact for a specified period in light of any injuries they may have sustained. They will also consider whether or not to license a fight based on the adequacy of matchmaking given the fighters' respective skill levels. Competitive balance is always front and centre, and overly one-sided matches are regularly investigated.

However, the level of oversight can vary from event to event. There can also be differences in level of scrutiny applied by one AC compared to another. This means that the supervision of an event at the pinnacle of the sport is frequently tighter than those taking place on the regional circuit. Intensive medical testing is sometimes neglected in lower level competitions, since something like post-match brain scans can cost in excess US$2,000 for individual competitors.

RULES OF COMBAT

Under the unified rules of MMA athletes will compete within a regulated system of multiple rounds of 3–5 minutes. Championship rounds will occupy five 5-minutes of ring or cage time.

As with boxing, scoring is undertaken within a 10-point system. The winner of the round will receive ten points and the loser nine points or less. Unlike boxing, MMA matches are scored not only for effective striking attacks, but also for ground-fighting effectiveness. Points are also added for submissions, takedown attempts and successful defensive strategies. Finally, points are allocated for ring-craft.

Bouts can end through a knock-out, a stoppage initiated by the referee, the participant's 'corner', or the attending doctor. The bout can also end as a result of one of the fighters submitting. When a bout ends by submission, the fighter either verbally or physically 'taps out', or signals that he has had enough.

CASE STUDY QUESTIONS

1   Could the old UFC have survived commercially without heavier regulation?

2   Is MMA now a legitimate sport?

3   Has regulation made MMA a better or worse sport from a spectator perspective?

4   As an MMA official or manager, would you be comfortable with the current regulatory arrangements?

5   What is missing from the current regulations, and what regulations would you like to see added?

6   From a management perspective what does the tighter regulation of MMA do for the sport?

CASE STUDY 2.2

Managing safety: Lifesaving clubs and lifeguard associations

The lifesaving movement has a rich and long history. So long as people wanted to engage with the sea and the ocean and enjoy the pleasures of the beach, there was always the risk that they would drown. Learning to swim was a crucial means of reducing the risk, but this valuable outdoors skill was often insufficient to deal with crashing waves, a powerful rip, or a leaky boat. As a result, even in the late nineteenth century, places where people swam, and spaces where they engaged with the sea, required professional supervision to ensure that catastrophes did not occur (Jaggard 2006). One of the first initiatives to help create an international forum for international lifesaving discussion occurred in France in 1878 when delegates from around Western Europe met to examine the ways in which the whole lifesaving function could be formalized and rationalized. In 1891 in the UK, the Royal Life Saving Association (RLSA) was created, and membership soon expanded to other members of the old British Empire, including Canada and Australia. In 1910 the first official international lifesaving organization (the FIS) was established, and included many European member countries, especially those, like Spain, France, Italy and Great Britain, which had extensive coastlines.

Lifesaving in the form of surf lifesaving – which centred on ocean, as opposed to bayside beaches – has an especially interesting history in Australia, which is not surprising given the warm climate and hundreds of miles of swimmable ocean beaches around most of the populated areas. Clubs were formed in Australia between 1903 and 1907 in response to a spate of drownings at local Sydney beaches. The Bronte surf lifesaving club claims to be the first 'surf' club in the world having been established in 1903. At the same time, the Bondi surf bathers lifesaving club also claimed to be the world's first lifesaving club, but as it turns out, it was not established until 1907. The first club to be formed outside of Sydney was the Kiama surf bather's club founded in 1908. These clubs, and others like them, became necessary following the relaxing of laws prohibiting daylight bathing on Australian beaches. As a result, thousands of swimmers took to the water, and volunteer groups of men – women were not initially invited to become members of lifesaving clubs – were subsequently trained in lifesaving methods and patrolled the beaches as lifesavers looking after public safety. There are now more than 300 surf lifesaving clubs in Australia that collectively patrol over 400 beaches. Lifesavers have undertaken so many valuable tasks, and done it with so much flair, and backed it up with so much physical skills and expertise, that they have also become one of the most iconic figures of the Australian sporting landscape (Jaggard 2006).

While the UK does not have the strong beach culture that exists in Australia, it still has a strong network of lifesavers and lifeguard services under the auspices of the RLSA. Nearly all of the UK's major tourist beaches now have lifeguards and which provides the opportunity for children to join lifesaving clubs. Like the situation in Australia this enables them to start from an early age, build their aquatic confidence, improve their knowledge of the sea's many turbulent features, and develop the skills required to save lives in the future. A lot of the UK's smaller coastal resorts get very busy and therefore have lifeguards on duty throughout the summer. Cardigan Bay for example, which sits along the west coast of Wales has many beaches that not only fills with tourists over the summer months, but also provides an array of professional lifesavers and lifeguards (www.ilsf.org).

In 1971 the World Lifesaving Organisation (WLS) was formed, and it brought together countries such as NZ, the UK, South Africa and the United States, where they proclaimed their mission of protecting the public on beaches worldwide. This organization later merged with the FIS and became the International Life Saving Federation (ILSF) in 1993 (Jaggard, 2006). Its mission statement says in part that its role is to 'lead{...}support and collaborate with national and international organizations engaged in drowning prevention, water safety, water rescue, lifesaving, lifeguarding and lifesaving sport' (www.ilsf.org). As a result of its global initiatives we now find that all around the world on any popular coastline there are either lifesavers or lifeguards.

The other important point to note is that lifesaving and lifeguard work is not just physically demanding, it is also costly to mount. This is because it 1) is a labour intensive practice, 2) is something that requires extensive training, and 3) has to be carried out in quite different terrains and conditions. In Europe, for example, there are also several coastal areas that are patrolled by lifeguards, including in Belgium which has a limited coastal area of just under 70 kilometres. In Germany work is done by the Red Cross group, while Italy is covered by the Italian Swimming Federation and the National Life Saving Society. In some European countries such as Portugal and Spain coastal areas are so long that they sometimes have to be patrolled by lifeguards on quad bikes (www.ilsf.org).

In Britain, as with Australia, there are distinctions to be made between surf-beach, bayside beach, and pool lifeguards. The Royal Life Saving Society and the Swimming Teachers Association train individuals for their national pool lifeguard qualification, and additionally teach the National Aquatic Rescue Standard. The lifeguard course comprises around 40 hours of instructional time, and is valid for two years once qualified. If anyone wishes to continue as a lifeguard they must complete a further 20 hours of training. The Royal Lifesaving Society also has an individual qualification for beach work known as the National Beach Lifeguard Qualification (NBLQ) and involves training in several modules such as rescue-boat training and VHF radio operation. This is all very impressive, and ensures that the pools and beaches of Britain are properly managed and supervised.

All of these global developments are essential for the creation of safe beaches and pools, but they beg the question as to how they are funded. Well, they are funded very heavily by government. Take, for example the recent developments that have occurred in Australia. Between 2008 and 2013, the New South Wales State government provided AUS$20 million for surf lifesaving facilities on top of the annual funding arrangements. The money went into projects that contribute to beach safety, which includes things like improved access to rescue equipment and better sight lines between clubs and swimming areas. Some of the funding was also used to assist surf lifesaving clubs in making their facilities more accessible to the broader community through improved disability access, the inclusion of young people from non-English speaking backgrounds, and female-friendly amenities. In the case of the national governing body for surf lifesaving, Surf Life Saving Australia (SLSA), nearly 30 per cent of its total annual revenue of around AUS$30 million comes from the Australian national government (SLSA 2012). This means that like most other nations around the world that provide extensive lifesaving facilities, it would not have been possible without the very generous support of the government.

This begs the additional and crucially important question of why government should want to involve itself in the funding of lifesaving and lifeguard services when the community who use the services could, alternatively, pay for it. What do you think, and what arguments can you mount to confirm that communities around the world will be far better off with government assistance to surf lifesavers and lifeguards than without government assistance? So, when we consider the role of surf lifesavers, beach lifeguards and pool lifeguards, and the role that might be played by government in making things happen in these very important public spaces, seven pivotal questions need to be asked.

CASE STUDY QUESTIONS

1   What is the core role of lifesaving clubs and agencies?

2   What are their likely sources of income, and why?

3   How feasible would it be to get the people being rescued to actually fund the operations of lifesaving clubs and agencies?

4   Why should governments want to assist lifesaving clubs and agencies?

5   What are lifesaving clubs and agencies expected to do with the funds that are allocated to them by government?

6   What are the benefits we expect to secure from the activities of surf lifesavers and guards?

7   Would these benefits arise if the lifesaving clubs were not funded by government?

CHAPTER 3

Nonprofit sport

OVERVIEW

This chapter examines the role of the nonprofit sector in the provision of sport participation and consumption opportunities and explores the reasons why the nonprofit sector plays such a large part in the provision of sport participation opportunities. The scope of the nonprofit sector's involvement in sport around the world is examined, with a particular emphasis on the role of volunteers in administration, officiating and coaching and the role of nonprofit sport organizations in facilitating people's enjoyment of sport as active participants, supporters, or consumers. The chapter also provides a summary of the relationship between nonprofit sport organizations and the state.

After completing this chapter the reader should be able to:

- describe the scope of the nonprofit sector's involvement in sport;
- understand the differences in the roles performed by the state and nonprofit sport organizations;
- understand the ways in which nonprofit sport organizations provide sport participation and consumption opportunities around the world; and
- understand some of the challenges facing the nonprofit sector in delivering these opportunities.

INTRODUCTION

The model presented in Chapter 1 presents the sport industry as comprising three distinct but overlapping sectors: the state or public sector, the commercial or professional sport sector, and the nonprofit or voluntary sector. This chapter focuses on the nonprofit or voluntary sector of the model; the various sport organizations that would be classified as nonprofit. Many terms have been used to refer to nonprofit organizations that operate in a variety of industry sectors and countries around the world. These terms include voluntary, not for profit, non government, community, club based, associations, co-operatives, friendly societies, civil society, and the third sector. For the purposes of this book we have chosen to use the term nonprofit organizations to describe those organizations that are institutionally separate from the state, do not return profits to owners, are self-governing, have a significant element of voluntary contribution, and are formally incorporated.

The nonprofit sport sector comprises organizations that are markedly different from state organizations discussed in Chapter 2, and also profit seeking organizations that are discussed in Chapter 4. Nonprofit organizations vary in size, focus and capability, and include groups as diverse as community associations, chambers of commerce, private schools, charitable trusts and foundations, welfare agencies and sporting organizations. Nonprofit organizations are a major part of many industries in health services, education, housing, welfare, culture and sport. Describing these organizations as nonprofit does not mean they run at a financial loss or do not generate a surplus of revenue versus their expenses; the term nonprofit refers merely to the fact they do not exist for the primary purpose to make profits to reward their owners.

NONPROFIT SECTOR AND SOCIETY

Nonprofit organizations exist to develop communities, meet the needs of identifiable and discrete groups in those communities, and work for the benefit of public good rather than wealth creation for individuals. Nonprofit organizations have evolved to fill gaps in the provision of services such as welfare assistance that are not provided by the state or market sector, and are driven largely by the efforts of volunteers with the occasional support of paid staff.

A review of nonprofit organizations in Canada (Statistics Canada 2004) noted that these organizations were vehicles for citizen engagement – they enable individuals to contribute their talent, energy and time to engaging in group activities and causes that are not otherwise provided by the public or private sectors. Nonprofit organizations are in general governed by volunteers, run on the time and money contributed by volunteers, and enable volunteers to contribute to enhancing their local, regional, national and global communities. In Canada there are more than 161,000 nonprofit organizations, that collectively utilize more than 2 billion volunteer hours, and receive more than CAN$8 billion in donations to deliver their services. According to Statistics Canada (2004) Canadians take out 139 million memberships in these organizations, an average of four per person. These figures show us that the nonprofit sector represents a major part of the economic activity of many nations and plays a pivotal role in encouraging people to engage in social, religious, charitable, philanthropic and sport-related activities.

Nonprofit organizations usually focus on delivering services to very specific population groups or within defined geographic areas. Many of them provide services to targeted groups and only a few focus solely on providing services to members. The variety of activities carried out by nonprofit organizations is very broad and ranges from providing sporting opportunities to funding hospital and medical services. As a result, the revenue sources, cost base, numbers of paid staff and volunteers, and the sophistication of management systems also vary between nonprofit organizations.

The nonprofit sector is not without its problems. The larger organizations such as independent schools, colleges and hospitals receive the majority of funding and almost half the funding for most nonprofit organizations comes from government. The resourcing of nonprofit organizations in some sectors continues to be inadequate as they struggle to keep up with demand, particularly in the welfare, housing and charitable sectors. By far the biggest problem facing nonprofit organizations is the inability to fulfil their missions due to problems securing adequate numbers of volunteers, finding board members, and attracting enough sustainable funding (Cuskelly 2004). As governments around the world seek to decrease their costs and devolve responsibility for service delivery to the private and nonprofit sectors without adequately funding such delivery, nonprofit organizations will find it increasingly difficult to operate.

In Practice 3.1 The Australian nonprofit sector

According to a recent review by the Australian Productivity Commission (2010) many not-for-profit organizations (NFPs) feel they are poorly understood by government and the general public. Pressures to be more efficient have seen overhead spending reduced that in turn, reduces effectiveness. While the Australian nonprofit sector is diverse, NFPs display some common behavioural patterns. First, in contrast to for-profit organizations, the behaviour of NFPs is driven mostly by their mission or community purpose. Second, demonstrated commitment to their community purpose underpins support for their activities, whether by members for member-serving NFPs, or by donors and government who provide funding for community-serving NFPs. Third, processes, often highly participatory, matter to NFPs because they provide value to the volunteers and members, and because of their central importance to maintaining trusting relationships that form the basis for effective service delivery. Finally, control can be a major motivating factor for the managers of NFPs. While generally motivated by altruism, NFP management also benefit personally from their role when it confers status or power, builds their skills and contacts, and where it improves the environment for their other activities.

The Productivity Commission argued that these characteristics have implications for the drivers of efficiency and effectiveness, namely:

1   Processes that appear messy and inefficient to outsiders can be essential for effective delivery of services, especially those requiring engagement with clients who face disadvantages and are wary of government and for-profit providers.
2   They can also be important to attract and retain volunteers, the involvement of which can be valued as much for the engagement outcomes as for replacing the need for paid labour.
3   It is possible that, for some managers, 'doing' can take precedence over 'achieving'. Unless NFP boards are able to act decisively, such behaviour can undermine efficiency and effectiveness and threaten the sustainability of an NFP.
4   While greater scale and sharing of support services can improve production efficiency, NFPs can be reluctant to merge or collaborate where other interests might be eroded or where the purchase of support services adds to overheads.

Community-serving NFPs may also lack adequate feedback mechanisms on their effectiveness (or lack thereof) as clients are often grateful for the assistance. This contrasts strongly with member-serving organizations, particularly small grassroots organisations, where member satisfaction is paramount to survival.

While historically Australia fits in the 'liberal' social origin category (where government social spending is low and NFP activity is relatively large); since the 1970s, government funding of the sector has grown. From the 1980s, this has increasingly been under competitive allocation arrangements, with greater use of the sector to deliver government-funded services. More recently, social enterprise is being seen as a way to harness network governance to address social issues. Along with demographic, ethnic and cultural changes (such as increasing environmental awareness), these forces are increasing demand for NFP activities. In responding to rising demand, NFPs report constraints arising from growing regulation and contract requirements, and challenges in accessing funding, finance and skilled workers. Government can assist in addressing these constraints to facilitate sector growth and development; nevertheless the sector remains responsible for its own future.

Source: Productivity Commission. (2010). *Contribution of the Not-for-Profit Sector*, Canberra: Commonwealth of Australia, pp. 13–14.

NONPROFIT SECTOR AND SPORT

The International Classification of Nonprofit Organizations (ICNPO) has a designated category for sports and recreation organizations. This category includes three broad groups:

1 sports including amateur sport, training, fitness and sport facilities, and sport competition and events;
2 recreation and social clubs such as country clubs, playground associations, touring clubs and leisure clubs; and
3 service clubs such as Lions, Rotary, Kiwanis and Apex clubs.

Of particular interest are those organizations that operate on a nonprofit basis in sport including professional service organizations, industry lobby groups, sport event organizations and sport governing bodies.

Nonprofit professional service organizations operate in sport in similar ways to professional associations like accrediting medical boards, or associations for lawyers and accountants. These organizations assist in setting standards of practice in their respective industries, provide professional accreditation for qualified members and offer professional development opportunities through conferences, seminars or training programs. They operate in a business-like fashion but the aim is to return surpluses to members through improved service delivery rather than create wealth for owners.

In Australia, the Australian Council for Health, Physical Education and Recreation (ACHPER) is a national professional association representing people who work in the areas of Health Education, Physical Education, Recreation, Sport, Dance, Community Fitness or Movement Sciences. The roles of ACHPER include advocating for the promotion and provision of sport opportunities, providing professional development programs for teachers, and accrediting and training people wanting to become community fitness instructors. Similar groups operate in Canada (Canadian Association for Health, Physical Education, Recreation and Dance), the USA (American Alliance for Health, Physical Education and Dance), the UK (British Institute of Sports Administration) and New Zealand (Physical Education New Zealand).

A number of industry lobby groups, representing the interests of nonprofit sport organizations, also operate throughout the world. A leading example is the Central Council of Physical Recreation (CCPR) in the UK, the representative body for national sports organizations. It acts as the independent umbrella organization for national governing and representative bodies of sport and recreation in the UK to promote their interests to government and other players in the sport industry. This role is undertaken by Sport Industry Australia, a similar nonprofit organization in Australia.

Some of the largest and most influential sport event organizations in the world operate on a nonprofit basis, including the International Olympic Committee (IOC) and the Commonwealth Games Federation (CGF). The IOC was founded in 1894 by Baron Pierre de Coubertin, and is an independent nonprofit organization that serves as the umbrella organization of the Olympic Movement. The IOC's primary role is to supervise the organization of the summer and winter Olympic Games.

The IOC has come under much criticism in recent years for poor governance practices, corruption allegations against some officials and for not doing enough to share the proceeds of Olympic Games with those nations in most need. In reaction, the IOC has greatly improved its reporting to member organizations, providing far greater transparency for how revenues are distributed to National Olympic Committees and through a variety of sport development programs around the globe.

Similar to the IOC, the role of the CGF is to facilitate a major games event every four years but it also provides education assistance for sports development throughout the 53 Commonwealth countries. There are more Commonwealth Games Associations (CGA) (71) than countries (53) because some countries like the UK have seven CGAs (Scotland, England, Northern Ireland, Wales, Isle of Man, Jersey and Guernsey) that all compete in the Games as separate nations (www.commonwealthgames.com). Both the IOC and CGF fund their operations through contributions from governments that host the games, and the sale of international broadcasting rights, corporate sponsorship, ticket sales, licensing and merchandising sales.

There are also a range of specialist nonprofit organizations that focus on discrete community groups. Foremost among these is the International Paralympic Committee (IPC) which is the international representative organization of elite sports for athletes with disabilities. The IPC organizes, supervises and coordinates the Paralympic Games and other multi-disability sports competitions at elite level (www.paralympic.org). Other similar nonprofit organizations include the Cerebral Palsy International Sports and Recreation Association and the International Blind Sport Federation which facilitate major events for athletes.

Our focus for the remainder of the chapter is on those nonprofit sport organizations that provide sporting competition or event participation opportunities for their members and other members of the public – sport governing bodies and sports clubs. In countries such as Australia, the UK, Canada, New Zealand, Hong Kong and others with club based sporting systems, almost all sporting teams and competitions are organized by nonprofit sport organizations (Lyons 2001). These organizations take many forms. They include small local clubs that may field a few teams in a local football competition; regional associations that coordinate competitions between clubs; and state or provincial organizations that not only facilitate competitions, but also manage coach development, talent identification, volunteer training, marketing and sponsorship. They also comprise national sporting organizations that regulate the rules of competition in a country, coordinate national championships between state or provincial teams, manage elite athlete programs, employ development officers to conduct clinics, and undertake many other tasks that facilitate participation in sport. Finally, there are international sports federations that coordinate the development of sport across the globe and facilitate rule changes and liaison between countries on issues like international competitions.

The common element amongst all these sport organizations is their nonprofit focus – they exist to facilitate sporting opportunities for their members who may be individual athletes, coaches, officials or administrators, clubs, associations, or other sport organizations. They are also interdependent, relying on each other to provide playing talent, information to access competitions, resources for coach, official and player development and funding to support their activities. It is important to note that volunteers are at the heart of these organizations, playing significant roles in service delivery and decision-making at all levels of nonprofit sport organizations. At the same time though, many of the larger nonprofit sport organizations contain a significant number of paid staff who support their ongoing administration and service delivery to member associations and clubs.

GOVERNING BODIES OF SPORT

Sport clubs compete against other clubs in competition structures provided by regional or state/provincial sporting organizations. State based teams compete in competitions facilitated by national sporting organizations, and nations compete in leagues or events provided by international federations of sport, such as the Fédération Internationale de Football Association (FIFA), or major competition organizations such as the International Olympic Committee or the Commonwealth Games Association. These organizations are known as governing bodies for sport, that have the responsibility for the management, administration and development for a sport on a global, national, state/provincial level, or regional level.

The structure of the International Netball Federation Limited (IFNA) typifies the relationships between these various governing bodies of sport. The members of IFNA comprise 39 national associations from five regions: Africa, Asia, Americas, Europe and Oceania. Each region elects 2 members to direct the activities of the world governing organization who are responsible for setting the rules for netball, running international competitions, promoting good management in the regions, striving to seek Olympic accreditation for netball, and increasing participation levels around the globe.

Netball Australia, one of the 39 members of IFNA, has more than 350,000 registered players who participate through eight state/provincial associations. They in turn have a total of 541 affiliated associations. Each of the state/provincial associations has a delegate to the national board who, along with the staff of Netball Australia, are responsible for communicating rule changes from IFNA to their members, managing a national competition, promoting good management in the state/provincial organizations, increasing participation nationally, and bidding to host world events.

One of the largest members of Netball Australia, Netball Victoria, has 110,000 registered players who compete in 250 affiliated associations, organized into 21 regions and six zones across the state. Netball Victoria's role differs markedly from Netball Australia and IFNA, with responsibility for coach, official and player development, managing state competitions, promoting good management in the clubs, providing insurance coverage for players, assisting in facility development, trying to increase participation in the state, bidding to host national events, and managing two teams in the national competition. Finally, netball clubs field teams, find coaches and players, manage volunteers, conduct fundraising and may own and operate a facility.

It is important to remember that these sport governing organizations are volunteer based, with volunteers involved in decisions at every level from clubs to international federations. As discussed in Chapter 12, nonprofit sport organizations do not operate as top-down power hierarchies, with clubs always abiding by regional directives, or national governing bodies agreeing with international policy initiatives. Communication and agreement can be difficult between these organizations that may have competing priorities and localized issues. A spirit of cooperation and negotiation is required to make the nonprofit sport system operate effectively. The simple exerting of authority in a traditional organizational hierarchy is not appropriate for most nonprofit sport organizations.

THE SPORTS CLUB ENVIRONMENT

At the centre of sport development in countries such as Canada, New Zealand, Australia and the UK is the local or community sports club. It is worth taking some time to reflect on the role of the sports club, how volunteers and staff work in the club environment and how clubs contribute to sport development.

A background report initially prepared in 2001 and updated in 2002 for Sport Scotland provides a snapshot of sport clubs in Scotland (Allison 2002). The most striking thing about local sport clubs is their diversity. Sport clubs have many functions, structures, resources, values and ideologies and they provide an enormous range of participation opportunities for people to be involved in sport. Most clubs provide activity in a single sport, and have as their focus enjoyment in sport, rather than competitive success. Sport clubs in Scotland come in various sizes, with an average membership size of 133, and most tend to cater for both junior and adult participants. They operate with minimum staffing, structures, income and expenditure, and often rely on a small group of paid or unpaid individuals to organize and administer club activities. The majority of club income comes from membership payments, so they tend to operate fairly autonomously. The management of local sport clubs in Scotland is regarded as an 'organic and intuitive process based on trust and experience rather than formal contracts and codes of practice' (Allison 2002, p. 7).

The characteristics of local sport clubs in other countries are similar. The vast majority of sport clubs rely almost exclusively on volunteers to govern, administer, and manage their organizations and to provide coaching, officiating and general assistance with training, match day functions and fundraising.

Administrators

Administrators who fill roles as elected or appointed committee members have the responsibility for the overall guidance, direction and supervision of the organization. According to the Australian Sports Commission (2000, p. 2) the responsibility of the management committee of a sports club extends to:

1 conducting long-term planning for the future of the club;
2 developing policy and procedures for club activities;
3 managing external relations with other sport organizations, local governments or sponsors;
4 managing financial resources and legal issues on behalf of the club;
5 carrying out recommendations put forward by members;
6 communicating to members on current issues or developments;
7 evaluating the performance of officials, employees (if any), and other serviced providers;
8 ensuring adequate records are kept for future transfer of responsibilities to new committee members;
9 acting as role models for other club members.

While governance is covered in detail in Chapter 13, it is important to note here that the ability of clubs to carry out these tasks effectively will vary according to their resources, culture and the quality of people willing to be involved. The important administrative roles within local sports club are the chairperson or president, secretary, treasurer and volunteer coordinator. Other committee roles might involve responsibility for coaching, officiating, representative teams, match day arrangements, fundraising or marketing.

The chairperson or president should be the one to set the agenda for how a committee operates, work to develop the strategic direction of the club, chair committee meetings, and coordinate the work of other members of the committee. Club secretaries are the administrative link between members, the committee and other organizations and have responsibility for managing correspondence, records, and information about club activities. The treasurer has responsibility for preparing the annual budget, monitoring expenditure and revenue, planning for future financial needs and managing operational issues such as petty cash, payments and banking. The position of volunteer coordinator involves the development of systems and procedures to manage volunteers such as planning, recruitment, training and recognition.

Coaches

Coaches working in the sport club system may be unpaid or paid, depending on the nature of the sport and the resources of individual clubs. The role of the coach is central to developing athlete's skills and knowledge, in helping them learn tactics for success, and enjoy their sport. Coaches also act as important role models for players and athletes.

Most sports provide a structured training and accreditation scheme for coaches to develop their skills and experience to coach at local, state/provincial, national or international levels. In Australia, for example, the National Coaching Council established a three-tier National Coaching Accreditation Scheme (NCAS) in 1978. Coaches can undertake a Level 1 introductory course, Level 2 intermediate course and Level 3 advanced course in coaching. NCAS training programs comprise three elements:

1   coaching principles that cover fundamentals of coaching and athletic performance;
2   sport-specific coaching that covers the skills, techniques, strategies and scientific approaches to a particular sport; and
3   coaching practice where coaches engage in practical coaching and application of coaching principles.

Officials

Sports officials include those people who act as referees, umpires, judges, scorers or timekeepers to officiate over games or events. The majority of officials are unpaid, but some sports such as Australian Rules Football, basketball, and some other football codes pay officials at all levels, enabling some to earn a substantial salary from full-time officiating. Other sports such as netball, softball or tennis rarely pay officials unless they are at state or national championship level. Sports officials are critical to facilitating people's involvement in sport but are the hardest positions to fill within the nonprofit sport system since they absorb a lot of time and often have low status.

All sports provide a structured training and accreditation scheme for officials in much the same way as coaches to develop their skills and experience at local, state/ provincial, national or international levels. The Australian National Officiating Accreditation Scheme (NOAS) was established in 1994, modelled on the NCAS, but does not prescribe formal levels of officiating as these vary greatly between sporting codes. The NOAS aims to develop and implement programs that improve the quality, quantity, leadership and status of sports officiating in Australia through training programs that comprise three elements: (1) general principles of officiating and event management, (2) sport-specific technical rules, interpretations, reporting and specific roles, and (3) practice at officiating and applying the officiating principles.

General volunteers

Sports clubs also depend on people to perform roles in fundraising, managing representative teams, helping with match day arrangements such as car parking or stewarding, or helping to market the club. The majority of general volunteers have an existing link to a sports club through being a parent of a child who plays at the club, having some other family connection, or through friends and work colleagues involved in the club.

The Volunteering Australia 2004 publication, *Snapshot 2004: Volunteering Report Card*, provided a detailed picture of volunteer involvement in a range of activities. In the 12 months prior to April 2004, an estimated 4.3 million persons over the age of 15 in Australia were involved in organized sport and physical activity – 27 per cent of the total population. Of those, 1.5 million persons were involved in non-playing roles such as coach, official, administrator, scorer, medical support or other role, and about one third of them had more than one non-playing role. Only about 12 per cent of these people received payment for their role, which means that 88 per cent of these 1.5 million people involved in non-playing roles were volunteers. Of these 1.5 million people, 60 per cent also played sport. The majority of non-playing involvement was associated with junior sport. While making comparisons between data sets is difficult due to differences in sampling methods and instruments, the data between 1993 and 2004 indicated that while the numbers of people coaching remains constant, the numbers of people involved in officiating and administration has declined. The majority of these would be volunteers, highlighting the potential fragility of a sport system dependent on volunteers to facilitate involvement.

Figures on voluntary participation in New Zealand show that just under 20 per cent of the adult population was involved as a volunteer in the physical leisure sector in 1998 (Hillary Commission 2000). These roles included 11.1 per cent as coaches, 8.7 per cent as officials, and 8.8 per cent as administrators, with people donating an average of 2.7 hours/week volunteering. This voluntary contribution was estimated to be more than 77 per cent of the equivalent full-time workforce, and worth nearly NZ$900 million a year. These figures clearly illustrate the enormous contribution volunteers make in roles such as coaches, officials and administrators in order to facilitate people's involvement in sport. However, there are some worrying signs that such voluntary involvement may be on the wane and that in order to sustain current levels of involvement in sport, the management of sport volunteers needs to improve.

GOVERNMENT INTERVENTION

The substantial funds allocated to nonprofit sport organizations by governments to support their activities in areas of mass participation or elite performance has meant that governments are increasingly trying to influence the way in which the nonprofit sector of sport operates. Examples of these attempts include the Australian Sports Commission Volunteer Management Program and the policy of Sport England to have national organizations develop 'whole of sport' plans. These are briefly reviewed below to highlight the increasingly interdependent nature of government and sport organizations in seeking improvements in nonprofit sport.

The Australian Sports Commission developed the Volunteer Involvement Program in 1994 in partnership with the Australian Society of Sports Administrators, the Confederation of Australian Sport, and state departments of sport and recreation. The program aimed to improve the operation of nonprofit sport clubs and associations by providing a series of publications on sport club administration. In 2000, the Volunteer Management Program (VMP) and the Club and Association Management Program (CAMP) resources were published, and the ASC encouraged all clubs to join a Club Development Network and engage in strategic planning and other management techniques.

Another example is the policy developed by Sport England to require national sport organizations to develop 'whole of sport plans'. In 2003 Sport England identified 30 priority sports, based on their capability to contribute to Sport England's vision of an active and successful sporting nation, and is now working with the national sport organizations to develop and implement these plans. The plans are designed to outline how a sport from grassroots right to the elite level will attract and keep participants, and improve their sporting experiences. The plans will drive decisions by Sport England to provide funding to national organizations based on clearly articulated ideas of the resources they need to drive their sport. The plans will also provide for measurable performance results and assist Sport England to evaluate the benefits that accrue from funding nonprofit sport organizations.

The CLUBMARK program developed by Sport England is indicative of the approach many governments have taken toward trying to enhance the capacity of the nonprofit sport sector at the community club level. Because approximately 60 per cent of young people in England belong to a sports club outside of school (where government can influence delivery standards via the education system), the government sought to improve the standard of service delivery that young people receive from community sport clubs by creating CLUBMARK, a cross-sport quality accreditation for clubs with junior sections run by Sport England. The main purpose of CLUBMARK was to encourage sport clubs to seek accreditation as a CLUBMARK club. National governing bodies of sport (NGBs) and county sport partnerships (CSPs) award CLUBMARK to proven high quality clubs. The national scheme has been in place since 2002 and midway through 2011 there were more than 10,750 accredited clubs in the CLUBMARK scheme.

CLUBMARK accreditation is awarded to clubs that comply with minimum operating standards in four areas: the playing program, duty of care and child protection, sports equity and ethics, and club management. Clubs working towards accreditation can receive support and advice from their NGB and other partners such as county sports partnerships (CSPs). Circumstances vary between clubs and sports but the process of accreditation is the same. The benefits of implementing a single, national standard for sport club operations gives structure and direction to sports clubs of all types, specifically in areas such as:

- Club development – The foundation for any club is its youth structure. By encouraging and attracting young members, it is building a strong future.
- Increased membership – Addressing issues like equity and child protection gives parents confidence when choosing a club for their children.

- Developing coaches and volunteers – As part of CLUBMARK, clubs receive help in developing the skills of those involved in their organization.
- Raised profile – Once CLUBMARK accredited, clubs are listed on a national database and in other directories, to help them attract new members and grow.

The CLUBMARK program provides sports clubs a framework for volunteer management as well as a series of templates that they can adapt for their specific circumstances. CLUBMARK is managed by Knight, Kavanagh & Page (KKP) on behalf of Sport England. It is responsible for validation of NGBs and CSPs, for moderation of its impact on clubs and for the marketing and promotion of the programme throughout England (Sport England 2011a).

In Practice 3.2 Sport England Sport Makers

One of the more ambitious government intervention programs aimed at influencing the direction and capacity of the nonprofit sport sector is the Sport Makers program, an initiative tied to the London 2012 Olympic Games. According to the Sport England website before the 2012 Games, the intention was that the Sport Makers program would recruit, train and deploy 50,000 new sports volunteers aged 16 years and over to organize and lead community sporting activities across England. The program was designed to grow the volunteer base who would have:

> A positive and inspiring introduction to the world of sport volunteering via a series of workshops delivered locally through a training provider and in conjunction with a county sports partnership. We anticipate that many volunteers will continue to give of their time, further increasing sport participation long after the 2012 Games are held in the UK. These Sport Makers will organise and support hundreds of thousands of new hours of grassroots sport, creating new opportunities across the country. While doing so, they will bring the Olympic and Paralympic values to life in every community. Sport Makers will be fully inclusive and target participants including people who have a disability, both males and females and participants from BME groups.
>
> (Sport England 2011b)

The Sport Makers program was originally scheduled to run from April 2011 until September 2013 with a budget of £4 million drawn from National Lottery Funding, with approximately half delivered via county sport partnerships. The outcomes were planned to include:

- 50,000 new Sport Makers recruited and invited to an orientation workshop delivered locally through a CSP and by an inspirational trainer.
- 40,000 Sport Makers are provided with deployment opportunities to increase participation for a minimum of 10 hours each by their CSP. Of those deployed, we anticipate 20,000 will continue to volunteer in sport beyond these 10 hours.

- Olympic and Paralympic values are brought to life for the Sport Makers through their orientation workshop so that they feel part of the Olympic movement and role model these values in raising participation.
- As a result of their deployment, thousands of new opportunities for people aged 16 and over to participate will be created.

(Sport England 2011b)

This ambitious program involved the British Olympic Association, London Organising Committee of the Olympic Games, national governing bodies, county sports partnerships, local authority sports development teams, local governments, and a range of national and county/sub-regional voluntary partners. A review published in March 2013 (Nichols et al.) concluded that while it had assisted the work of county sports partnerships, it had failed to meet its original targets. Such a centralized, target driven approach highlights the complexities of achieving significant sustainable change in the nonprofit sport sector where partnerships and collaboration across all the stakeholders involved in delivering sport is required.

Source: Sport England (2011b). *Sport Makers factsheet*. London, UK: Sport England; Nichols, G., Ferguson, G., Grix, J. & Griffiths, J. (2013) *Sport Makers: Developing Good Practice in Volunteer and Sports Development*, University of Sheffield.

ISSUES FOR THE NONPROFIT SPORT SECTOR

A range of challenges exist for the nonprofit sport sector around the globe. Foremost among these is the dependence on volunteers to sustain the sports system in areas such as coaching, administration and officiating. As highlighted earlier in this chapter there is evidence to suggest that the rate of volunteerism is declining for roles such as officiating and administration in sport. Governments and nonprofit sport organizations will need to address this issue if their mutually dependent goals of increasing participation in organized sport are to be achieved.

The increasingly litigious nature of society and the associated increase in costs of insurance for nonprofit sport organizations directly affects the cost of participation. In Australia fewer insurers are providing insurance cover for sporting organizations and insurance premium prices have risen significantly in recent years. For example, the public liability insurance premium for the Australian Parachute Federation increased from AUS$127,000 to AUS$1.1 million in two years. Public liability insurance is vital to run sport events and programs and these costs are passed on to participants for no additional benefits, which raises the question of whether people can afford to keep playing sport in traditional nonprofit systems.

A further issue for nonprofit sport organizations is the trend away from participating in traditional sports, organized through clubs and associations, to a more informal pattern of participation. Some people are unwilling to commit to a season of sporting involvement, and are seeking ways to engage in sport and physical activity on a more casual basis, either through short-term commercial providers or with friends in spontaneous or pick-up sports (Stewart et al. 2004). The increase in options available to young people to spend their discretionary leisure dollars, euros or pounds has also presented challenges for nonprofit sport organizations to market themselves as an attractive option.

As highlighted earlier, nonprofit organizations, including nonprofit sport organizations face significant capacity problems. They are often constrained by the size of their facilities or venues, and may struggle to attract enough quality people to manage the operations of their organization. They are also constrained by the interdependent nature of sport – they require other clubs, teams and organizations to provide competition – so they need to work cooperatively with other nonprofit sport organizations to expand their 'product'.

The very nature of nonprofit sport organizations requires adherence to frequently cumbersome consultative decision-making processes, often across large geographic areas and with widely dispersed and disparate groups of stakeholders. The additional complexity of the governance and management requirements of these organizations present their own set of challenges in terms of making timely decisions, reacting to market trends, being innovative, or seeking agreement on significant organizational changes.

Lyons (2001) also suggests that nonprofit organizations are unique because they have difficulty in judging performance relative to their commercial counterparts, have to be accountable to a wide range of stakeholders, and must deal with tension and possible conflict between paid staff and volunteers. These tensions are due to a lack of clarity about paid staff and volunteer roles, and are exacerbated by the lack of clear performance measures. Nonprofit sport organizations are particularly susceptible to these problems, especially where there is a coterie of paid staff in senior administrative positions. In Practice 3.3 explores the challenges facing the nonprofit sport sector in the area of recruiting and retaining volunteers.

In Practice 3.3 Volunteer retention and capacity issues

A report from the UK based Institute for Volunteering Research (2008) concluded that sport and recreation organizations were most likely to report difficulties with recruiting enough volunteers compared to other categories of nonprofit organizations. They also found that these organizations were more likely to say that they experienced difficulties with the retention of volunteers in the last year and that they were most likely to say that they wanted to involve more volunteers. Crucially the report concluded that organizations in the sports (and arts and culture) fields were less likely to have structured volunteer management practices in place or to have funding to support volunteers. Unsurprisingly, it was also more common for sport and recreation organizations to report difficulties in recruiting sufficient numbers of volunteers compared to other fields of activity. Another report from the same year identified three main problems faced by sports clubs in England: a shortage of volunteers, difficulty in recruiting new volunteers and the fact that work is increasingly left to fewer people. These are common problems in most westernized countries of the world where sport is primarily delivered through nonprofit sport organizations.

The reasons why this may be the case can be found in an earlier report commissioned by the top government agency responsible for sports development in England, Sport England, that (in part) identified the challenges faced by volunteers and volunteer managers in the English sports industry (Leisure Industries Research Centre, 2003). Sport volunteering in England has many of the same problems facing the sports industries of Australia, New Zealand and Canada. The 2003 report concluded that the sport system and its volunteers were subject to a variety of often competing pressures, driven by changes in government policy, technological change, and market competition for leisure expenditure. Core sport volunteers, those people who work, have children, and participate in sport, were most affected. As national government and sport organizations pursue policies that attempt to increase participation at the grassroots as well as drive improvements in elite performance, volunteers are being asked to deal with an ever-increasing complexity and required level of professionalism in organizational procedures and systems. Government funding is increasingly tied to the ability of a sports organization to deliver measurable outcomes and be more accountable for their activities.

Improvements in technology and subsequent demands from end users for sport organizations to use the latest technology have placed increased demands on sport volunteers. An example of this is the shift to artificial playing surfaces for field hockey. These surfaces undoubtedly improve the playing and spectator experience but require volunteers at club level to fundraise continuously to meet significantly increased financial obligations.

The increasingly competitive leisure market has also meant volunteers at the club level have to manage their organizations to meet the demands of diverse 'customers' rather than the traditional member. People who are new to a sport may find it hard to differentiate between community club providers and commercial facilities and expect volunteers to meet their demands without becoming engaged in the life of the club. An example is the parent who treats the nonprofit sporting club as a cheap child minding option by dropping off and picking up their child without donating any time, energy or skills to the running of the club.

The capacity of nonprofit sport organizations and their volunteers to deal with these pressures varies enormously. Some have well-established systems and resources; others flounder from one crisis to the next, continuously playing catch up. The organizations and volunteers at the community level are the ones most affected. The 2003 report recommended the use of a range of flexible and practical solutions to assist nonprofit sport organizations deal with these pressures. These included the provision of better education and training resources, simplified government funding requirements, reducing the compliance burden of reporting for sports organizations, and talking to nonprofit sports organizations in language more attuned to their core values of individual volunteer motivations and commitment than overly sophisticated business and management language.

Sources: Leisure Industries Research Centre (2003). *Sports Volunteering in England 2002: A Report for Sport England*. Sheffield, UK: Leisure Industries Research Centre; Institute for Volunteering Research (2008). *Management Matters: A National Survey of Volunteer Management Capacity*. London, UK: Institute for Volunteering Research; and Institute for Volunteering Research and Volunteering England (2008). *A Winning Team? The Impacts of Volunteers in Sport*. London, UK: Institute for Volunteering Research.

SUMMARY

Nonprofit organizations were defined as those organizations that are institutionally separate from the state, do not return profits to owners, are self-governing, have a significant element of voluntary contribution and are formally incorporated. Nonprofit organizations exist to develop communities, meet the needs of identifiable and discrete groups in those communities, and work for the benefit of public good rather than wealth creation for individuals. The majority of nonprofit organizations are driven largely by the efforts of volunteers rather than paid staff.

Sport organizations that operate on a nonprofit basis include professional service organizations, industry lobby groups, sport event organizations and sport governing bodies. By far the greatest numbers of nonprofit sport organizations are those that provide sporting competition or event participation opportunities for their members and other members of the public – sport governing bodies and sports clubs. The common element amongst all these sport organizations is their nonprofit focus – they exist to facilitate sporting opportunities for their members who may be individual athletes, coaches, officials or administrators, clubs, associations, or other sport organizations. They are also interdependent, relying on each other to provide playing talent, information to access competitions, resources for coach, official and player development, and funding to support their activities.

Sport governing bodies and clubs rely almost exclusively on volunteers to govern, administer and manage their organizations and to provide coaching, officiating and general assistance with training, events and fundraising. The substantial funds allocated to nonprofit sport organizations by governments to support their activities in areas of mass participation or elite performance has meant that governments are increasingly trying to influence the way in which the nonprofit sector of sport operates. Finally, a number of challenges exist for the nonprofit sport sector including the dependence on volunteers to sustain the sports system, the increasingly litigious nature of society and the associated increase in costs of insurance for nonprofit sport organizations, the trend away from participating in traditional sports, significant capacity problems, and the additional complexity of the governance and management requirements of these organizations.

REVIEW QUESTIONS

1 What is the role of the nonprofit sector in relation to sport?

2 What are the unique aspects of nonprofit sport organizations that set them apart from profit oriented or privately owned sport organizations?

3 Describe the role of a local community sport club.

4 Explain how the state and the nonprofit sector may contribute to sport development.

5 In what ways are volunteers important to the delivery of sport?

6 What are the important management roles in nonprofit sporting clubs?

7 Explain the role of a national governing body for a sport.

8 Why does the government attempt to intervene in the management of nonprofit sport organizations? Explain how governments do this in your own country.

9 How can nonprofit sport organizations reduce the costs to participants?

10 Explain how nonprofit sport organizations have to work cooperatively with each other but still compete on the playing field.

FURTHER READING

Cuskelly, G., Hoye, R. & Auld, C. (2006). *Working with Volunteers in Sport: Theory and Practice*. London: Routledge.

Green, M. (2006). From 'sport for all' to not about 'sport' at all: Interrogating sport policy interventions in the United Kingdom. *European Sport Management Quarterly*, 6(3), 217–238.

Houlihan, B. & Green, M. (2007). *Comparative Elite Sport Development Systems, Structures and Public Policy*. London: Elsevier.

Houlihan, B. & White, A. (2002). *The Politics of Sports Development: Development of Sport or Development through Sport?* London: Routledge.

Hylton, K. & Bramham, P. (eds) (2007). *Sports Development: Policy, Process and Practice*. 2nd edn. London: Routledge.

May, T., Harris, S. & Collins, M. (2013). Implementing community sport policy: understanding the variety of voluntary club types and their attitudes to policy, *International Journal of Sport Policy and Politics*, 5(3), 397–419.

Misener, K. & Doherty, A. (2013). Understanding capacity through the processes and outcomes of interorganizational relationships in nonprofit community sport organizations, *Sport Management Review*, 16(2), 135–147.

Productivity Commission (2010). *Contribution of the Not-for-Profit Sector*, Canberra: Commonwealth of Australia.

Sport England (2011a). *Clubmark factsheet*. London, UK: Sport England.

Sport England (2011b). *Sport Makers factsheet*. London, UK: Sport England.

RELEVANT WEBSITES

The following websites are useful starting points for further information on nonprofit sport organizations:

- Association for Research in Nonprofit Organizations and Voluntary Action at www. arnova.org
- Australian Sports Commission at www.ausport.gov.au
- Sport New Zealand at www.sportnz.org.nz
- Sport Canada at http://pch.gc.ca/eng/1266246552427
- Sport England at www.sportengland.org
- Sport Scotland at www.sportscotland.org.uk
- Volunteering Australia at www.volunteeringaustralia.org
- CLUBMARK website at www.clubmark.org.uk/about/about-clubmark

CASE STUDY 3.1

Gymnastics Australia

This case study explores the difficulties faced by nonprofit sport organizations in delivering sport through a network of volunteer controlled community based organizations but with the added complexities of being a multi-disciplinary sport and with commercial operators involved in the sport delivery pathway.

Gymnastics Australia's purpose is to represent the interests of gymnastics in Australia as the Australian affiliate of the International Gymnastics Federation (FIG). Gymnastics Australia, in cooperation with the association members (state associations), coordinates and provides for the participation by Australian athletes, coaches and officials in gymnastics and approved national and international competitions. Gymnastics Australia is made up of eight association members:

- ACT Gymnastics Association Inc.
- NSW Gymnastics Association Inc.
- NT Gymnastics Association Inc.
- Queensland Gymnastics Association Inc.
- Gymnastics South Australian Inc.
- Tasmania Gymnastics Associations Inc.
- Victorian Gymnastics Association Inc.
- Gymnastics Western Australia Inc.

The organization covers seven core disciplines of Gymsports: men's artistic and women's artistic (the 'traditional' forms of gymnastics), rhythmic, trampoline, aerobic, acrobatic and cheerleading. In addition, Gymnastics Australia runs *Gymnastics for All*, a program that is the basis of all Gymsports and a Gymsport in its own right. Clubs can utilize *Gymnastics for All* as a starting point for teaching the fundamentals, before gymnasts specialize in any of the other Gymsports. Alternatively, clubs may focus on *Gymnastics for All* which develops gymnasts with diverse skills, adaptable to a variety of movement experiences. *Gymnastics for All* has been categorized by the International Federation of Gymnastics (FIG) into the following areas: Gymnastics with apparatus and Gymnastics and Dance. Display Gymnastics is a large and dynamic aspect of *Gymnastics for All* with opportunities for gymnasts to perform at club, state, national and international display events. KinderGym activities for children under the age of five years also come under the banner of *Gymnastics for All*. Club programs which follow the KinderGym Guiding Principles, have an underlying philosophy of learning through play.

A perennial issue for any nonprofit sport organization is the struggle to maintain minimum standards of service delivery with limited resources and when a variety of 'agents' (clubs, schools, businesses) are delivering the sport opportunities (i.e. the sport 'product'). Gymnastics Australia's approach has been to develop a quality assurance and risk management approach – Club 10 for affiliated gymnastics clubs. Involving a series of checklists and application processes, clubs can move through the five levels of accreditation via self-assessment, external assessment and endorsement. There are five Club 10 Accreditation Categories (Star 1 to Star 5) each with unique compliance requirements. Star 3 is the benchmark for all clubs (the 'middle ground') where clubs are required to demonstrate compliance with all Club 10 National Standards through submission of documentation and evidence.

Club 10 was developed to help people who run gymnastics clubs understand how to establish and maintain management systems that will assure quality and give the necessary information to enable clubs to build such systems. Management systems, if well planned and written, will underpin any service business such as a gymnastics club. Although not all gymnastics clubs will need to restructure all processes to meet National Standards, Club 10 can make good business sense and should also lead to improvements within each club.

There are many advantages for implementing quality management systems within a gymnastics club. The benefits associated with quality assurance and risk management can include improvements to both internal processes and external operations. Through Club 10, gymnastics clubs can experience:

- assurance that risk management strategies are in place which could reduce the likelihood and impact of liability claims;
- enhanced recognition nationally that can create new opportunities in membership recruitment and retention;
- continuous improvement of club performance through ongoing accreditation and compliance;
- boosted staff morale through increased management efficiencies; and
- bottom-line benefits through increased efficiency, reduced waste and better utilization of resources.

The system enables clubs to improve their performance in promotion and marketing, technical development, membership, information, services, compliance, planning, leadership, management, communication, and facilities and equipment – all common issues for any nonprofit sport organization. The GA website states that Club 10 is designed to assist gymnastics clubs measure current performance and build a solid foundation for future success. Rigorous, objective assessment provides an overview of the extent to which the systems and operations of the club are aligned to the principles and National Standards of Club 10. Club 10 is a review of the club's management processes and performance against a standard model of excellence as determined by and for gymnastics clubs. Assessment through Club 10 enables your club to clearly:

- assess the performance of its leadership and management systems;
- build those results into strategic planning processes;
- benchmark where the club stands in terms of the sporting marketplace and competitors; and
- drive and focus business improvements to achieve measurable results.

While Club 10 has been developed by GA, the implementation of the process is actually delivered by the eight affiliated state and territory associations to clubs that wish to affiliate with their respective state or territory association. GA imposes, via its member associations, minimum standards for clubs to be able to be affiliated which form the basis for achieving the first level of the Club 10 accreditation ratings.

In addition to clubs becoming members, individual athletes, coaches and judges can become members. Athletes become registered members so that their performance and progression can be monitored, while coaches and judges become members so that GA can be assured that the right people receive the right training and have acquired the correct skills to be able to perform their roles as either coach or judge.

Source: Much of the material for this case study is based on the contents of the Gymnastics Australia website that can be found at www.gymnastics.org.au

CASE STUDY QUESTIONS

1 Visit the Gymnastics Australia website and document all the roles where volunteers are involved in the governance, management and operations of gymnastics. Do these roles differ between the disciplines of Gymsports?

2 Explain how the Club 10 accreditation system for gymnastics operates across Australia.

3 What are the roles of volunteers versus paid staff in this system?

4 Identify the strengths and weaknesses of the club accreditation system used by GA to ensure good quality in service deliver.

5 What alternative structures or systems could be used to improve the experience of people wanting to be involved in gymnastics in Australia?

CASE STUDY 3.2

England Hockey

This case study also explores the difficulties faced by nonprofit sport organizations in delivering sport through a network of volunteer controlled community based organizations. As the chapter has highlighted, the capacity of nonprofit sport organizations varies enormously according to the local environment in which it operates, the degree of support it receives from its local government authority, its asset base, the competitiveness of the local market (i.e. how many other sports can people choose to play), and crucially, the management system used by its volunteers and their individual abilities, skills and experience in managing a sport organization.

England Hockey is the national governing body (NGB) for field hockey in England. England Hockey officially commenced operations in January 2003, taking over from its predecessor, the English Hockey Association (EHA) which, in turn, was formed in 1996 to unite the then separate men's, women's and mixed associations. England Hockey employs over 70 full-time staff who work with volunteers at club, county, regional and national level to coach, officiate and administer the sport. England Hockey is affiliated to the European Hockey Federation (EHF) and International Hockey Federation (FIH). The FIH is responsible for the production of the 'Rules of Hockey' which are the rules that are followed worldwide by all players and umpires participating in the game. The role of England Hockey is to govern hockey in England from grassroots to the elite end of the sport.

Governance of the game is devolved at a regional and local level to Regional and County Associations. There are six Regional Associations – East, Midlands, North, South, West and the Combined Services who represent the three single service Associations. Counties affiliate to their respective Region. These bodies bring clubs together at a local level and ensure that information is cascaded up and down through the game. They are also responsible for implementing the Disciplinary Code of England Hockey.

The Regional Associations are represented on the Regional Consultative Committee (RCC) which supports the work of the Board to ensure it is operating in line with the agreed Memorandum & Articles of England Hockey and follows best practice in terms of the financial management of the company's affairs. England Hockey has more than 1050 affiliated clubs. These clubs also affiliate to their County and Regional Associations. The England Hockey website states that 'the bedrock of club activity is league hockey played mostly on Saturdays almost exclusively on artificial turf pitches'. This is organized through Regional and County Leagues with the top Men's and Women's clubs playing nationally in the English Hockey League of which the men's game is played on Sunday. Parallel umpiring associations and committees ensure that the games are controlled, where possible, by suitably qualified officials and just as there is a progression through leagues for teams so umpires will progress from the grassroots of the game through to national and international level.

Clubs consist of between one and 20 teams who usually have a regular booking at a local hockey pitch or field, either at a school or a leisure centre and will use a pub (hotel) for post-match social activity. Other clubs will own their own clubhouse and pitch(es). Other club activity will include midweek training, and an increasing number of clubs undertake youth development work on weekdays after school, in the evenings and on Sundays. Hockey is a very popular sport with young people and is played in schools as well as junior sections of clubs. Regions and Counties play an important role in the promotion of the game through the work they undertake with development schemes and initiatives and organizing age group representative sides – often in partnership with other local agencies.

A key aspect of the delivery of hockey throughout the country is Hockey's Single System, the development pathway for players, coaches and officials. It is based on a set of principles for long-term athlete development that puts the participant at the centre and is based on scientific research that has been widely accepted by the majority of other major sports within England. The system delivers opportunities for people of most ages to participate in hockey and is based on a complex system of service providers, clubs, schools and associations working together to coach and support players.

A cornerstone of the England Hockey model (and many other sports) is the affiliation fees charged to members which enable England Hockey to deliver the strategy to develop hockey. Affiliating to England Hockey provides clubs access to:

- ClubsFirst, an industry wide and hockey-specific club accreditation scheme linked to Sport England's CLUBMARK accreditation, which means your club can be recognized as safe, effective and child-friendly;
- over 40 different organised and managed competitions for clubs and teams to compete in;
- Grow Your Own resources and support;
- industry approved coaching qualification courses;
- regional support offices – staff with local knowledge to help support your club on issues relevant to you;
- safeguarding guidance and templates to make it easier for clubs to provide a safe environment for children, helping you to protect young people and your club;
- the provision of coaches, umpires, tutors and assessors for clubs, counties and regions who help raise the standards of hockey and ensure a more enjoyable playing experience;
- easy to understand, fair and transparent player pathways, from picking up a stick for the first time through to representing your country in hockey;
- discounted and exclusive insurance for your club, to cover liability and personal accident insurance for your members;
- awards in officiating, safeguarding young people and leadership, to support individuals and club development;

- a quarterly copy of *Hockey News* magazine keeping you up-to-date with club and national hockey news;
- benefits from funding and sponsorship such as reduced fees in junior and adult competitions;
- access to Capital Funding;
- individual guidance and support on how to develop your club, or how you as an individual can develop your skills on or off the pitch;
- information, resources and website downloads so you can get the latest hockey news and information relevant to you;
- CRB checking at a low cost, designed to help clubs meet government requirements of working with young people, and including all the follow-up required when a CRB reveals detrimental information.

Source: Much of the material for this case study is based on the contents of the England Hockey website that can be found at www.englandhockey.co.uk

CASE STUDY QUESTIONS

1   Visit the England Hockey website and document all the roles where volunteers are involved in the governance, management and operations of hockey in England.

2   Explain how the Single System for hockey operates across England. What are the roles of volunteers versus paid staff in this system? If the 2013 review report of the Single System is available on their website this would be a useful starting point to help answer this question.

3   Identify the strengths and weaknesses of the voluntary system used by England Hockey to deliver hockey throughout England.

4   What alternative structures or systems could replace the nonprofit sector for hockey in England?

CHAPTER 4

Professional sport

OVERVIEW

This chapter examines the key features of professional sport organizations and provides examples of the unique features of professional sport leagues and clubs. The chapter does not examine community, state or national sport organizations, but does comment on the relationship between these organizations and professional sport, as well as the impact professional sport has on the sport industry in general.

After completing this chapter the reader should be able to:

- identify the ways in which professional sport dominates the global sport industry;
- understand and explain the ways in which the media, sponsors and professional sport organizations engage in corporate synergies to market and sell their products and services; and
- understand and explain the roles of players, agents, sponsors, leagues, clubs and the media in professional sport.

WHAT IS PROFESSIONAL SPORT?

Professional sport, wherever it is played, is the most expensive, most visible and most watched sporting activity. It captures the lion's share of media coverage, as well as almost all sponsorship revenue and corporate support that is on offer. Professional sport is played in cities all over the world, from Kolkata, India to Rio de Janeiro, Brazil to Melbourne, Australia, in the very best stadiums (Eden Gardens, Maracana Stadium, Melbourne Cricket Ground), by athletes who often earn, depending on the size of the market, millions of dollars. Professional sport, and the industry that surrounds it, dominates world sport and those who play it are cultural celebrities on a global scale. Local, regional, state and national sport organizations are often geared around feeding professional sport leagues by developing player talent or spectator interest. These same organizations are also often forced, somewhat ironically, to compete in vain with professional sport for media coverage, sponsorship and general support (from fans, governments and communities). At its best, professional sport is the peak of the sports industry that supports those organizations below it by generating financial resources and cultural cachet. At its worst, it is a rapacious commercial animal with an insatiable appetite for financial, cultural and social resources.

Professional sport leagues, such as the National Football League (NFL) in the United States of America, dominate weekly media and social interests within the cities in which they are popular, with fans attracted to plots and sub-plots each week in the form of winners and losers, injuries and scandals, player or coach sackings, player transfers and crisis events (financial, human and organizational). In the late nineteenth century American college football games were played on an ad hoc basis, largely special events that captured the attention of some football followers and some media outlets. College football only became a part of the US national psyche and identity when games were organized around seasons, when media outlets and fans alike could plan their sport production and consumption around a weekly routine. The constancy and consistency of professional sport leagues has been the foundation upon which their popularity has been built. In many cities around the world, professional sport leagues have become an ingrained part of what it means to belong to a cultural or social group. In other words, professional sport leagues and their clubs have become, for many fans, an essential way of understanding and defining who they are.

Professional sport events, such as the Football, Rugby Union or Cricket world cups have also become part of our cultural and commercial consumption. They are held periodically (usually every four years) and capture audience attention because they provide out-of-the-ordinary sport action and are typically fuelled by nationalism. At a lower level, we are also exposed to annual events, such as world championships, and to circuits, such as the world rally championship, which hosts rounds in countries such as Sweden, Mexico and Finland. Each day of our lives we are bombarded by saturation media coverage of sport events through television, radio, magazines, newspapers and the internet. There is no escaping the reach of professional sport in contemporary society.

Professional sport is now big business. It is not simply about what happens on the field of play, like it once was (in broad terms prior to the commercialization of sport in the 1970s), but is also about what happens in the boardroom and on the stock exchange. Table 4.1 lists *Forbes* magazine's estimation of the football/soccer teams with the highest value in the world in 2014. The list demonstrates that many of these teams are significant corporate entities – all of the top ten have estimated annual revenues in excess of US$300 million, with the top four recording estimated annual revenues in excess of US$550 million across three different Leagues (Spain's La Liga, England's Premier League and the German Bundesliga), a clear indication that sport is an established global business.

In the first chapter of this book you were introduced to the three sector model of sport: public, nonprofit and private. In Chapters 2 and 3 the public and nonprofit sectors were examined, while this fourth chapter examines professional sport. It would be a mistake, however, to assume that the terms private and professional are synonymous in the context of sport organizations and their operations. Rather, in this chapter we are examining those sport organizations in which competitive commercial revenue is used to sustain their operations, as opposed to organizations that are funded by the state or almost exclusively through membership fees or subscriptions. It is important to recognize that many of the organizations featured in this chapter are actually nonprofit, and are not

TABLE 4.1 Highest value football/soccer teams 2014

Team	Country	Value (US$)
Real Madrid	Spain	3,440,000,000
Barcelona	Spain	3,200,000,000
Manchester United	England	2,810,000,000
Bayern Munich	Germany	1,850,000,000
Arsenal	England	1,331,000,000
Chelsea	England	868,000,000
Manchester City	England	863,000,000
AC Milan	Italy	856,000,000
Juventus	Italy	850,000,000
Liverpool	England	691,000,000

Source: www.forbes.com

privately owned. Professional sport organizations have two important features that define them. First, they share a scale of operations (particularly commercial and financial) that means they exist at the apex of the sport industry, and second, all the players or athletes are 'professionals' – sport is their job and they are paid to train and play full-time. Sports in which the players or athletes are required to find additional employment to supplement their income cannot be considered professional.

The example of the Australian professional football landscape is useful for illustrating and understanding the distinction between private and nonprofit organizations within professional sport, as well as the differences that exist between sports. In the Australian Football League (AFL) all the clubs are essentially member-based organizations (in which supporters or fans who buy memberships are entitled to attend games, as well as vote to elect a board of directors to govern their club). AFL clubs have annual revenues of up to AUS$80 million, but they are nonprofit organizations – all the money is used on club operations (e.g. to pay players and staff, maintain facilities or promote the club) and none of the money earned by the clubs is returned to an owner or to shareholders. Although it is essentially a collection of nonprofit organizations, the AFL is the wealthiest and most popular professional sport organization in Australia, which captures the greatest share of sponsorship and broadcast rights revenue. Like the AFL, Australia's National Rugby League (NRL) consists of many member based clubs, but there are also some which are privately owned. In the instances where a club is privately owned, the annual profit or loss is either returned to or borne by the private owner. For example, if the Melbourne Storm, one of the NRL's most successful and controversial clubs in the first decade of the twenty-first century, secures a profit, it is returned to its owners, headed up by New Zealand businessman Bart Campbell, who bought the club from multinational media conglomerate News Corporation in 2013. In contrast to the AFL and NRL, all eight clubs in the Australian A-League (soccer) are privately owned, but the governing body, Football Federation Australia, is a nonprofit organization. In this case the responsibility for ensuring a healthy and viable professional league is shared between private and nonprofit organizations. Throughout this chapter, and the remaining chapters of the book, it is important to keep in mind that both nonprofit and private organizations compete in professional sport leagues.

In Practice 4.1 FC Bayern Munich

In 2014 *Forbes* magazine ranked FC Bayern Munich as the fourth most valuable football team in the world, with an estimated value of US$1.85 billion, behind only Real Madrid, Barcelona and Manchester United, the powerhouses of European football. Bayern won its 24th German championship in the 2013/14 season of the Bundesliga, its sixth title of the previous ten seasons. In 2013 the club won the prestigious UEFA Champions League, after finishing runners-up in 2012 and 2010 (to Chelsea and Internazionale respectively), a title that it has won five times, placing it third on the all-time list behind Real Madrid and Milan (10 and 7 wins respectively).

Bayern's on-field success has been mirrored by its off-field success. Bayern's home, Allianz Arena, is a state-of-the-art football stadium, with a capacity of 71,000 and a luminous exterior that makes it one of the most recognizable stadiums in world football and a piece of architectural sport art when it is lit at night. The stadium is sold out for all of Bayern's home games, which means that more than 2 million fans attend the stadium each season, with most of the matches selling out as soon as the fixture for the forthcoming Bundesliga season is released. That Bayern's home games sell out so fast is not surprising given that in the 2012/3 season the club reported a record 223,985 paid-up members (each of whom pay €65), in a city of less than 1.4 million people.

In the 2012/13 financial year the FC Bayern München AG Group (the consolidated accounts for FC Bayern München AG and Allianz Arena München Stadion GmbH) posted a record turnover of €432.8 million, an increase from the 2011/12 financial year in which the turnover was €373.4 million. FC Bayern München AG, the corporate arm responsible for the club's professional football operations, recorded an annual turnover of €393.9 million. Bayern's major sponsor is T Deutsche Telekom, a sponsorship that is estimated to be worth US$43 million per year, and its uniform sponsor is Adidas, a deal estimated to be worth US$37 million per year. In 2014 the *Brand Finance* magazine rated Bayern Munich as the number one brand in world football at US$896 million, citing not only its on-field success, but perhaps more importantly its financial stability and the scale of its operations. In late 2013 Bayern sold an 8.33 per cent equity share in the club to Allianz for US$150 million, meaning that its three premier partners – Adidas, Audi and Allianz – now have a combined equity stake of 25 per cent. A clause in the Allianz agreement allows the company to extend its current stadium naming rights deal to 2041, an indication of Bayern's long-term commercial potential.

Sources: Bayern Munich website at www.fcbayern.de; Brand Finance website at www.brandfinance.com

CIRCUITS OF PROMOTION

In order to describe and explain the interconnections between professional sport, the media, advertisers and business, Whitson (1998) used the concept of 'circuits of promotion'. The key premise that underpins the circuit of promotion concept is that the boundaries between the promotion of sports and the use of sport events and athletes to promote products, which were previously separate, are now being dissolved. In other words, it is becoming increasingly more difficult to see where the sport organization ends and where the sponsor or media or advertiser begins. They are becoming (or have become) one, where one part of the professional sport machine serves to promote the other, for the good of itself and all the other constituent parts.

The relationship between Nike and former Chicago Bulls and Washington Wizards player Michael Jordan is a perfect example of a circuit of promotion at work. The Nike advertising campaigns that featured Jordan contributed to building the profile of both the company and the athlete, while Jordan's success in winning six NBA championships with the Bulls enhanced the corporate synergy between the two 'brands' and helped to increase the return on Nike's investment. Furthermore, the success of Jordan and the global advertising campaigns developed by Nike increased the cultural, social and commercial profile of the National Basketball Association (NBA) in America. In turn, the global promotion and advertising by the NBA, that either did or did not feature Jordan, helped to promote both Jordan, as the League's most visible and recognizable player, and Nike, as a major manufacturer of basketball footwear and apparel, either by direct or indirect association. Lastly, any advertising undertaken by Jordan's other sponsors, such as Gatorade, served to promote Jordan, but also the NBA and Nike through their association with Jordan. At its best, a sporting circuit of promotion is one of continuous commercial benefit and endless leveraging opportunities for the athletes and organizations involved.

SPORT CIRCUITS

Sport circuits involve a league or structured competition. NASCAR has been one of the most popular sports in the United States of America for over 50 years. It is broadcast on the FOX and NBC television networks and stations (such as Fox Sports 1). Like some other professional sports such as the National Hockey League (NHL) in America, the Bundesliga in Germany and the National Rugby League (NRL) in Australia, NASCAR operates on the basis of a seasonal calendar, with races in different American cities and towns each week, from February through to November at race tracks such as the Texas Motor Speedway (Texas; 191,000 seating capacity), Daytona International Speedway (Florida; 168,000 seating capacity) and the Talladega Superspeedway (Alabama; 175,000 seating capacity). Scheduling races at different venues ensures good live attendances, but also enables NASCAR and its competing teams and drivers to capitalize on an array of sponsorship opportunities.

The European Champions League is an example of a global sport circuit that is based around a league model, whereby teams play in different cities depending on who qualifies for the tournament and teams are progressively knocked out until a winner is determined. The men's and women's professional tennis tours are examples of a global circuit in which a series of events represent the structured competition. Each event or tournament on the tour may be entered by ranked players (who may have qualified through a lesser 'satellite circuit'), who compete for prize money, as well as points that go towards an overall ranking to determine the world's best player. In both the above cases, the circuit is managed or overseen by a governing body, although in the case of tennis the responsibility for managing and running individual tournaments is devolved to the host organization. For example, the Australian Open, the Grand Slam of the Asia-Pacific region, is managed and run by Tennis Australia, the sport's governing body in Australia.

The locations of events or tournaments that are part of national and global sport circuits are often flexible and cities or countries are able to bid for the right to host the event. In the case of the European Champions League the teams that qualify for the tournament are entitled to host their home games (a performance based flexibility), while in tennis the Grand Slam tournaments of the Australian Open, the US Open, the French Open and Wimbledon are the only marquee events (there is no flexibility). In other circuits, such as the World Rally Championship (WRC), the location of the events on the yearly calendar can change as cities and nations bid for the rights to host rounds. In 2014, the WRC held rounds in the European nations of Portugal, Poland and Spain yet ten years earlier these nations were not on the calendar. Similarly, Cyprus, Greece and Turkey hosted rounds in the 2004 season but not in the 2014 season. Bidding for these types of events can often be very competitive, as cities and nations seek to secure the prestige, status, tourism and potential economic benefit that are associated with popular global sport circuits.

The biggest global sport circuits are the Olympic Games and the FIFA World Cup, which are also the biggest events of any type staged in the world. Both events are held every four years and have a complex arrangement whereby countries and cities can bid to host the event. For a city to win the right to host the summer or winter Olympic Games it must go through a stringent two phase selection process. In the first phase – the 'candidature acceptance procedure' – national Olympic committees may nominate a city, which is then evaluated during a ten month process in which an International Olympic Committee (IOC) administrative committee examines each city based on technical criteria such as venue quality, general city infrastructure, public transport, security and government support. The cities accepted as applicants for the 2016 summer Olympic Games were Chicago (USA), Prague (Czechoslovakia), Tokyo (Japan), Rio de Janeiro (Brazil), Madrid (Spain), Baku (Azerbaijan) and Doha (Qatar). The selected 'candidate' cities move through to the second and final 'candidature phase'. Chicago, Tokyo, Rio de Janeiro and Madrid were selected as candidates for the 2016 Games. In this phase the cities must submit a comprehensive candidature file to the IOC and are visited by the IOC's evaluation commission. The evaluation commission's report on the candidate cities is made available to all IOC members, who subsequently elect a host for the Games at a full session of the IOC (for the election of the 2016 Games the IOC session was held in Copenhagen in October, 2009, at which it was announced that the Rio de Janeiro bid had been successful).

There are also global sport circuits in which participation in the event is dependent almost entirely on money, which situates them at the peak of the professional sport apex. Like the Olympic Games, the America's Cup is held every four years, but unlike the Olympic Games, a team can only enter if it has enough financial support to mount a challenge. For example, Oracle Team USA, the team which won the 34th America's Cup in 2013, is supported by Oracle, one of the world's largest software companies, which had revenues of US$37 billion in the 2013 fiscal year. It is estimated that each of the teams that challenged for the 34th America's Cup allocated between US$80 million and US$200 million to the task of winning the event, with yachts costing approximately US$10 million each.

In Practice 4.2 Formula 1

The Formula 1 racing circuit consists of a series of rounds held in locations throughout the world, typically from mid-March to the end of November. The circuit is based around Europe, but events are also held in Asia and North and South America. The races are broadcast to more than 185 countries, while cities or nations are often encouraged to bid for rights to host an event by the promise of economic benefits that might accrue as a result of securing a long-term contract. In 2014 the circuit was staged in the following 19 cities/locations:

1. Melbourne, Australia; 2. Kuala Lumpur, Malaysia; 3. Sakhir, Bahrain; 4. Shanghai, China; 5. Catalunya, Spain; 6. Monte Carlo, Monaco; 7. Montreal, Canada; 8. Spielberg, Austria; 9. Silverstone, England; 10. Hockenheim, Germany; 11. Budapest, Hungary; 12. Spa-Francorchamps, Belgium; 13. Monza, Italy; 14. Singapore; 15. Suzuka, Japan; 16. Sochi, Russia; 17. Austin, USA; 18. Sao Paulo, Brazil; 19. Yas Marina, Abu Dhabi.

Some of the cities and nations listed above have been hosting a round of the Formula 1 circuit since the formation of the World Drivers' Championship in 1950. For example, the Italian Grand Prix has been staged at the Autodroma Nazionale Monza (Monza) from 1950 (except for one year) while the Monaco Grand Prix has been staged on the Monaco street circuit since 1955. However, many of the cities and nations listed above are relative newcomers to Formula 1 – China was added to the circuit in 2004, with racing held at the purpose-built Shanghai International Circuit, Singapore in 2008 at the Marina Bay Street Circuit and Abu Dhabi in 2009 at the Yas Marina circuit as a day-night race under lights. Cities and locations also compete internally within nations to hold the event – the USA Grand Prix has been held at various locations throughout its history and most recently at the Circuit of the Americas in Austin, Texas, while in Australia the city of Melbourne secured a round of the circuit at the expense of neighbouring city Adelaide.

In October 2010 it was announced that a Russian Grand Prix would be held in the Black Sea resort city of Sochi, the location of the 2014 winter Olympic Games, at a purpose-built racing street circuit, the Sochi Autodrom. The deal to finally secure a Russian Grand Prix was negotiated between the CEO of Formula One Management Bernie Ecclestone and Vladimir Putin, the then Prime Minister of Russia. The seven-year agreement was reportedly worth US$40 million per year. Race fees of this magnitude are typically paid by the host city or nation to Formula One Management for a specified time period, such as five, seven or ten years. This means that there is often intense competition between cities and nations to secure a round of the circuit when a contract expires or there is an opening for an additional round.

Sources: Formula 1 website at www.formula1.com; Sochi Autodrom website at www. sochiautodrom.ru/en

MEDIA

Media organizations have become essential partners for professional and nonprofit sport organizations alike. The breadth and depth of coverage that media organizations provide their professional sporting partners is of such significance that it has the capacity to influence the social and commercial practices of millions, if not billions of people. The scale and scope of the financial relationship they enjoy is also important, so much so that sport and the media are often regarded as interdependent (Bellamy 1998; Nicholson 2007). The impact of sport news on the popularity and profitability of new media forms has only been equalled by the transformation that sport has undergone, as a result of its interplay with the media. It might have been possible in the 1890s to think about sport and its social and commercial relevance without reference to the media, but by the 1990s the task was impossible. It is now as if 'one is literally unthinkable without the other' (Rowe 1999, p. 13).

Whereas sport organizations once relied on ticket sales as their primary source of income, they now rely on the sale of broadcast rights (and to a lesser extent sponsorship revenue). For example, in 1930, 85 per cent of FIFA's income was derived from ticket sales and subscriptions from its member associations, yet at the beginning of the twenty-first century these revenue sources accounted for only 1 per cent. During the period 2007 to 2010, FIFA's revenue was US$4,189 million, of which the 2010 World Cup in South Africa provided US$2,408 million in television broadcast rights and US$1,072 in marketing rights, which were largely dependent on media coverage. The Olympics is also an outstanding example of the growth in broadcast rights fees paid by broadcasting networks across the globe, as well as the actual and perceived popularity of sports. Figure 4.1 illustrates the magnitude of broadcast rights for the Olympics over the previous quarter of a century. Clearly, sport is effective in attracting both audiences and advertisers. Importantly, the relationship between professional sport and the media has reached a point where professional sport would not survive in its current form without the media. More information about the relationship between sport and the media is provided in the media chapter of this book.

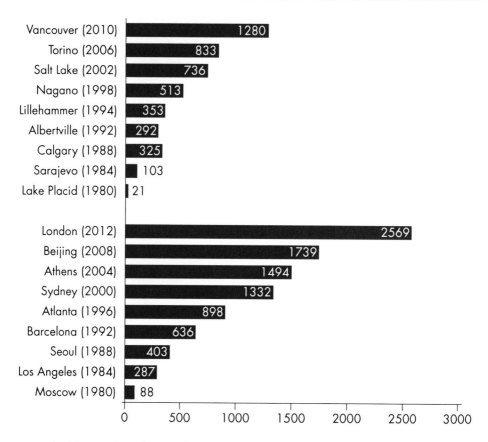

FIGURE 4.1 Olympic broadcast rights 1980–2012 for Summer and Winter Olympic Games (figures in US$ millions)

Source: www.olympics.org

SPONSORSHIP

The amount of money available to professional sport organizations through sponsorship arrangements or deals is directly related to the return on investment that the sponsor is able to achieve. In broad terms, the return on investment is dependent on an increase in sales or business, which a sponsor achieves through increased awareness or direct marketing. Sport organizations with large supporter bases, such as Manchester United, are able to secure significant sponsorship deals because the sponsor is able to market its product directly to a large number of supporters, as well as increase its awareness through media coverage of the club and the league. Sport organizations with global, regional or strong national profiles have a distinct advantage in the sponsorship market.

Sponsors want to be involved with a club or league that has very good network television coverage, which reaches a broad audience. This is most often achieved through exclusive broadcast rights arrangements. However, the general 'news' media coverage that a club or league receives in a variety of media forms and outlets, including television, radio, newspapers, magazines and the internet, can also influence its attractiveness to sponsors. This media coverage promotes the club or league and generally encourages fans to consume the sport, either by attending the game live or by accessing a mediated version. The club or league that is able to attract a greater amount of this 'news' media coverage is more likely to be embedded in the commercial consciousness of audiences and consumers. Thus, the amount of media coverage received is a measure of the audiences that can be reached by advertisers (or sponsors) through a commercial association with a professional sporting club or league and is directly proportional to the worth of the sponsorship.

The value of sponsorships differs between sports, between leagues, between clubs and across countries. At the highest level the IOC created 'The Olympic Partner Program' (TOP) in 1985, in order to provide companies with exclusive worldwide marketing rights to the Games. The Top VII partnership program, which included the 2010 Winter Olympic Games in Vancouver and the 2012 Olympic Games in London, comprised the following companies: Coca-Cola, Acer, Atos Energy, GE, McDonalds, Omega, Samsung, Visa and Panasonic; BMW, BP, British Airways and Adidas were among the official partners of 2012 London Olympic Games. At other levels of professional sport, the sponsorship or marketing arrangements may go further, as clubs and leagues are willing to enter into sponsorship arrangements whereby commercial organizations are able to acquire naming rights or enter into arrangements that give them either exclusive or increased access to fans. The development of the internet and online marketing has been particularly instrumental in this respect.

The English Premier League provides an example of the proliferation of sponsors within professional sport leagues and clubs. The competition is known as the Barclays Premiership, sponsored by a United Kingdom based financial services group engaged in banking, investment banking and investment management. The English Premier League also has a range of secondary or associate sponsors. For example, EA Sports, Nike and Carlsberg are the three 'official partners' of the League: EA Sports is the official 'Sports Technology Partner and Interactive Games Licensee'; Nike is the official 'Ball Supplier' and Carlsberg is the official beer. Furthermore, the clubs that play in the Barclays Premiership have significant sponsorship deals. The primary sponsor of each club is entitled to place its brand prominently on the front of the playing strip: Arsenal is sponsored by Emirates, one of the world's leading airlines (previous sponsors of Chelsea); Manchester City is sponsored by Etihad, another of the world's airlines and competitor to Emirates; Chelsea is sponsored by Samsung, an electronic goods manufacturer; Liverpool is sponsored by Standard Chartered, a bank; Everton has been sponsored by Chang, a Thai beer, since 2004; and Tottenham Hotspur is sponsored by AIA, a pan-Asian life insurance company based in Hong Kong.

Like broadcast rights revenue, sponsorship revenue within professional sport has grown exponentially. In the early 1960s, NASCAR driver Fred Lorenzen's sponsorship, from a Ford dealership, was US$6,000 for an entire season. By the late 1980s, it was estimated that approximately US$3 million in sponsorship was required for a NASCAR team to break even over the course of the season. In 2000 UPS announced its sponsorship of the Robert Yates No. 88 team driven by Dale Jarrett, which was estimated to be worth US$15 million per year. The cost of sponsoring an elite NASCAR team is now US$20–30 million per year.

The sponsorship of professional sport goes further than commercial agreements between clubs and leagues. Individual athletes also have sponsorship agreements that provide them with additional income to supplement their playing contracts (for team sports) or prize money (for individuals). Well-chosen brands with a global profile can enhance an athlete's overall image and in the case of more popular athletes a sponsor can establish the athlete as a brand in their own right. Sponsorship of professional athletes is not restricted to superstar athletes like David Beckham (formerly of football teams Manchester United, Los Angeles Galaxy, Real Madrid and Paris Saint-Germain), Tiger Woods (golf) or Kobe Bryant of the Los Angeles Lakers (basketball). Rather, sponsorship of professional athletes exists wherever there is a market, whether it a mass market in the case of global athletes or a niche market in the case of small or cult sports.

In Practice 4.3 Leveraging fans into media and sponsorship revenue

Manchester United is a commercial juggernaut, as well as a very successful football team. Using data gathered by market research agency Kantar, the club claims to have 659 million followers worldwide, an increase on the 139 million core fans and 333 million followers it claimed as part of its 2010 bond prospectus and research conducted by TNS Sport. 659 million followers is a staggering figure, particularly when it is acknowledged that this equates to approximately 1 in every 10 people on the planet. Kantar surveyed 54,000 respondents across 39 countries and then extrapolated this data, suggesting that Manchester United has 325 million followers in Asia, 173 million in Africa and the Middle East, 90 million in Europe and 71 million in the Americas. A follower of the club included 'a respondent who either watched live Manchester United matches, followed highlights coverage or read or talked about Manchester United regularly'. Even when a stricter definition of 'favourite football team' is applied, Manchester United can apparently claim 277 million of the 659 million followers as their own, which is still impressive, despite potential methodological questions relating to the data and broader population assumptions.

Given these figures regarding Manchester United fans and supporters, it is not surprising that the club is prominent in servicing its worldwide market through both traditional and new media. In July 2010 Manchester United launched a page on the influential social networking site Facebook. By early 2011 the club's page had more than 11 million fans and by 2014 the club's page had almost 55 million Likes. Manchester United's Twitter account attracted 345,000 followers in the first 24 hours after being launched in July 2013 and a little over a year later had 2.97 million followers. According to its 2013 annual report, Manchester United estimates that on average 47 million people watch each of its matches. This large number of committed fans means that the club has been able to spread itself across a range of different media platforms, of which its internet site and content delivery via mobile phones are prominent. Manchester United's website, which is published in seven different languages, attracts an average of more than 63 million page views per month. In the 2012/13 financial year Manchester United's broadcasting revenue was £101.6 million and new media and mobile revenue was £23 million.

Manchester United's fan base and media exposure allows it to capture additional sponsorship and merchandising revenues that fall outside match day and media revenues. In 2012/13 Manchester United sold more than five million items of branded licensed products, including more than two million jerseys. Retail, merchandising and product licensing revenue was £38.6 million in 2012/13, while sponsorship revenue was £90.9 million. In 2014 Manchester United's primary sponsors were AON, an international insurance and risk management company, Nike and Chevrolet. In 2014 Chevrolet signed a seven-year agreement worth £53 million per year to replace AON as the primary sponsor on the front of the club's playing strip, while at the same time the club chose to replace long-term partner Nike with Adidas for the 2015/16 season. Nike's sponsorship deal with Manchester United was worth £23.5 million per year, while the new deal with Adidas is for ten years at £75 million, a significant increase on the previous record of £31 million a year for the deal between Adidas and Real Madrid. Manchester United also has a diverse stable of sponsors that illustrates both the complexity of contemporary professional sport as well as the ways in which the commercial landscape can be segmented: Chevrolet is the official automotive partner; Singha is the official beer; Bulova is the official timekeeping partner; Aeroflot is the official carrier; Epson is the official office equipment partner; bwin is the official online gaming and betting partner; Aperol Spirtiz is the official global spirits partner; Nissin Food Group is the official global noodle partner; Kansai Paint is the official paint partner and DHL is the official logistics partner.

Sources: Manchester United website at www.manutd.com; BBC website at www.bbc.com

PLAYER MANAGEMENT

As sport has become increasingly professional and the amount of money secured through broadcast rights and sponsorship deals has increased, the salaries of players and athletes have also increased. The growth in player and athlete income has been mirrored by a concurrent rise in the expectations of clubs and leagues, an increase in the complexity of contract negotiations and greater off-field commercial opportunities for prominent 'sport stars'. These developments in the world of professional sport have led to the evolution of an industry focussed on player and athlete management, which is essentially geared towards providing players and athletes with services in return for a share of their income.

One of the most prominent player and athlete management companies is the International Management Group (IMG), which was formed in the 1960s and employs in excess of 2,000 staff in 70 offices in 30 countries. What began exclusively as a player management business has evolved into a complex commercial operation that includes television and publishing divisions. Golfer Arnold Palmer, winner of the US Masters golf tournament in 1958, 1960, 1962 and 1964, the US Open in 1960 and the British Open in 1961 and 1962, was the first athlete in the world to be branded by Mark McCormack, the creator and head of IMG. Back in the 1960s the 'brand-name' principle by which Palmer and McCormack approached sport was the first attempt to transform the business activities of leading athletes. Sport and business were previously related, but the scale of their operation was unique. The level of vertical and horizontal integration was essential to what became known as 'Sportsbiz' (Boyle & Haynes 2000). McCormack took the relationship of the agent further than before, and began to handle contract negotiations, proactively sought business opportunities, and planned the sale of the Palmer brand on a long-term basis, rather than previous attempts that might be characterized as ad hoc. McCormack set an important precedent by selling people as marketable commodities.

Octagon is a global sport marketing company and competitor to IMG. It represents and promotes more than 800 athletes in 35 different sports across the world. Octagon provides a broad range of services for the athletes it manages, including the following:

- contract negotiations;
- marketing initiatives and endorsements;
- public relations and charity involvement;
- financial planning;
- media management;
- property development;
- speaking engagements.

Octagon claims that it generates annual marketing revenues of in excess of US$300 million by maximizing its athletes' off-field corporate relationships. The company states that it does this by developing a unique and individual marketing plan for each of its athletes. Octagon represents American swimmer Michael Phelps, winner of the most Olympic medals of all time (22), including 18 gold medals (six in 2004 at Athens, eight in 2008 at Beijing and four in 2012 at London). The company claims Phelps is a perfect case study in what successful sport marketing and management can provide for an athlete in the contemporary hyper-commercial sport environment. Octagon suggests that Phelps laid the foundation with his performances in the pool, but that Octagon enhanced the Phelps story with a targeted publicity campaign, which included appearances in *Time, People*, the *Wall Street Journal* and *USA Today*. The result was what Octagon claims to be the creation of a connection between Phelps and corporate America, including the largest ever endorsement deal in swimming with Speedo and subsidiary deals with VISA, Omega and AT&T Wireless.

In many respects, athletes competing in individual sports are logical targets for both agents and sponsors; however, athletes in team sports are often as valuable, if not more so. In the United States the term 'multiples' is used to refer to an athlete that has the ability to attract multiple media and endorsements. The multiples' play on the field is at the highest level, they help to bring fans to the game, help the team to secure broadcast contracts or sponsorships deals, help the team in merchandising and licensing and in the extreme cases have the potential to increase the net financial worth of the organization. Thus, the athlete's commercial potential can be calculated in individual earnings (through the team or an agent), but also in terms of the growth of the club or league of which they are a part.

Professional sport stars are well paid by any measures. Importantly, their salaries are relative to revenue of the clubs, leagues, tournaments and events of which they are a part. In fact, in some professional sports with strong player unions, the level of remuneration for players is set as a percentage of league revenue. Table 4.2 is an estimate of the highest paid football/soccer players in the world in 2014. Their annual earnings are indicative of their on-field worth and the significant investment made by their respective teams, as well as their commercial worth off the field. Until 2014 David Beckham was by far the world's highest paid soccer player, with annual earnings of US$50 million, but since his retirement Cristiano Ronaldo and Lionel Messi, both of whom play in Spain's La Liga, have taken over as the highest paid and best known football/soccer players in the world.

TABLE 4.2 Highest value football/soccer players 2014

Player	Team	Annual earnings (US$)
Cristiano Ronaldo	Real Madrid	73,000,000
Lionel Messi	Barcelona	65,000,000
Zlatan Ibrahimovic	Paris Saint-Germain	34,000,000
Neymar Jr	Barcelona	28,000,000
Radamel Falcao	AS Monaco	26,000,000
Gareth Bale	Real Madrid	24,000,000
Wayne Rooney	Manchester United	22,000,000
Sergio Aguero	Manchester City	21,000,000
Yaya Toure	Manchester City	21,000,000
Fernando Torres	Chelsea	20,000,000

Source: www.forbes.com

In Practice 4.4 Sponsoring Serena

Serena Williams is one of the most recognizable athletes in the world. Williams turned professional in 1995 and has become one of the most successful tennis players of all time. Williams has won 17 Grand Slam titles, comprising five Australian Open titles, five Wimbledon titles, five US Open titles and two French Open titles; Williams has also won 13 Grand Slam doubles titles with her sister Venus and also won Olympic Games gold medals in the doubles in 2000, 2008 and 2012. As of 2014, Williams' on-court prize money was US$56 million, the highest of any female athlete in history. Williams' on-court successes have been mirrored off court by her commercial endorsements and media profile. According to *Forbes* magazine, Williams' income in 2014 was US$22 million, approximately half of which was earned off court. In 2014 she was sponsored by four key companies and products:

- Nike: One of the world's largest manufacturers and distributors of athletic apparel and equipment;
- Wilson: One of the world's leading manufacturers of ball sports equipment, including for tennis, baseball, American football, golf, basketball, softball, badminton and squash;
- Gatorade: The leading brand of sport drink in America;
- OPI: A company that specializes in professional beauty products, such as nail polish.

Three of Williams' four sponsorships are sport or tennis related – Nike, Wilson and Gatorade – where there are obvious commercial benefits for Williams and the sponsor. For example, through the Nike website consumers can purchase items from the 'Serena Williams Collection', which allows tennis fans and players to look like Williams on the court – shoes, tennis shorts, tank tops, tennis dresses, jackets and hats. Nike invites its consumers to 'dominate the court in styles from this collection inspired by – and worn by – a true tennis champion'. In many team sports the clothing and apparel are relatively generic, with fans able to customize products by adding their favourite player's name and number. By contrast, individual athletes such as Williams allow companies such as Nike to manufacture and market a diverse range of themed products. Williams has been a particularly good investment for Nike in this respect, as she has become known as a tennis fashion icon.

In the 2010 edition of *Sports Illustrated*'s list of the top 50 American athletes by earnings, Tiger Woods ranked number 1 with US$20 million in winnings and US$70 million in endorsements, despite off-field scandals that reduced his sponsorship value. Williams did not make the top 50, an indication of the power and popularity of male dominated sports such as football, basketball and baseball in the US market. By 2014, boxer Floyd Mayweather topped the list with US$105 million in earnings, while Williams' on-court dominance in 2013 combined with her endorsement earnings meant she captured position 39.

Sources: Serena Williams official website at www.serenawilliams.com; Sports Illustrated website at sportsillustrated.cnn.com; Nike website at www.nike.com.

OWNERSHIP AND OUTCOMES

Professional sports utilize different ownership and governance models in order to regulate and manage their businesses effectively. Some of the models have strong historical traditions, while others have been selected or adapted for their utility. One of the key distinctions is between professional sport teams and leagues that can be considered 'profit maximizers' and those that are 'win maximizers'. There is some debate as to whether these terms accurately reflect the practice of professional sport teams and franchises, but they are useful for broadly categorizing operational and financial priorities. Profit maximizing teams, such as those in the major American professional sport leagues, are typically owned by individuals or businesses who seek to maximize the financial return on investment. In some sports, however, such as English, Scottish and Australian football and cricket (Quirk & Fort 1992), the need to win is a greater priority than the need to make a profit. In fact, in some instances win maximizing teams will place the club in financial jeopardy, particularly by purchasing players they cannot afford.

In some cases, the ownership model has adapted to meet specific conditions brought about by commercial change. In the J-League, Japan's professional football (soccer) competition, teams like the Kashiwa Reysol are privately owned. The Reysol is owned by the Hitachi Corporation that specializes in the manufacturing of electrical goods and equipment. Originally established as an amateur team of the Hitachi Corporation, the Reysol was professionalized in order to participate in the inaugural J-League season in 1993.

Whether teams are win maximizing or profit maximizing, they must cooperate with each other at some level to ensure that fans, sponsors and the media remain interested and involved with the sport. Sport leagues that are dominated by one or two teams are often perceived to be less attractive to fans than leagues in which the result of games is uncertain. There is, however, a long history of leagues in which strong rivalries have maintained interest in the game (Los Angeles Lakers versus Boston Celtics in the NBA and Rangers versus Celtic in the Scottish Premier League, for example), although often the teams that are part of the rivalry benefit at the expense of teams that perform poorly. A league that is not dominated by only a couple of teams and in which there is an uncertainty of outcome (of a game or season) is said to have 'competitive balance' (Quirk & Fort 1992). Leagues across the world have instituted a range of measures to try to achieve competitive balance, which is often elusive. Perhaps the most obvious and publicized measure is the draft system that operates in football leagues such as the National Football League in America or the Australian Football League. The draft allows the league to allocate higher draft preferences (the best athletes on offer) to poorer performed teams, in order to equalize the playing talent across the league and create more competitive games.

SUMMARY

This chapter has presented an overview of professional sport and some of the central relationships that are essential to its ongoing prosperity and survival. The media, sponsors, agents, owners, advertisers, leagues, clubs and athletes are part of a self-sustaining commercial alliance, in which each of the partners promotes and supports the activities and interests of the others. Commercial networks are the binding forces that are holding professional sport together in the twenty-first century. Since the middle of the twentieth century, professional sport leagues and clubs have increasingly become willing partners in the promotion of their activities (sports and events), as well as the promotion of subsidiary products and services, and in the process have become major players in a multi-billion dollar industry.

REVIEW QUESTIONS

1 Use the circuit of promotion concept to explain the role of sponsors and the media in the professional sport industry.

2 Explain the rationale behind a company sponsoring a professional sport club, league or athlete.

3 Is the media important to the survival of professional sport? Why?

4 Identify an international and a domestic professional circuit and examine its operation. What are the special features that attract fans and media?

5 Choose a professional sport league and identify the fees paid by television broadcasters over the previous 20 years for the broadcast rights. Has it increased or decreased over the period? Explain why.

6 Choose a sport in which the location of events or tournaments is not fixed. Imagine that the city you live in is going to bid for the right to host the event and create a list of potential benefits – consider such features as the economy, environment, transportation, public services and housing.

7 Choose a high profile athlete and identify what companies or products sponsor the athlete. Is the athlete represented by an agent or did they secure the sponsorships or endorsements themselves?

8 Choose a sporting league of the world and identify whether it should be classified as 'win maximizing' or 'profit maximizing'. Provide a rationale for your answer that includes a commentary on the ownership of teams in the league.

9 Create a list of the top five paid sportspeople in the world. What does the list tell you about the size of the commercial markets that the sports are played in and the popularity of the sports?

10 Create a fictional international sport circuit. What cities of the world would host your events and why?

FURTHER READING

Bellamy, R. (1998). The evolving television sports marketplace. In L. Wenner (ed.), *MediaSport*. London: Routledge, pp. 73–87.

Boyle, R. & Haynes, R. (2000). *Power Play: Sport, the Media and Popular Culture*. London: Longman.

Cousens, L. & Slack, T. (2005). Field-level change: The case of North American major league professional sport. *Journal of Sport Management*, 19(1), 13–42.

Euchner, C. (1993). *Playing the Field: Why Sports Teams Move and Cities Fight to Keep Them*. Baltimore: Johns Hopkins University Press.

Fielding, L., Miller, L. & Brown, J. (1999). Harlem Globetrotters International, Inc. *Journal of Sport Management*, 13 (1), 45–77.

Nicholson, M. (2007). *Sport and the Media: Managing the Nexus*. London: Elsevier Butterworth-Heinemann.

O'Brien, D. & Slack, T. (2003) An analysis of change in an organizational field: The professionalization of English Rugby Union. *Journal of Sport Management*, 17(4), 417–448.

Shropshire, K. (1995). *The Sports Franchise Game*. Philadelphia: University of Pennsylvania Press.

Stewart, B. (ed.) (2007). *The Games are not the Same: The Political Economy of Australian Football*. Melbourne: Melbourne University Press.

RELEVANT WEBSITES

Americas
- National Football League at www.nfl.com
- National Basketball Association at www.nba.com
- Women's National Basketball Association at www.wnba.com
- Major League Baseball at www.mlb.com
- National Hockey League at www.nhl.com
- Ultimate Fighting Championship at www.ufc.com
- NASCAR at www.nascar.com
- Professional Golfers' Association at www.pga.com
- Ladies Professional Golf Association at www.lpga.com

Australia and New Zealand
- Australian Football League at www.afl.com.au
- Cricket Australia at www.cricket.com.au
- National Rugby League at www.nrl.com
- Super 15 Rugby Union at www.superxv.com

Great Britain
- English Premier League at www.premierleague.com
- British Rugby League at www.superleague.co.uk

Asia
- JatLeague at www.jatleague.or.jp/eng
- Japanese Sumo Association at www.sumo.or.jp/en
- Chinese Professional Baseball League at www.cpbl.com.tw/html/english/cpbl.asp

Europe
- European Champions League at www.uefa.com

- Serie A (Italy) at www.legaseriea.it
- La Liga at www.lfp.es/en
- Bundesliga (Germany) at www.bundesliga.de
- European Professional Golfers' Association Tour at www.europeantour.com

Global
- Olympics at www.olympic.org
- World Cup at www.fifa.com
- America's Cup at www.americascup.com
- Tour de France at www.letour.fr/indexus.html
- Formula One at www.formula1.com
- Association of Surfing Professionals at www.aspworldtour.com
- Association of Tennis Professionals (men) at www.atptennis.com/en
- Women's Tennis Association at www.wtatour.com
- World Rally Championship at www.wrc.com

CASE STUDY 4.1

National Basketball Association

This case explores the organization and operations of the National Basketball Association (NBA). The National Basketball Association is a professional sport league in the United States of America and competes with the National Football League (NFL), Major League Baseball (MLB), the National Hockey League (NHL) and NASCAR for public support, media coverage, media revenue and sponsorship revenue, as well as the ability to retain and promote its players as brand icons.

The National Basketball Association began in 1949 after a merger between the Basketball Association of America (which began in 1946) and the rival National Basketball League. Throughout the 1940s, 1950s and 1960s the league expanded and contracted as teams attempted to establish basketball in various towns and cities throughout America. Teams also moved from city to city in search of financial sustainability. The rival American Basketball Association formed in the late 1960s, but despite a period of limited success was merged with the NBA in the mid-1970s; the NBA has remained unchallenged as the premier professional basketball competition in America ever since.

The NBA consists of 30 teams, 29 of which are located in the United States of America and one of which is located in Canada. There are also two leagues that operate in their own right, but are affiliated with and promoted by the NBA: the Women's National Basketball Association (WNBA), the premier professional basketball competition for women in America and the NBA Development League (D League), which acts as a minor league for the NBA, in a similar way to the established minor league system in baseball. The WNBA, which was formed in

1997, consists of 12 teams, some of which are in established basketball markets such as Los Angeles, New York and Chicago, whereas others are located in lesser markets that do not have significant competition from other professional sports such as Tulsa and Connecticut. The D League consists of 18 teams, each of which is affiliated to at least one team in the NBA. D League teams are located throughout America, typically in small markets.

The NBA is split into the Eastern and Western conferences and each conference is split further into three divisions (Atlantic, Central and Southeast in the Eastern conference and Northwest, Pacific and Southwest in the Western conference). The divisions are geographically based, in order to minimize travel as much as possible within the confines of the scheduling rules. Teams play an 82 game season in which each team plays their division opponents four times (16 games), teams in the other two conference divisions three or four times (36 games) and teams from the opposing conference twice (30 games). In order to qualify for the play-offs, teams must finish in one of the top eight places in either conference. The play-offs consist of a series of in-conference elimination rounds (1 versus 8, 2 versus 7, 3 versus 6 and 4 versus 5 in the first round), until the Eastern and Western conference champions play each other for the NBA Championship.

As noted previously, the NBA consists of 30 teams. Although teams have been added to the league during the last 25 years and some teams have relocated, the league has remained relatively stable. Teams such as the Los Angeles Lakers and the Boston Celtics are well known in America and throughout the world because of their recent successes and high profile, as well as their past rivalries and the exploits of former players such as Magic Johnson (Lakers) and Larry Bird (Celtics). The Chicago Bulls became equally well known in the late 1980s and 1990s as a result of the exploits of Michael Jordan, who won six NBA championships, including three in a row twice. Like the WNBA, the teams in the NBA are spread throughout America and Canada. Table 4.3 lists all 30 NBA teams in order of the size of the population of the city in which they are located. It is clear from the table that some teams such as the New York Knicks, Los Angeles Lakers, Chicago Bulls and the Houston Rockets are located in large urban centres of America, while other teams such as the Utah Jazz, New Orleans Pelicans and the Milwaukee Bucks are located in relatively small cities. The Toronto Raptors have the advantage of not only being located in a large city, but the only Canadian city with an NBA franchise. The Los Angeles Clippers, by contrast, are located in a large city, but compete with perhaps the most famous basketball team in the world, the Lakers, which essentially makes them Los Angeles' second team.

TABLE 4.3 NBA teams by city population size

Team	City population	Metropolitan area population
New York Knicks	8,175,133	22,085,649
Brooklyn Nets	8,175,133	22,085,649

TABLE 4.3 *continued...*

Team	City population	Metropolitan area population
Los Angeles Lakers	3,792,621	17,877,006
Los Angeles Clippers	3,792,621	17,877,006
Chicago Bulls	2,695,598	9,686,021
Toronto Raptors	2,631,725	5,113,149
Houston Rockets	2,099,451	6,051,363
Philadelphia 76ers	1,526,006	6,533,683
Phoenix Suns	1,445,632	4,192,887
San Antonio Spurs	1,327,407	2,142,508
Dallas Mavericks	1,197,816	6,731,317
Indiana Pacers	820,445	2,080,782
Charlotte Bobcats	731,424	2,402,623
Detroit Pistons	713,777	5,218,852
Memphis Grizzlies	646,889	1,316,100
Boston Celtics	617,594	7,559,060
Washington Wizards	601,723	8,572,971
Denver Nuggets	600,158	3,090,874
Milwaukee Bucks	594,833	1,751,316
Portland Trail Blazers	583,776	2,226,009
Oklahoma City Thunder	579,999	1,322,429
Sacramento Kings	466,488	2,461,780
Atlanta Hawks	420,003	5,618,431
Miami Heat	399,457	5,564,635
Cleveland Cavaliers	396,815	2,881,937
Golden State Warriors	390,724	7,468,390
Minnesota Timberwolves	382,578	3,615,902
New Orleans Pelicans	343,829	1,214,932

Team	City population	Metropolitan area population
Orlando Magic	238,300	2,818,120
Utah Jazz	186,440	1,744,886

Source: US Census 2010 website at http://2010.census.gov/2010census/; Statistics Canada website at http://www.statcan.gc.ca

Table 4.4 lists the NBA teams by their estimated worth and estimated annual revenue in 2010 and 2014, in order to illustrate the absolute values of the teams, as well as recent growth. In 2014 former Microsoft CEO Steve Ballmer purchased the Los Angeles Clippers for US$2 billion, which suggests that the *Forbes* values are underestimates, particularly for large markets such as Los Angeles.

TABLE 4.4 NBA team values

Team	Estimated worth 2010 (US$ million)	Estimated worth 2014 (US$ million)	Estimated annual revenue 2010 (US$ million)	Estimated annual revenue 2014 (US$ million)
New York Knicks	655	1,400	226	287
Los Angeles Lakers	643	1,350	214	295
Chicago Bulls	511	1,000	169	195
Boston Celtics	452	875	151	169
Houston Rockets	443	775	153	191
Dallas Mavericks	438	765	146	162
Miami Heat	425	770	124	188
Phoenix Suns	411	565	147	137
San Antonio Spurs	404	660	135	167
Toronto Raptors	399	520	138	149
Orlando Magic	385	560	108	139

TABLE 4.4 *continued...*

Team	Estimated worth 2010 (US$ million)	Estimated worth 2014 (US$ million)	Estimated annual revenue 2010 (US$ million)	Estimated annual revenue 2014 (US$ million)
Golden State Warriors	363	750	119	160
Detroit Pistons	360	450	147	139
Portland Trail Blazers	356	587	127	140
Cleveland Cavaliers	355	515	161	145
Utah Jazz	343	525	121	131
Philadelphia 76ers	330	469	110	117
Oklahoma City Thunder	329	590	118	144
Washington Wizards	322	485	107	122
Denver Nuggets	316	495	113	124
Brooklyn (New Jersey) Nets	312	780	89	190
Los Angeles Clippers	305	575	102	128
Atlanta Hawks	295	425	105	119
Sacramento Kings	293	550	103	115
Charlotte Bobcats	281	410	98	115
New Orleans Pelicans (Hornets)	280	420	100	116
Indiana Pacers	269	475	95	121
Memphis Grizzlies	266	453	92	126

Team	Estimated worth 2010 (US$ million)	Estimated worth 2014 (US$ million)	Estimated annual revenue 2010 (US$ million)	Estimated annual revenue 2014 (US$ million)
Minnesota Timberwolves	264	430	95	116
Milwaukee Bucks	258	405	92	109

Source: www.forbes.com

The financial success of NBA teams is built in large part on the revenue secured through the sale of broadcast rights. In 2003 the NBA entered into agreements with broadcasters ABC, ESPN and TNT, which were subsequently extended in 2007. Both ABC and ESPN are owned by the Walt Disney Company, which declared in 2007 that contractual commitments relating to broadcast rights for the NFL, NBA, NASCAR, MLB and college football were worth US$19,200 million, spread over eight years. It is estimated that the NBA receives approximately US$930 million annually from the broadcast agreement extended to the 2015–2016 season. Through ESPN primarily, the NBA is broadcast in more than 200 countries worldwide, capitalizing on the global popularity of the game.

The NBA's media profile extends beyond television, although television coverage remains the most important way in which the league ensures its financial sustainability and maintains its fan base. The NBA's games are broadcast on both national and local television. Many of the games are broadcast into specific markets, so that the fans in the home city are able to watch their favourite team. NBA fans are also able to purchase a 'League Pass', which enables them to watch games via the internet. The ability to watch NBA games on the internet is a relatively recent phenomenon; for international NBA fans it has been revolutionary, as they were previously restricted to watching a small number of games purchased by local free-to-air or pay television providers.

The media coverage that the NBA receives is enhanced by the profile of its players. As with all professional sports, the organization, its players and importantly its sponsors play a major role in promoting basketball. The company most often associated with the sport of basketball is Nike, the global footwear and apparel company. Nike has long been associated with the game of basketball, particularly through its association with Michael Jordan. Nike is currently confirming its relationship with basketball and the NBA through its association with contemporary players such as Kobe Bryant, LeBron James, Kevin Durant and Kyrie Irving. Nike's promotion of basketball is heavily focussed on personalities and individual athletes, an acknowledgement that personalities such as Kobe Bryant, and his Nike alter ego, The Black Mamba, are essential in driving the sales of basketball footwear in particular.

CASE STUDY QUESTIONS

1 Is there a correlation between where an NBA team is located and its estimated revenue or total worth? Why might this be the case?

2 The *Forbes* valuations in 2010 and 2014 show that there have been some teams that have jumped in the rankings. Investigate these teams and suggest why their valuations might have risen during the period 2010 to 2014.

3 As noted in the case, the NBA is responsible for the management and promotion of the WNBA and the D League. Do these leagues operate as competition or a complementary product to the NBA?

4 Visit the Nike basketball website and investigate the ways in which NBA players are featured, particularly the use of social media and the creation of alter egos such as Kobe Bryant's 'The Black Mamba'. Does the NBA benefit from this promotion, and if so, how?

Sources: National Basketball Association website at www.nba.com; Walt Disney Company website at corporate.disney.go.com/index.html; US Census 2010 website at 2010.census.gov/2010census; Nike website at www.nike.com; Forbes website at www.forbes.com

CASE STUDY 4.2

UEFA Champions League

This case explores the organization and operations of the UEFA Champions League, with specific reference to the nexus between national and global leagues. As the chapter highlighted, the success of professional sport leagues is dependent on their levels of public support, media coverage, media revenue and sponsorship revenue, as well as the ability to retain and promote their players as brand icons. The Champions League is no different, as it has high levels of corporate support and is popular with fans. However, it cannot be regarded as equivalent to national football leagues because it is based on a model which rewards national and regional excellence, and is supported by regional and global interest. Its relatively unusual structure means that the Champions League provides an interesting perspective on a range of issues that are pertinent to the study and practice of professional sport.

FIFA is the world governing body for football. It is comprised of six regional football confederations: Africa, Asia, South America, North and Central America and the Caribbean, Europe and Oceania. Although the African football confederation has the largest number of members, the European confederation is by far the most powerful – it contains many of the world's best football nations, as well as being home to the most prominent leagues, including the English Premier League, the Italian Serie A, the Spanish La Liga and the German Bundesliga. The Union of European Football Associations (UEFA) is the governing body for football in Europe. UEFA organizes elite club competitions such as the UEFA Champions League and the Europa League, as well as national competitions such as the European Championships at senior and youth level.

In 2012/13, UEFA's income was €1,699 million. Broadcast rights revenue of €1,325 million represented 77 per cent of total revenue, with €313 million in commercial rights (sponsorship) equivalent to 18 per cent. By contrast, ticket and hospitality revenue (€39 million or 2.3 per cent) was a relatively minor contributor to UEFA's overall income. A closer examination of EUFA's finances reveals that its premier competition, the Champions League, accounted for a significant proportion of the confederation's overall revenue. In 2012/13 the UEFA Champions League accounted for 83 per cent of UEFA's overall revenue, with the UEFA Europa League contributing an additional 14 per cent. Every four years UEFA also runs the European Championship, which is similar to the FIFA World Cup but limited to European countries. In these years, such as 2008 and 2012, UEFA's revenue increases substantially – by €1,351 million in 2008 and €1,391 million in 2012. In 2012/13 the European Champions League was worth more to UEFA than the EURO 2012 tournament held in Poland and Ukraine.

Most national sport leagues are fairly static in that they contain a fixed number of teams from year to year and have well-defined promotion and relegation rules. For example, there are 20 teams in the English Premier League, and each year the three lowest teams from the Premier League are relegated to the Football League Championship (the next highest League in England) and three teams from the Football League Championship are promoted based on their performance (the top two teams plus a third as a result of a play-off system). European football leagues such as the Italian Serie A and the German Bundesliga operate on similar principles.

By contrast, the total number of teams that compete in the Champions League is fixed, but the composition of the League is dependent on national league performances, as are the number of teams that are able to compete from a single competition. The number of teams that are able to compete in the Champions League from individual national leagues is dependent on their recent performance (over the previous five seasons), which EUFA uses to calculate a coefficient ranking. In 2014, the top nine ranked nations were: 1. Spain; 2. England; 3. Germany; 4. Italy; 5. Portugal; 6. France; 7. Ukraine; 8. Russia; and 9. Netherlands. The national performance-based entitlements for the 2014/15 season are illustrated in Table 4.5:

TABLE 4.5 National performance-based entitlements

Position	Entitlement
1–3	Four clubs in the Champions League Three clubs in the Europa League
4–6	Three clubs in the Champions League Three clubs in the Europa League
7–9	Two clubs in the Champions League Four clubs in the Europa League
10–15	Two clubs in the Champions League Three clubs in the Europa League
16–32	One club in the Champions League Three clubs in the Europa League
33–54	One club in the Champions League One to Three clubs in the Europa League

The European Champions League is conducted from July until May the following year, with three qualifying rounds, a play-off, a group stage and a knock-out stage (round of 16, quarter-finals, semi-finals and final). There are 90 matches played in the qualifying rounds and play-off, which are used to determine the 32 teams that progress to the group stage, which consists of 96 matches – the top two teams in each of the eight groups of the group stage progress to the knock-out round of 16. Participating clubs are allocated to the various rounds and stages of the League based on their League and their League position in the previous season.

Not surprisingly, the clubs that dominate the Champions League come from the most powerful European leagues, particularly those ranked in the top 6 based on UEFA's coefficient system, which have at least two clubs in the group stage. Since the inception of the Champions League in 1992, a select number of clubs have consistently competed at the group stage of the tournament, including the most prominent and powerful clubs in Europe, as illustrated in the following table. Table 4.6 lists those clubs that have made 12 or more appearances at the group stage. Teams from the larger established leagues in Spain, England, Germany and Italy are also more likely to qualify for the knock-out rounds. As illustrated in Table 4.1, many of these clubs are estimated to be in the top ten most valuable football (soccer) clubs in the world.

TABLE 4.6 Clubs that have made 12 or more appearances at the group stages of the Champions League

Club	Country	Number of appearances at the group stage, 1992–2014
Barcelona	Spain	19
Real Madrid	Spain	19
Manchester United	England	19
Bayern Munich	Germany	18
Porto	Portugal	18
AC Milan	Italy	17
Arsenal	England	16
Olympiacos	Greece	16
Juventus	Italy	15
Dynamo Kiev	Ukraine	14
PSV Eindhoven	Netherlands	13
Ajax	Netherlands	13
Chelsea	England	13
Galatasaray	Turkey	13
Lyon	France	12

Some of the reasons that the same clubs dominate the Champions League from year to year are that the composition of the tournament is based on national league performances and the biggest and most powerful European leagues lack competitive balance. In other words, in these leagues the governing body has not enforced regulations, such as a salary cap or a player draft, which would spread the playing talent evenly and ensure competition. In the main, these types of regulations work well in football leagues in countries such as America or Australia, where global or regional player migration is either severely limited or non-existent. As a result of the organization of the European leagues, the richest, most powerful and most prominent clubs are able to purchase the best players, which enables the team to win national and regional competitions, which ensures they remain highly profitable, which in turn means that they are able to attract the best players. This cycle invariably means it is very difficult for lowly ranked clubs to break the stranglehold of those that occupy the top echelon.

In 2012/13 UEFA distributed €1.2 billion, equivalent to 70.5 per cent of its revenue, to teams that participated in UEFA's competitions. In 2012/13 €905 million was distributed to the 32 clubs that participated in the group stage of the Champions League, compared to €585 million to the 32 clubs that participated in the group stage in 2006/7 and the €23.5 million distributed to clubs in 1992/3, the first season of the Champions League. In 2012/13 each club in the group stage received a participation bonus of €8.6 million, a significant increase compared to the participation bonus of €3 million in 2006/7. Each of the 16 clubs that made it through to the knock-out stage received a participation bonus of €3.5 million in 2012/13 compared with €2.2 in 2006/7, quarter-finalists an additional €3.9 million (€2.5 million in 2006/7) and semi-finalists an additional € 4.9 million (€3 million in 2006/7). The winners received €10.5 million (€7 million in 2006/7) and the runners-up received €6.5 million (€4 million in 2006/7). In 2012/13, FC Bayern Munich won the title and received €55 million, while runners-up Borussia Dortmund received €54 million.

Excluding the final, the home club keeps all gate receipts during the Champions League, a significant source of income for clubs with large stadiums and supporter bases. Furthermore, clubs also receive a share of Champions League distributions based on the value of the club's national television market. This is referred to as the 'market pool', which is distributed based on the size of the television market in the country the club is from, how far the club progresses in the tournament and the performance of rival clubs in the same country. In the 2012/13 season Juventus received €65 for being eliminated at the quarter finals, of which €45 million was from the market pool. AC Milan, the other Italian club in the group stage secured €36 million from the market pool and earned €51 million overall, almost as much as the runners-up, despite being eliminated at the group of 16.

CASE STUDY QUESTIONS

1 As noted in the case, distributions to clubs via the Champions League increased from €23.5 million in 1992/3 to €585 million in 2006/7 to €905 million in 2012/13. What are some possible reasons for the increase in distributions?

2 Is the proportion of media revenue higher within UEFA and the Champions League than it is within European national leagues, or for individual clubs? Why is this so?

3 Do the top European clubs earn more from their participation in their national leagues or from their participation in the UEFA Champions League?

4 Would the top European clubs be better off in a European 'Super League'?

5 Would mechanisms to induce or improve competitive balance, like those used in the National Football League (America) or the Australian Football League, work in Europe's national football leagues?

Sources: UEFA Financial Reports available via the UEFA website at www.uefa.com/index.html

PART II

Sport management principles

CHAPTER 5

Strategic sport management

OVERVIEW

This chapter explains the processes and techniques of strategic management. Specifically, it focuses on the analysis of an organization's position in the competitive environment, the determination of its direction and goals, the selection of an appropriate strategy, the leveraging of its distinctive assets, the evaluation of its chosen activities, and the relationship to organizational change. These processes are reviewed within the context of a documented plan.

After completing this chapter the reader should be able to:

- understand the difference between strategy and planning;
- appreciate why strategic management should be undertaken;
- differentiate the steps of the strategic management process;
- identify the tools and techniques of strategic management;
- specify the steps involved in the documentation of a strategic plan;
- explain how the nature of sport affects the strategic management process;
- consider the relationship between strategy and organizational change.

STRATEGIC MANAGEMENT PRINCIPLES

In the simplest terms possible, strategy is the match or interface between an organization and its external environment. Looking at strategy in this way is a helpful start because it reinforces the importance of both the organization itself and the circumstances in which it operates. At the heart of strategy is the assumption that these two elements are of equal importance. Furthermore, strategy concerns the entirety of the organization and its operations as well as the entirety of the environment. Such a holistic approach differentiates the strategy management process from other dimensions of management.

One troublesome aspect of strategic management relates to its complex, multi-faceted nature. Johnson et al. (2014), for example note several important features associated with strategic decision-making:

1   Strategy affects the direction and scope of an organization's activities.
2   Strategy involves matching an organization's activities with the environment.
3   Strategy requires the matching of an organization's activities with its resource capabilities.
4   The substance of strategy is influenced by the views and expectations of key stakeholders.
5   Strategic decisions influence the long-term direction of the organization.

With the above points in mind, it is easily concluded that the management of strategy requires a keen understanding of the organization and the environment, as well as the consequences of decisions. But these points miss one vital outcome in the strategy process. The central purpose of strategy is to become different to the competition. From this viewpoint, strategy should help explain how one football club is different from the next, or why a customer should choose to use a recreation facility over another in the same area. The match between an organization and its environment should result in a clear competitive advantage that no other organization can easily copy.

Before we proceed, it is necessary to make several important distinctions in definition and terminology. First, strategy and planning are not the same. Strategy can be defined as the process of determining the direction and scope of activities of a sport organization in light of its capabilities and the environment in which it operates. Planning is the process of documenting these decisions in a step-by-step manner indicating what has to be done, by whom, with what resources, and when. In short, strategy reflects a combination of analysis and innovation; of science and craft. Planning identifies in a systematic and deductive way the steps and activities that need to be taken toward the implementation of a strategy. Strategic management marries strategy and planning into a process.

Second, the term strategy can be legitimately used to explain three levels of decision-making. At the first level, a sport organization is faced with the task of establishing clarity about what business it engages in. For example, is the core business providing sport competitions, managing facilities, developing players, winning medals, championships and tournaments, selling merchandise, making a profit, or improving shareholder wealth? At the second level, the term strategy is commonly used to identify how the organization will compete successfully against others. Strategy here offers an explanation of how competitive advantage is going to be created and sustained. Strategy can also be used at an operational level to identify how regular activities are to be undertaken and how resources are to be deployed to support them. For example, a broader strategy to improve player scouting methods might be supported by an operational strategy specifying the purchase of some computer software. Keep in mind that strategic management forms both a process and way of thinking that can be applied to multiple levels of a sport organization.

WHY UNDERTAKE STRATEGIC MANAGEMENT?

Surprisingly, the need for management of the strategy process is not always considered necessary. Some managers believe that the fast-paced nature of the sport industry precludes the use of a systematic strategic management process. Strategy for these managers is developed 'on the run' and in response to emerging circumstances and events. However, this approach contradicts the principles of strategic management, which emphasize the importance of actively shaping the future of one's own sport organization rather than waiting for circumstances to prompt action. Proactivity drives good strategy because it helps to reduce the uncertainty that accompanies chaotic and changeable industries like sport, where on-field performance can have such a radical effect on an organization's success.

Those versed in the concepts of strategic management would argue that with more uncertainty comes the need for greater strategic activity. Thus, a sport club that can generate a sizeable surplus with a performance at the top of the ladder, but a dangerous deficit with a performance at the bottom of the ladder, should engage in the strategy process in order to seek new ways of managing its financial obligations. In addition, those who favour reactive approaches to strategy assume that opportunities are always overt and transparent. This is seldom true. Identifying new opportunities that have not already been leveraged by competitors rarely proves easy and requires thorough analysis and innovative thinking. Neither of these can be achieved easily without the investment of time and energy in strategy development.

Allied to the notion of proactivity is the importance of coordination. Without a broad approach to the strategy process, different parts of the organization are likely to pursue their own agendas. Scarce resources need to be deployed in a coordinated and integrated manner consistent with an overarching strategy. Such a coordinated approach to strategy ensures that new strategy delivers change. In many sport organizations for which change is a necessary condition for survival, strategy represents the intellectual part of management that can be planned. The result of this process should be a coordinated attempt to achieve goals that have been agreed upon by organizational stakeholders that takes into account a balance between the achievement of goals and the resources required to do so. Efficiency arrives as an important benefit from sound strategic management.

STRATEGIC SPORT MANAGEMENT

One of the biggest issues in sport strategy comes in finding the balance between two or more divergent obligations. For example, sport organizations commonly seek both elite success as well as improved participation levels. Deploying resources to both of these commitments may be troublesome from a strategic viewpoint because they are not necessarily compatible. International success for a particular sport can motivate people to participate. However, the retention of new participants in sport tends to be poor in the medium term and negligible in the longer term. To make matters more complex, the choices of direction inherent in sport can be distracting, from the necessity to develop players or increase participation, to the pressure to make more money or win at all costs.

In Practice 5.1 The Comrades Ultramarathon:
                    Worth running?

A marathon appears to most running enthusiasts as the ultimate challenge. For most people, 42 kilometres of endurance is about the limit. And, of course, the marathon represents the culminating, definitive event in any summer Olympic schedule, often held in awe as a test of the mind, body and spirit. However, marathon running has diminished in its following over recent years leading sport managers to consider new opportunities for extending the challenge of running to the next level with even longer and more testing distances. Enter the age of the ultramarathon.

What can an ultramarathon offer? Ultramarathon running events occur over 50, 80, 100 or 161 kilometre courses involving varying terrains. Add to this the more arduous multiday or 'extreme conditions' events and you have a distance running program for nearly all types of extreme running enthusiasts. Competition in ultramarathons has escalated since the 1970s when trail running first gained momentum. International ultramarathon events subsequently blossomed, with now over 70 countries hosting some sort of ultramarathon event. Initially, the sport's main tactic emphasized participation as a method of conditioning to expand runners' marathon capabilities, but today the events attract their own specialist competitors.

Participation in ultramarathon has increased exponentially with, on average, one ultramarathon race staged in the United States every month. The majority of participants are in the over 40 age bracket, with women accounting for nearly 20 per cent of runners. The governing sport federation, The International Association of Ultrarunners, guides event organizers, providing them with the necessary protocols for official sanctioning of ultramarathon events.

Understanding the motives that drive runners to compete in extreme conditions can be pivotal in holding a successful event. A SWOT analysis for staging events enables organizers to accommodate the potential opportunities a unique event can bring to a region. In addition, developing a strategy to safeguard the welfare of ultramarathon competitors and volunteers demands the highest consideration. For example, the Australian based 2011 Kimberley Ultramarathon event had tragic consequences when miscommunication and a natural disaster caused participants to become trapped by a bushfire, prompting an Australian government enquiry into the organization of the event.

Comrades Marathon Association (CMA) was formed in 1921 and soon became a regular event for distance running enthusiasts on the South African calendar. In the first year, the 89-kilometre event played host to 34 runners, but now there are over 14,000 participants enjoying the support of both large spectator and television audiences. In the early days, CMA was not unlike any other amateur sporting body at the time. Most strategic decisions were ad hoc and volunteers managed the organization of the event. By the 1980s, however, CMA organizers had recognized that the consistently popular Comrades event had evolved into what they saw as 'heritage' status, and strategies were needed to protect it as a 'national treasure'. An executive committee was formed in 1985 and a Board of Trustees was installed in

1989 to protect and promote the event's unique identity. The formation of a separate Board to the management committee represented an important strategic decision because it distanced decision-making from CMA's daily operations. Trustee members were also encouraged to hold influential positions outside the CMA and forge stronger links to external stakeholders.

In 2004, CMA re-assessed their strategy, leading to a new vision and a restructure. By now the ultramarathon had become a popular event for local and overseas entrants. It was attracting some of the world's best ultra-distance runners such as Belarusian born South African Marathon champion, Vladimir Kotov and Russian world champion, Tatiana Zhirkova. Entrant numbers were steadily rising and by alternating yearly between a mainly uphill and a mainly downhill course between Pietermaritzburg and Durban, the Comrades marathon offered a unique competitive dimension. Four key components of the vision were developed, which remain relevant today: 1) to be world-class in racing, administration, customer service and innovation; 2) to recognize the event's rich heritage; 3) to deliver service excellence; and 4) to hold values of transparency, equality, integrity, diversity and mutual respect.

A functional structure supported the operational activities of the event, focussing largely on professionalizing its implementation and marketing. Event Operations were managed under a Race Directorship while Business Operations were separated into conventional portfolios of marketing, finance, media, international athletes, and the event museum. This new structure allowed the day-to-day logistics of the event to be undertaken separate from the broader, strategic decisions needed to position it successfully. For example, event staff tend to be transient and the operations relevant to the event need to be more flexible than those strategies associated with managing the overall organization. Recently, the event has added information technology to its portfolio of business operations.

Currently over 800 official ultramarathons are staged around the world, with nearly 700 of them in Europe and North America. The Comrades Marathon has become one of the largest events, a legacy of its 2004 vision and restructure. In order to control its quality, entries are now capped at 18,000 participants and athletes belong to 'teams', much like a Tour de France arrangement. An estimated 250,000 spectators line the route each year.

THE STRATEGIC MANAGEMENT PROCESS

Strategic management is a process designed to find the intersection of preparation and opportunity. This way of thinking has emerged from the first uses of the strategy concept, which came from the military. On the battlefield, the importance of imposing conditions that disadvantage the enemy in combat is paramount. For example, one of the key principles of military strategy is to manoeuvre an adversary into a position where they are outnumbered at the point of conflict. Variables like terrain and the opportunity to outflank, or attack the enemy from both the front and side simultaneously, make strategic decisions more complicated. These principles are also applied in the strategic sport management process, which is illustrated in Figure 5.1.

Strategy analysis	Internal analysis (capabilities, deficiencies and stakeholders)	Strengths Weaknesses
	External analysis (environment, competitors and customers)	Opportunities Threats
Strategy direction	Mission Vision Objectives	Performance measures
Strategy formulation	Strategic options	Generic strategies Cost leadership Differentiation Focus
Strategy implementation	Deployment of strategy	Products Services Systems Structure Culture
Strategy evaluation	Performance measurement	Corrective action

FIGURE 5.1 The strategic management process

Like an army general, the sport manager must first make an assessment of the 'battle' conditions. They do this by studying the capacities and deficiencies of their own organization, competing organizations, stakeholder groups and the business environment or 'battlefield'. This first stage in the strategic management process is known as *strategy analysis*.

Next, and in light of the information obtained from the first stage, the sport manager must make some decisions about the future. These are typically concentrated into a 'mission' statement recording the purpose of the organization, a 'vision' statement of the organization's long-term ambitions, and a set of objectives with measures to identify the essential achievements along the way to the vision. This second stage of the strategic management process is called *strategy direction*.

Setting a direction only determines what an organization wants to achieve. In the next step, the sport manager must consider how the direction can be realized. This is the most creative part of the strategic management process. Here, the sport manager, and his or her team, must work together to imagine the best methods or strategies for the organization. At this time, sport managers attempt to match the unique circumstances of the organization to its unique environmental conditions. When undertaken well, opportunities are found. This stage is called *strategy formulation*.

With a clear direction and a sharp idea of how that direction can be achieved, the task of the sport manager becomes one of implementation. At this point the range of products, services and activities that the organization engages with, and the systems that support them, are adjusted in line with the overarching strategy that was developed in the previous step. This is known as the *strategy implementation* stage.

Finally, strategy is rarely perfect the first time around. Modifications are always essential. Mostly this means a minor adjustment to the way in which the strategy has been implemented. However, sometimes it does require a re-think about the suitability of the strategy itself. Neither of these can be successfully undertaken without some feedback in the first place about the success of what has been done. That is why the final stage in the strategic management process, *strategy evaluation*, is necessary. In this stage, the organization reviews whether objectives have been achieved. Most of the time, some corrective action will need to be taken. Typically, the catalysts for these changes are unexpected events that affect the environment in which the sport organization operates, necessitating a return to strategy analysis. In this sense, the strategic management process never stops. In fact, moving back and forth between the stages in order to develop the best outcomes is normal. The strategy process works best when management takes the view that it is not linear or discrete but rather a circular and continuing activity.

STAGE 1: STRATEGY ANALYSIS

One of the biggest challenges facing sport managers lies in combating the desire to set strategy immediately and to take action without delay. While a call to action is a natural inclination for motivated managers, many strategies can fail because the preliminary work has not been done properly. This preliminary work entails a comprehensive review of the internal and external environments. The tools for doing this include: 1) SWOT analysis; 2) stakeholder and customer needs analysis; 3) competitor analysis; and 4) the five forces analysis.

SWOT analysis

One of the basic tools in the environmental analysis is called the SWOT analysis. This form of analysis helps to examine an organization's strategic position, from the inside to the outside. The SWOT technique considers the strengths, weaknesses, opportunities and threats that an organization possesses or faces.

There are two parts to the SWOT analysis. The first part represents the internal analysis of an organization, which can be summarized by its *strengths* and *weaknesses*. It covers everything that an organization has control over, some of which are performed well, and can be viewed as capabilities (strengths), while others are more difficult to do well, and can be seen as deficiencies (weaknesses). The second part of the SWOT technique is concerned with external factors; those which the organization has no direct control over. These are divided into *opportunities* and *threats*. In other words, issues and environmental circumstances arise that can either be exploited, or need to be neutralized.

The SWOT technique helps sport managers to find the major factors likely to play a role in the appropriateness of the organization's direction or the success of its strategy. With this in mind, the sport manager should be looking for overarching issues. A good rule of thumb is to look for no more than five factors under each of the four headings. This way the more important issues receive higher priority.

Given that the strengths and weaknesses part of the analysis concerns what goes on inside the organization, it has a time-orientation in the present; what the organization does right now. Strengths can be defined as resources or capabilities that the organization can use to achieve its strategic direction. Common strengths may include committed coaching staff, a sound membership base or a good junior development program. Weaknesses should be seen as limitations or inadequacies that will prevent or hinder the strategic direction from being achieved. Common weaknesses may include poor training facilities, inadequate sponsorship or a diminishing volunteer workforce.

In contrast, the opportunity and threats analysis also has a future-thinking dimension, because of the need to consider what is about to happen. Opportunities are favourable situations or events that can be exploited by the organization to enhance its circumstances or capabilities. Common opportunities tend to include new government grants, the identification of a new market or potential product, or the chance to appoint a new staff member with unique skills. Threats are unfavourable situations that could make it more difficult for the organization to achieve its strategic direction. Common threats include inflating player salaries, new competitors, or unfavourable trends in the consumption of leisure such as the increased popularity of gaming consoles with young people over playing traditional sports.

Stakeholder and customer needs analysis

Before an analysis of the environment is complete, an assessment of the organization's stakeholders and customers remains essential. Stakeholders are all the people and groups that have an interest in an organization, including its employees, players, members, league or affiliated governing body, government, community, facility-owners, sponsors, broadcasters and fans. The constant question that a sport manager has to answer is concerned with whom they are trying to make happy. Either deliberately or inadvertently serving the interests of some stakeholders in preference to others has serious implications for the setting of strategic direction, and for the distribution of limited resources. For example, some professional sport clubs tend to focus on winning to the exclusion of all other priorities, including sensible financial management. While this may make members and fans happy in the short term, it does not reflect the interests of governing bodies, leagues and employees, for whom a sustainable enterprise is fundamental.

Sponsors and government sport funding departments sometimes withdraw funding if their needs are not met. A careful analysis of the intentions and objectives of each stakeholder in their affiliation with the sport organization must therefore be completed before a strategic direction can be set. The substance of strategy is influenced by the beliefs, values and expectations of the most powerful stakeholders.

Competitor analysis

Opportunities and threats can encompass anything in the external environment, including the presence and activities of competitors. Because the actions of competitors can greatly affect the success of a strategic approach, *competitor analysis* ensures that an investigation is conducted systematically.

There are many forms of competitor analysis, and they can range in detail considerably. However, most competitor analyses consider the following dimensions, as summarized in Table 5.1. For each competitor, these eight dimensions should be considered. Time and care should be taken in assessing competitors' strategies, their strengths, vulnerabilities and resources, and as well as their next likely actions.

TABLE 5.1 Competitor analysis dimensions

Dimension	Description
Geographic Scope	Location and overlap
Vision and Intent	Ranges from survival to attempts at dominance
Objective	Short- to medium-term intentions
Market Share and Position	From small player to virtual monopolist
Strategy	Methods of gaining a competitive advantage
Resources	Volume and availability
Target Market	To whom the products and services are directed
Marketing Approach	The products, services and the promotions, pricing and distribution behind them

Five forces analysis

An extension of the competitive environment analysis is the *five forces analysis*, which was developed by Michael Porter. It is the most commonly used tool for describing the competitive environment. The technique does this by focussing upon five competitive forces (Porter 1980).

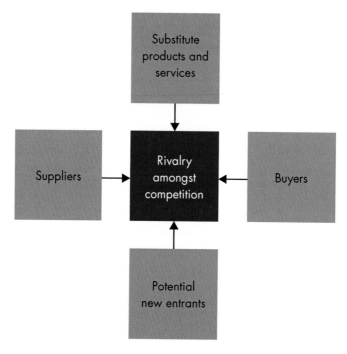

FIGURE 5.2 Five forces competitive analysis

The threat of new entrants: Every organization is faced with the possibility that new competitors could enter their industry at any time. In some forms of professional sport, this is unlikely as the barriers preventing entry are very high. For example, it would be extremely difficult for a private independent league to enter the market against any of the professional football leagues in Europe. On the other hand, new sport facilities, events, sport apparel companies and new equipment manufacturers are regular entrants in the sport industry.

The bargaining power of buyers: Buyers are those individuals, groups and companies that purchase the products and services that sport organizations offer. The nature of the competitive environment is affected by the strength, or bargaining power, of buyers. For example, most football fans in the UK hold little power, if the price of football tickets is any indication. When there is buying power, prices are lower. Despite some extravagant sums paid by broadcasters for the media rights of certain sports, the bargaining power of media buyers should be relatively strong. For most sport organizations, however, the chief buyers – fans – do not work together to leverage their power, and therefore the bargaining power of buyers is limited.

The bargaining power of suppliers: When suppliers of raw materials essential to sporting organizations threaten to raise prices or withdraw their products or services, they are attempting to improve their bargaining power. This may come from suppliers of the materials necessary in the building of a new facility or from sporting equipment suppliers.

The most important supplier issue in sport has come about with the unionization of professional players in an attempt to increase their salaries and the salary caps of clubs. Where player groups have been well organized, their bargaining power has proven significant.

The threat of substitute products and services: Increasingly, the traditional sport industry sectors are expanding, and it is more common for different sports to compete against each other. When this threat is high, a sport organization is faced with the problem of being out-competed by other kinds of sports, or worse, by other forms of leisure activity.

The intensity of rivalry among competitors in an industry: The more sport organizations offering virtually identical products and services, the higher the intensity of rivalry. For example, in the sport shoe marketplace, the rivalry between Nike and Adidas is extremely intense. Rivalry is more ambiguous between sport clubs in the same league that share a general geographical region. London football clubs, Melbourne Australian football clubs and colleges in the same state in the United States, are examples. In these cases, it is unlikely that one club would be able to 'steal' supporters from another local club. Nor is the alumnus of one college likely to start attending the home games of another college team. However, these clubs do intensely compete for media exposure, corporate sponsorship, players, coaches, managers and management staff. Of course, they also compete with the most intense rivalry imaginable for the championship.

STAGE 2: STRATEGY DIRECTION

Once the strategic analysis has been completed, the strategic direction can be set. There are four conventional tools used to clarify and document this direction: 1) mission statement; 2) vision statement; 3) organizational objectives; and 4) performance measures.

Mission statements

A *mission statement* identifies the purpose of an organization. While it may seem strange to need to put this in writing, such a statement reduces the risk of strategic confusion. For example, players, members, spectators, staff, coaches, media, sponsors and government representatives may all hold different interpretations of the purpose of a sport organization. The mission statement should define why an organization was set up, what services and products it provides, and for whom it provides them. When reduced to a single statement, this mission is a powerful statement of intention and responsibility. It usually does not exceed one paragraph.

Vision statements

It goes without saying that behind the idea of setting a strategic direction is the need to be visionary: to look into the future and form a clear mental image of what an organization could be like. Thinking in this manner means being able to interpret the information collected during the analysis stage and find the opportunities they present. A *vision statement* represents the culmination of this kind of thinking. It is a statement that declares the medium- to long-range ambitions of an organization. The statement is an expression of what the organization wants to achieve within a period of around three to five years. The statement is normally no longer than a sentence.

Organizational objectives

Given that the vision statement is a reflection of the medium- to long-term ambitions of an organization, *organizational objectives* serve as markers on the way to this destination. Objectives reflect the achievements that must be made in order to realize the vision. For example, if a club is situated at the bottom of the championship ladder, their vision might be to finish in the top three. However, achieving this vision inside a single season is unrealistic, so an objective might indicate the ambition to improve by three places by next season, as a progression toward the overarching vision. Objectives are normally set in each of the major operational areas of an organization, such as on-field performance, youth development, finances, facilities, marketing and human resources. However, it is essential that objectives stay measurable.

Performance measures

Key Performance Indicators (*KPIs*) are used in combination with organizational objectives in order to establish success or failure. KPIs are therefore inseparable from objectives and should be created at the same time. Each time a performance measure is used care should be taken to ensure that it can indeed be measured in a concrete way. For example, a marketing objective of 'improving the public image' of an organization is meaningless unless it is accompanied by something quantifiable. It is worth noting that measures do not have to focus exclusively on outputs like volumes, rankings and trophies. They can also be used to measure efficiency; that is, doing the same with less or doing more with the same resources.

STAGE 3: STRATEGY FORMULATION

Strategic analysis reveals the competitive position of a sport organization and setting the strategic direction plots a course for the future. The next question is how to get there. In the strategy formulation stage of the strategic management process, the sport manager and his or her team face the task of positioning their organization in the competitive environment. This necessitates a combination of imagination and scenario thinking. In other words, they must consider the implications of each potential strategic approach. To help matters, however, from a strategic positioning viewpoint there are a finite number of strategies available to the sport manager. These are called *generic competitive strategies*.

In Practice 5.2 Speed skating tactics in Canada

It would seem if you were only the slightest bit interested in succeeding in speed skating as a sport, you would want to be Dutch. The Netherlands has cultivated an outstanding reputation for speed skating on the world stage. Since the 1924 Olympics, the Dutch have accumulated a total of 105 medals, a number surpassing any other nations by a significant margin. Canada has also traditionally focussed on winter sports but their Olympic medal total has languished at a more modest 35. Undeterred by stiff competition, Speed Skating Canada launched a strategy to develop speed skating throughout the country. Under previous plans the resources they had invested into the sport concentrated on talent identification and international competition. Consequently, the financial rewards and media recognition normally associated with achieving Olympic and World Championship success had overtaken the strategic necessity to build a solid foundation of participants from which talented athletes can then be selected. Shifting their thinking meant taking a long-term view of the sport's strategic development. As a result, Speed Skating Canada acknowledged that strategic plans focussing exclusively on medals and world championships often miss the crucial need to develop athletes for the future.

Whilst excellence is hardly ignored in Speed Skating Canada's current strategic plan, a dual focus has emerged combining grassroots development and elite performance. This more holistic approach is now referred to as the Long Term Participation and Athlete Development (LTPAD) Model. It embodies the vision and principles of the Canadian Sport For Life movement (CS4L), prioritizing the implementation of a seven-stage development strategy to improve the quality and proficiency of physical activity in Canada. Each stage of the model encourages the participation of all Canadians from infancy to old age in numerous facets of participation including getting started, appreciating the fun of sport, learning to train, training to train, competing and winning in sport, and remaining active throughout life. A unique principle driving the CS4L movement holds that its delivery requires no governing authority or formal infrastructure. Rather, the CS4L relies on industry experts across education, government, provincial and national sport programs to lead sport participation in Canada. Since its implementation in 2005, CS4L has expanded its approach to include a leadership team from 17 supporting sport organizations across Canada with the intention of nurturing its long-term athlete development (LTAD) framework.

Speed Skating Canada have embraced the CS4L model and incorporated a long-term athlete development plan into its overall strategy. The plan addresses the issues of growth and development within the sport, motivated by the intention to maximize its use of resources in channelling high potential skaters towards career participation and eventual elite competition. The plan has also addressed some of the limitations of the current strategies, which tend towards short-term outcomes. Speed Skating Canada have recognized that getting more people involved in speed skating needs a greater focus on the skill development process. In practice, for example, the most experienced coaches work on the elite end of participation, when in fact they should be reassigned to the developmental stages of participation so that the fundamentals of the sport are acquired earlier and at a higher quality of skill performance. A major consequence of such short-term strategy is a curtailed natural progression from participation and fun to competitive participation and elite competition. Under the new strategic plan, the luck-driven process of talent identification will give way to an emphasis on participation rates and talent development programs over the long term. Perhaps unsurprisingly, the new Speed Skating Canada strategy mirrors the Dutch approach so renowned for sustainable outcomes.

Generic competitive strategies

Porter (1985) contended that there are only three fundamental or generic strategies that can be applied in any organization, irrespective of their industry, products and services, environmental circumstance and resources. Generic competitive strategies answer the most basic question facing a sport manager while forming a strategic choice: What is going to be our source of *competitive advantage*? To put it another way, every sport organization must take a position somewhere in the marketplace. The challenge is to find a position that is both opportune *and* advantageous. As a result, some sport organizations try to out-compete their adversaries because they can provide their products and services cheaper; others compete on the basis of a unique product or service that is hard for others to replicate; others still attempt to position themselves as the exclusive supplier to a small but loyal niche in the marketplace. These three strategic positions are described below:

Cost leadership: To become a cost leader by supplying products and services at the lowest possible cost to as many customers as possible. The logic of this strategic approach is driven by volume and market share where more sales than any other competitors lead to greater profitability. Essential to this generic competitive strategy is efficiency and the ability to keep costs to a minimum. While this approach is common in consumer products like shampoo, it is less common in sport. However, some equipment and sport apparel manufacturers do provide their products at the cheap end of the market in the hope that they can significantly outsell their more expensive competitors. Similarly, many leisure facilities try to attract customers on the basis of their lower prices.

Differentiation: To provide a differentiated set of products and services that is difficult for competitors to replicate. The logic of this strategic approach is underpinned by an assumption that consumers will place a high value on products and service that are unique. Typically, this approach is supported by an attempt to build a strong brand image, incorporate regular innovations and new features, as well as responsive customer service. Many sport organizations are thrown into this position almost by default because of the nature of their offerings. A tennis club, for example, offers a range of services that are by definition differentiated, at least when compared to other sports or leisure activities. However, when two tennis clubs compete in a similar area, it may become necessary for one to take a new strategic position. One option is to further differentiate their services, perhaps by offering something new or innovative like a crèche for mid-week players or a gym for conditioning the more seriously competitive players.

Focus: To provide a set of products and services to a niche in the market with the intention of dominating market share. The logic guiding this strategic approach is that being dominant in a small section of a larger market allows an organization to have early success, without having to compete with much larger and better resourced organizations. To succeed with this strategic approach it is necessary to choose the market segment very carefully, aware that the products and services provided must fill particular needs in customers very well. Many sport organizations take this approach. Examples include specialist sport equipment and less mainstream sport clubs and associations like rock climbing and table tennis.

The key to making a decision between these three alternatives returns to the analysis and direction stages of the strategic management process. A strategy-savvy sport manager is always looking for a way to position the organization in a cluttered market. Part of the choice is in determining what the sport organization is likely to be able to do better than others; their competitive advantage (like keeping costs low or delivering great customer service). The other part is in finding the opportunity in the environment that is worth exploring. Where there is a match between these factors consistent with strategic direction, strategic formulation is born. It is worth remembering that the worst place to be is 'stuck in the middle' between strategies, but that combining strategic options can be advantageous if managed effectively.

STAGE 4: STRATEGY IMPLEMENTATION

Strategy implementation represents the introduction of the organization's choice of competitive strategy. For example, if a differentiation strategy has been selected, the implementation stage considers how it can be brought about across the organization's products, services and activities. There is an important distinction to be made here between the strategic level of decision-making and the implementation level. To return to the military analogy, strategy concerns how an entire army is deployed. At the implementation level, tactical and operational decisions are made as well. These are like the choice of what each battalion, unit or platoon does. Always the overarching goal is a reflection of the army's objectives, but each smaller part of the army works towards bite-sized achievements that will eventually bring about success in the battle.

Once decisions have been finalized concerning the strategy that will be employed to achieve organizational objectives, the task of converting them into action begins. This means that representatives from each major area or department of the organization must become involved in deciding how they can contribute towards the generic strategy. For example, if one objective in a club is concerned with on-field performance, it is likely that the leaders of the developmental programs will play a role in planning. Equally, an objective associated with financial performance will require marketing staff responsible for sponsorship to become involved. As a result, the strategy implementation process should permeate the organization including junior development, community liaison, coaching, facilities, governance, marketing, finance and human resources, for example. In each of these areas a plan should be developed that illustrates the set of activities that will be performed at the tactical and operational levels to support the generic strategy.

Like objectives, each of these actions requires a measure or KPI of some sort. Often the implementation process also requires changes to resource allocation, organizational structure, systems for delivering products and services, organizational culture and leadership. These areas are considered in subsequent chapters.

In Practice 5.3 Crafting a customer needs analysis for online personal training

Recent reports indicate that team sport participation is steadily declining. For example, in the United States participation in the four most popular sports – basketball, soccer, baseball and football – has dropped by nearly 4 per cent over the last few years alone. To combat such declining interest, sport managers need to undertake environmental analyses wherein they seek to better understand the motivations and decisions of their customers in order to respond with more compelling offerings. In short, sport managers need to know their customers if they are going to formulate the most effective strategies for the success of their sporting enterprises.

As an example, the typical team sport consumer shares several important psychographic and behavioural characteristics, such as an historical interest in the sport inherited from family or regional traditions. In addition, from an economic perspective, team sports can offer more affordable sport-playing opportunities because more participants utilize the same facilities simultaneously, thereby diluting the direct costs of involvement. Since sport clubs originally emerged from local communities, participants relied on convenient access and a parochial sense of belonging. Team sports can promote camaraderie akin to fighting for your country; it improves skills and coordination and creates positive interactions with others. Add to this the opportunity to win acclaim or heroic status and the appeal of team sports is secured for most participants. Given these underpinning motivations, common to participation in most team sports, and the proliferation of competing offerings from the competitive to the recreational, the importance of conducting an environmental analysis has only increased in importance.

Building customer 'intelligence' remains an essential component of strategy formulation. Profiling the demographic, psychographic and behavioural attributes of the consumer reveals the opportunities available for exploitation as well as the sporting alternatives that they might be swayed to try. With the decline of team sport participation and the rise of individual fitness-related pursuits, sport consumer needs and wants have changed. For example, customer research has shown that a large contingent of sport participants have dropped out of team sports because they do not enjoy its competitive ethos. Despite initial fun at a young age, team sport can quickly escalate to emphasize elite competition and specialization, from which talent identification occurs. Other perceived limitations include concerns over safety, time commitments and privacy, while cultural barriers tend to exclude some from feeling as though they fit in.

Based on the available evidence, sport and recreation consumers are seeking less competitive and more personalized participation activities that focus on health and fitness rather than on trophies and performance. For these individuals uninterested in team sport, as well as those who are time poor, working with a personal trainer provides an ideal substitute to traditional, organized team sports. Although the demand for personal trainers can be influenced by the social and economic circumstances of potential customers, such as discretionary wealth and individual concerns about a healthy lifestyle, interest in personal training has accelerated significant over the last few years.

In the United States, the personal training industry has blossomed into a new sport and recreational experience. Primarily it consists of individual and group face-to-face sessions indoors or in parks during the early morning light and in the cool of the evening, driven and inspired by a trainer. 'Personal' is seen as the major source of appeal, reflecting a new understanding of what the contemporary customer wants. From a psychographic perspective the personal trainer is a mentor, guardian angel, and inspiration. But now even this industry is evolving and more and more consumers are pursuing advice from an online personal trainer. An online personal trainer can provide the service to anyone around the globe at a time and place that specifically suits the consumer. Their personalized approach appeals to a customer who may have self-esteem concerns, be time poor, or practise a nomadic work and social life. As long as there is internet access, personal trainers can deliver their services.

Individualized online programs for fitness, well-being and specialized sport training such as marathons, cycling, triathlon, crossfit and ironman are typically available. In developing a targeted strategy to attract consumers to this growing industry, the sport manager must review the psychographic, behavioural and demographic preferences of current consumers for personal training, and develop strategies to entice potential new participants.

STAGE 5: STRATEGY EVALUATION

One of the more difficult aspects of strategic management is the control or evaluation of what has been done. In sport there are numerous issues that make this process more complicated including the obvious one that on-field performance can have a tendency to overwhelm the other elements of strategy. Chapter 14 on performance management considers these important issues in detail.

The *strategic evaluation* stage requires an assessment of two related aspects of the strategy. First, the KPIs associated with each organizational objective need to be compared with actual results, and second, the success of the implementation actions needs to be ascertained.

STRATEGY AS CHANGE

For managers taking a strongly strategic perspective, organizational change requires a coherent framework in which to manage the process. From this viewpoint, successful organizational change remains intractably connected to strategy implementation, as change should materialize as an outcome. Strategy and change are therefore often conflated and treated as the same thing. Confronted by a deteriorating bottom line, a bad run on the field, an unexpected shift in technology, underwhelming merchandise sales, or one of a hundred other possibilities, strategists confront organizational change problems that previously seemed too difficult or too entrenched. Unfortunately, many sport organizations get side-tracked or distracted by the minutiae of how to come to grips with the need for change without considering the simple need to plan for it.

Strategic change is typically seen as a difference in the form, quality, or state over time in an organization's alignment with its external environment. Yet, most change leaders scarcely have time for definitions when it comes to strategy. Strategy is like great art in that we know it when we see it. Assuming a strategic approach to change assumes that the idealized final destination shapes change attempts in the same way that the top of a mountain defines the end of a climb. A strategic method requires a sport organization and its leaders to apply both logic and honesty to define a current position and then to determine precisely where it would like to be at the end of the change process. The difference between the two positions then dictates the requirements for change. While an oversimplification, the gap method characterizes strategic change because the inspiration for action focuses on bridging the difference between the current and desired state. Of course, traversing a gap in performance leads to decisions about the deployment of scarce resources, taking into account the complexities of environmental boundaries and the relative importance of different objectives. A strategic perspective also assumes that organizations behave with purposeful, adaptive proactivity. Change occurs because senior managers and other change agents deem it necessary, proceeding in a rational and linear fashion with leaders as the pivotal instigators and arbiters. As a result, a strategic approach maintains that sport managers wield the ultimate control of their organizations. Leaders introduce various processes, structures and products until they either reveal the most successful recipe, or catastrophe strikes. Conversely, unsuccessful change must be due to managerial or leadership inadequacy, or poor strategy selection in the first place. Strategic change takes a managerial, interventionist approach. It emphasizes the manipulation of organizational parts by strategically aware leaders in response to environmental circumstances. Such thinking remains obvious in sport organizational leaders today whose use of strategic language and methods uncovers a certainty about the cause and effect relations between strategic decisions and performance consequences.

When change emanates from the formulation of an organizational strategy it presumes the sequential, planned pursuit of optimal solutions to clear and well-understood problems. Sport managers believe that they optimize their organization's performance by finding the fit between a vision and the environment. In this respect, change relies on the conventional interpretation of strategy outlined in this chapter in that it reflects an alignment between organizational objectives, internal capabilities and environmental opportunities. Repetitive sequences of goal formulation, implementation, evaluation and modification always feature as stalwarts. While unfair to suggest that a conventional model does not attempt to accommodate the complexities of organizational change, it does present it in a linear fashion. Change can be controlled because everything in a sport organization should be subservient to the will, vision and action of its leaders.

Notwithstanding the presumption that strategic change operates as a clearly determined process envisioned at the outset, often sport organizational change exhibits emergent properties. Change programs change. Leaders and commentators tend to offer neat and systematic reconstructions after the event, implying a careful calculation behind every move. In contrast, the personal experiences of observers and employees within sport organizations can depict a lot of muddling and messiness. A strategic presentation of change might be clean and neat, but few operational sport managers and employees experience change as anything but fuzzy. Original plans seldom come to fruition in exactly the way they were conceived. While plans can go wrong and unanticipated issues can arise in the environment, disconnections between strategic planning and strategic thinking are probably inevitable. In addition, it may be argued that the need for organizational change in the first place demonstrates a failure of organizational planning and strategy. The proper response, of course, means proceeding with some more strategic change.

No matter how well planned, how strongly agreed by the majority of staff, how well led, or how important the strategic change plan, someone or some group of individuals within, or, occasionally outside the organization, will attempt to derail it. This may occur because an individual or group feels that the proposed strategy will adversely affect them, because they misunderstand the requirements of the plan, because they genuinely lack the capability to readily accept change, or because they believe the plan flawed. When faced with change, not everyone reacts with the same rationality that is supposedly driving the change process. Almost all commentaries on strategic change will acknowledge the prospect of possible obstruction from some element of the workforce. Most will provide sensible suggestions for improvement, but it remains problematic to plan for resistance while employing a strategic mindset.

It should also be noted that the strategic change model does not perform equally well for all sport organizations or for all levels of change. However, for substantive change across a large sport organization, the strategic model offers a powerful organizing framework. Given committed leadership together with a clear impetus for change, we think that the concepts associated with strategic change offer a useful, if sometimes too rigid, initial guide. Sport organizations are not always rational actors in the change process. Their fate is not exclusively determined by a leader's ability to make correct analyses and to formulate appropriate plans to meet predetermined objectives.

Strategic change methods suggest that change works in a one-dimensional way. However, change occurs at different levels, and with varying magnitudes and directions. Moreover, while not an immutable force, the external environment cannot always be mitigated with clever tactics. Sport organizations contribute to, and interact with, their environments in ways that make choices about responses far more ambiguous and complex than a strategic plan can always capture. In some cases, change managers find that more analysis leads to more complexity as the subtle idiosyncrasies of various possibilities become apparent. Another obvious limitation of the strategic approach to change accompanies its treatment of management decision-making as a 'black-box' that produces the correct outputs when the correct inputs are computed. For example, in sport, it is especially difficult for organizations to gain objective distance from their socio-historical circumstances. In practice, the result is that organizational change can be messy and non-linear due to environmental turbulence and historical baggage, not to mention the unpredictable 'human factor'. Despite the wisdom of conducting environmental analyses and establishing clear goals, the future often runs contrary to expectations based on linear trends. The challenge for sport managers is not just about planning for change but in knowing when to change the plan.

In Practice 5.4 Monitoring and evaluating Sportivate

The London Olympics was by most accounts a successful event. Every major strategy proposed was delivered as planned. Stakeholder groups expressed satisfaction that the London Olympic Committee delivered on its promise for improved social, economic, health and environmental benefits for London and its surrounds through regeneration and sustainable development. Developing and implementing a strategic plan is only half the battle, however. Monitoring and evaluation are integral concluding elements of the strategic planning process. Monitoring confirms that the strategy will be effective and deviations can be corrected. Evaluation encompasses the systematic and objective process of measuring the strategic plan. The London Olympics underwent a stringent series of evaluation procedures. One of the key legacy programs from the London Olympics under evaluation is Sportivate.

Sportivate is a Sport England initiative aimed at helping young people connect to the sports that interest them. The aim of the program is to offer free or low-cost coaching for 11–25 year olds to guide them to a new sporting experience with sport organizations around the country. Initially funded by a £56 million lottery investment, the program must undergo an objective evaluation in order to be funded again now that the euphoria of the Olympics has faded.

Consultancy firm Sport Structures was charged with responsibility for the evaluation of the Sportivate program. They primarily focussed on the impact the program has had on sport development as well as how well it has serviced the needs of more than 40 National Governing Sport authorities. External evaluation agencies like Sport Structures tend to provide their own set of tools for measuring performance and offer comparisons with other sports independent of the organizing committee's values and judgements. In evaluating the program, Sport Structures focussed on six main areas:

- portal analysis;
- intention postcard analysis;
- online survey analysis;
- cross data analysis;
- raw data;
- year-on-year comparisons.

The portal analysis examined the quantitative aspects of Sportivate participation such as demographics, attendances, locations, projects and sessions, and measures of participation at the national level. Evaluating a portal can also assist Sportivate to improve its web layout by better matching its web content to the targeted audience. In addition, it can identify the need for new or modified features and functions. Portal analysis may help locate key user groups accessing the portal and compare the users' behaviours online with Sportivate's mission and objectives.

Feedback from postcard analysis revealed participant satisfaction levels and the potential intention to participate in future sessions, or the likelihood of joining a club as a result of the participants' Sportivate experiences. For those participants who did not continue with sport participation after the Sportivate program, their online survey responses were evaluated to better understand the reasons why the program did not sustain their interest. Statistical programs were applied to assess raw data using cross comparisons and year-on-year comparisons so that participant characteristics could be measured over time to help detect deviations in behaviour and satisfaction.

Sportivate's performance objectives are important in drawing conclusions about the consequences of evaluation data. Sustainability has been a major legacy output from the London Olympics. Sport Structures reported sustainability of client participation in Sportivate, particularly in the costly membership to private gyms. The consultants recommended that Sportivate continue to build strong relationships with its community sport providers and create more opportunities to increase staff capacity through internships. The utility of an independent evaluation is not necessarily realized exclusively through data collection and analysis, but also in the future recommendations that emerge. Carrying out independent evaluations and acting on recommendations represents a critical and often ignored phase of the monitoring and evaluation process.

STRATEGY AS PRACTICE

An emerging issue in strategy emphasizes the blurred line between strategy and the practice of management, particularly where organizing forms are considered an integral part of the strategizing process. This position is reflective of the wider strategy-as-practice trend in strategic management, which is concerned with how managers 'do strategy', or strategize. The view that organizing forms within structures remains subservient to strategy may be considered old-fashioned, as it demands a sharp distinction between the two as different properties and processes. However, strategy and organization are not necessarily distinct states. Organization does not follow strategy. Instead, the more contemporary view holds that organization *is* the strategy. For example, investment in sophisticated IT infrastructure may be instrumental in enabling a sport organization to enter new markets and reach more fans. The assumption here is that a change to organizing forms is a strategic change. In addition, the use of the terms organizing and strategizing lies central to this proposition. As verbs, the terms impart the importance of continuous rather than static change processes. Organization and strategy therefore become organizing and strategizing.

From the standpoint of a sport manager, success is not so much a function of getting strategy and structure right in the first place, but rather is about having the capability to adjust them continuously alongside shifts in competitive and market forces. A sport organization's knowledge – its know-how – relies on managers' abilities to think about strategy and organizing decisions at the same time. Like a sport team without designated playing positions, strategizing without organizing is limited in scope. The strategizing-organizing way of thinking also suggests that middle and lower level managers need to engage in the strategy-making process.

SUMMARY

This chapter is concerned with the process of strategic management. This process is founded on the principle that opportunity is discovered by analysis rather than luck. Strategic management, we have argued, is therefore at the heart of the success of a sport organization.

Five stages in the strategic management process have been identified. The first stage is *strategy analysis*, which demands the assessment of both internal organizational capacities as well as external environmental conditions. The second stage is *strategy direction*, which sets the vision and objectives of an organization. The third stage is *strategy formulation*, where a definitive strategic position is selected for an organization. The fourth stage is *strategy implementation*, where the strategy is directed to action across organizational areas. The final stage, *strategy evaluation*, involves the control and measurement of the process so that improvements can be made.

Strategic management in sport organizations requires preparation, research and analysis, imagination, decision-making and critical thinking. It demands an equal balance of systematization and innovation. This chapter is weighted heavily toward the system side, but that is simply a necessity to convey the principles and techniques of strategic management. It is up to the readers to provide the imagination in their own strategic management activities.

REVIEW QUESTIONS

1   Why is strategic management important in the turbulent world of sport?

2   What is the basic principle that underpins strategic management?

3   Name the five stages of strategic management.

4   What is the relationship between a SWOT analysis and competitor analysis?

5   How do stakeholders influence the setting of strategic direction?

6   Explain the differences between the three generic strategies.

7   What is the relationship between KPIs and strategy evaluation?

8   Select a sport organization that has a strategic plan on its website. Conduct an analysis of this plan, and comment on its approach to each of the five steps of strategic management explained in this chapter.

9   Select a sport organization that you know well and that does not have a strategic plan available. Based on your background knowledge, make point form comments under the

headings of the five steps in strategic management to illustrate your approach to forming a plan.

10 Provide an example where a new kind of organizing method in a sport organization could impart a strategic effect.

FURTHER READING

Johnson, G., Whittington, R., Scholes, K., Angwin, D. & Regner, P. (2014). *Exploring Corporate Strategy*. 10th edn. London: Prentice-Hall.

Porter, M. (1985). *Competitive Strategy: Creating and Sustaining Superior Performance.* New York: Simon & Schuster.

Richelieu, A. (2014). Strategic management of the brand in the world of sport. *Journal of Brand Strategy*, 2(4), 403–415.

Robinson, L., Chelladurai, P., Bodet, G. & Downward, P. (eds) (2011). *Routledge Handbook of Sport Management*. London: Routledge.

Robinson, L. & Minikin, B. (2011). Developing strategic capacity in Olympic sport organisations. *Sport, Business and Management*, 1(3), 219–233.

RELEVANT WEBSITES

- Formula 1 at http://www.formula1.com
- UAE Automobile and Touring Club (ATCUAE) at www.atcuae.ae
- The International Association of Ultrarunners at www.iau-ultramarathon.org
- Canadian Sport for Life Program http://canadiansportforlife.ca
- Speed Skating Canada at www.speedskating.ca
- Sport England at www.sportengland.org
- Comrades Ultramarathon at www.comrades.com
- Sport Structures Consultancy at www.sportstructures.com
- SANZAR Super Rugby at www.sanzarrugby.com

CASE STUDY 5.1

The FIA on track for strategic progress in the Middle East

As part of the Middle Eastern strategic focus towards attracting global business entities, sport and entertainment events have risen to the top of the growth agenda for the region. Attitudes and perceptions about doing sport business in the Middle East seem to be changing as well. For example, Ernst & Young recently reported a growing appetite within the West for doing business in the region. With a population of over 175 million and a youthful median age for residents of 25, the Middle East offers more than just an oil-rich, cashed-up market. Ambitious economic and social goals in the wealthy Arab states have driven an exploration of new sport business opportunities, where attracting international sport events represents a viable and powerful platform for further development within the region.

The need for a strategic perspective has never been greater for the promotion of sport in the Middle East and Northern Africa (MENA) region. Fast changing sport consumer preferences, the rapid expansion of powerful new economies, and online leveraging advantages for global events, figure as key strategic issues affecting the expansion of sport event activity in the region. However, success demands at least three underpinning strategic foundations. First, the public must be interested in the sport. Second, government involvement is crucial to ensure that the immediate environment is supportive financially, legally and politically. Finally, local and international media must be willing to spread a positive message on the sport's behalf.

At the same time, corporate sport organizations interested in mobilizing the power of an untapped population are interested in high-growth strategic markets such as Saudi Arabia, Qatar, Kuwait and Bahrain. So far, their preferred approach has been to apply existing global strategies to the Middle East on the assumption that expansion into the region will work in a similar way as it has in other locations. Consequently, the Middle East is emerging as a key region for elite sport with the pursuit of Olympic Games and Football World Cup events, as well as horse racing, EPL football and Formula One. In some instances, the international governing entity, such as the International Cricket Council, has relocated to the Middle East in a bid to be closer to the highly lucrative market. Other major sports such as Formula One motor racing have devised new events to be staged in the Middle East for their annual calendars.

Formula One motor racing delivers the cream of motor sport competition worldwide. With over 500 million unique television viewers, Formula One's global appeal is incentive enough for countries in the Middle East to lure the race to the region. However, no matter how financially successful motor sport might be generally, a strategy unique to the MENA region must underpin a sustainable regional sport business development strategy. For the motor sport governing body FIA, the opportunity to expand into new markets with a regional expansion strategy exploits untapped revenue potential. Yet, with a long-standing history of poor strategic decision-making, under-developed infrastructures, and a sport with lower race outcome uncertainty, motor racing has faced a difficult challenge in establishing a foothold in the Middle Eastern market.

Motor racing offers a wide variety of 'products' from formula, touring, sports, production and stock car racing to rallying, off-road and karting forms of racing. In the MENA region, motor sport activities are already a popular recreational endeavour, steadily rising in support behind football (soccer), swimming and cricket. On the commercial side, motor sport has become the fastest growing sport in the Middle East to receive sponsorship and government funding. With such a wide variety of auto racing products to develop strategies for, motor racing organizations in the region have needed to understand the intricacies of the strategic management process in order to remain competitive. To lift motor sport from the doldrums of a regional leisure recreation, to an elite sporting pursuit, begins with the local governing authority charged with securing and orchestrating events.

The Automobile and Touring Club UAE (ATCUAE) was established in 1965, shortly after becoming one of the first organizations to attract Grand Prix motor racing to the region. Today the ATCUAE holds responsibility for overseeing more than 140 motor sports events in the region under the endorsement of FIA, FIM and FIVA, the key stakeholders in global motor sports. Attention to the strategic development of motor racing in the region has been a joint focus of both the FIA and the ATCUAE. Sound strategy development has linked the ATCUAE to its external environment in a systematic and profitable way. A number of key aspects of the strategy have ensured the success of Formula One Grand Prix events in the region, including decisive leaders and regional champions, a clear purpose, and the ability to capitalize on native resources.

For sport organizations to expand into new geographies, local champions are needed to drive support, activate resources, and generate interest and exposure. For example, UAE national Mohammed ben Sulayem attracted FIA interest in the Middle East, leading to the eventual staging of Formula One racing. Not only a fierce political advocate and savvy commercial operator, Mohammed ben Sulayem is the region's most successful championship rally driver with a career spanning three decades, starting with driving, moving into training young motor racing drivers for the future, and currently involving senior management roles within key governing motor racing authorities. Collectively, Sulayem's efforts have provided the impetus for expanding motor racing activities such as circuit racing, rallying, drag racing and moto-cross in the region. As an avid supporter of motor racing research and education, Mohammed ben Sulayem possesses an unrivalled passion for bringing motor racing to his home region. Standing out from other local enthusiasts is his commitment to progressive, commercially viable events.

In 2008 Suleyam was invested as Vice President of the FIA and quickly became instrumental in delivering the first Formula One event to Abu Dhabi and the Middle East in 2009. For strategic initiatives to be successful, strong and committed leadership remains critical. Change initiatives can be costly and the FIA needed reliable and well-funded organizations to support any expansion plans. Sulayem was able to steer the FIA to support the Middle East initiative and at the same time prepare the Middle East community and facilities to embrace Formula One. Initially volunteers and event management staff were brought in from Europe, but Suleyam began a home-grown volunteer training program, which attracted local enthusiasts and expatriate workers in the region. Eventually Formula One in the Middle East became a successful event with a local contingent comprising over 15 per cent of the event management staff.

In 2013 the FIA Middle East set up a task force with the intention of producing a 10-year development strategy for the sport's global development. The key issues addressed in the strategy included:

- a need for continued government support in finances, logistics and materials;
- the imperative for future motor sport initiatives to be fan driven and not technically/sporting led;
- the development of grassroots motor sport to be the main focus of all national sporting authorities in the region;
- the need for ongoing research in order to monitor the progress of motor sports and to follow emerging trends in participation and spectatorship;
- the importance of supporting all stakeholders, and in particular the media, on both national and regional levels.

The progress of motor sport in the Middle East has been exciting for the region. In 2014 the ATCUAE achieved the top level of accreditation in the FIA Institute's Young Driver Safety Programme and became the region's primary training provider for emerging drivers. The ATCUAE are also the authorized provider of training for officials as well, firmly establishing their credibility as a global player in elite motor sport competition and feeder structures.

From motor sport's first event in Lebanon in 1919 to the first FIA endorsed Formula One Grand Prix in 2009, motor sport in the Middle East has developed significantly, underpinned by a strategic plan that enabled the ACTUAE to make informed decisions about the development of the sport in all of its aspects: the expansion of motor sport clubs; the staging of international events; and the participation as drivers, volunteers and sport managers. Critical support from government authorities and well-placed champions has also confirmed the sport's regional success. Also, focussing on financial contributions from the corporate sector to grassroots mass participation activities like karting, just as much as for the staging of mass events like Formula One, has proven to be a highly successful strategy. In the end, motor sport in the Middle East has demonstrated the strategic impact that accompanies collecting reliable data from a wide variety of partners and stakeholder groups before making strategic decisions to capitalize on environmental opportunities.

CASE STUDY QUESTIONS

1 The 'Driving Motorsport Forward Together FIA Middle East Strategy 2010–2014' outlined in the previous case is a joint initiative between the FIA and the ACTUAE exemplifying their intentions in the region. What environmental analyses have the two entities used to develop their strategy and take motor sport racing to the next level in the Middle East?

2 In the preparation of a strategy for the region, the ACTUAE identified that the approach must be public-led and not sport- or technical-led. What does this mean? Why would a public-led strategy work for motor racing?

3 In the light of your understanding of a strategic sport management process, what kind of competitive strategy has been adopted by the FIA and by the ACTUAE?

CASE STUDY 5.2

Expanding Super Rugby across the gain line

Sport organizations wishing to maintain a competitive edge should always be on the lookout for growth opportunities. Once a sport enterprise becomes well established in the marketplace, and has cultivated a distinctive brand identity, a temptation towards expansion in the form of new markets or new products tends to enter the minds of many sport leaders. Evaluating any risks associated with expansion requires the sport strategist to develop a thorough strategic plan and incorporate that plan into other existing organization-wide plans.

Super Rugby comprises an amalgamation of competitive teams from South Africa, Australia and New Zealand and has emerged as the most financially successful Rugby Union competition in the Southern Hemisphere. Originally, a traditional tri-nation round-robin competition existed between these three nations as the high point of the Rugby Union calendar, but when the amateur status of rugby changed in 1996, South Africa, New Zealand and Australia formed a separate entity, SANZAR, to govern the tri-nation competition more professionally. SANZAR maintained independence from the individual rugby union associations of its constituent nations. This was the first step in building an expansion strategy for rugby union in the region.

SANZAR developed Super Rugby as a separate product from its original competition between the three regional nations. Initially, the new competition used the 'Super 12' name in reference to its 12 competing, franchised teams. Rugby union enjoys tremendous popularity in each of the participating nations, ranking first in South Africa and New Zealand, and arguably second or third behind the AFL and rugby league in Australia. However, individually, the national rugby union authorities had very little commercial power to compete with other sports. But with the consolidation of resources and the formation of the separate organization, SANZAR, rugby union became a more compelling commercial prospect, unencumbered by national agendas and managed strategically by an independent governing body. By 2006, Super 12 had grown into Super 14, as the competition attracted higher levels of financial backing and media support leading to the involvement of two additional franchises. Another team joined in 2011, leading to a rebranding from the colloquial Super 15s to Super Rugby. SANZAR's expansion enacted a penetration strategy. That is, more teams mean more of the product permeated the existing markets.

While tri-nations delivers the flagship competition as it engages the national identities of its participants, the Super Rugby challenge has proven the real growth opportunity for SANZAR and the reason it has attracted valuable sponsorships and broadcasting contracts. In order for SANZAR to expand successfully, it had to maintain a strong relationship with each national rugby union governing agency, as they hold responsibility for the game's rules and regulations and provide the feeder players for the competition.

Once an economy of scale has been established, progressing into new markets becomes the natural progression for a sport competition. SANZAR's strategy unfolded in this direction. Having built its Super Rugby competition to an optimal size, deeper market development was sought. Markets can differ significantly in their structure and dynamics. Seeking growth in untapped markets presents a risk. Some markets lie dormant and unlikely to be attracted to a sport product no matter how much effort is directed towards them. For example, expanding Super Rugby to China may seem on the surface an attractive proposition, given the market size, increasing wealth, interest in football (soccer), and an aspiration to achieve global sporting success, but if there is no desire for the code in China, then expansion strategies will fail. Sports that already command an international presence are more likely to succeed in expanding their products to new regions. Market development represents a competitive strategy that enables a sport or organization to present its current product to new geographical territories as well as to unfamiliar audiences. By targeting new supporters and franchises of the Super Rugby competition, SANZAR augmented its international expansion strategy. After analysis, considerable deliberation, and some pivotal broadcasting negotiations, SANZAR determined to move aggressively into the Asian market. Presently, SANZAR has plans to develop into an 18 team franchise competition, incorporating four conference regions in 2016.

Managing the complexities associated with a vast geographical expansion can present numerous challenges. For example, it is essential to establish business partnerships with local agencies and partners from the region so that the regulatory environment, political climate and prospective customer base can be appropriately targeted. In addition, SANZAR now have parties from Japan and Singapore contending for the eighteenth franchise in the 2016 competition. Encouraging sport clubs to compete for franchise positions within professional sporting leagues represents an important tactical move for SANZAR in itself, modelled on the North American system, which has maximized the commercial potential of sporting competitions. In the US, Major League Soccer and the National Hockey League have demonstrated the approach in their own competitions. In the case of Major League Soccer, one recent franchise fee exceeded US$40 million. However, unlike SANZAR's bold strategy, even the US major leagues have not yet ventured beyond national boundaries.

Speed into the market will undoubtedly prove critical for the expansion strategy. Supportive networks in Asia will accelerate success for the SANZAR Super Rugby model. In one important development, Frenchman and rugby enthusiast, Eric Series has become the champion for the Singapore bid. As a leading businessman and CEO of the Asian Pacific Dragons, Series can stimulate interest in the local market and facilitate access for SANZAR. Singapore rugby shifted from a volunteer-run entity to a professional governing body less than 20 years ago. However, despite its modest rugby playing population, Singapore has hosted numerous Rugby Sevens competitions and has shown an appetite for growth in the sport's support base. Singapore offers SANZAR an ideal location for expansion because of its close links to New Zealand rugby, its centralized flight hub in the Asia region, and its predictable, thriving economy.

Japan's immense and lucrative market appeals to SANZAR's strategic thinking as well. By far the stronger rugby nation, Japan's playing population is 10 times that of Singapore with the fourth largest number of registered rugby union players in the world, while its national side holds the 10th place ranking in the world. Helping the political cause, former Prime Minister Yoshiro Mori holds office as Japan Rugby Football Union CEO. In 2019 Japan will hold the Rugby World Cup, making it the first Asian nation to host the event. However, access to Japan's major cities may introduce problems for the Super Rugby competition's logistics. Where it takes a South African team 11 hours to reach Singapore, it will take them 23 hours to reach Japan. SANZAR remains confident that expanding into Asia represents a strategically advantageous and financially sound decision, and have the luxury of choosing between bids that can each demonstrate reliable commercial and business support.

The existing competitive structure in desired markets must be explored in order to better identify rugby's opportunities and threats. In Japan, football and the successful J-League present the strongest rivals. Baseball too is a popular sport, but its competition does not follow the same calendar as rugby. Conversely, Singapore's population is much smaller and more diverse than Japan's population, leading it to operate a wider variety of sports, consequently precluding any one competition from dominating. For the multi-million dollar price tag and a five-year contract to secure a franchise, SANZAR are driving a hard bargain with prospective franchises. To put the opportunity into perspective, the entire Asian Rugby Football Union's regional budget to run 28 countries amounts to only around US$2 million, while SANZAR is reportedly asking for US$100 million to secure franchise rights.

The Super Rugby brand is strong in three competing nations while the sport itself enjoys considerable global interest. Yet, SANZAR has determined that expanding market potential offers the best strategy for the sport's regional development. Their strategic intentions reveal how market development and market penetration strategies translate from theory to practice.

CASE STUDY QUESTIONS

1 In order to understanding where growth can come from in a strategy, the sport manager must analyse its product offering. SANZAR have two distinct products, the tri-nations and the Super Rugby competitions. Describe each of the products in the portfolio in terms of their potential market share and growth opportunities.

2 For SANZAR the idea of expanding the franchises into America and Canada has also been a consideration. What are the opportunities and threats that exist for Super Rugby when entering the North American market?

3 Continued expansion may dilute the competition. Can you suggest reasons why this might happen to SANZAR?

CHAPTER 6

Organizational structure

OVERVIEW

Organizational structure is a phenomenon that receives a significant amount of attention from managers as they seek to organise their staff and volunteers to optimize their impact on organizational performance, employee behaviour, organizational culture and meeting their strategic goals. Rather than replicate the myriad of existing material on this topic, this chapter highlights the unique aspects of the structure of sports organizations. Consequently, this chapter reviews the key concepts of organizational structure, provides examples of the unique features of sport organization structures, and summarizes the key research findings on the structure of sport organizations. The chapter also provides a summary of principles for managing organizational structures within community, state, national and professional sport organizations.

After completing this chapter the reader should be able to:

- describe the key dimensions of organizational structure;
- understand the unique features of the structure of sport organizations;
- understand the various models of organization structure that can be used for sports organizations;
- identify the factors that influence the structure of sport organizations; and
- understand some of the challenges facing managers and volunteers involved in managing the structure of sport organizations.

WHAT IS ORGANIZATIONAL STRUCTURE?

An organizational structure is the framework that outlines how tasks are divided, grouped and coordinated within an organization (Robbins et al. 2010). Every sport organization has a structure that outlines the tasks to be performed by individuals and teams. Finding the right structure for an organization involves juggling requirements to formalize procedures and ensuring accountability for tasks are clear whilst fostering innovation and creativity. The 'right' structure means one in which owners and managers can exert adequate control over employee activities without unduly affecting people's motivation and attitudes to work. It also provides clear reporting, accountability and communication lines while trying to reduce unnecessary and costly layers of management.

An organization's structure is important because it defines where staff and volunteers 'fit in' with each other in terms of work tasks, decision-making procedures, the need for collaboration, levels of responsibility and reporting mechanisms. In other words, the structure of an organization provides a roadmap for how positions within an organization are related to each other and what tasks are performed by individuals and work teams within an organization.

In Practice 6.1 Netball Queensland

Netball is the largest female participation sport in Australia and has more than 47,000 registered participants in Queensland, one of the major states of Australia. Netball Queensland (NQ), the state sporting organization responsible for the management and development of netball across Queensland, uses a typical nonprofit sport organizational structure.

NQ was established in 1971 and incorporated in 1985 and provides a range of programs and services for netball players, coaches, umpires, administrators, associations and clubs with the aim of increasing and enhancing participation experiences. More than 410 clubs affiliate with NQ, which provides access to netball events, programs and services as well as a pathway to state, national and international representation. These clubs are affiliated to one of 85 associations across the state that are geographically grouped into one of nine regions.

Associations that choose to affiliate with NQ do so to receive a number of benefits:

- insurance including public liability, professional indemnity, personal accident, property insurance (for associations), and association liability – including directors and officers;
- coach development and pathways for grassroots to elite through the provision of courses, resources, workshops, accreditation and networking opportunities;
- umpire development and pathways from grassroots to elite through courses, accreditation, mentoring, testing and resources;
- player development and pathways from grassroots to elite through NetSetGO!, training, clinics, Firebirds Netball Camps, regional academies, state teams and resources;
- community development through Volunteer Recognition Program, Inclusion and the Quality Member Program (QMP);
- management and administration support through the Netball Queensland constitution, policy and procedures advice, facility development advice, complaint handling, NMAS administration support and MyNetball training and support;
- information and access to Netball Queensland sponsors and preferred suppliers opportunities;

- voting rights at the Netball Queensland Annual General Meeting and General Meetings;
- representation and advocacy to Netball Australia and stakeholders such as local and state government.

The relationship between clubs, associations, regions and the state governing body is often described as the governance structure of a sport, and is covered in more detail in Chapter 13 when we examine sport governance in detail.

In addition to facilitating participation opportunities, NQ holds the licence for the Queensland Firebirds, the Queensland team that competes in the trans-national netball competition, the ANZ Championship. NQ is responsible for the management and marketing of the team, and staging the ANZ Championship games in Queensland in liaison with Netball Australia. NQ also manages a second tier elite team, the Queensland Fusion that competes in the Australian Netball League.

A team of over 30 staff work with a board of management and an extensive network of volunteers to deliver these programs, services and events across Queensland. The organizational structure for the NQ state office staff is based around the key functional departments of financial management, the high performance sport program, communications and events, membership services for affiliated associations and the sports participation and development functions. These functional departments broadly align with the main themes in the NQ strategic plan for 2014 to 2016: to grow their brand through promotional campaigns, media partnerships and quality service to affiliated associations; to increase participation as players, coaches, umpires and bench officials through development programs and support services; to improve the capacity of people working and volunteering throughout the various clubs and associations as coaches and administrators; and to build a sustainable financial platform for NQ through good governance and management practices, close relationships with all levels of government that support netball through facility and program funding, and increasing commercial revenue streams through events, sponsorship and merchandise sales. The structure allows individuals to be appointed to carry out specialized tasks and for the establishment of clear communication between the lower levels of the organization and the Chief Executive. The six dimensions of organizational structure help us understand why an organization such as NQ is structured this way.

Source: Netball Queensland website at qld.netball.com.au

DIMENSIONS OF ORGANIZATIONAL STRUCTURE

When designing any organization's structure, managers need to consider six elements: work specialization, departmentalization, chain of command, span of control, centralization and formalization (Robbins et al. 2010).

Work specialization

Creating roles for individuals that enable them to specialize in performing a limited number of tasks is known as work specialization. This concept can easily be applied in organizations that manufacture things such as sporting goods, or need to process a large volume of resources such as distributing uniforms and information to volunteers for a large sporting event. The advantage of breaking jobs down into a set of routine repetitive tasks is an increase in employee productivity and reduced costs through the use of a lower skilled labour force. This advantage must be balanced against the risks of making work too boring or stressful for individuals which can lead to accidents, poor quality, lower productivity, absenteeism and high job turnover.

The majority of sports organizations employ small numbers of staff who are often required to perform a diverse range of tasks over a day, week or year. In these cases, the structure of the organization will require a low level of work specialization. For example a sport development officer within a state or provincial sporting organization would be involved in activities such as conducting skills clinics with junior athletes, designing coach education courses, managing a database of casual staff, or representing the organization to sponsors or funding agencies over the course of a season. These roles require very different skill sets and in such an organization the structure would benefit from a low level of work specialization.

Departmentalization

Departmentalization is the bringing together of individuals into groups so that common or related tasks can be coordinated. In essence, people are assigned to departments in order to achieve organizational goals. Organizations can departmentalize on the basis of functions, products or services, processes, geography or customer type.

The most common form of departmentalizing is based on assigning people or positions to various departments according to the function a person may perform. For example, a state or provincial sporting organization might group their staff according to athlete development, competition management, special events and corporate affairs departments, with each department having a very specific function to perform.

Alternatively, a sport organization that manufactures cricket equipment may group their staff according to the product line they produce, with groups of people handling the manufacturing, sales and service for cricket apparel, cricket bats and training aids. In this case, the functions of marketing, human resource management, financial management and production are all replicated in each department. These criteria can also be applied to service based sport organizations. For example, an athlete management firm may offer a range of services under financial planning, career development, life skills and public relations training. Again, each department would manage their own marketing, human resource management and financial management systems.

Sport organizations can also design departments on the basis of geography. For example, the operations for a sports law firm may be split into departments for capital city offices or regions. Each of the offices or regions would have responsibility in regard to their operations in a designated geographical region. Finally, sport organizations can arrange their departments on the basis of their various customer types. This approach could be used by an organization like the Australian Institute of Sport, which might create departments that support individual athletes or team sports.

It is important to note that organizations may choose to use more than one criterion to devise departments and their choice will depend on organizational size, capabilities and operational requirements.

Chain of command

The chain of command is the reporting trail that exists between the upper and lower levels of an organization. In essence it is the line of authority that connects each position within an organization to the Chief Executive. It encompasses the notions of establishing clear authority and responsibility for each position within the organization. Authority refers to the rights managers have to give orders to other members in the organization and the expectation that the orders will be carried out. If managers at certain levels of an organization are provided with the authority to get things done, they are also assigned a corresponding level of responsibility. Having a single person to whom an employee is responsible is known as the unity of command. Having a single 'boss' avoids employees having to deal with potential conflict when juggling the demands of two or more managers and it helps achieve clear decision-making.

Robbins et al. (2010) argue that the basic tenets of the chain of command are less relevant today due to the increase in the use of information technology, and the corresponding ease with which most employees can communicate with each other at all levels of the organization and access information that was previously restricted to top level managers. Nevertheless, managers of sports organizations should be cognizant of the basic principle of the chain of command when designing their organizational structure.

Span of control

Span of control refers to the number of staff which any manager can directly supervise without becoming inefficient or ineffective. The exact number which any manager can effectively control is determined by the level of expertise or experience of the staff – the logic being that more experienced and skilled staff require less supervision. The complexity of tasks, the location of staff, the reporting mechanisms in place, the degree to which tasks are standardized, the style of managers and the culture of an organization also play a role in determining what the ideal span of control might be for an individual manager in an organization. The span of control impacts on how many levels of management are required in any given organization. The wider the span of control, the more employees can be supervised by one manager which leads to lower management costs. However, this reduced cost is a trade-off with effectiveness, as this single manager must devote more of his or her time to liaison and communication with a large number of staff.

The trend over the past 10 years has been for organizations to introduce wider spans of control and a subsequent flattening of organizational structures. This must be done in conjunction with the provision of more employee training, a commitment to building strong work cultures and assistance to ensure staff are more self-sufficient in their roles.

Centralization and decentralization

Centralization refers to the degree to which decision-making is located at the top of an organization. An organization is deemed to be highly centralized when the majority of decisions are made by senior managers with little input from employees at lower levels. Alternatively, an organization is decentralized when decisions are able to be made by employees and lower level managers who have been empowered to do so. It is importnat to understand that the concepts of centralization and decentralization are relative, in the sense that an organization is never exclusively one or the other. Organizations could not function if all decisions were made by a small group of top managers or if all decisions were delegated to lower level staff.

Nonprofit sport organizations tend to be more centralized than decentralized due to the influence of their traditional structures. Decision-making is often concentrated at the board level, where volunteers make decisions related to strategy for paid staff to implement at an operational level. This can lead to problems (see Chapter 12) of slow decision-making or politics. On the other hand, the nature of nonprofit sport organizations that are often made up of disparate groups and spread over a wide geographical area, requires local level decision-making for clubs, events and sporting competitions to operate effectively.

Formalization

Formalization refers to the extent jobs are standardised and the degree to which employee behaviour is guided by rules and procedures. These rules and procedures might cover selection of new staff, training, general policies on how work is done, procedures for routine tasks, and the amount of detail that is provided in job descriptions. Formalizing an organization increases the control managers have over staff and the amount of decision-making discretion individual staff may have. An organization such as a local sport club may have very few procedures or rules for how things are done, but the tribunal for a professional sports league will have a very detailed set of procedures and policies in regard to how cases are reported, heard and prosecuted.

In Practice 6.2 Melbourne Cricket Club

The Melbourne Cricket Club (MCC) is a private club, incorporated under the Melbourne Cricket Club Act 1974, boasting by far the biggest membership of any sporting club in Australia. In 2014, the MCC had 233,000 people on a waiting list to become a member and while there is no definitive waiting period, the most recent intake of members had been on the waiting list for more than 18 years!

The MCC has the public responsibility of managing the iconic sporting arena, the Melbourne Cricket Ground (MCG), home of many an Ashes victory by Australia over the old enemy England, and home to one of the world's great sporting events, the Australian Football League Grand Final each September. It has also hosted the 1956 Olympic Games, the 2006 Commonwealth Games, Bledisloe Cup games between Australia and New Zealand, music events and opera.

The MCG also houses the National Sports Museum within the Olympic Stand. The Museum has a number of exhibitions focussed on Australian football, basketball, boxing, cricket, cycling, golf, netball, Olympic and Paralympic Games, rugby union, rugby league, soccer and tennis. It also tells the MCG story and includes an extensive interactive area that reinforces the MCG's traditional role as the spiritual home of Australian sport and curator of some of the finest sports-related memorabilia and interactive technology in the world.

The MCG is built on Crown land and is a significant asset of the Victorian community. The Melbourne Cricket Ground Trust, established by the Melbourne Cricket Ground Act 1933, is responsible for the ground management of the MCG. Section 7(1) of the Act states 'the function of the Trust is to manage and control and make improvements to the Ground at its discretion'. In 2003, following the signing of the Management and Indemnity Deed between the Melbourne Cricket Club, the Melbourne Cricket Ground Trust and the Treasurer of Victoria, the MCC is contracted to manage the MCG until 2042. Under the terms of the Deed the MCC has the exclusive rights to manage the MCG in accordance with the terms of the Management and Indemnity Deed.

The business and affairs of the MCC are overseen and controlled by a committee. The committee comprises members of the club elected to honorary office bearer positions, namely, a president, three vice-presidents and a treasurer, and nine other club members elected to the committee. To assist in the execution of its responsibilities, the committee has established a number of sub-committees to which the President appoints committee members. Committee members are also involved in the following additional sub-committees and related funds or corporate bodies: MCC Sporting Sections, Cricket, Legal, AFL, MCC Foundation and MCC Nominees.

Additionally, the committee reviews the performance of the club's management team in consultation with the Chief Executive Officer (CEO), measuring results against the business plan objectives, ensuring compliance with legal requirements and monitoring the strategic and operational risk management plan. The MCC manages the ground through seven departments responsible to the CEO: Membership and Heritage, Events, Executive, Facilities, Finance and Information Systems, Commercial Operations, and People and Culture. There are about 140 permanent club employees and event staff are drawn from a pool of 900-plus for match day duties at the ground.

Source: MCC website at www.mcc.org.au

STRUCTURAL MODELS

The types of structure adopted by sports organizations can be categorized into four common types: the simple structure, the bureaucracy, the matrix structure and the team structure. Let's examine each of these briefly and explore their relevance for sport organizations.

The simple structure has a low degree of departmentalization and formalization, wide spans of control and would most likely have decisions centralized to few people. Such a structure would be used by a small sporting goods retail store that might have 10 casual and full-time staff and an owner/manager. There would be no need for departments, as most decisions and administrative tasks would be performed by the owner/manager and all other staff on the sales floor. The majority of procedures would be executed according to a simple set of rules and the owner/manager would have all staff reporting directly to him or her. The advantages of the structure in this case are obvious: decisions can be made quickly, it ensures a flexible workforce to cater for seasonal needs and busy periods, and accountability clearly rests with the owner/manager.

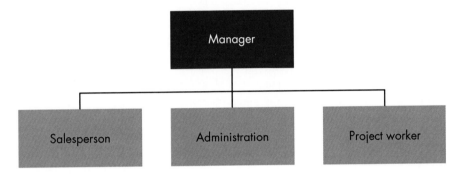

FIGURE 6.1 Simple structure

If the owner/manager wanted to expand the operation and open other stores in other locations, he or she would require a different structure to cope with the added demands of controlling staff in multiple locations, making decisions across a wider number of operational areas, and ensuring quality products and services are provided in each store or location. The owner/manager might consider adopting a bureaucratic structure.

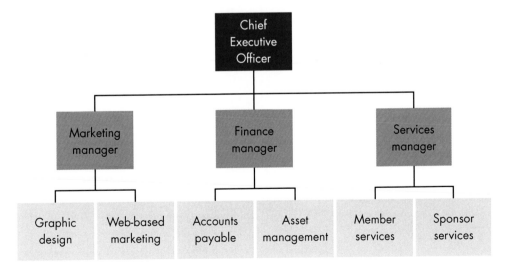

FIGURE 6.2 The bureaucratic structure

The bureaucratic structure attempts to standardize the operation of an organization in order to maximize coordination and control of staff and activities. It relies on high levels of formalization, the use of departments to group people into discrete work teams that deal with specific functions or tasks, highly centralized decision-making and a clear chain of command. An organization such as Sport England, the Australian Sports Commission, or a state or provincial government department of sport would be structured along these lines. Obviously, as an organization expands in size, increases the number of locations it delivers services, or diversifies its range of activities, the more likely it is to reflect some elements of bureaucratization.

The matrix organization structure reflects the organization of groups of people into departments according to functions and products. For example, an elite institute for sport might group specialists such as sports psychologists, biomechanists, skill acquisition coaches and exercise physiologists into discrete teams. At the same time, individuals in these teams might be involved in providing services to a range of different sporting groups or athletes, effectively creating two bosses for them. This breaks the unity of command principle, but allows an organization to group specialists together to maximize sharing of expertise while facilitating their involvement in a number of projects or service delivery areas. The argument for this arrangement is that it is better to have the specialists work as a team than to appoint individuals to work in isolation to provide their services. While this allows the organization to provide a range of services, it does increase the potential for confusion in regard to managing the demands from two bosses, which in turn may lead to an increase in stress.

	Football operations division	Corporate services division	Marketing division
Team 1	Manager 1	Project worker 1	Worker 1
Team 2	Manager 2	Project worker 2	Worker 2
Team 3	Manager 3	Project worker 3	Worker 3

FIGURE 6.3 The matrix structure

A relatively new structural design option is the team structure. The team structure requires decision-making to be decentralized to work teams that are made up of people with skills to perform a variety of tasks. A football club franchise might employ such a structure with teams formed for club events or marketing campaigns as it will allow quick decision-making in regard to finance, staffing, or impacts on players.

While these generic structures can be applied to all types of organizations, there has been some research that has attempted to categorize the various structures that exist within nonprofit sport organizations. Kikulis et al. (1989) developed a structural taxonomy for provincial (state) Canadian amateur sport organizations based on the organizational dimensions of specialization, standardization and centralization. The evolution of Canadian sport organizations in the 1980s to a more professional and bureaucratized form prompted the researchers to attempt to establish exactly what form this evolution had taken. Kikulis et al. (1989) identified eight structural designs for

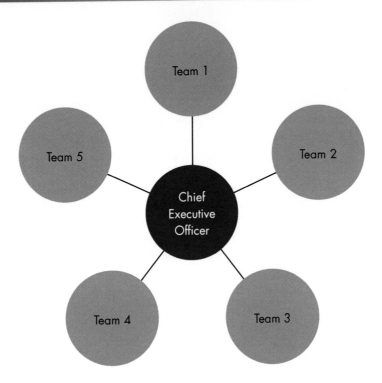

FIGURE 6.4 Team structure

voluntary sport organizations (VSOs), ranging in scale of complexity for the three structural dimensions. Theodoraki and Henry (1994), in a similar study, defined a typology of structures for British sport governing bodies. They too utilized the structural elements of specialization, standardization and centralization to distinguish between various structural designs.

Identifying design types for national level sport organizations was the focus of a study by Kikulis et al. (1992) in which organizational values and organizational structure dimensions were used to identify three distinct designs – kitchen table, boardroom and executive office. Each design represents a distinct mix of organizational values comprising their orientation toward private or public interests; the domain of activities conducted (ranging from broad participation based to a focus on high performance results); the degree of professional involvement in decision-making; and the criteria used to evaluate effectiveness.

Now that we have explored the elements of structure and the various ways they can be used, we can examine the factors that influence the structure adopted by a sport organization.

WHAT INFLUENCES THE STRUCTURE OF A SPORT ORGANIZATION?

There are generally four factors that influence the structure of an organization: strategy, size, technology and environmental uncertainty. Each of these is briefly reviewed.

Strategy

In a perfect world, an organization's structure would be designed purely around the requirement to maximize the chances of an organization's strategic goals being achieved. This is rarely possible, but strategy does play an important part in determining the structure adopted by a sport organization. Whether an organization is pursuing an overall strategy of innovation, cost minimization, or imitation will necessitate the design of a specific organizational structure.

An important trend to note in the development of structure for nonprofit sport organizations has been the impact of the introduction of paid professional staff, a very deliberate strategy in response to increases in government funding in sport in most club based sporting systems around the world. The impact of such a strategy on the structure of Canadian provincial VSOs was explored by Thibault et al. (1991). They found that specialization and formalization increased after the introduction of professional staff, but that centralization, after initially increasing, actually decreased over time. It was suggested that centralization increased because volunteer board members sought to retain control over decisions, and then decreased as the relationship between board members and staff stabilized. Such resistance to changes in structure were noted by Kikulis et al. (1995), who studied the changes in specialization, standardization and centralization of Canadian NSOs over a four year period. They found that incumbent volunteers resisted change across all three elements of organizational structure, highlighting the role of human agents and personal choice in determining organizational change outcomes.

Size

The size of an organization also plays an important part in the determination of what will be its best possible structure. Larger organizations tend to be more formalised, with more specialist roles and departments and more levels of management than smaller organizations. This makes sense as managers need to implement greater control measures to manage the volume and communication of information in a large organization. Amis and Slack (1996) state that much of the research into the relationship between organizational size and degree of centralization suggest that as 'organizations become larger, decision-making becomes more decentralized' (p. 83). In terms of nonprofit sport organizations they also found that with an increase in size of the organization, control over organizational decision-making remains at the voluntary board level, and concluded that a 'central role of decision-making as a means of control and the desire for volunteers to retain this control' (Amis & Slack 1996, p. 84) meant that the boards of many sport organizations were reluctant to relinquish control to professional staff.

Technology

Technology does have an impact on organizational structure. Robbins et al. (2010) argue that if organizations predominantly undertake routine tasks then there is a high degree of departmentalization, and a high level of centralized decision-making. This appears logical because non-routine tasks require decisions to be made at the level of organization where they actually happen. In regard to a sport organization, such as a professional sport club, the increased use of information and communication technology means that it requires additional specialist staff such as video technicians, statisticians and network programmers who may have replaced staff that used to perform tasks manually. The net effect is a higher level of departmentalization and specialization amongst the workforce.

Environmental uncertainty

Environmental uncertainty for sport organizations can be influenced by the actions of suppliers, service providers, customers, sponsors, athletes, volunteers, staff, stakeholder groups, government regulatory agencies, as well as general changes in economic or market conditions. For example, if a group of professional athletes behave inappropriately, their actions can affect the ability of their club or team to maintain or develop sponsorships, which in turn may affect their ability to retain staff and hence require a structural adjustment. Similarly, a downturn in the economy can directly affect sales of sporting merchandise, and organizations may have to adjust their structure accordingly to reduce costs or change product lines.

There are some additional drivers of structural change in sport organizations that are worth noting. These include poor on-field performance, changes in personnel due to politics, competition and market forces, government policy changes, and forced change via mergers and amalgamations. Poor on-field performance by professional sporting teams or clubs can lead to an end-of-season purge of playing or coaching personnel, and may entail a review of how the group of staff involved in coaching, athlete support or allied health services is organized. The political nature of some sport organizations that elect individuals to govern their activities can lead to structural change being implemented due to the personal preferences of elected leaders or a mandate for change. Competition and market forces affect all organizations, but the interdependent nature of clubs operating within a league or competition necessitates them sharing information. Consequently, these organizations tend to be structured in similar ways, making structural change difficult. Governments may also change the way they fund high performance programs or tie funding levels to the performances of international teams or individuals. Poor international performances may consequently reduce funding and therefore the capability of an organization to sustain their organizational structure. Finally, structural change may be forced upon sports organizations, either by economic conditions (such as population loss in rural areas forcing clubs to merge) or government policy (such as forcing single gender sport organizations to merge).

The example of Sport Scotland highlights how the four generic factors of strategy, size, technology and environmental uncertainty can influence the structure of a sports organization.

In Practice 6.3 Sport Scotland

Sport Scotland is the lead agency tasked with developing sports in Scotland, both in terms of developing participation in sport and increasing elite sport performances.

The website for Sport Scotland states that they work with partners to develop the Scottish sporting system, investing in and joining up the people, places, partnerships and planning that make sport happen, specifically:

- advising the Scottish Government and supporting delivery of its policies;
- leading, supporting and coordinating key organizations involved in sport;
- investing National Lottery and Scottish Government funding;
- delivering quality products and services in targeted areas;
- promoting the power of sport and the contribution it makes to life in Scotland;
- collaborating with UK and international sporting systems to ensure Scottish sport is well represented and integrated; and
- adding value to major sporting events and additional investment.

Sport Scotland's organizational structure is directly linked to their strategy. As their website proclaims,

> as the national agency for sport, we are a non-departmental public body, responsible through ministers to the Scottish Parliament. We are also a National Lottery Fund distributor and we are governed by National Lottery distribution rules. We invest Scottish Government and National Lottery resources to support people in Scotland to participate, develop and achieve in sport. We continually strive to ensure these resources are invested wisely so as to achieve best value and maximum impact.

Sport Scotland incorporates a head office in Glasgow and a high performance arm, the Sport Scotland Institute of Sport (SSIS), in Stirling. The Sport Scotland Trust Company also operates three national training centres, Glenmore Lodge, Inverclyde and Cumbrae. These centres provide quality, affordable and appropriate residential and sporting facilities for people to develop in sport.

The entire organization is based on a simple structure, with the CEO having three direct reports (or a span of control of three): a Director of High Performance who works with the SSIS; a Director of Sports Development who has four direct reports (Heads of coaching and voluntering, sporting pathways, school and community sport, and facilities); and a Director of Corporate Services who has five direct reports (office support, strategic planning, finance, communications and human resources).

It is clear that each of the four contingency factors noted earlier in the chapter have impacted on the structure of the organization. Sport Scotland has a very clear mandate to deliver professional services and support for elite athletes and to increase the number of people involved in sport in Scotland. Accordingly the structure reflects these core functions or strategic foci. Any increase in the number of elite sports or athletes supported by Sport Scotland would not necessarily lead to a change in structure, rather each of the existing teams would simply expand to cater for the increased service requirements. As a government owned enterprise, its structure is in part determined by its mandate to deliver services to the Scottish sport industry, and is unlikely to be unduly affected by environmental uncertainty. The drivers of change in structure would include any significant shifts in strategy or government policy, such as a move to focus on a selected number of priority sports, which would perhaps require a redesign in organizational structure.

Source: Sports Scotland website at www.sportscotland.org.uk

CHALLENGES FOR SPORT MANAGERS

An ongoing challenge facing sport managers is the need to strike a balance between lowering costs by using fewer staff and increasing productivity. This can be achieved through a greater use of technology for communication, data management and analysis, the appointment of skilled staff able to use technology, and the development of semi-autonomous work teams that are able to make operational decisions quickly. This requires the use of a more flexible organizational structure than perhaps is the norm for the majority of contemporary sport organizations.

A further challenge for sport managers is to ensure that their organizations are flexible enough to react quickly to opportunities in the market or to the demands of their stakeholders, while at the same time maintaining adequate forms of control and accountability. Sport managers will need to establish clear guidelines for decision-making and acceptable levels of formalization for standard procedures, without unduly constraining the flexibility to modify those guidelines and formal procedures.

An aspect of managing organizational structures that is relatively unique to sport is the presence of both paid staff and volunteers, often with volunteers directing the work of paid staff. Sport managers will need to be cognizant of the need to maintain close links between these two significant parts of their workforce and maintain a suitable structure that allows these groups to communicate effectively and work to achieve organizational outcomes.

Sport managers also need to ensure the structure can enable strategy to be realized. If strategic plans are devised, new markets identified, or new product and service offerings developed in the absence of concomitant changes to the organizational structure, then the ability of the organization to deliver such planned changes is questionable. It is imperative that sport managers pay attention to designing their structure to enable specific strategic directions to be achieved.

As illustrated in the previous chapters, organizations that work within the sport industry must work within a myriad of other organizations from the public, private and nonprofit sectors. Often, sport organizations have many stakeholders involved in setting the strategic direction of the organization. The organizational structure should therefore facilitate decision-making processes that engage all relevant stakeholders.

Finally, the interdependent relationships that exist between sports organizations that may be involved in a league, a collection of associations, a joint venture, or a funding agreement with multiple partners and sponsors, necessitate organizational structures that reflect these connections. This may extend to establishing designated roles for external liaison within the structure or incorporating representation from members of external organizations on internal decision-making committees.

The structure adopted by the British Basketball League represents an attempt to deal with many of these challenges.

In Practice 6.4 British Basketball League

The top men's professional basketball league in the UK is the British Basketball League (BBL). The BBL is an independent company owned by its 12 member clubs, each with an equal shareholding in BBL. Each club has a representative on the BBL Board of Directors who oversee the operation of a central BBL office in Birmingham, which manages administration, marketing and media functions. The interesting aspect of the structure of the BBL is that each club operates as a franchise in designated areas across the UK in order to maximize commercial and media value within their local community. In 2014, these franchises were:

- Bristol Flyers
- Cheshire Phoenix
- Durham Wildcats
- Glasgow Rocks
- Leeds Force
- Leicester Riders
- London Lions
- Manchester Giants
- Newcastle Eagles
- Plymouth Raiders
- Sheffield Sharks
- Surrey United
- Worcester Wolves

Unlike other sports where second division champions are promoted to replace the bottom ranked team in the top league, the BBL operates independently of the second tier competition, the English Basketball League (EBL). There is no promotion and relegation between the BBL and the EBL, and EBL clubs cannot join the BBL based on their performances in official competition alone. However, EBL clubs and any other organizations can apply for a franchise from the BBL.

The organizational structure or franchise system used by the BBL is used because of the significant costs of running a team in the BBL compared to running any other team in the UK. The structure attempts to provide financial security and protect investment into clubs by removing the threat that comes with relegation. A salary cap and income distribution policy amongst BBL clubs also assists with competitive balance and financial management.

Clubs can apply to join the BBL by submitting a detailed business plan to the BBL Franchise Committee that specifies venue details, proof of an acceptable level of financial backing, and an explanation of how the club will be sustainable. Because government funding for basketball goes to England Basketball, the BBL receives no government financial support. Instead, it derives its income from sponsorship, media partnerships, merchandising and ticket sales. Commercial and media rights generate the largest portion of income for the league and clubs.

The BBL has introduced player eligibility rules to provide more opportunities for British players, with each team allowed a maximum of five over-18 non-British players per game. There is no national draft system; players are recruited directly by clubs from their development programs or via direct application.

The challenge of organizing a viable professional basketball league in a country dominated by football, rugby and cricket is significant. Competition for sponsorship dollars, access to appropriate venues, securing media rights and maintaining market share in a crowded professional sport market are all challenges for the directors of the BBL and the managers of their member clubs. The organizational structure adopted by the BBL in using the US style franchise system is an attempt to combat these challenges. The structure allows the league and clubs to plan for future expansion, manage income and costs across all elements of the organization, and ensure equitable decision-making amongst the member clubs.

Source: British Basketball League website at www.bbl.org.uk

SUMMARY

Organizational structure was defined as the framework that outlines how tasks are divided, grouped and coordinated within an organization. An organization's structure is important because it defines where staff and volunteers 'fit in' with each other in terms of work tasks, decision-making procedures, the need for collaboration, levels of responsibility and reporting mechanisms.

Six key elements of organizational structure were reviewed: work specialization, departmentalization, chain of command, the span of control, centralization and formalization. In addition, four basic models for how an organization may use these six elements to design an appropriate structure were reviewed: the simple structure, the bureaucracy, the matrix structure, and the team structure.

The generic contingency factors that influence organizational structure – size, strategy, technology and environmental uncertainty – were reviewed as well as some unique drivers of change to the structure of sport organizations. Finally, a number of unique challenges for sport managers in dealing with structures were presented. Sport managers should be aware of these factors that drive structural change and the specific structural elements they can influence that are likely to deliver improved organizational outcomes and performance.

REVIEW QUESTIONS

1 Define organizational structure in your own words.

2 If you were to manipulate any of the six elements of structure, which do you think could have the most impact on the day-to-day role of the Chief Executive of a sports organization?

3 Do staff in small sports organizations have a low degree of work specialization? Why or why not?

4 Which structural model would suit a large sports event such as the Commonwealth or Olympic Games? Why?

5 How are organizational strategy and structure related?

6 How does a change in size affect the structure of a sports organization?

7 Compare the organizational structure of a sport manufacturing organization and a local community sports facility? How do each of the six elements of organizational structure differ? Which elements are similar?

8 Explain how environmental uncertainty can force change to the structure of a sports organization.

9 Interview the CEO of a medium sized sports organization. What is their most significant challenge in managing their organizational structure?

10 Explore the structure of a small community sport club. Are the principles of organizational structure outlined in this chapter directly applicable? Why or why not?

FURTHER READING

The use of organizational theory in the analysis of structures for nonprofit sport organizations is well established. Three broad questions have been addressed in these studies. These are: first, investigating the relationship between organizational structure and organizational effectiveness; second, attempting to categorize organizational types; and third, exploring the impact of professionalization on various elements of organizational structure.

Students interested in reading further should consult the following journal articles:

Amis, J. & Slack, T. (1996). The size-structure relationship in voluntary sport organizations. *Journal of Sport Management*, 10, 76–86.

Kikulis, L.M., Slack, T., Hinings, B. & Zimmermann, A. (1989). A structural taxonomy of amateur sport organizations. *Journal of Sport Management*, 3, 129–150.

Kikulis, L.M., Slack, T. & Hinings, B. (1992). Institutionally specific design archetypes: A framework for understanding change in national sport organizations. *International Review for the Sociology of Sport*, 27, 343–367.

Kikulis, L.M., Slack, T. & Hinings, B. (1995). Toward an understanding of the role of agency and choice in the changing structure of Canada's national sport organizations. *Journal of Sport Management*, 9, 135–152.

Relvas, H., Littlewood, M., Nesti, M., Gilbourne, D. & Richardson, D. (2010). Organizational structures and working practices in elite European professional football clubs: Understanding the relationship between youth and professional domains, *European Sport Management Quarterly*, 10(2), 165–187.

Stevens, J. (2006). The Canadian Hockey Association merger and the emergence of the Amateur Sport Enterprise. *Journal of Sport Management*, 20, 74–101.

Theodoraki, E.I. & Henry, I.P. (1994). Organizational structures and contexts in British national governing bodies of sport. *International Review for the Sociology of Sport*, 29, 243–263.

Thibault, L., Slack, T. & Hinings, B. (1991). Professionalism, structures and systems: The impact of professional staff on voluntary sport organizations, *International Review for the Sociology of Sport*, 26, 83–97.

RELEVANT WEBSITES

The following websites are useful starting points for further information on the structure of sport organizations:

- Australian Sports Commission at www.ausport.gov.au
- Sport New Zealand at www.sportnz.org.nz
- Sport Canada at www.pch.gc.ca/eng/1266246552427
- Sport England at www.sportengland.org
- Sport Scotland at www.sportscotland.org.uk

CASE STUDY 6.1

Racing Victoria Limited

Thoroughbred horse racing in the state of Victoria, Australia is governed by Racing Victoria Limited. RVL's vision is 'to enhance the Victorian thoroughbred racing industry's position as a leading world-class sporting industry, delivering integrity, quality and entertainment'. On 17 December 2001, Racing Victoria Limited was registered as a public company limited by guarantee under the federal Corporations Act. On 19 December 2001, RVL assumed the functions and responsibilities as the new Principal Club (now known as the Principal Racing Authority) governing thoroughbred racing in Victoria. This coincided with the commencement of the Racing (Racing Victoria Ltd) Act 2001.

Prior to RVL's establishment, the Victoria Racing Club, the race club that hosts the famous Melbourne Cup at their Flemington race track each November, had responsibility as the Principal Club in Victoria. RVL was established with the support of the racing clubs, racing industry bodies and the State Government to provide independent governance of thoroughbred racing in Victoria.

RVL's Member Shareholders consist of Country Racing Victoria Inc (CRV), Melbourne Racing Club Inc (Melb RC), Moonee Valley Racing Club Inc (MVRC) and Victoria Racing Club (VRC), along with the Thoroughbred Racehorse Owners Association (TROA), Thoroughbred Breeders Vic (TBV), Australian Trainers Association (Victorian Branch) (ATA), Victorian Jockeys Association (VJA), Australian Jumps Racing Association (AJRA), Victorian Bookmakers Association (VBA), and unions representing the Australian Liquor Hospitality and Miscellaneous Workers' Union (Vic Branch) (LHMU), Australian Services Union (Vic Branch) (ASU), Australian Workers' Union (Vic Branch) (AWU), Media, Arts & Entertainment Alliance (MEAA).

RVL's constitutional objectives are to develop, encourage, promote and manage the conduct of the racing of thoroughbred horses in Victoria by ensuring:

- Excellence: Victorian thoroughbred racing is, and is recognized throughout Australia and worldwide as a centre of racing excellence.
- Service of customers: Victorian thoroughbred racing competes effectively in the leisure and entertainment markets by providing excellent customer service to patrons, punters and other customers; and a source of exciting entertainment for a wide audience.
- Integrity: Victorian thoroughbred racing generally, and race meetings in particular, are managed and conducted to ensure the highest integrity, building continuously on the reputation and integrity of Victorian thoroughbred racing.
- Efficiency: Victorian thoroughbred racing is managed with optimal efficiency in order to best enable the meeting of the objectives.
- Participation: Victorian thoroughbred racing is managed to encourage the fullest participation by the widest range of people, particularly women and young people.
- Economic benefits: the management of RVL's and Victorian thoroughbred racing clubs' revenues, costs, assets and liabilities optimizes the economic benefits delivered by Victorian thoroughbred racing to all of its stakeholders and participants, including in particular the owners and breeders of thoroughbred racehorses, other participants and stakeholders in Victorian thoroughbred racing, the communities in which Victorian thoroughbred racing operates, and the Victorian economy generally.
- Social obligations: Victorian thoroughbred racing is conducted to ensure that it meets its social obligations to Victoria and the communities in which it operates, including but not only by promoting Victorian country thoroughbred racing, encouraging responsible wagering and gaming; and optimizing employment in the Victorian thoroughbred racing industry.
- Independence: RVL conducts its operations and exercises its powers and functions in a manner which ensures the public confidence in RVL's integrity and independence from any improper external influence.

RVL's organizational structure comprises three board portfolios (or mega-departments): Integrity, Racing Operations, and Marketing and Development. The RVL Integrity Department is broken into the two key areas of Integrity Services and Veterinary Services. Integrity Services manages all officials including Stewards, Starters, Judges, Clerks of Scales and Barrier Attendants at race meetings and race trials. Integrity Services comprises the following functions: Integrity Management, Betting Services, Chair Meetings, Form Analysis, Stewards' Operations, Investigations, and Race Day Administration and Licensing. Veterinary Services is responsible for such things as Race Day Vets, Drug Control Program, Research and Development, Quarantine Services and other activities dealing with the care and regulation of horses.

The Racing Operations group is responsible for the management and development of the racing program and optimizing opportunities for owners, trainers, jockeys and breeders. The Racing Operations department undertakes regular analysis, monitoring and review of the program and consults regularly with clients and stakeholder groups. It performs important tasks such as the handicapping of courses, developing the racing program and rating tracks on race days.

The Marketing and Development group is principally aimed at growing and developing the level of participation, interest in and awareness of thoroughbred racing in Victoria. Marketing and Development comprises of the following functions: Media & Public Relations, Publishing, Design & Website management; the Call Centre; Sponsorship & Marketing of RVL & the Australian Racing Museum; and working with Owners and Breeders for promotional efforts.

The strategy document 'Racing to 2020' written in 2009 stated:

> The Victorian thoroughbred racing industry is a major player in the global sports, entertainment and wagering market. It is also a key employer and contributor to the state's economy. Racing To 2020 has been developed to address Victorian thoroughbred racing's future and to ensure its continued vitality, growth and sustainability. This exciting new strategic vision provides the platform and framework for industry development over the next twelve years. It is a clear statement of our current and future objectives. Over the past decade, the landscape has changed dramatically for racing. Wagering on racing and sports is no longer the sole domain of the TABs and on-course bookmakers. Mobile telephones, the internet and competition policy have changed the racing environment forever. RVL perceives this as an opportunity to expand racing's popularity and to enhance its position as a mainstream sport and entertainment experience of choice. A sustainable future will be achieved by maintaining customer focus, maximising revenue, renovating and renewing racing's infrastructure and increasing the returns to participants.

Since that vision was articulated, RVL has developed a new strategic plan for the period 2013 to 2016 that specified seven strategic objectives (see Figure 6.5).

Strategic objectives	Goals
Build attendance, viewership and engagement in Victorian thoroughbred racing	Develop and engage the broadest possible audience through the compelling presentation of thoroughbred racing across all media platforms, on race days and in the community
High performance racing	To strengthen the quality and depth of Victoria's racing program to showcase Victorian racing on the world stage – while delivering growth in wagering, attendances and media reach, with whole of industry engagement
Best practice integrity assurance	To ensure the reputation of and confidence in Victorian racing is protected by best practice integrity assurance processes, implemented by a professional and progressive Integrity Team
Grow national and international wagering	To maintain Victorian thoroughbred racing as the nation's wagering product of choice, while growing international wagering revenue streams
World leading equine welfare	To promote a racing industry culture in which the safety and welfare of the thoroughbred racehorse is paramount
Great people and an inclusive industry	To build an inclusive, high performance culture that is accountable, rewards performance, provides clear career pathways and delivers leadership across the industry
Industry financial strength and optimum infrastructure	Ensure the Victorian thoroughbred racing industry is financially strong and has a sustainable infrastructure platform

FIGURE 6.5 Racing Victoria Limited Strategic Objectives 2013–2016

The plan also specified the criteria by which RVL would measure success of the plan over this three-year period:

1 Growth in feature event attendance above 1.4 million per annum.
2 Growth in free-to-air TV viewership on the Seven Network for marquee events, plus continuous growth in audience for year-round racing on TVN and SKY 1 (pay TV and digital TV audience).

3   Growth in total visitation to the aggregated Victorian thoroughbred racing's digital assets (Racing Victoria, Spring Racing Carnival, VRC, Flemington, Melbourne Cup, MVRC, MRC, CRV, websites) from 4.1 million unique users per annum.

4   Growth in total national wagering turnover on Victorian thoroughbred racing across all approved wagering service providers from AUS$5 billion per annum.

5   Growth in international turnover from AUS$275 million (FY 13) to AUS$366 million (FY 16).

6   Growth in total income earned from wagering from AUS$296 million per annum.

7   To arrest and reverse the trend of thoroughbred racing's declining market share of Victorian TAB three-code turnover from 68 per cent.

8   To raise annual prize money and other returns-to-participants from AUS$168 million.

9   To reduce Racing Victoria debt from AUS$27 million to AUS$6 million.

10 To increase average starter numbers for TAB flat races from 10.0 per race to 10.5 per race.

11 To increase Super VOBIS nominations from 2300 and the VOBIS Gold participation rate from 55 per cent [Super VOBIS is an incentive scheme designed to reward owners and breeders who invest in Victorian bloodstock].

12 To increase equine and participant drug tests and stable inspections.

13 To achieve a Racing Victoria Employee Engagement Index result well above the benchmark target that indicates a healthy engagement culture during a period of major change.

The RVL website provides a great deal of information on its strategies, more so than most sport organizations, probably because of the many stakeholders involved in racing. This provides a useful resource to get a fuller understanding of the racing industry in Victoria and why RVL has adopted its specific organizational structure.

CASE STUDY QUESTIONS

1   Access the RVL website at www.racingvictioria.net.au and read about the history of racing in Victoria. Why do you think racing in Victoria is now governed by an independent company?

2   How is the strategy for RVL toward 2020 aligned to its organizational structure?

3   What are the barriers or constraints that might limit the effectiveness of the structure adopted by RVL?

4   What are some of the economic and market forces that RVL needs to be mindful of in order to ensure its structure meets its needs?

5   Do you think the RVL would be able to quickly modify its organizational structure? Why or why not?

Source: RVL website at www.racingvictoria.net.au, Racing Victoria (2009). *Racing to 2020, Racing Victoria's Vision for the Victorian Thoroughbred Racing Industry.* Melbourne: Racing Victoria Limited and Racing Victoria (2013) *Strategic Plan 2013–2016.* Melbourne: Racing Victoria Limited.

CASE STUDY 6.2

New Zealand Rugby Union

The development of an organizational structure for a governing body for sport is often dependent on a combination of history, personal preference of the leadership team, regulatory requirements from government and the services that an organization provides to its members, supporters and customers. The New Zealand Rugby Union is one such organization with a history dating back to 1892 and a CEO (Steve Tew) who has been in that position for more than a decade. The NZRU is an incorporated society (New Zealand Rugby Union Incorporated), governed by the Incorporated Societies Act 1908, that distributes its surplus to its members (the Provincial Unions) to develop rugby, promote participation opportunities, organize matches, and manage New Zealand's national rugby teams, including the famous all-conquering All Blacks.

The NZRU website states that they are charged with responsibility to administer the game of rugby union at the national level; fostering, developing, administering, promoting and representing the game of rugby in New Zealand. The NZRU has offices in Wellington and Auckland and has direct relationships with its members, including all 26 Provincial Unions, Super Rugby Franchises, sponsors, and stakeholders such as the New Zealand Government. Given the popularity of rugby in New Zealand it is one of that country's largest sport organizations, and as of 2014 had a structure based on five key operational priorities: Rugby; the All Blacks; Relationships, Planning and Operations; Finance, ICT and People and Capability; and Content, Commercial and Public Affairs.

The Rugby team is made up of Community and Provincial Union Rugby, High Performance and Player Services. Community and Provincial Union Rugby provides support to New Zealand's biggest team – the players, coaches, referees and volunteers in New Zealand's clubs and schools – to ultimately help grow a lifelong love of the game. That support includes funding, coaching programs like Small Blacks, RugbySmart and educational resources. This team also supports the Provincial Unions and Maori Rugby and manages the Rugby Database, a collection of information about everyone involved in rugby in New Zealand. The Community Rugby Strategy 2013–2015 outlines key strategies and specific initiatives in each of the priority areas and provides a framework for the team's activities. The High Performance and Player Services teams are charged with winning pinnacle events that New Zealanders care about (Rugby World Cups, Olympic Gold Medals etc.) by supporting and working with New Zealand's High Performance players, coaches, referees and support personnel.

The All Blacks are the number one ranked team in world rugby with a coaching team that work with a Media Manager, specialist coaches, an Equipment Manager and medical team.

The Relationships, Planning and Operations team plans and delivers the world-leading rugby activity that teams and supporters deserve and ensures the NZRU has strong relationships with key partners in New Zealand and around the world in order to deliver those matches, tournaments, competitions and events. The team is made up of the Events, Rugby Operations, Major Projects and Project Support, Legal, and Junior World Championship 2014 teams.

The Finance, ICT and People and Capability team supports the rest of the organization. They support the day-to-day running of rugby and ensure they have the tools, resources and processes to enable all of NZRU to be the best it can be. The team is made up of Information Communication Technology (ICT), Finance, People and Capability, Office Services and Board Support.

The Content, Commercial and Public Affairs team manages relationships with commercial partners and sponsors, local and international broadcasters, and various license holders. The team is responsible for delivering the marketing and promotion of competitions, teams and the community game. The team also works on developing sustainable revenue and new partnerships to help fund rugby at all levels. They manage NZRU's brand, communications and media activity, government relations, publishing and online, video and social media activity, including allblacks.com – one of the world's most popular rugby websites. They also work with NZRU's charity partners and maintain NZRU's history and heritage program.

The Vision in the latest strategic plan is underpinned by six key pillars. These are:

Strong Community Rugby
- healthy Provincial Union, club and school rugby;
- rising participation numbers at all levels;
- a rugby community that is enjoyable, welcoming and inclusive;
- encouraging personal growth and development through rugby;
- rugby being a positive influence in New Zealand society.

Outstanding Competitions
- competitive, entertaining, aspirational, sustainable and safe;
- create pathways and support our development programs;
- loved, respected and valued by players, fans and other rugby people;
- roles that are clear and defined.

Winning All Blacks
- maintain their world-leading winning record;
- lead and support rugby development at all levels;
- promote rugby in New Zealand and internationally;
- ambassadors for New Zealand and for rugby in New Zealand.

Positive Global Presence
- contribute to the growth of rugby worldwide;
- share resources and expertise with developing rugby nations;

- maximise opportunities for the benefit of rugby in New Zealand;
- maintain New Zealand's influence with the IRB.

Effective structures
- appropriate and sustainable;
- challenge traditional structures;
- keep pace with New Zealand's changing society and lead those changes;
- clear roles and responsibilities for people and organizations.

Inspiring Rugby World Cup 2011 Legacy
- create a legacy from the Tournament for future generations to enjoy.

And their short-term goals, as of 2014, were:
1. All Blacks go Back to Back (i.e. win consecutive World Cups);
2. two Olympic Gold Medals in Rio;
3. New Zealand Rugby is financially healthy by driving revenue generation, cost and management and sustainability throughout the game;
4. New Zealand rugby is well led and delivered for fans, players and commercial partners;
5. rugby is the sport of choice in wider Auckland;
6. the key initiatives contained in the Community Rugby Plan are implemented to assist in rugby bringing communities together and being the sport of choice for teenagers; and
7. enhance our relationships and reputation with key international stakeholders and markets.

CASE STUDY QUESTIONS

1. Access the NZRU website at www.nzru.co.nz and read about the history of Rugby in New Zealand. Why do you think rugby in New Zealand is now governed by an independent charitable company?

2. How is the strategy for NZRU toward 2016 aligned to its organizational structure including the short-term goals?

3. In 2011, the NZRU successfully hosted the World Cup in New Zealand, beating France in the final 8–7 for their second Web Ellis Trophy. Hosting such a large event clearly has some implications for the organizational structure of a national sport governing body. If they were to host the event again, how would it affect their organizational structure?

4. What are some of the economic and market forces that NZRU needs to be mindful of in order to ensure its structure meets its needs?

5. Why is the high performance function in a separate department to the All Blacks?

Source: NZRU website at www.nzru.co.nz

CHAPTER 7

Human resource management

OVERVIEW

This chapter reviews the core concepts of human resource management, provides examples of the unique features of human resource management within sport organizations, such as volunteer and paid staff management, and summarizes the key phases in the human resource management process. The chapter examines human resource management within community, state, national and professional sport organizations, in order to illustrate core concepts and principles.

After completing this chapter the reader should be able to:

- identify the key concepts that underpin human resource management within sport organizations;
- explain why human resource management in sport organizations can be different to non-sport organizations;
- identify each of the phases within the human resource management process; and
- explain the ways in which each of the human resource management phases would be implemented in different sport organization contexts.

WHAT IS HUMAN RESOURCE MANAGEMENT?

Human resource management, in business or sport organizations, is essentially about first, finding the right person for the right job at the right time, and second, ensuring the organization has an appropriately trained and satisfied workforce. The concepts that underpin effective human resource management are not particularly complex. However, the sheer size of some organizations, as well as the difficulties in managing unusual organizations in the sport industry, make human resource management a complex issue to deal with in practice. Successful sport leagues, clubs, associations, retailers and venues all rely on good human resources, both on and off the field, to ensure they achieve their objectives. Conversely, organizations with staff that lack motivation, are ill suited to their work, under-paid or under-valued will struggle to perform.

Human resource management is a central feature of an organization's planning system. It cannot be divorced from other key management tools, such as strategic planning, financial planning or managing organizational culture and structure. Human resource management can both drive organizational success, and is a consequence of good management and planning. Importantly, human resource management is a process of continual planning and evaluation and is best viewed as part of a cycle in which an organization aims to meet its strategic goals. Human resource management, therefore, is a holistic management function in that it can be 'both person-centred and goal-directed' (Smith & Stewart 1999).

Human resource management can mean different things to different organizations, depending on their context and outlook. For professional sport organizations that are profit driven, such as the American National Basketball Association (NBA), Major League Baseball (MBL) or National Hockey League (NHL), successful human resource management is equated with profitability, long-term growth and success (on and off the court, diamond and rink). This is not to suggest that these things are pursued at the expense of employees, but rather that the success of the employees is measured by dispassionate business indicators and human resource management is a tool for driving the business towards its goals. For example, some player welfare and development programs within professional sport organizations are designed to produce socially, morally and ethically responsible citizens. This is viewed as a good human resource strategy, not only because of the intrinsic value to the athletes, but for the extrinsic value that comes from better public relations and sponsor servicing. In other words, better behaved athletes mean greater profitability and overall success for professional sport teams and franchises.

For nonprofit sport organizations, successful human resource management is not always about bottom-line financial performance. Rather, it can encompass a range of strategies and outcomes depending on the organizational context. A local sporting club that has had a problem with alcohol consumption among its junior players may develop a range of programs to educate its players, coaches and administrators (who may be paid or volunteer staff), in order to encourage a more responsible club culture. This player welfare program may actually be part of a human resource management strategy, as the inappropriate club culture may have been making it difficult to attract and retain volunteers with expertise and commitment. In the case of the professional team context the player welfare program can be used to manage its image and maintain brand credibility. In the case of the local community sport club the player welfare program can be used to retain volunteers who were being driven away from the club by poor behaviour and a dysfunctional culture. From these two examples it is clear that human resource management can be both person-centred and goal-directed at the same time.

One of the significant challenges of implementing effective human resource management within sport organizations is that not all sport organizations are alike. As Taylor et al. (2008) have illustrated, different types of sport organizations have different staffing profiles. These staffing profiles are dependent on an organization's type, as well as its purpose or reason for being. For example, a professional sport organization, such as a club in the Spanish La Liga, will have an extensive staff of full-time paid professionals engaged in marketing, coaching, sport science and general administration, whereas a voluntary organization, such as a local cricket or rugby club, is likely to have no paid staff. Other sport organizations might have a mixture of paid and voluntary staff, who work together in the day-to-day operations of the organization, or work together in their capacities as staff and members of a committee of management or board of directors. We will investigate the governance of sport organizations later in the book, but at this point it is sufficient to note that in many sport organizations paid staff are answerable to a voluntary board of directors. This relationship can be a challenge, for the overall management of the organization and the practice of human resource management more specifically.

Many of the functions of professional and voluntary sport organizations are similar – such as event management, promotion, fundraising, membership services and financial management – however, the scale of the organizations is different. While it is true that the scale and type of organization has an impact on the human resource management practices that can and need to be put in place, in many respects sport organizations are increasingly adopting human resource management practices that are underpinned by the notion of professional and standard practice. Indeed, the implementation of specific human resource management practices has been viewed as an important catalyst in the professionalization of voluntary or community sporting organizations. For example, in the early 1990s the Australian Sports Commission, in conjunction with the Australian Society of Sports Administrators, the Confederation of Australian Sport and state departments of sport and recreation, developed the 'Volunteer Involvement Program'. The original program was designed to encourage sport organizations to adopt professional volunteer management practices, which was viewed as essential given the large numbers of volunteers involved in sport organizations and the increasing professionalization of the industry.

The program has since been revised and improved to provide sporting clubs and associations with resources and training modules for volunteer management ('recruiting volunteers', 'retaining volunteers', 'volunteer management: a guide to good practice', 'managing event volunteers', 'volunteer management policy' and 'the volunteer coordinator'). These modules encourage Australian sporting clubs and associations to develop systematic processes and practices, although it should be acknowledged that the diversity of club based sporting system, such as that which is in operation in Australia, means that the capacity to professionalize varies considerably.

IS HUMAN RESOURCE MANAGEMENT IN SPORT SPECIAL?

Many of the core concepts that underpin human resource management apply to all organizations, whether they are situated in the world of business, such as soft drink manufacturer Coca-Cola or mining company BHP Billiton, or in the world of sport, such as the South African Rugby Football Union or the Canadian Curling Association. This is not surprising, given that all these organizations employ staff who are expected to execute a range of designated tasks at an appropriate level of performance. These staff will manage finances, undertake strategic planning, and produce products like Fanta, iron ore, coaching clinics and national championships. There are, however, significant differences between business and sport organizations, which result in modifications to generic human resource management practices.

In particular, professional sport organizations have special features, which present a unique human resource management challenge. Sport organizations, such as the Cincinnati Bengals in America's National Football League, revolve around three distinct types of employees. First, the Bengals employ people in what they call 'the front office', such as the director of business development or the director of corporate sales, marketing and broadcasting. Second, the Bengals employ people in what can be referred to as the 'football department', such as the coaches, trainers and scouts. Finally, the Bengals employ people that comprise 'the team', the players, who are the most visible people within any professional sport organization. It could be argued that non-sport businesses operate in the same way, with different levels of management, from the Chief Executive Officer all the way through to the employee on the factory floor. The obvious difference in the sporting context is that the human resources at the bottom of the staffing pyramid are the highest paid employees in the entire organization. The difference between sport and non-sport organizations is illustrated in Figure 7.1. It should be noted that sport organizations have employees that could be considered 'the lowest paid', but relative to non-sport organizations they are not equivalent, and as such a light blue arrow has not been included for the sport organization pyramid (sport organizations are not completely unique in this respect, however, for in many forms of entertainment, such as film or television drama, the actors are the highest paid).

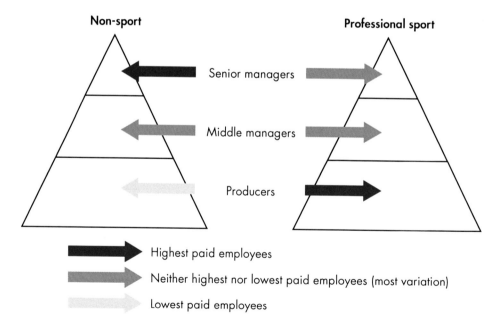

FIGURE 7.1 Pay and organization levels in professional sport and non-sport organizations

In non-sport organizations, Chief Executive Officers, General Managers and other senior executives often receive performance bonuses and have access to share options that allow them to share in the wealth and profitability of the company. The workers producing the product (at the Fanta bottling plant or the iron ore mine for example) do not have access to performance schemes and bonuses that might be worth millions of dollars. In professional sport organizations the situation is reversed and the performance bonuses are typically available to those who produce the product, the players. It is important to keep this special feature of sport in mind when considering the human resource management needs of professional sport organizations specifically and sport organizations more generally.

Additionally, a significant proportion of staff in semi-professional and nonprofit sport organizations are volunteers. The distinction between volunteers and paid staff in the effective management of these groups is a challenge for human resource management in sport organizations. Because sport is often played in a community environment (at a state, regional or local level), it necessarily requires the support of volunteers to maintain services, facilities and events. Some national sport organizations, like the South Africa Rugby Football Union or the Canadian Curling Association mentioned earlier, have paid staff at the national level, whose job it is to coordinate and develop programs, events, championships and national teams. Equivalent state or regional associations for sports like these might, depending on the size, popularity and government funding afforded the sport, also have paid staff in key management, development and coaching positions. In some instances these state or regional associations will have more staff than the national body because of the requirement to deliver programs and services, as well as manage and provide strategic direction for the sport. Local associations, again depending on the size and popularity of the sport, might also have some paid staff; however, at this level sports are supported by a significant core of volunteers. In Australia it has been estimated that sporting activities are supported by 1.5 million volunteers who collectively contribute in excess of 150 million volunteer hours per year, while in the United Kingdom it has been estimated that volunteers contribute in excess of 1 billion hours of labour (www.sportengland.org).

A significant proportion of sport is played on a weekly basis within leagues and associations across the world. Depending on whether the sport is played indoor or outdoor, the sport might have a winter season (football or ice hockey), a summer season (baseball) or might be played all year (basketball). The regularity of the season and the competition, whether at the elite or community level, means that the staffing requirements of sport organizations are predictable and remain relatively stable. There are, however, a range of sporting events and championship for which staff planning is difficult and staffing levels fluctuate greatly. These events are either irregular (a city might get to host the Olympics once in 100 years) or big enough that they require a large workforce for an intense period of time (the annual Monaco Grand Prix). The staffing for major annual sport events can be referred to as 'pulsating' (Hanlon & Cuskelly 2002), as illustrated in Figure 7.2.

In essence, major events need a large workforce, often composed primarily of volunteers or casual workers, for a short period of time prior to the event, during the event and directly following the event, and a small workforce of primarily paid staff for the rest of the year (events such as the Olympic Games or world championships will require a permanent paid staff for many years prior to the event, but most staffing appointments will conclude within six months of the event finishing). The rapid increase and decline in staffing within a one- or two-week period is a complex and significant

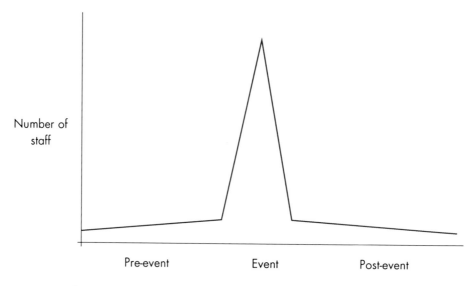

FIGURE 7.2 'Pulsating' sport event staffing

human resource management problem. It requires systematic recruitment, selection and orientation programs in order to attract the staff, and simple yet effective evaluation and reward schemes in order to retain them.

Large organizations with a large workforce have both the capacity and responsibility to engage in sophisticated human resource management. Often there is a dedicated team or department that manages human resources, led by a senior member of staff. In small to medium sized organizations, however, there is not always the human or financial capacity to devote to human resource management practices in a formal system. Human resource management in small to medium sized organizations is often the responsibility of the most senior staff member, such as the Chief Executive or General Manager or is combined with roles performed by another senior manager responsible for finances, planning or marketing, for example.

Sport leagues, clubs, associations and venues rarely have enough staff to warrant employing someone to be responsible solely for human resource management. Often the other key management roles, such as marketing, events or sponsorship are considered essential, and human resource management is considered either as a luxury or peripheral to the core management functions. Furthermore, human resource management can be confused with personnel management, which encompasses more mechanistic functions such as payroll and record keeping (leave, sick pay, etc.).

In Practice 7.1 The All England Lawn Tennis Club Championship

Each year the All England Lawn Tennis Club (AELTC), also known as the All-England Club, conducts one of the world's most well-known and prestigious tennis tournaments: Wimbledon, also known as The Championships. Held in late June to early July each year, Wimbledon is one of the four Grand Slam tournaments on the global tennis circuit.

The regular daily operations of The Championships are managed by the AELTC, which has a permanent staff including a Chief Executive, Championships Director, Financial Director, Marketing Director, Commercial Director, Information Technology Director and Club Secretary. These roles form the 'executive' body of the organization, or the senior management. These full-time staff members are in turn supported by a further 50 administrative staff, who are essentially working in sport management roles within the organization. In addition, there are 16 permanent members of the ground staff, led by the Head Groundsmen, who are responsible for the grass courts at the Club. A further 33 staff members are led by the Buildings and Services Manager. Four staff are allocated to the dressing rooms at the Club, while 11 full-time and part-time staff work in the Members' Dining Room. In all, the AELTC has approximately 120 staff who are working on delivering The Championships at Wimbledon each year, either in the 'commercial' arm of the business or within the building and grounds divisions.

These 120 permanent staff manage the daily business of the organization outside peak periods (i.e. when The Championships are not being played), but during the Wimbledon tournament they also facilitate a massive additional increase in specialized staff and volunteers. During the course of The Championships approximately 6,000 staff are employed or recruited as volunteers, including the following:

- 250 ball girls and boys, supplied through associations with local schools;
- 1,800 catering staff, employed by FMC, the official caterer to The Championships, for which 5,000 applications are received in a process that begins in January each year;
- 300 cleaners, employed in day and night shifts to service a 24-hour event operation during the two weeks of The Championships;
- 150 court attendants;
- 700 security guards, employed through GS4 Security Services;
- 320 drivers, working for the transport service provided by the AELTC to players and officials;
- 350 chair and line umpires, approximately 60 of whom are overseas professionals and the rest are members of the Association of British Tennis Officials.

The Championships at Wimbledon are the epitome of an annual 'pulsating' event referred to in the text, in which a relatively small number of permanent employees are complemented by thousands of annual paid and volunteer staff members at the time of event. This expansion (prior to and during the event) and contraction (post-event) in the number of staff and volunteers occurs year after year, as the AELTC manages an annual attendance of almost 500,000 spectators and seeks to ensure that The Championships continue to be regarded as a prestige global event.

Source: Wimbledon website at www.wimbledon.com

THE ESSENTIALS OF HUMAN RESOURCE MANAGEMENT

Human resource management in sport organizations aims to provide an effective, productive and satisfied workforce. Human resource management refers to the design, development, implementation, management and evaluation of systems and practices used by employers use to recruit, select, develop, reward, retain and evaluate their workforce. The core elements of the human resource management process are represented in Figure 7.3. The following phases are considered the core functions of human resource management, although it is important to keep in mind that these functions will differ significantly depending on the size, orientation and context of the sport organization in which they are implemented.

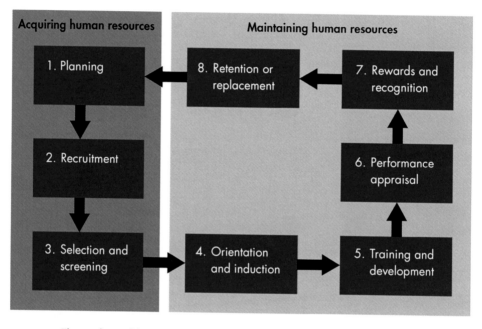

FIGURE 7.3 The traditional human resource management process

Phase 1: Human resource planning

Human resource management planning is essentially about assessing and forecasting the staffing needs of the organization and is often referred to as the most important phase for effective human resource (Smith & Stewart 1999). The planning phase of human resource management is short and fairly static for organizations in which the staffing levels remain fairly constant and the types of jobs performed by staff members varies little. For organizations that are dynamic or in a state of flux (as a result of economic pressures or opportunities for example), human resource planning is a cycle of ongoing development.

  In the planning phase an organization must assess whether current staffing needs will be adequate to meet future demand (or alternatively, whether fewer staff will be required), whether staff turnover is predictable and can be accommodated, whether the ratios of paid, full-time, part-time, casual and volunteer staff are appropriate or adequate, whether there are annual or cyclical fluctuations in staffing that need to be met and managed, and whether specific capabilities will be required in the future that the organization is currently lacking.

Once an organization decides that a new staff member is required or a new position is to be created, the organization must undertake a job analysis, in order to determine the job content (primary and implied tasks), requirements (skills, competencies, qualifications and experience) and context (reporting relationships and job characteristics). Once the job analysis has been completed in as much detail as possible, the organization is ready to develop a job description (a document that covers the job content and context) and a job specification (a document that covers the job requirements, especially skills and knowledge base).

There are four management principles that can be applied to job design. They are most useful for considering how a job might be positioned within an organization, as well as for identifying different types of organizations. These themes are job simplification, job rotation, job enlargement and job enrichment (Chelladurai 2006). Job simplification refers to the process in which a job (and the organization) is broken down into a series of simplified and specialized tasks. This simplification is intended to increase the specialization of employees, thereby increasing efficiency and productivity. Job simplification can be viewed as a positive management tool, particularly when it comes to evaluating the performance of an individual employee; however, job specialization, depending on the context, can lead to workers becoming bored and subsequently dissatisfied with their work.

The second principle, job rotation, is partly a remedy for the boredom and dissatisfaction that can result from simplification. Job rotation involves workers swapping jobs on a periodic basis, in order to keep fresh and stimulated, although clearly a sport organization will only have a finite range of jobs through which employees can rotate.

Job enlargement refers to a process in which employees are encouraged to enlarge the scope of their work and add tasks, even if they are simplified and specialized. The benefit of this approach is a happier workforce, but the downside is the perception of overwork.

Finally, job enrichment refers to the structuring of the job so that it maximizes employee motivation and involvement. This process relies on being able to design jobs that are flexible and have the capacity for growth and change, as well as the employment of people that can work autonomously. According to Chelladurai (2006), the greater levels of responsibility and challenging work that are available through job enrichment means that it is a superior method of job design.

Phase 2: Recruitment

Recruitment refers to the process by which an organization tries to find the person most suited to the job that has been designed. The greater the pool of applicants, the greater the chance the organization will find a suitable candidate. Generating a pool of applicants is not always simple, however, particularly if the job requires specific skills, knowledge, qualifications or experience that are in demand or short supply. Thus, for the chief executive position in a major professional club with responsibility for a multi-million dollar operation, the search might be extensive and costly. However, recruiting an attendant to check membership tickets at home games of the professional club might only require a small advertisement in a local newspaper. Finally, recruiting 10,000 people to act as volunteers for a major hallmark event might require a nationwide or international advertising campaign across various media forms. Increasingly, recruitment processes are becoming more sophisticated as organizations take advantage of rapidly developing communication technologies.

In Practice 7.2 New frontiers for the NBA

The National Basketball Association (NBA) is located in the United States of America, where it is one of the most popular and profitable sporting leagues. Until the 1980s the NBA was primarily a league for basketball players from the USA, although it was still considered the pre-eminent competition in the world. From the 1980s onwards NBA teams began to recruit players from outside the USA and during the last 30 years the number of non-American players in the NBA has grown exponentially. A record number of 92 players from 39 countries and territories outside the USA played during the 2013–2014 season, including 10 players on the championship winning San Antonio Spurs. The increasing number of non-American players, as well as the accessibility of NBA games via television and the internet, has resulted in the NBA being regarded as an international league with all of the world's best players. As such, the popularity of the NBA has grown and with it marketing and business opportunities outside the USA have also developed.

In 2014 the NBA advertised for a 'Senior Manager, New Business – Spain', whose role would be to 'lead the sponsorship new business acquisition process for the NBA in Spain, focusing on prospecting, pitching, negotiating and securing new marketing partners', located in Madrid, Spain and reporting to the Vice President of Marketing Partnerships. The job advertisement was divided into 5 sections: position summary (quoted above); major responsibilities; required experience/knowledge; required skills; and educational background required. A selection of responsibilities, experience/knowledge and skills are detailed below.

Major responsibilities

The overarching description of the role was as follows: 'Consult with both multinational and domestic-based companies to determine their marketing objectives and present, deliver, and sell integrated programs that will meet these objectives. These programs will include rights and assets across media, digital, marketing and events.' Specifically, the successful candidate was to 'develop and implement a sponsorship sales strategy' in consultation with the VP, Marketing Partnerships in Spain and the VP, Marketing and Emerging Markets based in London. The successful candidate was required to:

- lead the sale process to engage with potential sponsors;
- target, pitch and sell NBA marketing partnerships;

- meet financial targets for the NBA's marketing partnerships;
- develop and maximize relationships with potential and existing sponsors;
- maintain a strong understanding of advertising and marketing channels and technologies.

It is clear that job content and the job context were both covered in the section that detailed the major responsibilities of the role, which is typically part of a job description. The following sections on the required experience/knowledge and required skills for the role covered the areas most often found in a job specification.

Required experience/knowledge

The NBA were seeking an employee with significant experience and knowledge, who could take a leadership role within the organization immediately. It is also clear that they were seeking an individual who was working in Spain or who had very good networks within Spain and a well-developed understanding of the specific market context:

- a track record of securing sponsorship contracts for rights holders in sport in Spain;
- strong understanding of the sponsorship and commercial landscape in Spain;
- proven ability to meet and exceed financial and other targets;
- ability to work well within a matrixed organization;
- a persuasive and energetic character;
- gravitas and experience of dealing with and negotiating at Board level;
- a thorough understanding of the sports landscape (basketball and NBA knowledge desirable).

Many of the above points relate to an individual's experience or knowledge in the sport industry, but two of the criteria stand out, in part because they don't fit within the category of experience/knowledge, nor would they fit within the category of skills: 'a persuasive and energetic character' and 'gravitas'. These are personal qualities, rather than skills or experience. It is difficult for a job candidate in a written application to demonstrate these qualities, but it is expected that the organization will be looking for these in an interview if they are clearly stated as they are above.

Required skills

- strong persuading and negotiation skills;
- commercially minded and results driven;
- excellent presentation skills;
- must be fluent in English and Spanish; additional languages a plus;
- a passion for sports.

In addition a University qualification was required. It is evident from the list of required skills that some personal qualities or attitudes are part of the selection criteria, as they were in the experience section. For example, 'commercially minded' and 'a passion for sports' are not so much skills as they are frames of mind or attitudes to life and business. In each of the sections the NBA have attempted to make the type of person they want to employ in the organization as clear as possible – as such the job advertisement is part of the recruitment phase of the human resource management process, but perhaps more importantly is also a significant part of the selection phase.

Sources: NBA Website at www.nba.com; Sportspeople website at www.sportspeople.com.au

Phase 3: Selection

Selection and screening is the process of condensing the candidates that applied for the position during the recruitment phase to a short list, and then selecting the best candidate for the role. The selection phase will usually include at least one interview of the short-listed candidates, which will supplement the application form and curriculum vitae submitted by the applicants. These selection tools will be used to determine whether the applicant is appropriate in light of the job analysis and which of the applicants is the best person for the job. Depending on the geographic location of the applicants, the interview might be conducted in person, via telephone, via video conferencing or via the internet. Industrial relations legislation covers a range of organizational and employment issues in most countries. It is important to comply with these laws and regulations throughout the human resource management processes, such as the recruitment and selection phase, so that the organization is not exposed to claims of discrimination or bias (on the basis of race, colour, country of birth, ethnicity, disability, religion, sex, age, marital status, pregnancy or sexual preference). In this respect Smith and Stewart (1999) refer to the types of questions *not* to ask in an interview:

- How old are you?
- Do you have a problem working with younger people?
- Are you married?
- Do you have any children?
- How will you care for your children when at work?
- How long have you been a single parent?
- Do you intend to have any more children?
- Where do you attend church?
- Do you have a Christian background?
- What are your views on taking prohibited drugs?
- Please send a recent photo with your application form.
- What are you going to do about your weight problem?
- Do you have a communicable disease?
- What clubs do you belong to?
- Do you belong to a trade union or professional association?
- Tell us about your political affiliations?
- Have you undertaken any military service?

An interview is the most common way of determining whether a prospective employee will be best suited to the organization and the position. However, other techniques, such as sophisticated personality and intelligence tests, are increasingly being used to determine whether the applicant has the job requirements identified in the planning phase (skills, competencies, qualifications and experience). For example, the Myers-Briggs Type Indicator (MBTI) is a personality test which, based on questions about psychological processes such as the way people like to interpret information or make decisions, categorizes people into one of 16 personality types. Based on the psychological theories of Carl Jung, the MBTI can be used by sport organizations to determine whether an applicant not only has the appropriate skills and educational qualifications for the job, but also whether their personality, attitudes and values will be a good 'fit' for the organization.

In Practice 7.3 The NFL combine

The National Football League (NFL) is the most popular sporting league in America. The NFL consists of 32 teams throughout America in cities such as Miami (the Dolphins), Pittsburgh (the Steelers), Denver (the Broncos), Dallas (the Cowboys), Chicago (the Bears) and San Francisco (the 49ers). The NFL is one of the richest sporting leagues in the world, the foundation of which are multi-year, multi-billion dollar media rights and sponsorship deals; Monday Night Football and the Superbowl in particular are American institutions. Teams in the NFL spend in excess of US$100 million each on player salaries alone, which means that high school and college athletes throughout America compete to gain a lucrative contract in the NFL, while the NFL teams scout the nation looking for promising football talent.

In April each year the NFL conducts a draft, through which each NFL team has the opportunity to add players to its roster, typically secured through the well-developed college system. As with many sporting leagues around the world, in order to introduce a measure of competitive balance, the poorer performing teams each year are allocated higher 'picks' in the draft than the better performing teams, meaning that these poorer performing teams have priority access to the best players in that year's graduating college class (including those that nominate early for the draft). Because the NFL is such a competitive business, teams will go to great lengths to establish whether particular college players will be ready for the demands of the NFL, as well as determine whether the player will be a 'good fit' in their organization. Like many other organizations, NFL teams must go through the 'planning' phase of the human resource management process, whereby they assess their current playing talent and attempt to determine what future talent they will require. Like a standard business that has a marketing division, a finance division, a sales division and so on, with staff in each division, so too do NFL teams, with players in specific positions – quarterbacks, defensive backs, running backs, offensive lineman, wide receivers, etc. In each of these 'divisions' an NFL team must assess its future requirements and attempt through the draft (as well as through trades) to secure players that fulfil their needs.

The choice of college players through the draft is not left to chance. In February each year the best college prospects for the forthcoming draft are invited to participate in the annual NFL 'combine'. During the combine the draft prospects are put through a series of rigorous physical tests. These tests are standard from year to year, so that teams and coaches can assess the performance of one year's combine prospects relative to previous years. The following is the way in which the NFL describes each of the tests:

40-yard dash

The 40-yard dash is the marquee event at the combine. It's kind of like the 100 meters at the Olympics: It's all about speed, explosion and watching skilled athletes run great times. These athletes are timed at 10-, 20- and 40-yard intervals. What the scouts are looking for is an explosion from a static start.

Bench press

The bench press is a test of strength – 225 pounds, as many reps as the athlete can perform. What the NFL scouts are also looking for is endurance. Anybody can do a max one time, but what the bench press tells the pro scouts is how often the athlete frequented his college weight room for the last three to five years.

Vertical jump

The vertical jump is all about lower-body explosion and power. The athlete stands flat-footed and they measure his reach. It is important to accurately measure the reach, because the differential between the reach and the flag the athlete touches is his vertical jump measurement.

Broad jump

The broad jump is like being in gym class back in junior high school. Basically, it is testing an athlete's lower-body explosion and lower-body strength. The athlete starts out with a stance balanced and then he explodes out as far as he can. It tests explosion and balance, because he has to land without moving.

3 cone drill

The 3 cone drill tests an athlete's ability to change directions at a high speed. Three cones are arranged in an L-shape. The athlete starts from the starting line, goes five yards to the first cone and back. Then, he turns, runs around the second cone, runs a weave around the third cone, which is the high point of the L, changes directions, comes back around that second cone and finishes.

Shuttle run

The short shuttle is the first of the cone drills. It is known as the 5–10–5. What it tests is the athlete's lateral quickness and explosion in short areas. The athlete starts in the three-point stance, explodes out 5 yards to his right, touches the line, goes back 10 yards to his left, left hand touches the line, pivot, and he turns 5 more yards and finishes.

Sometimes the results in these tests, like a job application in a standard organization, are a good indication of whether a player will be a high selection in the NFL draft; however, this is not always the case as prospective players are also observed throughout the previous season by coaches and talent scouts, who will assess them on game sense and performance under pressure, amongst other things. Thus, the tests provide a valuable complementary selection tool for NFL teams. At the 2014 NFL combine defensive end Jadevedon Clowney recorded the best time in the 40 yard dash of all defensive linesmen (4.53 seconds) and was selected at pick number one in the 2014 draft by the Houston Texans. By contrast, running back Dri Archer recorded the best time in the 40 yard dash among all players (4.26 seconds), but was only taken at pick number 97 in the draft by the Pittsburgh Steelers.

Source: NFL website at www.nfl.com

Phase 4: Orientation

Once the employee has successfully navigated the recruitment and selection processes, they are ready to begin work in their new job within the sport organization. Before they start, however, they need to be orientated and inducted. This phase of human resource management is important, as a good quality orientation and induction program can make an employee feel both welcome and empowered, but a poor program, or no program, can make a new employee feel as if they have travelled to a foreign country, in which they can't speak the language, don't know where to go and can't read any of the signs. In short, being in a new organization can be a daunting and frightening experience. The implementation of successful orientation and induction programs can ameliorate some of the difficulties, concerns and anxieties. Potential problems are compounded if the employee is a volunteer and can be exacerbated further if the volunteer does not have any direct supervision from a paid employee of the organization. This is a recipe for disaster, both for the organization and the employee. Table 7.1 outlines some of the orientation and induction steps that the Australian Sports Commission recommended as part of a series of volunteer management modules.

Once an athlete has been selected to play for a team in a major professional sport league (passed the recruitment and selection processes), they are invariably faced with the completely new world of professional sport and all the demands that accompany it. The National Basketball Association (NBA) in the USA recognized that this was a difficult time for many young athletes and developed a comprehensive orientation and induction program. Since 1986, the rookie players of the forthcoming season have been required to participate in a week-long training and development camp in the month prior to the season's start. The rookie transition program is designed so that these young athletes can develop better life skills, which in turn will hopefully prepare them for the particular and peculiar stresses of a professional athletic career. Through the transition program, which includes a diverse range of topics such as sexual health, nutrition and anger management, the NBA hopes that its young players will be able to make better decisions.

TABLE 7.1 Australian Sports Commission volunteer orientation

Orientation Program Checklist

☑ Provide an orientation guidebook or kit

☑ Provide copies of current newsletter, annual report and recent marketing/promotional material

☑ Provide a copy of the constitution

☑ Enter the name, address and contact details of each volunteer into database

☑ Gather and file copies of qualifications and accreditation certificates from each volunteer

☑ Introduce the organization's culture, history, aims, funding, clients/members and decision-making processes

☑ Introduce key volunteers and/or staff (and organization chart)

☑ Outline the roles and responsibilities of key volunteers and staff

☑ Detail the roles and responsibilities and accountabilities of the volunteer in their new position

☑ Familiarize volunteers with facilities, equipment and resources

☑ Explain and 'walk through' emergency and evacuation procedures

☑ Familiarize volunteers with the organization's day-to-day operations (safety and risk management, telephone, photocopier, keys, filing system, tea/coffee making, office processes and procedures, authorizing expenditure)

Source: Australian Sports Commission website at www.ausport.gov.au

Successful orientation and induction programs revolve around forthright and effective communication of information about the organization and its operations. This information might include a general overview, policies and procedures, occupational health and safety regulations, industrial relations issues, a physical tour of the organization's facilities, an overview of the training and development programs available to employees or an explanation of the performance appraisal process (Slack 1997). The focus on orientation and induction is usually magnified when a large number of volunteers are required by the organization, such as at an Olympic Games. A total of 60,422 volunteers participated in running the Atlanta Olympics in 1996, 47,000 volunteers participated in Sydney in 2000, while the 2004 Athens Olympics received in excess of 160,000 volunteer applications from all over the world. At the 2008 Beijing Games, 74,615 volunteers provided services at Games venues, while another 400,000 volunteers provided information, translation services and emergency aid at 550 street stalls throughout the city.

Phase 5: Training and development

Training and development is at the heart of an organization that seeks continual growth and improvement. Sport organizations that do not engage in systematic training and development programs are destined to operate far below their optimum, not only because they will fall behind in current trends, practices and skills, but because they will not see themselves as learning organizations (Senge 1990). At its most basic, training and development is a process through which new and existing employees learn the skills required for them to be effective in their jobs. At one end of the spectrum these skills could be associated with learning how to operate automated turnstiles at a professional sport arena (training for the novice employee), or learning how to creatively brand the organization in order to compete in a hostile marketplace (training for the experienced existing employee). Where training was once a fairly mechanistic activity, it now includes more generic organizational skills that require development and implementation, such as when a major league sport franchise ensures product or service quality, or when a national sport organization develops an organizational culture that encourages compliance from state or regional sport organizations.

Dressler (2003) outlines a five-step training and development process that is useful for sport organizations. Step one is to complete a 'needs analysis', in which the organization identifies the necessary skills for its employees, analyses the current skills base and develops specific training objectives. Step two involves developing the actual training program, which may be done internally or externally. Most sport organizations, as previously noted, are too small to have sophisticated human resource management departments that have the skill and experience to design, develop and implement comprehensive training programs. Sport organizations will most often use external training providers, such as universities or consultancy firms, to provide tailored or standard programs, depending on the needs analysis. Step three, validation, is an optional step in which the organization is able to validate that the training program that has been developed or contracted satisfies the needs analysis. Step four is the implementation of the program, during which the staff are trained (this could be anything from a one-day short course, through to a two-year Masters program). In the fifth and final step the training program is evaluated. The successful program might be expanded to include more employees or more skills, while the unsuccessful program needs to be discontinued or re-worked, which requires the organization to re-assess the needs analysis. Like the entire human resource management process, the training and development process is best viewed as cyclical.

In Practice 7.4 All in one rhythm: Volunteers at the 2014 FIFA World Cup in Brazil

Most major sport events require both paid staff and volunteers in order to run successfully. Mega events such as the Olympic Games and the FIFA World Cup are far too large to be run by paid staff alone – they would not be able to operate without a significant volunteer labour force. In order to manage this labour force effectively and efficiently, mega events need to develop extensive policies and procedures for each of the human resource management phases examined within this chapter. In the 'planning' phase of the human resource management cycle, an event organization must assess its current and future staffing needs. For an organization such as a FIFA World Cup organizing committee, the 'current' staffing profile is relatively small for many of the years leading up to the World Cup; in the main the staff are full-time and paid. By contrast, the 'future' staffing needs are massive, with a mix of full-time, part-time, casual and volunteer staff required; World Cup organizers need to use the experience of previous events, as well as an assessment of their own specific needs, to plan for the event.

For the 2014 FIFA World Cup in Brazil the FIFA World Cup Volunteer Programme was instituted to recruit, select, train and retain the substantial volunteer labour force. According to FIFA, prospective volunteers were required to register on the FIFA.com website in order to be considered. During 2012 and 2013 a record number of 152,101 people registered to be part of the event, almost half of whom were aged 25 years or under. Once the prospective volunteer had registered, they were required to complete seven stages of what FIFA referred to as the 'selection' process, however, it is clear that orientation and training functions were built in to many of these seven stages.

Stage 1: Group exercise

In this stage of the selection process prospective volunteers were required to attend a group exercise at which their behaviour, attitude and ability would be assessed. These group interviews were held in ten host city locations throughout Brazil and were conducted on weekends during October to December 2013, more than six months prior to the event. At the completion of the group exercise stage, candidates were notified whether they would be advancing to the next stage or that they had been eliminated. Volunteer candidates outside Brazil were interviewed via Skype and not required to participate in the group exercise.

Stage 2: General internet-based training

In this stage volunteer candidates were able to undertake internet-based training, related to the World Cup, as well as more general information. At the conclusion of this training the volunteer candidates were required to complete a compulsory exam. Candidates were also required to undertake a mandatory English proficiency test. Similar to the conclusion of stage one, candidates were notified on the basis of these results whether they could advance or had been eliminated.

Stage 3: Placing volunteer candidates

In this stage the volunteer department of the World Cup analysed the information provided by volunteer candidates, such as their test results obtained in stage 2, their profile, availability and their self-nominated preferred area of work, in order to place the volunteer candidates. Candidates were placed in general areas for which there were no requirements or specialized areas that required specific abilities and qualities.

One of the important steps for the volunteer department in this stage was to determine how much time volunteer candidates could work for and then establish a work plan, for individual volunteers and the entire volunteer workforce.

Stage 4: Individual interviews

In this stage volunteer candidates who were assigned to specialized areas attended an interview, in part to assess their proficiency in conversational English. As with the previous stages, candidates were either allowed to proceed to the final stages or were eliminated at this point.

Stage 5: Tailored training

In this stage volunteers were offered a role and if they accepted were then provided with job-specific training via the internet. As per the previous stages, candidates could still be eliminated from the process if they did not complete the training or fulfil the requirements expected of them. In this way the selection process continued during the orientation and training stages of the program.

Stage 6 & 7: Fun day and specific training

In the sixth stage of the process, volunteers were invited to spend a day touring the stadium at the host city where they were based, led by staff from the volunteers department. This 'fun' day was designed to acquaint volunteers with their colleagues and place of work, as well as provide them with additional information as appropriate. In the seventh and final stage volunteers attended a compulsory training session, where they received specific instructions related to the area in which they would be working during the World Cup. At this final session the volunteers were able to meet their manager and the rest of the team working in their area.

It is evident from the seven stage 'selection' process for the 2014 FIFA World Cup detailed above that mega events are incredibly complex and that the human resource management processes and practices must be well planned and executed. It is also clear that the human resource management principle of the right person for the right job at the right time can be applied to one paid staff member or thousands of volunteers.

Source: FIFA website at www.fifa.com

Phase 6: Performance appraisal

This phase of the human resource management process is potentially the most dangerous, as it has the inherent ability to pit 'management' against 'employees' at the macro level, and at the micro level cause managers to feel uncomfortable in judging others or cause employees to feel unworthy, as part of a negative appraisal. The performance appraisal process must be approached carefully by sport organizations and human resource managers within an organization must seek to develop a collaborative process in which the employee, as well as the manager, feels empowered. As Chelladurai (2006) has noted, it is useful to think of performance appraisal in terms of its administrative and developmental purposes. The administrative purpose refers to the need within organizations to make judgements about performance that are directly related to rewards and recognition, such as promotions and salary increases. The administrative purpose often requires quantitative measures, so that employees can be appraised based on similar criteria. The developmental purpose refers to developing and enhancing the capabilities of an employee, which often requires a mix of quantitative and qualitative measures, and can be a catalyst for further training and development. The administrative and developmental purposes of performance appraisal demonstrate that the human resource management process is not always a neat cycle. Rather, there is a constant to and fro between the phases.

During the performance appraisal process, managers and leaders need the ability to review performance and suggest improvement, as a way of developing overall organizational capacity. On the other hand, employees need a forum in which they feel comfortable identifying the things they did well and the things they could have done better, as part of a process of ongoing professional and career development. In this respect the performance appraisal process within any sport organization, whatever its size or type, must be seen within the simple, but effective 'plan, do, review, improve' scheme, which is usually associated with the quality assurance agenda (Deming 1993, pp. 134–136).

In professional sports organizations in particular, the performance appraisal process is often very public, if at times convoluted. Athletes and coaches are constantly rated on their performance. In basketball the number of points, rebounds, assists, turnovers, steals, fouls and blocked shots are recorded meticulously. From year to year, goals are set for athletes and their ability to meet targets in key performance indicators can result in an extended contract with improved conditions. On the other hand, not meeting the targets can mean a player in a sport like baseball has to return to the minor leagues, to return to form or to see out their playing days. For coaches, performance appraisal is often based on one statistic alone, the win-loss record. The fact that the coach is adept at making the players feel good about themselves or has a great working relationship with the administrative staff, will count for very little when it comes to negotiating a new contract if he or she has posted a losing record.

Phases 7 and 8: Rewards and retention

Once a sport organization has planned for, recruited, selected, orientated, trained and appraised its staff, it makes good sense that it would try to retain them. Retaining good quality staff, whether they are in a paid or volunteer capacity, means that the organization will be better off financially and strategically. Organizational knowledge and intellectual property is lost when a sport organization fails to retain its staff. Constantly losing staff will mean that the organization may have the opportunity to encourage and develop new ways of thinking, but the more likely scenario is that it will lead to wasted resources, unnecessarily diverted to rudimentary induction programs.

The first six phases of the human resource management process all contribute to retaining staff. Poor orientation, training and performance appraisal programs in particular can all have a negative impact on staff retention. On the other side of the retention equation, rewards and compensation can encourage employees to remain with an organization. At a professional sport organization this may mean, rather than attempting to keep wage costs low, the senior managers will be prepared to pay the 'market rate' (Smith & Stewart 1999). In a primarily voluntary organization, the reward may take the form of a letter of appreciation for being part of a successful event and an invitation to participate next year. In other words, the reward and retention strategy will depend greatly on the context in which it is being implemented and the existing level of job satisfaction.

SUMMARY

Effective human resource management in sport organizations relies on the implementation of an interdependent set of processes. At one level this can be viewed as quite mechanistic, yet on another more positive level it can be viewed as a blueprint for the successful management of people through a clearly delineated set of stages. Human resource management planning, recruitment, selection, orientation, training, performance appraisal, rewards and retention strategies are essential for an organization to operate successfully in state, nonprofit or commercial sport environments, because good people management is at the core of every successful sport organization, irrespective of the context. Good human resource management allows sport organizations to deal with some of its unique and particular challenges, such as the place of athletes in professional sport organizations, the large casual and semi-permanent workforces required by major events (annual or periodic) and the large volunteer workforce within club based sporting systems. On the other hand, poor human resource management can result in a workforce that is not only uncommitted, but also subject to low levels of morale and job satisfaction. In short, effective and systematic human resource management should be seen as an important management tool in any sport organization, whatever the size or type.

REVIEW QUESTIONS

1   Which is the most important phase of the human resource management process? Why? Refer in your answer to organizations with primarily paid staff and organizations with primarily volunteer staff.

2   Is human resource management important for the effective management of sport organizations? Why?

3   Examine the human resource management processes of a local sport organization. Are the processes adequate?

4   Examine the staffing levels of a major annual event in your city/province/region. Are the staffing levels stable?

5 Should the human resource management role within sport organizations be combined with another functional division?

6 Should different human resource management strategies be applied to volunteers and paid staff?

7 Does the place of athletes in professional sport organizations make the need for effective human resource management practices more or less important?

8 Compare the orientation and induction processes of a sport organization and a non-sport organization. How and why do they differ?

9 Does the often public appraisal of employees in sport organizations diminish the integrity of the human resource management process?

10 Choose a small to medium sized organization without a human resource management specialist. Perform a job analysis for a new employee in the role of human resource management.

FURTHER READING

Chelladurai, P. (2006). *Human Resource Management in Sport and Recreation*. Champaign: Human Kinetics.

Cuskelly, G., Hoye, R. & Auld, C. (2006). *Working with Volunteers in Sport*. London: Routledge.

Doherty, A. (1998). Managing our human resources: A review of organizational behaviour in sport. *Journal of Sport Management*, 12(1), pp. 1–24.

Robinson, L. (2004). Human resource management. In Robinson, L. *Managing Public Sport and Leisure Services*. London: Routledge.

Taylor, T., Doherty, A. & McGraw, P. (2008). *Managing People in Sport Organizations: A Strategic Human Resource Management Perspective*. London: Elsevier Butterworth-Heinemann.

RELEVANT WEBSITES

The following websites are useful starting points for further information on the human resource management of sport organizations:

- Australian Sports Commission Resources at www.ausport.gov.au/supporting/clubs/resource_library/people_management
- Sport England's Running Sport Program at www.runningsports.org
- Sport and Recreation New Zealand Resources at www.sportnz.org.nz/managing-sport/search

CASE STUDY 7.1

Managing student athletes in the NCAA

The National Collegiate Athletic Association (NCAA) of America was 'founded in 1906 to protect young people from the dangerous and exploitive athletics practices of the time'. The NCAA began to have a significant impact on the conduct of college sport in the 1950s and as the extent and scope of college sport grew the NCAA took on a greater administrative role. In the early 1970s the NCAA adopted its current three division administrative structure (Divisions I, II and III). The NCAA is essentially an association that governs and organizes sport within the colleges and universities of America. The NCAA has media rights agreements with the major television networks in America to broadcast its games and national championships, as well as a range of sponsorship deals. In the 2013 financial year US$838 million was received by the NCAA in television and marketing rights fees, which comprised approximately 92 per cent of their total revenue. NCAA revenue has grown steadily, from US$558 million in 2005–2006 to US$750 million in 2009–2010 to US$912 in 2012–2013; the proportion of revenue associated with television and marketing rights fees has been in excess of 80 per cent in each of the five years since 2005–2006. According to the NCAA, more than 90 per cent of its revenue is returned to its member institutions in the form of direct distributions or services; however, it is evident that the higher profile schools in Division I receive the lion's share; in 2012–2013 the Division I schools received 62 per cent of the total distribution.

A significant component of the business of the NCAA can broadly be defined as human resource management, although as an organization its operations are special in many respects. As noted above, the Association was originally formed to protect young athletes from dangerous and exploitative practices. In essence the NCAA still exists to perform this role, monitoring the practices and performances of colleges, universities and their respective employees and students throughout the nation. However, it is clear that as an industry, college sport is manifestly more complex now than at the turn of the twentieth century and that the NCAA is now a large administrative organization. In 1950 there were 387 members of the NCAA, of which 362 were active, whereas by 2010 there were 1,315 members, of which 1,062 were active.

The NCAA provides a variety of what it refers to as 'student athlete benefits'. First, the NCAA provides scholarships to athletes. The scholarships provided by the NCAA to athletes directly are typically special scholarships, either available to athletes via a competitive process or to particular types of athletes. The NCAA also provides a distribution to Division I colleges and universities via an academic enhancement fund. Second, the NCAA provides financial support to athletes. This financial support is provided in the form of injury, disability and medical insurance programs, as well as Division I athlete opportunity and special assistance funds. Third, the NCAA provides health and safety programs, which include a cheerleading safety initiative, as well as in-season and championship drug testing, particularly for Division I and II members. The NCAA also produces a variety of resources to assist their member institutions to develop policies and practices that improve the health and well-being of student athletes. Finally, the NCAA runs a variety of other education programs, clinics and workshops that assist student athletes and their communities.

Through its committee structure and the employment of investigative officers, the NCAA also monitors violations of its rules and regulations, particularly the conduct of its member institutions in relation to their student athletes. There are a raft of rules related to issues such as the recruitment of student athletes, the training and development of student athletes and the compensation of student athletes. The issue of compensation is particularly noteworthy as the NCAA operates a strictly amateur competition, in which the student athletes at colleges and universities throughout America are unable to receive any form of remuneration for their participation in sport.

The NCAA runs the NCAA Eligibility Center, which certifies the academic and amateur credentials of all students seeking to play sport at a Division I or II institution. In order to be considered eligible to participate in a Division I or II NCAA program, a student athlete must meet the requirements sets out by the NCAA. The student must have graduated from high school, have completed a minimum of 16 core courses, meet the required grade point average (GPA) and achieve a qualifying score on one of the standard university admission tests. The GPA and admission test scores for Division I student athletes are calculated on a sliding scale, whereby a high score in one can offset a low score in the other. In addition, the student must complete an amateurism questionnaire and request amateurism certification. Some of the activities that may be reviewed by the NCAA include contracts with a professional team, receiving a salary for participation in sport, prize money received through sport, receiving benefits from an agent or prospective agent, the agreement to be represented by an agent or the provision of financial assistance based on sporting skill. By putting in place these academic and amateur eligibility rules the NCAA attempts to ensure that the integrity of the college and university system is maintained, and that the focus of college and university sport is student athletes, not simply athletes.

Individual member institutions of the NCAA compete with each other to attract the best student athletes across a wide variety of sports such as football, basketball, baseball, softball, track and field, golf, lacrosse, soccer and volleyball. Colleges and universities provide athletic scholarships, which enable the student athletes to attend college or university at no cost, but given that many colleges and universities offer these scholarships, the individual institutions need to provide other benefits to attract the student athletes. For some, the quality of the training and game facilities will be an important drawcard, while for others the opportunity to secure national television exposure or to play at a college or university that has a long history of success in a particular sport will be a deciding factor. As a result of the fierce competition to recruit student athletes, the NCAA has detailed rules that govern what is and is not allowed by students and their prospective colleges and universities. For example, the NCAA has rules regarding the allowable recruiting materials, number of telephone calls, official visits, unofficial visits and contact between a coach and a prospective player, which all increase as the student progresses through high school. These rules also differ depending on the sport; a coach may contact a prospective basketball player or their parents not more than three times in their senior year, whereas a coach may contact prospective football players up to six times.

Once the student has made a decision about which college or university they will attend, they sign a national letter of intent (NLI), a nationwide system governed by the NCAA, which is essentially a binding agreement between the student and the respective institution. The NLI guarantees the student financial support for one year pending eligibility and the institution receives certainty that the student is committed to it alone. Most student athletes within the NCAA have four-year sporting careers (freshman, sophomore, junior and senior). The very best student athletes that participate in sports that have professional leagues, such as football, basketball and ice hockey, are selected via draft systems. Those that participate in non-professional sports, such as swimming or skiing, may represent their country at an Olympic Games.

CASE STUDY QUESTIONS

1   The case refers to the operations of the NCAA as involving human resource management, but that its operations are special. What are some of the NCAA activities that make it a special human resource management business compared to a standard business, such as a sales or marketing company?

2   Which phases of the human resource management process does the NCAA focus its operations and activities on? Why might this be the case?

3   Beyond the fact that student athletes do not get paid, how does the human resource management of a college or university sport program (sometimes referred to as an athletic program or athletic department) differ from a professional sport team or franchise?

4   In which phase of the human resource management process does the NCAA Eligibility Centre belong? Why? How do the perspectives of the NCAA and its individual member institutions differ in respect to their focus in this phase of the process?

Sources: NCAA websites at www.ncaa.org; www.ncaa.com; www.eligibilitycenter.org

CASE STUDY 7.2

'In the spotlight': Sport's public performance appraisal

Manchester United is regarded by many as the most popular sport club in the world, with a large global fan base, high profile players, multi-million dollar sponsorship deals and high match-day attendances. The club has been extremely successful in the English Premier League and in European Cup competitions, including 20 Premier League/League Division 1 titles, 11 FA Cup titles and three European Cup/EUFA Champions League titles. In the 10 years between 2004 and 2013 Manchester United won five Premier League titles (2007, 2008, 2009, 2011 and 2013), one FA Cup (2004), one UEFA Champions League title (2008), three Football League Cups (2006, 2009 and 2010), one FIFA Club World Cup (2008) and five FA Charity/Community Shield titles (2007, 2008, 2010, 2011 and 2013).

During the period 1986 to 2013 Manchester United's manager (a head coach in other sports around the world) was Sir Alex Ferguson, perhaps the most celebrated manager of all time and certainly the most successful in the modern era. Under Ferguson, United claimed the League title in 13 seasons, and finished second in an additional seven seasons; in 22 consecutive seasons United finished in the top three places in the League. Ferguson presided over a total of 1,498 games with Manchester United – they won 894 (59.5 per cent); drew 337 (22.5 per cent) and lost 267 (18 per cent). In other words, during the Ferguson period, a Manchester United fan had less than a 1 in 5 chance that they would see their team lose. Ferguson was knighted in the 1999 Queen's Birthday Honours for his services to football, was one of the inaugural managerial inductees of the English Football Hall of Fame in 2002 and was awarded the Premier League Manager of the Season 11 times.

In May 2013 Sir Alex Ferguson announced that he would retire at the end of the 2012–2013 season, a season in which Manchester United would win the Premier League title yet again. Ferguson noted in his retirement announcement that it was important to him 'to leave an organisation in the strongest possible shape', that United's 'training facilities are among the finest in global sport and our home Old Trafford is rightfully regarded as one of the leading venues in the world'. He also praised Manchester United's owners, the Glazer family, for providing him with the platform to manage the club to the best of his ability and that he had been extremely fortunate to have worked with a talented and trustworthy Chief Executive (David Gill).

Ferguson's retirement meant that Manchester United needed to appoint a new manager, something that the club had not been required to do for an extended period. The new manager would be in charge of a large football department staff and budget and responsible for the on-field performance of one of the most successful and popular sports teams in the world. Ferguson's were clearly big shoes to fill. Two days after media reporting of Ferguson's retirement it was announced that David Moyes, manager of Everton, one of Manchester United's rivals in the English Premier League, was replacing Ferguson on a six-year contract. It was reported in the media that Moyes was personally chosen for the job by Ferguson and that the recommendation was unanimously accepted by the Manchester United Board of Directors. Ferguson was quoted as saying, 'When we discussed the candidates that we felt had the right attributes we unanimously agreed on David Moyes. David is a man of great integrity with a strong work ethic. I've admired his work for a long time and approached him as far back as 1998 to discuss the position of assistant manager here. He was a young man then at the start of his career and has since gone on to do a magnificent job at Everton. There is no question he has all the qualities we expect of a manager at this club.'

Upon being announced as the Manchester United manager, Moyes was quoted as saying 'It's a great honour to be asked to be the next manager of Manchester United. I am delighted that Sir Alex saw fit to recommend me for the job. I have great respect for everything he has done and for the football club. I know how hard it will be to follow the best manager ever, but the opportunity to manage Manchester United isn't something that comes around very often and I'm really looking forward to taking up the post next season.' Moyes joined English Premier League club Everton as manager in 2002 and in his 11 year reign presided over 518 games, of which he won 218, drew 139 and lost 161. During his period as manager Everton's best result was runners-up in the 2009 FA Cup, while in the English Premier League the club's best results were 4th in 2004/5, 5th in 2007/8 and 5th in 2008/9, in an era dominated by Manchester United, Manchester City, Chelsea, Arsenal and Liverpool.

In Ferguson's last season with Manchester United the club won the English Premier League by a convincing margin. They played 38 games, winning 28, drawing 5 and losing 5, with 86 goals for and 43 goals against and a total of 89 points for the season. Manchester City were runners-up with 23 wins, 9 draws, 6 losses, 66 goals for and 34 against and a total of 78 points for the season. In the 2013/14 season, Moyes' first in charge, Manchester United won its first game against Swansea City but by the end of September were 12th on the League table, with two wins and three losses from their first six games, the club's worst start to a season since 1989 and sport journalists began to question what was going wrong at the club. By early December Manchester United were 9th on the League table with six wins from 15 games, and 5 losses (including 3 at Old Trafford), as many as the entire 2012–2013 season. Moyes was forced to concede that it was 'tough because the expectancy is to win all the games' and to publicly claim 'complete responsibility' for the club's poor record. By mid-April 2014 United's positon had only improved slightly to 7th on the League table, with 17 wins, 6 draws and 11 losses from 34 games. After a season of media pressure and speculation, Manchester United released a statement on April 22, in which it announced that Moyes had been sacked: 'Manchester United has announced that David Moyes has left the club. The club would like to place on record its thanks for the hard work, honesty and integrity he brought to the role.' Following the announcement it was speculated that the hiring of Moyes would cost United up to £200 million, including £50 million from lost broadcast rights, prize money and gate receipts as a result of not qualifying for the European Champions League. At the same time the move to sack Moyes was well received by the market and shares in Manchester United rose by 6 per cent, equivalent to £110 million, following the announcement.

In Moyes' time at Manchester United he managed the club to 27 wins, 9 draws and 15 losses from 51 games across all fixtures, a winning ratio of almost 53 per cent, which was more than 10 percentage points higher than his average winning ratio at Everton. On these figures alone Moyes might have expected to retain his job as manager, but compared to previous seasons and the record of Sir Alex Ferguson, the performance of the club in 2013–2014 was completely unacceptable to Manchester United's owners and fans. It also left sport journalists questioning why he was hired in the first place, given his previous record, and speculating that he had not been the right person for the job from the beginning. Manchester United announced that club favourite Ryan Giggs would take over the managerial responsibilities for the remainder of the 2013–2014 season until a permanent manager was appointed. In mid-May Manchester United announced they had signed Dutch national coach Louis van Gaal to the position of manager and a three-year contract, emphasizing van Gaal's success in winning titles in three countries, including the UEFA Champions League. Van Gaal was quoted as saying 'To work as a manager for Manchester United, the biggest club in the world, makes me very proud{...}This club has big ambitions; I too have big ambitions. Together I'm sure we will make history.' In late July, prior to the start of the 2014/15 season, van Gaal said that he had inherited a 'broken squad' at Manchester United and when asked whether it would have been harder taking over from Ferguson rather than Moyes, van Gaal was quoted as saying 'No. I don't agree. I had to follow Bobby Robson at Barcelona the year after he won three titles and there wasn't a problem [Van Gaal won the league that year].{...} When there is success you have a very good squad and now I have to follow and the squad was broken I think.{...}It's more difficult to succeed in a difficult situation than in a fantastic situation.'

CASE STUDY QUESTIONS

1   The case refers to performance appraisal and selection outcomes within one of the most heavily scrutinized sporting leagues in the world. In what ways does the case illustrate that human resource management in clubs such as Manchester United are special, particularly relative to non-sport business operations?

2   Athletes, coaches/managers, officials and administrators associated with professional sport teams are often subjected to a public performance appraisal that is conducted through and by the media. In what other spheres of business or public life are performance appraisals conducted in a similarly public way? What implications does this have for human resource management within these organizations?

3   On what is the performance appraisal of coaches/managers in professional sporting leagues based? Is there one main performance criteria or are there many? Are different stakeholders likely to have different performance criteria for a coach/manager (think of fans, players, owners, shareholders, media, sponsors, etc.)?

4   What does the case illustrate about absolute and relative performance evaluations? How much of a role do expectations play in the performance appraisal of employees within sport organizations, particularly coaches/managers and players? Do you think this is more or less in sport compared to non-sport organizations?

5   The case study refers to Moyes taking 'complete responsibility' for the performance of the club. Is this reasonable to expect of a single employee within a large and complex organization? Why?

Sources: Manchester United website at www.manutd.com; The Guardian website at www.theguardian.com; BBC website at www.bbc.com

CHAPTER 8

Leadership

OVERVIEW

Leadership is arguably the most researched yet least understood topic in the context of management. What we define as excellent leadership and who are great leaders remain points of serious and widespread academic debate. In the United States alone, more than 2,000 books on the topic of leadership are published every year. In this chapter we provide a broad outline of the different approaches that have been used to describe and analyse leadership. We will also use a number of examples and cases to explore leadership. Much of this discussion will take place in reference to the leadership challenges that confront sport organizations.

By the end of this chapter the reader should be able to:

- describe the need for leaders and for leadership;
- distinguish between leadership and management;
- outline the different levels (in the organization) that leaders can work at and how this impacts their approach to leadership; and
- provide an overview of your personal leadership development needs.

WHAT IS LEADERSHIP?

It is not easy to find agreement among any group on a definition of leadership. Sometimes leadership is described as 'getting things done through people'. Others argue that leadership is about 'exercising power in order to influence others' or that true leadership is about 'envisioning a bright future and taking others by the hand towards it'. In other words, leadership can be many things to different people. Cotton Fitzsimmons, former coach of the Kansas City Kings argues that 'if you're a positive person, you're an automatic motivator. You can get people to do things you don't think they're capable of' (Westerbeek & Smith 2005). Vince Lombardi, the famous coach of the Green Bay Packers of the 1950s and 1960s once said that 'leaders are made, they are not born; and they are made just like anything else has been made in this country – by hard effort. And that's the price that we all have to pay to achieve that goal, or any goal' (Westerbeek & Smith 2005). According to former US President Theodore Roosevelt 'the best executive is the one who has sense enough to pick good men to do what he wants done, and self-restraint enough to keep from meddling with them while the do it', and Lou Holts, a former coach of the Notre Dame football team argued that 'all winning teams are goal-oriented. Teams like these win consistently because everyone connected with them concentrates on specific objectives. They go about their business with blinders on; nothing will distract them from achieving their aims' (Westerbeek & Smith 2005).

Harvard Professor and leadership expert Linda Hill (2008) argues that in today's global, fast changing, multiple stakeholder decision-making business environments we may well have to 'lead from behind' in order to let others take charge as leaders when it is most needed. According to these experienced, but very different leaders and leadership experts, leadership is:

- goal oriented;
- about influencing others;
- about empowering others;
- about seeing the big picture;
- about needing others; and
- about strength of character.

We can use these different components of leadership to construct a leadership definition. For the purposes of this book we define leadership as 'influencing and enabling others towards the attainment of aspirational goals'. We appreciate that there are many other definitions of leadership, but as an introduction to the topic in this book the above definition will serve its purpose. In the next section of this chapter we will further outline the ways that leadership can be viewed.

In Practice 8.1 Popular culture view of leaders

Type in the words 'sport' and 'leadership' into any web browser and more than 192 million results can be viewed. Leadership in sport by players, coaches, CEOs, Chairpersons, volunteers, consultants and government agencies is clearly a topic of interest for a lot of people. There are a myriad of sites that extol the leadership traits of successful sports people, recalling stories of leaders overcoming adversity, examples of young people developing leadership abilities through sport, arguments over the question of whether leadership in sport can be learned or whether it is intuitive to only a few individuals, and endless lists of the characteristics of effective sport leaders.

The popular culture view of sport leadership seems to revolve around what behaviours people see in good leaders. The concept of a great sport leader is invariably associated with coaches of successful teams – Sir Alex Ferguson at Manchester United FC, Vince Lombardi at the Green Bay Packers, John Wooden of NCAA Basketball fame at University of California Los Angeles, or Phil Jackson at the Chicago Bulls. A list compiled by *Fortune* magazine in 2014 of the world's 50 greatest leaders included Derek Jeter, aged 39, shortstop and captain of the New York Yankees ranked at #11, and three sport coaches ranked tied for #20 (Mike Krzyzewski, Head Coach of Duke University's men's basketball team; Gregg Popovich, Head Coach of the San Antonio Spurs; and Dawn Staley, Head Coach of the University of South Carolina women's basketball team) and at #36, they ranked George Kennedy, Head Coach of the Johns Hopkins University swim teams.

The fascination with leadership in sport is not restricted to the average sports fan or readers of *Fortune*. Each year, the Sport Business Summit, convened by a company called Leaders, hosts a forum dedicated to leadership in sport. The 2014 website promoting the summit provides this explanation:

> The Leaders Sport Business Summit brings together top industry influencers to share ideas, spark discussions and build relationships capable of helping shape the future of sport. When time is so precious the Leaders Sport Business Summit guarantees world class speakers, leading edge content and an invite only audience who are all leaders in their field. It ensures you maximise your time, learn something new and develop relevant business relationships. The event hosts 1500 senior people across 45 sports and 50 countries all in one place at one time. It's a must attend for anyone serious about the business of sport.

There is clearly an ongoing fascination with what makes effective leadership work, and in the high profile world of elite sport, whether as coach, CEO, or athlete, the leadership styles, traits, success and failures are played out on the world stage for all to see.

Source: *Fortune* magazine website (2014) at http://fortune.com/2014/03/20/fortune-ranks-the-worlds-50-greatest-leaders and the Leaders website (2014) at www.leadersinsport.com/attend/the-sport-business-summit

THEORIES OF LEADERSHIP

Northouse (2010) separates leadership theories into categories that relate to traits of leaders, their skills, their styles, the situation in which they have to lead or the contingency that they face. He also lists theories such as the path-goal theory, the leader member exchange theory, the transformational approach, the authentic approach, team leadership and the psychodynamic approach as separate categories. As this is an introduction to the concept of leadership, the dominant theories have been conflated into four approaches: trait or personality approaches, the behavioral approach, the contingency approach and the transformational approach.

Trait or personality approaches

Although the personality and trait approaches to leadership stem from the earliest of leadership research times, popular leadership literature continues to stress the importance of personality and innate ability in the demonstration of leadership. Locke (1991) argues that trait theories (or great man theories as they are also called), are incomplete theories of leadership, irrespective of traits and/or personality of the leaders being important contributors to, or detractors from excellent leadership. Locke (1991) suggests that the possession of certain traits, such as energy and honesty, appear to be vital for effective leadership. Basketball legend Michael Jordan, for example, has been credited with having an impressive range of innate leadership traits that will stand him in good stead for being an excellent leader in many different contexts. Leaders must use their traits to develop skills, formulate a vision, and implement this vision into reality. This being the case, it appears that traits only form part of the picture.

Although empirical evidence linking the personality of leaders with their success is weak, much of the popular literature still focuses on leadership traits as a way to better understand leadership. In general, trait theories are based on the assumption that social background, physical features and personality characteristics will distinguish good leaders from poor leaders.

Behavioural approach

When it became clear that good leadership could not simply be explained on the basis of the innate characteristics of the leaders, organizational research began to focus on discovering universal behaviours of effective leaders. Behaviourists argued that anyone could be taught to become a leader by simply learning the behaviours of other effective leaders.

Behavioural strategy takes behaviours as signs of learned responses to contingencies. If research shows that to behave in a certain manner results in success for a leader, then one can learn to discharge those behaviours in particular leadership situations. The behavioural approach to leadership was also a response to early approaches to management as a whole. Frederick Taylor was an early champion of the idea that managers should use science to improve efficiency. This approach became known as Taylorism or Scientific Management, a philosophy in which there was limited attention for the human side of the mass production movement. Rather, under Taylorism, humans were simply 'part of the larger machines' and standardization of human labour would lead to great efficiency and higher profits. Managers, according to Taylor, should begin by studying the tasks workers performed, break jobs down by analysing, measuring and timing each separate element of the job in order to determine the most efficient manner of doing the job. The most efficient method for each job became both the standard method that workers were supposed to adopt and a means for measuring worker productivity.

In response to Taylor's ideas, behaviouralists demanded a new 'human relations' approach to management of organizations involving an examination of the interaction between managers and workers. In the Hawthorne experiments, which were originally designed to study the effects of lighting upon factory workers, Elton Mayo discovered that human relations between workers, and between workers and supervisors were most important in ensuring efficiency. In other words, by focussing on interaction between humans, and by studying the best ways of interacting, managers could better lead the people that worked for the organization. Another behavioural approach to the study of leadership is the so-called Theory X and Theory Y, developed by Douglas McGregor. The theories are formulated based on the assumptions that leaders have about individuals. Managers that have Theory X assumptions argue that the typical employee dislikes work and needs direction at all times. They also think that employees need to be coerced to perform their duties. Theory Y managers believe that employees are self-motivated and committed to work and to the company. They naturally seek responsibility for the work they perform. As a result, Theory Y leaders behave in quite different ways from Theory X leaders.

Another behaviouralist approach was formulated by Blake and Mouton. They developed the managerial grid model along two dimensions: one with a concern for people and one with a concern for production. Blake and Mouton argued that differing levels of concern along those dimensions would lead to different styles of leadership. For example, managers with low levels of concern for people and production will have an impoverished style of leadership whereas those leaders with high concern for people and production can be typified as having team style leadership qualities. The Blake and Mouton approach has also been used to differentiate person-centred leaders from task-centred leaders. Ultimately it is important to conclude that the behaviouralist approach to leadership leads to the identification of different styles that can be described as more or less successful.

Contingency approach

It became increasingly clear to those studying leadership that traits and behaviours of leaders were often observed in relation to the situation at hand, or in other words, according to situational contingencies. Isolated behavioural and trait approaches failed to take account of how situational variables, such as task structure, the characteristics of the environment, or subordinate characteristics could impact and moderate the relationship between the behaviour of a leader and the different outcomes.

In contingency theories of leadership, the core argument is that different leadership styles and approaches will apply to a range of possible management situations. This is why, for example, the on-field leadership brilliance of Diego Maradona with the Argentinean team resulted in winning the 1986 World Cup, but when Diego was required to achieve similar results with club teams in different cultures (Napoli in Italy and Barcelona in Spain) or even as the national coach of the Argentinean side at the 2010 World Cup in South Africa, he failed dismally, also resulting in the exposure of a number of personal leadership flaws. The centrality of leader behaviour and/or personality needs to be de-emphasised, and in the contingency approach we turn our attention to the leader in conjunction with circumstances that are specific to the situation at hand, including characteristics of the subordinates and the work setting. In the next section we will present three situational theories of leadership that have influenced the ways in which leadership is understood and practised. They are:

*   Fiedler's Least Preferred Co-worker approach
*   Hersey and Blanchard's Situational Leadership Theory
*   Path-Goal Theory

Fiedler's Least Preferred Co-worker approach

Fiedler's (1967) model is based on the following three axioms:

1   the interaction between the leader's personal characteristics and some aspects of the situation determines the effectiveness of the leader;
2   leaders are either 'task oriented' or 'person oriented'; and
3   the effectiveness of the leader is determined by the leader's control of the situation.

Fiedler comes to his classification of task or person oriented leadership by the use of a measurement scale called the 'Least Preferred Co-worker' (LPC) scale. The instrument asks leaders to assess co-workers on a series of bi-polar descriptors including pleasant-unpleasant, cold-warm, and supportive-hostile in order to assess to what degree they think they would not work well together with that co-worker. A leader who obtains a low LPC is more motivated by task achievements and will only be concerned about relationships with subordinates if the work unit is deemed to be performing well. A leader who obtains a high LPC score will be more motivated to develop close interpersonal relations with subordinates. Task directed behaviour is of a lesser concern, and only becomes important once sound interpersonal relations have been developed. According to Fiedler, if the least preferred co-worker still scores relatively high it indicates that the leader derives a sense of satisfaction from 'working on good relationships', indicating a person oriented leadership style.

The model further suggests that control is dependent on three combined contingency variables:

1   the relations between the leader and the followers;
2   the degree of task structure (or the degree to which the followers' jobs can be specified clearly); and
3   the leader's position of power or amount of authority, yielding eight possible conditions presented in Figure 8.1.

Hersey and Blanchard's Situational Leadership Theory

A theory claiming that as maturity of the group changes, leader behaviour should change as well, is known as the Situational Theory of Leadership. Hersey and Blanchard (1977) argued that as the technical skill level and psychological maturity of the group moves from low to moderate to high, the leader's behaviour would be most effective when it changes accordingly. When low levels of maturity are enacted in relation to the tasks being performed, a high task-behaviour of the leader should be exhibited, or in other words, a 'selling' and 'telling' approach to communicating with the subordinates. At medium levels of maturity, leaders need to be more focussed on relationship-behaviours and at the highest levels of subordinate maturity, the leader needs to offer little direction or task-behaviour and allow the subordinate to assume responsibilities, or in other words, a 'supportive' and 'delegation' driven style of leadership communication.

	Situational favourability			
Condition	Leader-member relations	Task structure	Position power	Effective leadership
1	Good	High	Strong	Low LPC
2	Good	High	Weak	Low LPC
3	Good	Weak	Strong	Low LPC
4	Good	Weak	Weak	High LPC
5	Poor	High	Strong	High LPC
6	Poor	High	Weak	High LPC
7	Poor	Weak	Strong	High LPC
8	Poor	Weak	Weak	Low LPC

FIGURE 8.1 Fiedler's Situational Favourability Factors and leadership effectiveness

Source: Adapted from Fiedler (1967) p. 34

According to sport organization theory researcher Trevor Slack (Slack & Parent 2006), there have been few attempts to empirically test the concepts and relationships that Hersey and Blanchard (1977) have outlined in their work, even in the management and organizational literature. Some attempts have been made to apply the theory directly in sport settings, but results have been inconsistent.

Path-Goal Theory

The Path-Goal Theory (House 1971) takes a behavioural and situational approach to leadership. There are many roads that lead to Rome and therefore the Path-Goal Theory suggests that a leader must select a style most appropriate to the particular situation. The theory in particular aims to explain how a leader's behaviour affects the motivation and satisfaction of subordinates.

House (1971) is cited in Wexley and Yukl (1984), arguing that 'the motivational function of the leaders consists of increasing personal payoffs to subordinates for work-goal attainment, and making the path to these payoffs easier to travel by clarifying it, reducing roadblocks and pitfalls, and increasing the opportunities for personal satisfaction en route' (p. 176). In other words, characteristics of the subordinates and characteristics of the environment determine both the potential for increased motivation and the manner in which the leader must act to improve motivation. Subordinate preferences for a particular pattern of leadership behaviour may also depend on the actual situation in which they are placed (Wexley & Yukl 1984). Taking those different perspectives into consideration, the Path-Goal Theory proposes four styles of leadership behaviour that can be utilized to achieve goals (House & Mitchell 1974). They are:

- Directive leadership: The leader gives specific instructions, expectations and guidance.
- Supportive leadership: The leader shows concern and support for subordinates.
- Participative leadership: The subordinates participate in the decision-making.
- Achievement oriented leadership: The leader sets challenges, emphasizes excellence and shows confidence that subordinates will attain high standards of performance.

The theory is principally aimed at examining how leaders affect subordinate expectations about likely outcomes of different courses of action. Directive leadership is predicted to have a positive effect on subordinates when the task is ambiguous, and will have a negative impact when the task is clear. Supportive leadership is predicted to increase job satisfaction, particularly when conditions are adverse. Achievement-oriented leadership is predicted to encourage higher performance standards and increase expectancies that desired outcomes can be achieved. Participative leadership is predicted to promote satisfaction due to involvement (Schermerhorn et al. 1994).

From transactional to transformational leadership

As already noted earlier in this chapter, the scientific approach to management (Taylorism) reduced the individual to performing machine-like functions. The human relations approach to management took into consideration the human part of the labour equation, appreciating that much better results can be achieved if people's individual needs are taken into consideration when leading them towards achieving certain work outputs.

One of the most recent thrusts in leadership research is that of transactional and transformational leadership. Transactional leadership encompasses much of the theories based on rational exchange between leader and subordinate, such as the theories presented above, but transformational leaders, according to Bass (1985), are charismatic, and develop followers into leaders through a process that transcends the existing organizational climate and culture. The transactional leader aims to create a cost-benefit economic exchange, or in other words, to meet the needs of followers in return for 'contracted' services that are produced by the follower (Bass 1985). To influence behaviour, the transactional leader may use the following approaches:

- Contingent reward: The leader uses rewards or incentives to achieve results.
- Active management by exception: The leader actively monitors the work performed and uses corrective methods to ensure the work meets accepted standards.
- Passive management by exception: The leader uses corrective methods as a response to unacceptable performance or deviation from the accepted standards.
- Laissez-faire leadership: The leader is indifferent and has a 'hands-off' approach toward the workers and their performance.

However, leadership theorists have argued that transactional leadership merely seeks to influence others by exchanging work for wages. It fails to build on the worker's need for meaningful work and it does not actively tap into their sources of creativity. A more effective and beneficial leadership behaviour to achieve long-term success and improved performance therefore is transformational leadership. Sir Alex Ferguson, the long-time Manchester United manager can be described as a transformational leader. He envisioned a future for the club and the Board repaid him with the trust of keeping him at the helm at Manchester United since 1986 for more than 1,400 games. Under his guidance and supervision the club became the most successful team in the new English Premier League and the team won multiple Champions League crowns. Sir Alex also prepared the likes of Eric Cantona, Ryan Giggs, Roy Keane, David Beckham, Ruud van Nistelrooy, Wayne Rooney and Cristiano Ronaldo for the world stage of football leadership.

What is transformational leadership?

It has been argued by Bass and Avolio (1994) that transformational leadership is the new leadership that must accompany good management. In contrast to transactional models, transformational leadership goes beyond the exchange process. It not only aligns and elevates the needs and values of followers, but also provides intellectual stimulation and increased follower confidence. Bass and Avolio (1994) identified four 'I's that transformational leaders employ in order to achieve superior results. These are:

*   Idealized influence: Transformational leaders behave in ways that result in them being admired, respected and trusted, and ultimately becoming a role model. The transformational leader demonstrates high standards of ethical and moral conduct.
*   Inspirational motivation: By demonstrating enthusiasm and optimism, the transformational leader actively arouses team spirit and motivates and inspires followers to share in and work towards a common goal.
*   Intellectual stimulation: By being innovative, creative and supportive, and by reframing problems and questioning old assumptions, the transformational leader creates an intellectually stimulating and encouraging environment.
*   Individualized consideration: Transformational leaders pay special attention to each individual's needs for achievement and growth by acting as a coach or mentor.

Looking closer at the four it can be argued that charisma (the ability to inspire enthusiasm, interest, or affection in others by means of personal charm or influence) is an important component of transformational leadership. Purely charismatic leaders may be limited in their ability to achieve successful outcomes, due to their need to instil their beliefs in others which may inhibit the individual growth of followers. However, transformational leaders are more than charismatic in that they generate awareness of the mission or vision of the team and the organization, and then motivate colleagues and followers towards outcomes that benefit the team rather than merely serving the individual interest.

In Practice 8.2 AIS Centre for Performance Coaching and Leadership

This In Practice highlights a leadership training course designed for high performance program managers; the content of this course outlines some of the core issues for leadership development in sport. The Performance Leaders Program conducted by the Australian Institute of Sport Centre for Performance Coaching and Leadership is designed to deliver 'world's best approaches to learning and development to invoke discussion, transformation and practical applied solutions to frontline performance coaching and leadership challenges'. The Performance Leaders Program is for performance leaders in the high performance sports sector, including national sport organizations (NSOs) and the National Institute Network (the national and state institutes). The Performance Leaders Program is funded by the AIS and limited to 20 performance leaders each year. The program is delivered over a two-year period through a series of face-to-face residential labs, immersive experiences, project work, executive coaching, individual assessment and regular feedback and reflection.

The creation of this program has been driven by a desire to improve the quality of leadership within the Australian sport system, and to directly influence the next generation of sport leaders for Australia's NSOs, professional sports and high performance programs. There are three key themes to the program that highlight the dimensions of leadership development relevant to sport.

The Leadership theme focuses on leading adaptively in a complex networked environment. Key topics include complex adaptive systems, adaptive leadership and organization power, and systems with a focus on developing the following capability sets:

- ability to leverage the whole system – drawing upon expertise in all areas of the team;
- shift from an operational to a 'leaderful' mindset;
- high level influencing and negotiation skills;
- readiness to adapt and encourage continuous change;
- complexity of mind; developing the ability to hold the paradoxes (e.g. competition and collaboration).

Theme 2, Strategy, focuses on strategic thinking and execution including planning for the future: setting a vision. Key topics include values and organizing principles, holding multiple perspectives and questioning underpinning assumptions, strategic approaches and business models with a focus on developing the following capability sets:

- strategic thinking, planning and articulation;
- setting a vision and clearly defining a pathway to get there;
- high level accountability and alignment;
- processes and systems to support the strategy;
- the ability to hold the 'whole' in mind and constantly assess and adjust.

The third theme, Innovation, focuses on dealing with ambiguity and continuous change. Key topics include the role of 'change agents', working emergently and creative thinking with a focus on developing the following capability sets:

- complexity of mind to match complex systems;
- capacity to challenge own and system's assumptions and paradigms;
- commitment to continuous review and improvement;
- readiness to adapt and encourage continuous change, recognizing the 'competing commitments' which might need to be assessed and challenged.

Source: AIS website (2014) at www.ausport.gov.au/ais/australias_winning_edge/centre_for_performance_coaching_and_leadership/performance_leaders_program

LEADERSHIP AND MANAGEMENT

At this stage of the chapter it will be useful to briefly consider the debate about the relationship between leadership and management, and how to distinguish between the two. Kotter (1990) has conducted extensive research work in order to find out how to differentiate managers from leaders. He concluded that management effectiveness rests in the ability to plan and budget; organize staff; and control and solve problems. Leadership, however, is principally founded upon the ability to establish direction, align people, and to motivate and inspire. According to Kotter, leaders achieve change whilst managers succeed in maintaining the status quo. Bass (1990), however, states that 'leaders manage and managers lead, but the two activities are not synonymous' (p. 383). It goes beyond the scope of this book to further elaborate on the distinction between leadership and management. Suffice to say that in the context of discussing management principles in sport organizations, management without leadership is much less likely to be successful than a capable manager who can also provide excellent leadership. In the next section we will therefore put forward what can be described as the five key functions of leadership:

- to create a vision;
- to set out strategy;
- to set objectives and lead towards performance;
- to influence and motivate people;
- to facilitate change and nurture culture.

To create a vision

A vision can be described as 'a state of the future that lies beyond the directly imaginable by most people'. This view of the future, in the context of an organization, is a positive and bright state of being that only the 'visionary' (one who is characterized by unusually acute foresight and imagination) can see at that time. In other words, the leader is responsible for envisioning a future for the organization that can become reality if the people working in the organization can be aligned towards achieving that 'envisioned state'. It is often said that good leaders distinguish themselves from good managers because they do have a vision whereas managers do not. How to achieve the vision through strategy is the next function of the leader.

To set out strategy

The process of strategic planning is all about the different ways that a vision can be achieved. It constitutes two principal perspectives: that of the organization and that of the individuals making up the organization. Visionary leaders are not necessarily successful leaders if they are not capable of translating the vision into action strategies. The process of strategic management is therefore concerned with carefully managing the internal organization, including considering the individual needs of workers, and the external environment in which many opportunities and threats impact the ability of the leader to achieve the vision. To be better prepared for action, the leader needs to be involved in setting measurable objectives.

To set objectives and lead towards performance

Setting objectives is the next function of the leader. Once the broad strategies have been set out (and these strategies are never set in concrete, they need constant updating), it is time to link measurable outcomes to these strategies. In other words, what do we want to achieve in the short term, in order to work towards our visionary objectives that lie ahead in the distant future. Stated differently, the leader is often involved in setting objectives at different levels of the organization, ranging from 'visionary' and strategic objectives to delegating the responsibility to set more operational objectives at lower levels of the organization. Only when SMART (specific, measurable, achievable, resources available, time bound) objectives are set, will the leader be in a position to manage the performance of the organization and its employees effectively. An important part of the performance of an organization is achieved through the people management skills of the leader.

To influence and motivate people

In our overview of the different approaches to leadership, we have already commented on the different styles that leaders chose to develop (because they better fit their skill set) in order to influence groups of people and communicate with individuals or teams. Where setting objectives is important in making people aware of the targets of performance, the actual activation and application of people skills is critical when trying to steer people in a certain direction. This is where leaders with charismatic appeal will have an easier job. Their natural ability to inspire enthusiasm, interest, or affection in others by means of personal charm or influence will put these leaders in a favourable position in regard to achieving the objectives that were set.

To facilitate change and nurture culture

Finally it is important to acknowledge that in this day and age, change is constant. Leaders who are incapable of assisting others to understand why 'change' is needed and how this change can be achieved with minimal disruption and maximum outcomes will have a difficult time surviving in the organizations of the twenty-first century. Most organizations are required to keep close track of the market conditions that they are working under and the impact that changes in market conditions will have on their structures and strategies. Often a rapid response to changing market conditions is needed and this is where the interesting relationship with the organization's culture comes into play. Ironically, a strong and stable organizational culture can contribute to the need to constantly modify direction and change the systems and structures of the organization. It is the leaders' responsibility to create and nurture a culture in which change is accepted as part of the natural way of organizational life. A strong culture is the backbone of any successful organization and the maintenance of this culture is therefore one of the primary areas of leadership responsibility.

In Practice 8.3 Sir Alex Ferguson

In the October 2013 edition of the *Harvard Business Review*, a detailed case study of the leadership style and legacy of Sir Alex Ferguson, the manager of the Manchester United Football Club for 26 seasons, was published that offers some insights into what it takes to be a successful leader of a sport organization. During Ferguson's reign, MUFC won 13 EPL titles and 25 other domestic and international titles, a success rate of nearly double that of the next most successful English football club manager. The analysis of his leadership style revealed eight key dimensions to success as a leader:

1   Start with the foundation: Ferguson focussed on building a club rather than just a team so he always had his eye on the bigger picture and started by recruiting and developing younger players, something he recognizes would be a luxury in today's results driven industry.

2   Dare to rebuild your team: He was not afraid to refresh his pool of playing talent so that his resources were always a mixture of experience and youth; a very strategic, rationale and systematic way of managing a club. He was able to sell players while they still had value and use that reinvest in younger talent.

3   Set high standards and hold everyone to them: He instilled a sense of hard work and a commitment that every training session had a purpose and was of the highest standard.

4   Never, ever cede control: He maintained the position of leader at all times, even when dealing with players on huge salaries and even bigger egos.

5   Match the message to the moment: He thought very carefully about what to say, to whom and how. He recognized the power of the words said by a leader can be very influential, particularly when dealing with motivating people to give their best.

6 Prepare to win. His focus was on planning and preparation and let the result take care of itself (a classic sport cliché) but in this case it worked for 26 seasons.

7 Rely on the power of observation: He increasingly let his assistant coaches take over the running of training and dedicated time and effort to observing specific players, to see things he did not expect to see, that made his decision-making more informed.

8 Never stop adapting: He was at the forefront of many changes in practice as a football club manager, always seeking the next innovation to improve his club.

Source: Elberse, A. (2013). Ferguson's formula, *Harvard Business Review*, 10, 116–125.

SUMMARY

In this chapter we described what it takes to be a leader. We argued that irrespective of leadership type or style, leaders are goal oriented, they influence others, they empower others, they need to remain focussed on the big picture, they need others to achieve their goals, and they have strong characters. Based on these components of leadership we discussed a number of theoretical approaches to leadership including the trait/personality, behavioural and contingency approaches, ultimately resulting in a discussion about transactional versus transformational leadership. We also highlighted the differences between managers and leaders by outlining what are the functions of leaders: the creation of a vision; the setting out of strategy; setting objectives and measuring performance; influencing and motivating people; and finally, to facilitate change and nurture organizational culture.

REVIEW QUESTIONS

1 Are leaders born or can they be made? Justify your answer by comparing the different leadership theories discussed in this chapter.

2 Does sport offer valuable leadership lessons to business? What are the specific characteristics of sport organizations that challenge leaders in sport organizations more than leaders in business and how can this knowledge be transferred to a non-sport context?

3 'A good manager is also a good leader'. Do you agree or disagree with this statement. Justify your answer.

4 Explain how leadership is important for the performance of a sport organization. Interview the leader of a small sport organization. How would you describe their leadership style?

5 Is there any difference in the leadership skills required to be the CEO of a major professional sport franchise versus the leader of community sports club?

6 What criteria would you use to evaluate the leadership skills of a sport manager?

7 Is it possible to compare the performance of leaders of two different sport organizations? Why or why not?

FURTHER READING

Amar, A.D., Hentrich, C. & Hlupic, V. (2009). To be a better leader, give up authority. *Harvard Business Review*, 87(12), 22–24.

Bass, B. M. (1990). *Bass & Stogdill's Handbook of Leadership: Theory, Research, and Managerial Applications*. 3rd edn. New York: Free Press.

Hill, L.A. (2008). Where will we find tomorrow's leaders? *Harvard Business Review*, 86(1) 123–129.

Kotter, J.P. (1990). *A Force for Change: How Leadership Differs from Management*. New York: The Free Press.

Kouzes, J.M., & Posner, B.Z. (2006). *A Leader's Legacy*. Hoboken: Jossey-Bass.

Locke, E.A. (1991). *The Essence of Leadership: The Four Keys to Leading Successfully*. New York: Lexington Books.

Northouse, P.G. (2010). *Leadership: Theory and Practice*. 5th edn. Thousand Oaks, Sage Publications.

Slack, T. & Parent, M. (2006). *Understanding sport organizations: The Application of Organization Theory*. 2nd edn. Champaign, IL: Human Kinetics.

Thomas, R.J. (2008). *Crucibles of Leadership*. Boston: Harvard Business School Publishing Corporation.

RELEVANT WEBSITES

- The Centre for Creative Leadership at www.ccl.org
- The Test Café Leadership Test at www.testcafe.com/lead
- Leadership directories at www.leadershipdirectories.com
- Stephen Covey at www.stephencovey.com

CASE STUDY 8.1

The Leading Teams phenomenon

Leading Teams is a consulting firm specializing in facilitating change and improvement in organizations. Founded by Ray McLean, Leading Teams, according to their website, specializes in the delivery of culture change, leadership and team development programs that create elite teams and improve performance. Leading Teams shot to prominence through its work with a number of leading Australian

Rules Football Clubs, including many that have had a sustained period of success in the last decade such as Geelong FC, Sydney Swans FC and Hawthorn FC.

The website for Leading Teams describes their approach:

> Our Performance Improvement Program (PIP) is the cornerstone of our work at Leading Teams. It is a values-based approach to leadership, teamwork and culture change. The PIP is generally delivered over a sustained period for maximum impact and typically encompasses an all-of organisation approach. It is a behaviours-based framework for managing the entire life-cycle of any given team, from a member's induction to their eventual retirement from the team. The program provides a structure that empowers team members to become leaders, be accountable, and participate in open and honest reviews of performance. We provide teams with the necessary tools to develop functional dynamics within the group and create a shared vision, behaviours and expectations. The main areas that we address are:
>
> - Leadership Development
> - Team Development
> - Culture Change
>
> We work in a wide range of industries in organisations of various sizes. Our program can be rolled out with Board and Senior Executive teams, right through to entry-level teams. The Leading Teams program highlights the importance of functional team dynamics and builds a strong level of engagement, commitment and accountability within teams. Specifically the model centres on:
>
> - Building and strengthening current relationships within and across teams
> - Identifying a common purpose for each specific team
> - Defining the behaviours which are considered essential to the trademark of the team/organisation
> - Developing leaders who behave in a manner that has a positive impact on their peers and the performance of the organisation
> - Developing a framework for leaders to honestly assess their own performance as leaders and that of their staff. This enables them to make intelligent decisions around recruitment, retention and induction
> - Further develop managers as leaders who model and drive the Trademark behaviours of the team/organisation
> - Creating an environment where open and honest professional dialogue takes place in regard to behaviour and performance

In a recent article published by Adam McNicol on www.afl.com.au, an example of how it worked was explained:

When it comes to studying how the PIP has worked for AFL clubs, the Sydney Swans is among the best examples, for it was by using Leading Teams that the Swans were able to build their now-famous culture of success. In the case of the Swans, numerous team-building exercises were undertaken before players or coaches were asked to front a peer review. These included the players deciding what they wanted to stand for and how they believed they should act, which is where they came up with the idea of representing 'The Bloods'. The process continued with the Swans players identifying their teammates who best personified The Bloods. These players then formed the core of the club's leadership group.

When the first vote was taken at the Swans, star player Adam Goodes missed out. Goodes found out why when he fronted his teammates for his peer review session. He was told that although he was a great player himself, he wasn't doing enough to help others at the club. 'So then he started mentoring players, building relationships, helping them to get better, and it was a no-brainer that he came into the leadership group,' McLean says in The Rise of the Swans. Today, peer reviews are part and parcel of being a Swans player. 'We're hard but we're fair,' 2012 premiership co-captain Jarrad McVeigh says in Blake's book. 'We want that player to improve, and therefore we improve as a group. We stress all the time that it's not personal. We want him to improve as a person and a player. We make sure everyone's honest, there's no tiptoeing around it. We say what we have to say and move on.'

Leading Teams has not only been involved in AFL, it was also engaged by the Australian Netball Diamonds Head Coach Lisa Alexander in their ultimately successful quest to secure a Commonwealth Games Gold Medal at the 2014 Glasgow Games. Players were asked to provide feedback on their own performances and their training sessions. In an article by Chris Barrett of The Age at www. theage.com.au, he cited the Diamonds Captain, Laura Geitz, as saying

> It's about creating an honest environment. We've probably not had that in the Australian netball team before and it's speaking volumes. It was implemented at the beginning of last year [2013] and we went on to have our most successful series against New Zealand in 15 years. I think there's definitely something to be said for creating that environment where a lot of research goes into each individual, that's for sure. We've seen great things because of it.

The Leading Teams approach has not been without its critics, with some saying it can be too confronting for some athletes, and actually counterproductive to good performances. While this case study is not an endorsement of the Leading Teams approach, there does seem to be some merit in sport organizations engaging in a conscious attempt to develop their culture, their communication and ultimately their leadership capacity at all levels of their organization.

CASE STUDY QUESTIONS

1 What might be some of the signs in an organization's performance that might trigger a decision to engage in a process such as that provided by Leading Teams?

2 What might be some of the reservations players might have about engaging in such a process?

3 What are the potential problems or benefits for organizations in seeking to develop leaders at every level of their organization?

4 Do sport organizations have to seek external expertise to help them develop their leaders? Why can't they do it themselves?

Sources: The Adam McNicol article from 20 July 2013 at www.afl.com.au/news/2013-07-20/leading-teams-explained; the Leading Teams website (2014) at www.leadingteams.net.au; and the Chris Barrett article from 23 July 2014 at www.theage.com.au/commonwealth-games-glasgow-2014/commonwealth-games-news/lisa-alexander-has-some-homework-for-the-diamonds-20140723-zvw3y.html

CASE STUDY 8.2

Developing women leaders in sport

Both the UK and Australia have developed national programs conducted by their national sport agencies to support the development of women as leaders in their respective sport systems. In Canada, a similar development program is conducted by the Canadian Association for the Advancement of Women and Sport and Physical Activity (CAAWS).

UNITED KINGDOM
The UK Sport program website states that the Women and Leadership Development Programme (WLDP) has been developed by UK Sport in partnership with the British Olympic Foundation (BOF) and the Central Council of Physical Recreation (CCPR) to help tackle the issue of women's representation within the highest ranks of British sport. The program is a key part of UK Sport's work in building a high performance system of 'world class people'. The program was established to address the low level of women in senior administrative positions in sport and involves periods of intense training and continuous support to build leadership skills and enable the participants to maximize their potential. Designed to create a level playing field for women in a competitive environment like the sport industry, it forms a key part of UK Sport's commitment to gender equality in sport.

The overarching aims are four-fold:

- to increase representation by women in leadership positions in sport;
- to build the competence and confidence of women in decision-making positions;
- to increase support among organizations for the contribution women can make to sports leadership; and
- to foster networking between women leaders, both in the UK and internationally.

Each participant has a Personal Development Plan which identifies skill and knowledge requirements and set out how these will be met. A variety of learning methods are utilized, from workshops and presentation, to attendance at relevant international events. All participants are also teamed up with a mentor, usually an established woman leader, to provide additional support. In addition to equipping individuals with leadership skills, the program also contributes to each organization's influencing work in terms of international representation, developing excellence in sports leadership and advancing governance in sport.

The UK Sport website explains that the first program ran from 2006 to 2009, with all individuals stating the program had made a positive impact on themselves and their organizations. Approximately 70 per cent had been promoted and 80 per cent stated their confidence had improved at least a lot, if not a huge amount, as a result of the bespoke training received.

AUSTRALIA

The Women Leaders in Sport (WLIS) grant program (formally Sport Leadership Grants and Scholarships for Women) is an Australian Government initiative that is managed by the Australian Sports Commission (ASC) in partnership with the Australian Government Office for Women. The WLIS grant program provides female administrators, coaches and officials with opportunities to undertake intermediate or advanced training within an existing pathway in the sport industry to reach their leadership potential. There are two types of grants available for individuals (grant of up to AUS$5,000 per annum) or for organizations (grant of up to AUS$10,000 per annum).

Grants are available in the following categories:

- coaching
- communications, media and marketing
- governance (board/committees)
- management and administration
- officiating.

As part of the Women Leaders in Sport (WLIS) grant program, the Australian Sports Commission (ASC) conducts a two-day residential sport leadership workshop for grant recipients. The workshop aims to develop the participant's leadership capabilities to progress within sport as an administrator, coach or official, and to enable them to effectively manage the challenges within their sport and life in general. All individual grant recipients are required to attend an allocated sport leadership workshop, and all organization recipients are required to nominate an aspiring female leader from within the organization who is participating in the proposed project to attend the workshop. Topics covered in the workshops include:

- Effective leadership – what does it take?
- Leadership styles – what works best when?
- Personal leadership attributes.
- Leadership vs management.
- Emotional Intelligence.
- The essentials for effective communication.
- Active listening – the power of questioning.
- Visionary leadership – developing your own vision for your organization.
- Achieving life balance – establishing priorities and time management.

CANADA

CAAWS' Women and Leadership Program consists of a series of five professional development sessions that blend theory with practical applications, and provide an opportunity for women working or volunteering in the sport or physical activity sector to share experiences, reflect on ideas and apply specific techniques. The sessions also allow for networking opportunities among participants. The Canadian Association for the Advancement of Women and Sport and Physical Activity (CAAWS) delivers the program through strategic partnerships within the Canadian sport and physical activity system to actively engage women as leaders (senior administrators, coaches, officials, board members, etc.). The collaboration through the Women and Leadership Program is intended to:

- increase provincial/territorial and national sport and multi-sport commitment to taking action to engage women and girls as participants and leaders;
- increase capacity to address the barriers limiting women's leadership throughout the system; and
- integrate the workshops into ongoing professional development and support services delivered by partner organizations during the project period, and into the future.

The workshops are focussed on five key themes as outlined on the CAAWS website:

Effective communication

In the workplace, effective communication is the foundation for better job performance and relationship building. During this workshop participants will:

- Consider the importance of their personal brand.
- Learn about four distinct communication styles, and identify their preferred style.
- Discuss electronic communication and social media etiquette, and how to avoid common pitfalls.

Conflict resolution

Conflict, in its many forms, is an inevitable part of our personal and professional lives. This workshop will ensure participants can understand and resolve conflict professionally.

- Consider sources of conflict and the cost of leaving conflict unresolved.
- Consider five styles for dealing with conflict, identify your preferred style, and discuss situations when each style should be employed.
- Review tips for effective conflict management.

Influencing change

Whether influencing change in your organization, across the sport and physical activity system, or more broadly in society, this workshop will provide participants with theory and practical tools for success.

- Identify elements of effective change movements.
- Discuss the (under)representation of women in society.
- Review tips for being heard and improving your listening skills.
- Discuss approaches on how to influence others.

Creating work-life balance

For many women, balancing the demands of work, family, friends and personal time is a challenge. This workshop will provide participants with an opportunity to explore a variety of strategies to add more balance to their lives.

- Explore the need for balance in your life.
- Examine 10 key solutions to help you find and maintain balance.
- Share tips and success stories.

Effective networking

Strong networking skills can be a valuable tool, both personally and professionally. From building organizational partnerships to knowing about upcoming events, building your network is a long-term investment with great payoffs.

- Explore the value of personal and professional networks.
- Identify strategies to build and maintain your network.
- Rehearse networking scenarios.

CASE STUDY QUESTIONS

1   Why is it necessary to have specific programs devoted to advancing the capacity of women to serve as leaders in the sport systems of such westernised countries as Australia, Canada and the UK?

2   In what type of roles and at what level of organizations are women less represented in leadership roles within sport? Why do you think this is the case?

3   Identify the similarities and differences between these three programs. Do you think the content and focus of these three programs is what is needed most to assist women succeed in sport leadership roles or are additional things required to make that happen? What might they be?

4   In addition to these development programs should there be mandatory minimum quotas for women to serve in leadership roles in sport imposed on nationally funded sport organizations? Justify your argument.

Sources: The UK Sport website (2014) at www.uksport.gov.uk/pages/women-and-leadership-development-programme; the ASC website (2014) at www.ausport.gov.au/participating/women; and the CAAWS website (2014) at www.caaws.ca/leadership/women-and-leadership-program

CHAPTER 9

Organizational culture

OVERVIEW

This chapter explores the influence organizational culture imparts upon sport organizations. It examines why organizational culture is pivotal, highlights its impact and explains how it can be diagnosed. Several cases and numerous examples will be used throughout the chapter to help explain the role of culture in a sport organization's performance.

By the end of this chapter the reader should be able to:

- define the meaning of organizational culture;
- specify why culture is important to sport organizations;
- explain how different contexts can affect an organizational culture;
- connect organizational culture and organizational identity;
- identify how sport organizational cultures can be diagnosed;
- show the dimensions across which sport organizational cultures can be measured; and
- discuss how sport organizational culture can be changed.

THE CULTURE-PROOF SPORT MANAGER

This chapter explores the role played by organizational culture in sport, and explains its development, expression and potency. Moreover, this chapter is for readers who want to destroy the tyranny of tradition that keeps organizations in the managerial Dark Ages, and transform clubs, associations, agencies and businesses into something of greater value. It reveals how to understand cultures and helps to signpost how to create sport enterprises characterized by strong attachments and high performance. However, our task is not as simple as it appears, since culture presents a slippery concept. Securing an early agreement on exactly what constitutes culture, and how it works, will help us to introduce the concept and its importance to sport managers. In short, organizational culture comprises the shared values, beliefs and assumptions that influence the attitudes, habits, customs and behaviour of an organization's members. The 'culture-proof' sport manager needs to be able to diagnose these shared ideas and determine how to use or adjust them to make a positive impact upon their organization.

Culture also reflects the internal and external perceptions of an organization. Examining an organization's culture enables a better understanding of how groups, or sub-cultures within them, behave and work together, and consequently how others perceive them. The significance of culture has intensified since the 1980s, when the concept first flourished, because it offers a window through which organizational leaders can reflect upon how to adapt to or resist changes in the environment, and either enhance or squander any competitive advantage.

All sport organizations have become embedded with their own unique culture, even when dysfunctional or in disarray. In fact, under-performing sport organizations notoriously covet old traditions and customs, even when faced with marginalization at best, or irrelevance at worst. Culture operates as the underlying force preserving old ways of doing things. Culture is like the elephant in the room. Everyone knows it is there, everyone knows it is shaping the agenda, but no one wants to talk about it, much less try to change it. Culture can be a repository for crazy beliefs under the guise of historical truth and wisdom passed down through the ages. It can also be a recipe for redundancy and chronic failure. Not all cultures deliver good outcomes, even those renowned for their strength and resilience. In reality, old cultures can often be disastrous cultures. Moreover, dysfunctional cultures can be so embedded within an organization's identity – that is, the ways in which they see themselves – that nothing seems to be able to change them. For the outside observer the amount of effort that some sport organizations invest into preserving old identities does not make sense.

On the other hand, appropriate cultures drive performance, leverage powerful histories and change quickly in turbulent conditions. Sport organizations with great cultures find ways of winning because success lies at the heart of their identities. Organizational culture provides an understanding of how and why an organization does things, the way the people within the organization behave, and the perceptions held sovereign by stakeholders. Put another way, culture provides a means by which a sport organization's members interpret the way things are done, and what happens in daily working life.

All sport organizations possess cultures, but some are stronger than others, and these cultures can exert a powerful influence on individual behaviour and organizational outcomes. Given the emergence of sport business as an independent discipline of theoretical study, in concert with a growing body of literature demonstrating sport's peculiar economies, an argument has developed suggesting that sport cultures may possess unique characteristics. We share this view and argue that the key to successful sport culture lies with understanding how it is created, transmitted, maintained and challenged within a specific context.

WHY IS ORGANIZATIONAL CULTURE SO IMPORTANT?

The notion of culture tends to receive only superficial treatment by practitioners and educators. Part of the reason lies with culture's social and anthropological background, which does not intuitively appeal to the commercially minded, market-oriented, number-crunching sport executive. Sometimes, interrogating culture may be seen as too distant from work-related outcomes, or that too much arms-length 'critiquing' of sport and organizations fails to accommodate the commercial realities of business. These arguments can then be easily fused with the view that the examination of culture may create a chronic tension within an organization about its identity, strategic management, and commercial outlook. For some, the critical analysis of culture contains the inevitable danger that the organization will be declared socially or culturally 'flawed'. But our view remains that the history and tradition associated with any sport organization needs to be understood in order to achieve any subsequent improvement in performance. Furthermore, any attempt to diagnose and improve sport culture must also account for how sport is wielded as a tool for communication and shared understanding.

Sport simultaneously incurs global and local implications, rarely best described in absolute terms. It is within the texture and grain that the idiosyncratic features of sport and organizations should be explored. As a result, we caution against a view that constrains the analysis of sport or organizations to a single interpretive lens. Such an approach leaves little room for complexity in the relationships between sport fans, organizational members, and the sport enterprise, which can range from the rational cost-benefit appraisal of an entertainment experience to the subtle devotion of quiet mourning after a heavy loss. If sport were reducible to simple, one-dimensional cultural structures, then we would all be Manchester United and New York Yankees supporters. We should also be careful not to dismiss the realities of sport's context, from its commodification to its media impact.

WHAT EXACTLY IS ORGANIZATIONAL CULTURE?

Culture was originally defined by anthropologists as the values and beliefs common to a group of people. These researchers set themselves the task of investigating, interpreting and translating the behavioural and social patterns of groups of individuals by trying to understand how they relate to their environment. From a sport perspective, although people in organizations run the technology and invent the processes, they in turn, as part of the process, have much of their behaviour determined by the systems they operate including an often rich and voluminous suite of traditional practices. In other words, there are underlying forces that impact upon behaviour. The concept of culture is a way of putting a name to these forces.

There is no single accepted definition of organizational culture. For example, some view organizational culture as the 'personality' of an organization, while for others it represents the things that make an organization unique. However, several assumptions about organizational culture are well accepted. These include:

1   Culture tends to be inflexible and resistant to easy or rapid change.
2   Culture is shaped by an organization's circumstances, its history and its members.
3   Culture is learned and shared by members of an organization and is reflected in common understandings and beliefs.

4   Culture is often covert; the deep values and beliefs causing behaviour can be hidden from organizational members making them difficult to identify.

5   Culture is manifested in a variety of ways that affect the performance of an organization and its members.

Although elements of commonality exist in the way in which researchers conceive and define culture in organizations, much inconsistency and controversy can still be found. However, for the purposes of this chapter, we shall discuss organizational culture in a way consistent with the view of Schein (2010), who invokes a more psycho-dynamic view. This means that he believes culture is, in part, an unconscious phenomenon, driven by deep level assumptions and beliefs, and where conscious views are merely artefacts and symbolic representations. For example, most sport clubs' members would report that on-field winning is important. Schein's interpretation of organizational culture would lead to questions about *why* winning is important. Does it have to do with a need to belong to a successful group, the pressure of peers, or some other more mysterious explanation? While many people involved in sport would think this question easy to answer, it is less easy to specify the underpinning values that drive unusual rituals, ceremonies, myths, legends, stories, beliefs, memorabilia and attitudes. For example, in current and former nations of the British Commonwealth, cricket is played with enormous enthusiasm, but can take up to five days to complete a single match, which often ends in a draw. Similarly, to the uninitiated, American football seems quite strange with each team comprising separate players for offensive and defensive manoeuvres. Off the field can be just as odd. In Australia, many (Australian rules) football clubs have 'sausage-sizzles' (BBQs), 'pie-nights' (involving the traditional meal of a meat-pie), and a host of rituals associated with drinking beer. In addition, many sport organizations are packed with memorabilia and expect their employees to work during evening training sessions and weekend games. Sport organizations are rich with strong, meaningful cultural symbols, which on the surface seem easy to interpret, but sometimes are only superficial symptoms of deeper, more complex issues.

What we are searching for is not the superficial, but rather the unconsciously held, fundamental concepts of right or wrong; what an organization might perceive as correct or incorrect values. These values, which are the foundation of an organization's culture, do not simply exist or come into being by their own volition. Instead, members of the organization painstakingly build them up as they gradually learn to interact and achieve their collective and individual aims. An organization's founders, together with the more influential of the organization's past and present members, are usually the most influential in determining the culture. For this reason, we prefer to examine the long-held assumptions and beliefs in an organization.

For the purposes of this chapter, we shall define sport organizational culture as follows:

> Sport organizational culture is a collection of fundamental values, beliefs and attitudes that are common to members of a sport organization, and which subsequently set the behavioural standards or norms for all members.

This definition reflects the view that sport organizations have ways of approaching things that have evolved over time. In many ways, organizational culture answers questions about solving problems. Culture is how 'things are done around here' and how 'we think about things here'.

SPORT ORGANIZATIONAL CULTURE: FROM THE KITCHEN TABLE TO THE BOARD ROOM

We can expect that different types of sport organizations will possess different kinds of cultures. For example, professional clubs and major national leagues are more likely to emphasize dispassionate business values, while smaller, not-for-profit associations are more likely to value participation and fun. Some sport organizations like Italian and Spanish football clubs are geared almost exclusively to winning and are prepared to go heavily into debt in order to do so. Others, like the company Formula One Holdings, manage the commercial rights to major events and have little other interest than to make money. While the *Fédération Internationale de l'Automobile* seeks to regulate motor sport, others still, like the International Olympic Committee are interested in developing elite, Olympic sports around the world, and in so doing acquire vast sums of money and spend it liberally.

Sports organizations are increasingly compelled to join the commercial world, and are under great pressure to adopt the operational and structural characteristics of business enterprises. The influence of modern communication has been profound, with sporting results available from any smart device connected to the internet. Many sporting organizations have realized that in order to remain competitive they must provide high levels of entertainment value, just like any compelling leisure option from television to gaming consoles. Consequently, corporate boxes line major sporting venues, sport is blanketed across pay, cable and free-to-air television, high profile athletes earn extraordinary sums, and politicians associate themselves with certain teams. The commercial and competitive pressures placed upon sport organizations from local football clubs, universities and colleges, to professional leagues and teams, has encouraged sport managers to embrace business tools and concepts like organizational culture.

Perhaps the most powerful argument in favour of considering culture in sport organizations is that its understanding can help to bring about change. Since culture commands such an influence on the performance of an organization's members, it is critical that cultural traits remain both appropriate and strong. In the case of sport, it is common to have strong cultures that have been forged by tradition and a fierce sense of history. At the same time, some cultural characteristics like excessive drinking and on-field violence may no longer suit the more professional management approach that needs to be assumed in a media-savvy world where almost every individual carries a smart phone with a video camera.

Commentaries on organizational culture, while as disparate as the number of researchers pursuing its investigation, generally emphasize its most superficial manifestation. Moreover, sport culture is frequently seen as mono-cultural: perceived at one level, and as one entity. Here, a sport organization is distinguished as a giant cultural mass, constructed equivalently throughout, and with little or no internal variability. However, this way of thinking is difficult to sustain when analysing a sporting organization. Sporting club cultures possess numerous cultural themes, and can be perceived readily at several levels, or as several sub-cultures. For example, as an organizational or administrative unit comparable to other business organizations, as a supporter organization, whose aims, objectives and traditions may be different (such as winning matches in preference to making a financial profit), and as a player unit, where motivation may vary from glory to money. While a player may perform for a club because of loyalty or remuneration (or any number of other reasons), supporters are usually passionately attached to a club's colours and traditions, expecting only on-field success in return. At the same time, some sport organizations are driven by broader social and health agendas or values that relegate both winning and profit to background issues. Others still are held accountable to business returns by shareholders, owners and sponsors.

In Practice 9.1 Cultural diversity in sport

Most countries around the world have embraced immigrants and visitors from different cultures. Cultural diversity enhances the economic, social and political milieu in which sport organizations operate. Sport for many multicultural nations is a means for integrating people from culturally and linguistically different circumstances into a new local context. For example, African athletes have traditionally moved towards Europe. However today, athletes from Africa, participating in a wide variety of sports, have migrated to all parts of the world including Asia, North America and the Middle East. Sport can also provide a vital pathway for migrants to break away from the political and economic hindrances that affected the quality of living they experienced in their homelands.

For some countries, attracting and embracing athletes from culturally different backgrounds can bring with it some challenges. Australia offers a good example, illustrating an established tradition of sport blended with new influences. A typical Australian values his or her leisure time, and sport is instrumental in bringing meaning to those leisure experiences. With over 70 per cent of the population engaging in physical activity of some kind, it is clear that sport and leisure are key attributes of Australia's cultural identity.

The dominant sports in Australia, such as Australian Rules football, cricket, rugby and netball, all possess strong cultural identities. However, people from culturally diverse backgrounds are under-represented. Despite the effort by clubs and administering organizations to implement policies on racial vilification and inclusivity, the acceptance of non-Anglo players remains burdened with controversy. A sport organization must do more than just design and execute rules and regulations as a means of preventing racism and exclusivity. Sport organizations must pursue a deep acceptance of diversity by changing the very core of their cultural identities.

What's the Score? A Survey of Cultural Diversity and Racism in Australian Sport, a report commissioned by the Australian Human Rights Commission, cautioned that for individuals from culturally or linguistically different backgrounds, the fear of racial abuse was a clear barrier to engaging in sport at any level. However, changing the culture of a 'traditional' sport can prove problematic. The AFL, for example, has had policies against racial vilification since 1995, but their presence or overt acceptance in the community has not stopped fans, sports commentators or players from making inappropriate and often public remarks. How can a sport manage its cultural identity positively and hence encourage involvement from culturally and linguistically different backgrounds?

For successful cultural change to come about, a sport organization must question the most fundamental assumptions it holds about its game, history and membership, and subsequently make a commitment to a new, more appropriate cultural identity. Identity change may incorporate three mechanisms. First, it is the responsibility of management to ensure that the information disseminated is clear and consistent, and that appropriate control systems are in place to encourage diversity in order to protect the interests of participants. Second, leadership behaviour can drive culture by establishing a clear vision, propagating constructive story-telling and instituting positive behavioural examples and suitable role models. Finally, the application of persuasive and even coercive power to prevent stakeholder deviation from the new cultural mindset, can be used to reinforce and justify the desired cultural direction.

SPORT, BUSINESS AND SUB-CULTURES

In sporting organizational cultures there is the additional hurdle of translating and adopting a culture directly from traditional business theory. It is dangerously simplistic to assume that a sporting organization should adopt the methods and practices of a traditional business without addressing the cultural variables. While business methods can be transferred to accommodate the organizational strategies of a sporting club, a direct transfer fails to confront the issue of what it is that makes the culture of a sporting organization differ from that of a traditional business enterprise.

Ideal business culture tends to reflect a willingness by an organization's employees to embrace a standard of performance that promotes quality in the production of goods and services, in the attempt to generate a financial profit. This cultural ideology, while cognizant of business necessities, is unable to cater for the more diverse structures that exist in a sporting organization. In any business, financial realities must be acknowledged, but in a sporting business, additional behavioural variables require recognition and respect. While different businesses have different cultures, they are less variable than the cultural differences between individual sports. It cannot be assumed, for example, that a single unified culture exists for all sports. Sport managers must be aware of the cultural nuances of their respective sports and the influence they have upon players, employees, members, fans and the general public.

Culture is not a simple matter within a single sport either. Professional players, for example, have a different cultural attitude from most amateurs and spectators. This variability of attitudes is symptomatic of a wider, more troublesome area: the clash of cultures within sports. This is illustrated best at an international level, where players from different countries have been brought up with profoundly different ideologies of the game, and how it should be played. Football – the 'world game' – is indicative of this culture clash, in addition to the immense cultural significance inherent in the game. Like all living cultures, sport is incessantly changing, dynamic in nature and subject to constant reinterpretation by its participants and viewers. The only apparent consistencies in sporting culture are the pursuit of competition, the love of winning, and the ability to summon strong emotional responses in both victory and defeat.

Undeniably there is a need to study organizational cultures, accounting for the effect of the sport itself. For example, in the same way that we might expect that accounting firms might share some cultural traits, so might we predict that bocce clubs do as well. Similarly, the tradition and discipline central to a bocce club might be expected to encourage cultural characteristics different to the youthful and eclectic philosophy found in a BMX club. Other sports, like ultimate fighting and mixed martial arts, laud different values again, reinforcing masculinity, toughness and power. These cultural characteristics can even seep into the behaviours of executive officers and employees of the clubs, especially since many sport organizations like to hire past players. Given that so many sporting organizations covet tradition and the accomplishments of the past, they also tend to be resistant to change. However, before any change can occur, an organization's culture needs to be accurately diagnosed in the form of a coherent identity.

In Practice 9.2 Can an online sports entity have a culture? The birth of eSports

eSports is the new sports genre for the twenty-first century, foreshadowing the implications of radically shifting terrain in the sport-media-technology nexus. Electronic sports, or eSports, combines electronic gaming activity with sporting competition. Instead of utilizing a physical space, enthusiasts compete in a virtual space. An online sport megatrend comprised of several growing governing bodies and commercial enterprises, eSports seeks to co-create sport engagement experiences with participants through global online networks. As such, eSports exemplifies the growing intersection between the recreational and the relational interfaces available through sport products.

eSports is relatively young, having first established a presence in the late 1990s, but is now blossoming and building its own definitive cultural identity. For example, the eSports league recently reported a staggering 3.6 million participants, a number growing exponentially. South Korea has become the leading hub for practising eSports professionals with over 430 individuals making a professional living out of their performances. Yet, where physical activity is seen as a positive and healthy lifestyle choice, computer-based gaming does not command the same glowing perception. Online games have often been viewed as little more than pointless forms of entertainment, or worse, as an activity that undermines the health benefits of physical sport by encouraging indolence. Arguably eSports can overcome that perception. eSports justifies its existence in the sport domain by staging physical and online events, professional players, practice facilities and sessions, all with sport media support. Events are staged in more than 10 countries, and of course, are available for viewing from anywhere in the world through a smart, internet-connected device. Just as with any sport, eSports participants aim to be better, faster, more skilled than their competitors, and to win.

Can online sport gaming bodies develop an organizational culture akin to other traditional sport organization cultures? For eSports, the growth of competitive computer games and the rapid evolution of digital technologies, have fostered a community of enthusiasts who share similar values as well as a common belief in the product, irrespective of their locations and inability to meet face-to-face. In fact, when looking below the surface it becomes clear that the cultural forces at the core of eSports have arisen from the co-created values, beliefs and assumptions made by its numerous stakeholders, including its governing body, the International eSports Federation, as well as media and technology corporations, sponsors, players, and communities of players. With corporate sponsors like Coca-Cola throwing significant money in support of a recent World Championships in a capacity-filled Staples Arena in Los Angeles, it is no wonder that part of the culture reflects the confluence of sport, entertainment, media, business and marketing, which exemplifies contemporary global sport. With around US$20 million on the line in prize money each year in the eSports competition pool, we might expect that its escalation will build strongly upon a cultural emphasis on professionalization. Stadiums are being filled with fans just to watch professional sport gamers compete as avatars in a virtual world. Millions more watch remotely online.

In a curious mix of technology and tradition, cultural 'clans' have evolved around geographical boundaries, especially within Asia and the United Stated as the two key founding regions responsible for building the eSports culture. Spreading across all regions, the Cyberathlete Professional League was founded in 1997 as the first organized body to offer prize money for competitive gaming. Since then the prize pool has steadily increased with over US$3 million in prize money distributed, alongside an additional US$2 million in merchandise sales. Globally cast events have accelerated the exposure in recent times and reinforced cultural attributes. The World Cyber Games for 2013 was held in China with over 500 participants from more than 40 nations. In this sense, the Games were just like any major sporting event where participants travelled to a specific location, even though they could have competed in an exclusively virtual format. However, this way the organizers were able to marshal a large group of fans to attend and watch, in so doing amplifying the atmosphere and reinforcing the event's cultural strength through personal connections. Like its mega-sized compatriot governing Olympic sports, the Olympic Games, the World Cyber Games promotes three primary values. For those competing in eSports, the central principles include a sense of belonging, working together, and achieving clarity in what they want and what they stand for. Unlike a conventional sport organization, where tangible physical facilities linked to a geographical region have influenced cultural features over a long period and through a myriad of historical events, the cultural identity of the eSports online community has developed and diffused rapidly. Yet, like a football club and its game, the characteristics of online gaming can be recognized in the lauded identities of the organizations governing eSports. Adding to its claim for sporting legitimacy, eSports reinforces its culture with an annual symposium staged in conjunction with the eSports world championship.

Noteworthy from a sub-cultural viewpoint, the specific online games participants select to compete in provide a distinguishing point of identification for membership to different clans. In the United States, for example, the focus is on first person shooting games where competitors meet head-to-head, battling it out until a single (only-living avatar) winner is determined. In the Asian eSports sub-cultural clan, competition prioritizes real-time strategy games.

One important change is sweeping the eSports environment, shifting the cultural values of the key governing organizations: where gaming began as an activity strongly dominated by males, now nearly half of eSports participants are female. This change has enhanced the importance of social cultural values, where eSports participants are drawn to both the visual game features offered by technological advances, as well as the social engagement opportunities with other players.

ORGANIZATIONAL IDENTITY

Like all social concepts, organizational identity allocates meaning to largely intangible but pivotal organizational behaviours. From a social perspective, identity describes how individuals perceive themselves, as well as how they are perceived by others. Because identity represents an individual's self-perception, it also tends to be durable, providing a long-term, stable, distinctive and enduring image. Similarly, as social entities, sport organizations exhibit identities established by the adoption, reinforcement and rejection of particular characteristics created by its members over time. The process operates as an extension of personal identity where individuals adopt or reinforce characteristics they perceive advantageous while discarding the negative. For example, an organization might adopt team-based work practices if its members expect collaboration to be advantageous. An organization establishes its identity through the collective self-perceptions of insiders, which in turn accompanies how it performs (culture), the way it expresses itself, and the way it is perceived by outsiders (image). However, a sport organization might perceive itself in a manner incompatible with outside perceptions. Change to bring the two into alignment is difficult because identity reflects long-term, stable perceptions about an organization's idiosyncratic characteristics. Such perceptions determine not only an organization's understanding of itself, but also how such statements are received and accepted (or rejected) by stakeholders.

Culture is about the way we do things and identity is about how we perceive or are perceived. Furthermore, things are done in a particular way due to culture, but also to reinforce or change perceptions. In this respect, organizational culture and identity work together in a reciprocal and dynamic manner. Culture is the more contextual, tacit and emergent side, whereas identity is the more textual, explicit and instrumental side. Another way of looking at it expresses identity as a manifestation and artefact of culture. However, like culture, identity reveals an organizational contradiction. Change is necessary in order for an organization to survive a competitive environment, but at the same time, identity has to endure long enough to maintain a sense of continuity. Appropriate cultures change while strong cultures endure. Understanding the role identity plays in organizations is also essential to culture's diagnosis.

DIAGNOSING AND MANAGING ORGANIZATIONAL CULTURE

In order to grasp the concept of culture and its relationship to the individual, the group and the sport organization, an in-depth approach is required. Sport organizations create intentions and atmospheres that influence behaviour, routines, practices and the thought systems of members. These systems and processes subsequently form patterns that are acquired primarily through socialization, or learning over time from the reactions and behaviours of others. In essence, individuals within a sport organization are exposed to what researchers call 'culture revealing' situations, which might include the observable behaviour of other members, their organizational methods, 'artefacts' – the photos, honour boards and other memorabilia on show – and interactive communication, or the way in which individuals talk to each other. Some of these common, superficial and observable representations of organizational culture are reproduced in Table 9.1. These are important to recognize because the driving values and belief systems behind them can never be seen as anything more than observable 'symptoms'.

Although the superficial aspects of culture can be observed, the difficulty comes in their interpretation because they are merely surface representations of deeper values. Thus, a useful cultural diagnosis will always seek to understand what drives the observable behaviour. For example, what does it mean if an employee makes a mistake and is severely reprimanded by his or her boss? What does common jargon imply? Why are certain rituals typical, like the moment when a new player is allocated a number or jersey?

The key question remains as to how overt observations relate to deeper values. Most researchers recommend some form of classification system that describes organizational culture in the form of 'dimensions', each one a deeper, core value. These dimensions reflect on particular organizational characteristics as an aid to categorizing cultures. The summation of these characteristics may be used to describe an organization's culture, which can then allow for comparisons to be undertaken between organizations. For example, observable evidence in the form of an end-of-season awards night in a sporting club might be suggestive of the nature of the organization's reward/motivation values. Enough observable evidence can lead a sport manager to make some tentative conclusions about each dimension. Table 9.2 lists some common dimensions used to describe organizational culture. They can be seen as continua, an organization's position somewhere between the two extremes.

TABLE 9.1 Observable symptoms of sport organizational culture

Symptom	Explanation
Environment	The general surroundings of an organization, like the building it is housed in and the geographical location, like the city or in a grandstand.
Artefacts	Physical objects located in the organization from its furnishings to its coffee machine.
Language	The common words and phrases used by most organizational members, including gestures and body language.
Documents	Any literature including reports, statements, promotional material, memos and emails produced for the purpose of communication.
Logos	Any symbolic visual imagery including colours and fonts that convey meaning about the organization.
Heroes	Current or former organizational members who are considered exemplars.
Stories	Narratives shared by organizational members based at least partly on true events.
Legends	An event with some historical basis but has been embellished with fictional details.
Rituals	Standardized and repeated behaviours.
Rites	Elaborate, dramatic, planned set of activities.

TABLE 9.2 Cultural dimensions

Dimension	Characteristics
Stability/changeability	Disposition toward change: Degree to which organization encourages alternative 'ways of doing things' or existing ways.
Cooperation/conflict	Disposition toward problem resolution: Degree to which organization encourages cooperation or conflict.
Goal focus/orientation	Clarity and nature of objectives and performance expectations.
Reward/motivation	Nature of reward orientation of organizational members: Degree to which organization encourages seniority or performance.
Control/authority	Nature and degree of responsibility, freedom and independence of organizational members.
Time/planning	Disposition toward long-term planning: Degree to which organization encourages short-term or long-term thinking.

Any analysis that captures the complexity of organizational culture may have great difficulty in separating the interwoven strands of organizational history and personal relationships. As a result, concrete conclusions may be difficult to establish. It is therefore important to take advantage of the symbolism created by sport's abundant myths, rituals and ceremonies in order to gain a complete understanding of the full range of human behaviour within a complex organization. The traditions, folklore, mythologies, dramas, and successes and traumas of the past, are the threads that weave together the fabric of organizational culture.

ORGANIZATIONAL CULTURE IN MIND

A psychological approach is helpful in identifying and interpreting human behaviour in organizations as a cultural phenomenon. Psychologists, originally stimulated by the work of Carl Jung, suggest that there are different levels of behavioural awareness, from the conscious to unconscious. Organizational psychologists have appropriated this kind of thinking and transposed it to culture. The key analogy is that an organization is like a mind.

From the psychological viewpoint, the readily apparent and observable qualities of a sporting organization are the same as the conscious part of an individual mind. These include the physical environment, the public statements of officials, the way individuals interactively communicate, the form of language used, what clothes are worn, and the memorabilia that fills the rooms and offices. Another of the most important observable qualities involves the place of sporting heroes. They represent rich and highly visible indicators of the culture being sought. Heroes offer an insight into the culture of an organization, since the members as well as power brokers select them. In addition, heroes signpost those qualities in individuals respected and admired by a wider audience. The hero is a powerful figure in a sporting organization, and may be simultaneously an employee and ex-player. The hero may also be charismatic, entrepreneurial, or just plain administrative, which often characterizes business enterprises. By understanding the orientation of hero figures, both past and present, it is possible to map trends in cultural change. Heroes can be both reactionary and progressive. For example, heroes that reinforce the dominant culture will not change the values and attitudes that the culture emphasizes. On the other hand, a hero that transcends and transforms the dominant culture will be a catalyst for change in the behaviours and values of a club. Often a hero is the most powerful medium for change to be successful.

Tradition is another window into the culture of an organization. Like heroes, traditions are readily observable through memorabilia. However, the underlying values and assumptions that give meaning to heroes and traditions reside in the deeper levels of a culture. Tradition may on the one hand be preserved by the present cultural identity, while on the other hand the sporting organization may have developed a contemporary cultural personality. Thus, it is useful to acknowledge the importance of tradition and history to a sporting organization because it may be a cultural lynchpin, or a stepping stone from which their contemporary cultural character has been launched.

In order to bypass the obstacles (in the form of stereotypical views and superficial signs) that can block an assessment of culture, it is essential to analyse and explore natural, observable outcroppings of culture; places where the cultural understandings can be exposed. By analysing these sites, it is possible to gain a practical insight into the underlying culture of the organization. This level deals with organizational rites and rituals because their performance is readily apparent, and in performing these rites, employees generally use other cultural forms of expression, such as certain customary language or jargon, gestures and artefacts. These rites, which are shared understandings, are additionally conveyed through myths, sagas, legends, or other stories associated with the occasion, and in practical terms may take the form of barbecues or presentations. In order to actively assess this level of culture, not only must observational techniques be employed, but meanings must be attached to them. This requires more than a superficial level of analysis.

There are also 'unconscious' parts of organizations as well. In effect, it is the unconscious that controls the individual. This incorporates the beliefs, habits, values, behaviours and attitudes prevalent in a sporting organization. An accurate assessment of this level of culture is difficult and fraught with the danger of misrepresentation. For example, how employees say they behave and what they state they believe, has to be compared to their actual behaviour.

As a cautionary note, sport managers should be aware that multiple interpretations can be made based on the same evidence. For example, one way of looking at culture is to focus attention on the consistency and congruence of policies and practices within a sport organization, as members are confronted with problems to solve. In contrast, it is also valid to consider ambiguities and inconsistencies in behaviour. These anomalies often represent the difference between espoused values and actual values. Cultural manifestations can be interpreted in multiple ways, and change over time and location. It is important to look for patterns, exceptions and values targeted for change.

In Practice 9.3 Changing beliefs in Rwandan cycling

In 1994, Rwanda's sad media association rested with civil war atrocities. Sporting accolades were hardly newsworthy stories, and, in reality, any notions of sport management, let alone organizational culture, would have been viewed as trivial. Unfortunately, Rwanda is best known as an African nation riddled with violence, corruption, economic, health and welfare problems. It is no surprise, then, that cultural activities of any sort have rarely featured on the nation's agenda. Any cultural activity was primarily related to religious ceremonies or traditional community-level performances. Sport participation was limited to passive activities between friendly neighbouring communities. However, the aftermath of devastation included the opportunity to rebuild the nation and change its cultural mindset, including the values and beliefs of its most significant sporting organizations. Since national cultural values enforce a strong influence upon the organizational cultures of its constituent enterprises, the birth of Rwandan sporting culture can be viewed as an illustrative expression of an emerging sport management industry.

Initially the government ministry for culture focussed on respecting the burial rites and memories of lost lives. But they shortly introduced a vocational training agenda aimed at developing the country's ailing economy by bolstering the skills of its citizens. Amongst this vocational commitment was an endeavour to grow sport participation and elite performance by solidifying and professionalizing its sporting organizations. Today, the Rwandan Ministry of Sport and Culture embraces 'a winning culture in various sports disciplines and promotes culture as foundation to the development of our country'. Increased exposure to international sport prompted individuals and groups to stimulate life back into Rwanda through sport. Team Rwanda Cycling was one such project created to unite an unsettled and despairing nation by providing a central organizational hub for identity and performance.

Prior to 2002, cycling was seen as a mode of daily transport for those lucky enough to afford a bike. Competitive cycling in Rwanda simply did not exist. By 2007 though, Team Rwanda was born and cycling became an opportunity for Rwandan men to focus on a positive activity. Team Rwanda was different from other sports entities in terms of the culture it was seeking to foster. Competition in sport is normal; competition between riders, for sponsors and new participants is expected. But the values and beliefs of Team Rwanda are firmly based in community-building where supporting and regenerating the Rwandan community through cycling activity hold precedence. It was the drive of an American elite cyclist, Jock Boyer, along with Tom Ritchey, who reinforced the cycling passion. It was this leadership combination that laid the groundwork for a strong culture within Team Rwanda. Combined with financial support, the international UCI graded Tour of Rwanda was born in 2008, and cycling rapidly transformed into an institution within the country. Today over three million people watch the race and it remains the nation's largest sporting event.

Adrien Niyonshuti was the first Rwandan to be signed by a professional cycling team and in 2012 became the first Rwandan to represent the country at an Olympic Games. His profile helped Team Rwanda to develop its athletes and attract important sponsorship and government funding. Team Rwanda now races in events across Africa, including Morocco, Gabon and Eritrea. It has also recently expanded to include a women's team.

Team Rwanda's cultural identity goes beyond just competition. Instead it emphasizes the transition of cyclists into non-cycling roles in order to sustain the future growth of cycling and sport in Rwanda. Team Rwanda also values the notion of nurturing the community by ensuring that its cyclists become mentors for others. For example, their agenda includes developing young cyclists as community role models and supporting local sport and education with contributions from their team earnings and race winnings. This philanthropic approach to sport is not unusual, but it does highlight how collective communities operate and find ways through sport to build a stronger and more positive identity. All of these developments emanated from a single sport organization driven by a deep cultural commitment to making a positive difference.

MAPPING SPORT ORGANIZATIONAL CULTURE

Cultural understanding stems from successfully translating information into meaning. Every aspect of a sporting organization is symbolically representative in some way of its culture. All information is not equal, however, yet all possible data must be analysed in order to establish the most comprehensive image possible of the existing culture. In order for a culture to be created and bolstered, shared values and beliefs must in some way be reinforced and transferred to organizational members through tangible means.

A cultural map summarizes the predominant features of a sporting organization's culture, and provides a means through which raw data can be interpreted into measurable criteria. It works by providing sets of categories in which information can be collected and summarized with the intention of identifying the main themes that continuously emerge. Some researchers believe that this approach can also be used in a more statistical form, the numbers attached to responses from questions derived from the dimensions and answered by organizational members.

While the range and diversity of information available for cultural analysis is profound, many cultural studies ignore all but the most apparent and accessible data. A holistic cultural analysis will utilize every available piece of information, with the more obvious elements becoming vehicles for the transmission of less tangible, more subjective facets of culture. However, the culture of any one sporting organization cannot be classified into one of just a few categories, even though many models offer a handful of neatly predetermined types. In reality, there are as many organizational cultures as there are sporting organizations, and they cannot be generically categorized into one of a fixed number of groups. Sporting clubs are immersed in tradition, history, values and myths, and these should figure prominently in any diagnosis. From an accurate diagnosis, change becomes far easier.

The main lesson for cultural change is that it cannot be tackled without a clear, prior understanding of an organization's chief cultural traits and how they manifest themselves. Once an accurate diagnosis has been undertaken, through some form of formal or informal cultural map, elements of culture can be managed. Since a sport manager cannot literally change peoples' minds, they instead have to change peoples' actions. To some extent this can be imposed or encouraged, but it is a slow process. For example, new rituals can be introduced to replace older, less desirable ones, like a club dinner instead of a drinking binge. Entrenched values and beliefs can be extremely difficult to change, and, even with the right introduction of new symbols, language, heroes, stories, employees and so on, genuine cultural change in an organization can take many years or even a new generation of organizational members before it takes hold.

CULTURAL COMPLEXITIES

Culture and identity cannot be avoided by any member of an organization. Although a slippery concept, hard to conflate to the simple or tangible, culture shapes the collective conduct of all organizational members. It does this by inculcating bundles of values and beliefs into members' minds. In turn, values and beliefs channel and restrict ways of thinking. In short, culture shapes conduct and individual behaviour. For example, cultural values and beliefs might have to do with how men should relate to women, why profit should override environmental sensitivity, or why winning and success are more important than participation. As a result, some cultures create socially valued outcomes, while others create dysfunctional cultures. Culture can be changed for the better, but it requires astute and sophisticated management. Perhaps more than anything else, it demands a deep understanding of how culture works.

We emphasize the importance of building cultural understandings. Every aspect of a sporting organization is symbolically representative in some way of its culture. Cultivating a successful culture relies on shared values and beliefs that have been reinforced and transferred to organizational members through tangible means like rituals. Cultural change cannot be tackled without a clear, prior understanding of an organization's chief cultural traits and how they manifest. Once an accurate diagnosis has been undertaken, elements of culture can be managed. Of course, since sport managers cannot literally change peoples' minds, they can influence behaviour. For this reason, organizational rituals provide a mechanism through which entrenched values and beliefs can be influenced by new symbols, language, heroes and stories. Keep in mind that cultivating a successful sport culture relies on translating information into meaning. And, meaning is the path to a powerful cultural identity.

SUMMARY

In the world of sport management, organizational culture has gained prominence as a concept useful in assessing and managing performance. Sport organizational culture can be defined as the collection of fundamental values and attitudes that are common to members of a sport organization, and which subsequently set the behavioural standards or norms for all members. The difficulty remains, however, that the deep values common to organizational members are not easy to access. As a way of getting around this inaccessibility problem, sport managers can use cultural dimensions that suggest some of the possible values that are present. A step further, cultural maps show the variables and observable manifestations of culture that need to be investigated. These maps use the tip of the cultural iceberg (the accessible aspects of culture like symbols and artefacts) to estimate the iceberg's underwater composition (the deep values and beliefs of organizational members). Once a thorough diagnosis has been completed, sport managers can work toward adapting and replacing undesirable cultural characteristics.

REVIEW QUESTIONS

1 Why is organization culture important to sport managers?

2 Explain how organizational culture can be manifested at different levels.

3 Describe the difference between superficial elements of culture and deeper elements of culture. What is the difference between organizational culture and identity?

4   What is a cultural dimension?

5   How can organizational culture be measured in a sport organization?

6   How does measuring organizational culture help in changing it?

7   Select a sport organization you belong or have belonged to. Create a list of attributes or values that you believe embodies its organizational culture. Which are the characteristics that distinguish it from other similar sport organizations?

8   Select a sport organization you belong or have belonged to. Describe 10 artefacts that are on show in its premises and explain how each illuminates organizational culture.

FURTHER READING

Girginov, V. (2010). Culture and the study of sport management. *European Sport Management Quarterly*, 10(4): 397–417.

Jarvie, G. (2013). *Sport, Culture and Society: An Introduction*. London: Routledge.

Markovits, A.S. & Rensmann, L. (2010). *Gaming the World: How Sports are Reshaping Global Politics and Culture*. Princeton, NJ: Princeton University Press.

Schein, E. (2010). *Organizational Culture and Leadership*. 4th edn. San Francisco: Jossey-Bass.

Smith, A., Stewart, B. & Haimes, G. (2012). *Organizational Culture and Identity: Sport, Symbols and Success*. New York: Nova Science Publishers.

RELEVANT WEBSITES

- Australian Human Rights Commission at www.humanrights.gov.au
- Australian Football League Community at www.aflcommunityclub.com.au
- International eSports Federation at http://ie-sf.orgI
- Cyberathlete Professional League at www.wcg.com
- Rwandan Ministry of Sport and Culture at http://minispoc.gov.rw
- Team Rwanda at http://teamrwandancycling.org
- Swimming Australia at http://swimming.org.au
- USA Swimming at http://usaswimming.org
- Australian Rules Football (AFL) at http://afl.com.au

CASE STUDY 9.1

Swimming: Drowning in a toxic culture?

The idea of an organization possessing a 'culture' has been pre-eminent in management vernacular since the 1980s. Yet, the 'collective programming' of culture has been acknowledged as the underlying and unconscious core of sport for centuries. In sport, culture acts as a filter for all participants to cope with order and to contribute to the sport in a meaningful way, where the collective outcome in performance is sovereign over any individual. However, when values and beliefs are challenged with deviant behaviour, an organization's fundamental culture is challenged, leading to dissonance and fracturing.

As an elite sport, swimming has enjoyed the spotlight on the world stage and is one of the premier events in the Summer Olympics program. In fact, as a tangible measure of the sport's global spectator and sponsor attractiveness, seats for the swimming at the London Olympics (2012) were the most expensive competition event tickets to buy in the secondary market at 242 per cent over their face value. A successful sport must balance participation rates, on- and off-field performance, and commercial sustainability. Building a strong culture around these dimensions has been the reason for swimming's success, especially in Australia. Despite its high profile and performance success, the culture of elite swimming has experienced numerous problems, intensifying in recent times.

Waves of reputational issues have swept over swimming over the last 50 years. Mischievous pranks in the 1960s were supplanted by systematic doping during the 1970s and 1980s in the Eastern Bloc, while Chinese and European teams allegedly employed performance-enhancing drugs in the 1990s and 2000s. In the modern era swimming has revealed inappropriate behaviour of coaching personnel and the current use and abuse of prescription and social drugs by its elite athletes. This has caused the governing authority, the *Fédération Internationale de Natation* (FINA) and associated national associations, to question the culture of elite swimming. For example, USA Swimming suffered criticism on its management of misconduct cases by swim coaches and support staff well after its preventative Safe Sport program was implemented. The culture of USA Swimming today is markedly different to the ideals set out in its organizational constitution.

In Australia, swimming is often likened to riding a bike in that nearly every Australian learns to do both from an early age. Australians value sport and leisure highly and swimming is a powerful representation of the country's cultural beliefs. Participation in an almost limitless supply of swimming activities combined with the Australian penchant for sports competition has shaped the nation's desire for successful in-pool performance at international competitions. Australia is presently ranked first in Commonwealth competition and fifth in the world, but it was an unexpectedly poor team performance at the most recent Olympic Games that caused authorities within Swimming Australia serious concern. Added to the underwhelming performances was an increasing media exposure of reckless athlete behaviour and reports of a poor team work ethos. The worldwide notoriety of a number of Australia's great swimming personalities such as Dawn Fraser, Shane Gould and Ian Thorpe had been replaced by the more disturbing behaviours of some of its modern stars. The culture of swimming had changed, leading fans and authorities in the broader Olympic movement to brand it toxic.

An organization's culture can be a reflection of the culture of a society. Countries like Australia and the United States are passionate about sport. Sport organizational culture values in these two countries tend to reflect the prevailing, broader social values. Sport connects people in a way that very few other activities can achieve. For Americans, there are only two days in a calendar year where professional sport is not televised. For Australians, there are sporting events so important that they command a public holiday in commemoration.

A strong, united organizational culture has a positive effect on performance. While difficult to define, when its underlying values and beliefs are tested, an organization's cultural weaknesses are easily exposed. For example, organizational culture is reflected by the manner in which participants and representatives interact with each other, and with competitors, fans, sponsors and officials. In practice, Swimming Australia's strategic goals had been challenged. Performances at both the World Championships and the Olympic Games were below expectations, and coupled with numerous, high profile athlete behavioural transgressions, a cultural conflict had become evident. Media reporting had cited poor governance from Swimming Australia and an eroding team culture as the two major reasons for the lack of results in the pool. A new face of swimming was emerging and the previously unwavering universal principles of fairness, competitiveness and pride were being replaced by more discouraging standards.

Arguably, the combination of increased media access to athletes, the commercialization of successful athletes, and the necessity for sport to entertain its fans, may contradict Swimming Australia's traditional values. Nevertheless, by the 2012 London Olympics, Australian swimming was floundering against the tide of public expectations, severely threatening its credibility.

At the same time, athlete misbehaviour and poor results cannot be entirely blamed on the athletes. An organization's policies must at least in part account for dysfunctional behavioural expectations since governance is the overriding framework for cultural practices. Governance exists to balance social and economic goals with stakeholder and partner goals, while ensuring proper legal compliance. Existing strategies and structures had failed and management was accountable for overlooking deviant activity such as pranks, inappropriate harassment, and recreational drug use. The perception within Swimming Australia seemed to be that when the time came to perform, coaches and athletes would 'step up'. When a sport becomes too insular, unacceptable behaviours may be overlooked. Over time, a strong positive culture can erode, and a new, less attractive set of values and behaviours can emerge. Changing dysfunctional cultural values and behaviours must begin with management.

As a result of public scrutiny, Swimming Australia underwent a significant review of its managerial hierarchy and the policies and practices that had been blamed for destroying team dynamism and podium results. The Bluestone Review (Grange 2013) assessed the culture and leadership in Australian swimming. It identified not one single significant issue that was damaging the culture of swimming, but rather a 'confluence of circumstances' that had been building for some time. Rigorous new standards were recommended for personal athlete behaviour, social media usage, and accountability at all levels of the sport. The consideration of successful role models such as Dawn Fraser also appeared in an effort to reinforce more traditional values and standards.

In the United States, the Safe Swim Program was enacted to protect the well-being of swimmers at all levels of the sport. In addition, the Funnest Sport campaign (2014) is an attempt to refresh the positive perception that swimming as a sport had held for most people. The campaign aims to highlight the positive aspects of competitive swimming, with the intention of attracting more people to get involved. Simultaneously, governing body USA Swimming is endeavouring to reinforce strong ethical values and practices from the elite level to grassroots participation. Its vision 'to inspire and enable our members to achieve excellence in the sport of swimming and in life' reflects the desired culture.

An organization's culture can often be resistant to change. Without serious threats like losing financial support or participants, most sport organizations would not tamper with the existing culture. However, when an organization seemingly loses its way, and its culture becomes labelled as toxic, change can be brought about swiftly. Constant media exposure of the competitions, and the celebrity capabilities of athletes, exposes elite sport to negative influences, which if not managed suitably, can undermine performance by destroying positive cultural values, beliefs and practices.

CASE STUDY QUESTIONS

1   How reflective of the national culture is the culture of swimming's governing body in either Australia or the United States?

2   Can the recommendations made by the Bluestone Review be implemented quickly for Swimming Australia so that its positive culture can be revived and a stronger organization can return?

CASE STUDY 9.2

In a man's football world: Women with an eye on the ball

Australian Rules football lies at the heart of Australian sporting culture. Put simply, Aussies love their 'footy'. Australian Rules football has been in existence since the 1850s and commands the largest participation base, live and television audiences, and commercial revenues in Australia. Like all the other football codes, Australian Rules Football (AFL) is predominantly a man's game: men play it, men coach it and men manage it (but everyone can watch it). The values of dynamism, physicality and heroism have traditionally been associated with the AFL, exemplifying the stereotypical bonds of masculine team sport. Yet, one value, egalitarianism, has always been missing. Men have played football while women have watched.

It was not until relatively recently that the AFL's obsession with masculinity was challenged, mostly as a result of the sizeable numbers of females involved in the sport. Women had formed teams and competitions of their own, both in Australia and overseas. Women were fans, spectators and paid-up members of all Australian Football League (AFL) clubs. In fact, the current numbers undeniably compel an argument for changing the culture of the AFL:

- 40 per cent of AFL and club members are female;
- 41 per cent of game day attendees are female;
- 43 per cent of the television audience are female;
- 35 per cent of volunteers within local clubs are female;
- 78,224 females are now playing Australian Football;
- 30,524 girls are participating in the junior development program Auskick;
- 18,986 females are playing in a dedicated female competition;
- 1,497 female coaches are accredited;
- 700+ female umpires are working across Australia.

Overturning the prevailing culture of a sport, its governing organizations and its clubs is a significant task, achieved at least to some degree in this case by the presence of women in all aspects of the game. Yet, women involved in football did not want to compete with their male counterparts, they wanted to collaborate. For a sport steeped in a culture of masculinity, the AFL has had to take several uncomfortable steps to embrace a cultural change giving weight to the contributions of female managers, players, officials, coaches, support staff, volunteers and supporters.

Sport managers work within contexts that shape what they do and what they can change. The AFL context provides an example of the classic value common to sport of 'hyper masculinity', where a sport and its entire identity have been shaped by a single, prevailing value. Accepting females as players, managers, reporters and playing staff has challenged the AFL's core identity. Some progress has occurred. For example, girls are able to participate in modified competitions with boys. At the same time, all-women competitions have emerged around the country, with over 160,000 participants registered in 2013 representing an increase of 24 per cent from the previous year.

Women have also been employed as administrators, managers and board members. In 2009, the AFL actively sought to attract women to senior management positions within their Community Development program. For example, the governing board for the competition, the AFL Commission, has two female representatives. In addition, the first female AFL senior umpire, Chelsea Roffey, made her debut as a goal umpire in 2004, and umpired her first Grand Final in

2012. This constitutes a remarkable achievement, not only because Roffey is female and had successfully challenged the traditional institutionalized practice, but also because she came from the rugby-mad Australian state of Queensland. Presently, three female goal umpires officiate in the AFL. AFL media commentary has also been restricted to senior (male) journalists and past players and coaches until the past decade when female journalists became more prominent in providing regular expert commentary and analysis. With women accounting for more than 40 per cent of the AFL television audience, club membership and spectatorship, the media has been forced to respond to their viewers and listeners. However, despite all of this, coaching at the elite level represented an important, final, glass ceiling to break through.

While females could be part of the medical team at AFL clubs, no female had yet been appointed a coach to an AFL team. The egalitarian value so much a part of the national culture did not translate to the country's largest and most popular sport. In 2014 the AFL broke new ground with the employment of the first, elite female coach. The core values synonymous with the popular and financially successful heritage sport of 'footy' were again challenged. Victorian, Peta Searle, became a specialist coach for Melbourne AFL team Saint Kilda. Her 'rise' through the AFL ranks was distinctive and not without critics. The sceptics voiced hesitation about whether a female could handle the physicality of AFL, its ego-driven playing stars, and the harsh critical analysis of its many thousands of fans, mainstream media authorities, and social media pundits. Such critics accepted that the game was 'owned by the people', but remained unable to accept that the game could be run by women at the elite level.

Searle rose to the position of Development Coach at Saint Kilda Football Club in 2014 after a successful stint at Victorian Football League (VFL) club, Port Melbourne from 2012. It was with Port Melbourne that a shift in cultural values and norms became most evident. Prior to her Port Melbourne appointment, Searle had produced five grand final successes in the Women's Football League. She also held a physical education teacher qualification. Comparing her career trajectory to the senior AFL ranks with Brisbane Football Club head coach, Justin Leppitsch, it becomes clear that the AFL and its clubs lionize past players rather than choose coaches with a steady track record. Leppitsch is a well-regarded AFL player who retired in 2006 and was immediately appointed Assistant Coach at the Brisbane Lions Football Club. In 2009 he moved to the Richmond Football Club as an assistant coach, but returned to The Lions in 2013 to assume the position of Head Coach on a three-year contract. Of the current AFL head coaches, three have less than three years of coaching experience. Searle's rise highlights how the AFL socialization process has been an impediment to diversity and equality in the coaching ranks.

Changing cultural perceptions takes time, and for 'outsiders' like Searle, champions driving change play a pivotal role. Searle was well supported in her pursuit of a football coaching career by the head coach of Port Melbourne at the time, Gary Ayres. Ayres recognized Searle's coaching credentials, her formidable track record, and her drive to achieve at the highest level of the sport. With the support of club authorities, Searle was nurtured through the development process and effected a transformation of cultural values. However, even with support at the second tier of the competition, Searle was initially unable to secure a position in the elite AFL ranks, and for financial reasons resumed her previous employment as a teacher. The AFL acknowledged Searle as a talented coach but it took time for senior management and clubs to employ her as a fully fledged elite coach.

Although a traditional male dominated sport, the AFL has taken numerous steps in recent times to accommodate a changing environment that needs a more diverse and egalitarian culture to meet the needs and aspirations of their stakeholders. The AFL Community Program serves as a beacon for attracting a committed and diverse group of participants and employees. Searle's appointment at the highest level sends a clear message that a culture can evolve, be accountable to its stakeholders, and yet still remain strong and cohesive.

CASE STUDY QUESTIONS

1   In sport, historical organizational values underpin the cultural understandings sport participants infer from their sports. How would other sports that have a strong traditional culture respond to social changes such as the employment of non-traditional employees?

2   Identify the factors that influence the socialization processes at the AFL and build new values into the culture.

3   How does the AFL communicate its cultural values to its stakeholders?

CHAPTER 10

Financial management

OVERVIEW

This chapter introduces readers to the financial management function in sport organizations. Through the use of incidents and cases, a number of core accounting principles will be discussed. Special attention will be given to the budgeting process and the analysis of balance sheets, profit and loss statements, and cash flow statements, together with the key principles of sound financial management. Throughout the chapter reference will made to a range of accounting terms and financial management concepts. The overall aim is to have readers build a broad accounting vocabulary that will give them a basic level of financial literacy, which can, in turn, be used to better understand the administrative processes required to build a sport organization's financial viability.

After completing this chapter the reader should be able to:

- explain how sport has changed over the last 50 years, and what that means for the effective financial management of sport organizations;
- understand the importance of professional financial management in sport;
- identify the ways in which the financial operations of sport organization can be best reported;
- explain how assets are organized, and how they differ from liabilities;
- explain how profits and or surpluses are calculated for sport organizations, and the difference between operating profit and net profit;
- understand the importance of cash, and the use of cash flow statements to ensure ongoing liquidity; and
- explain how budgets operate and explain why they are crucial to effective financial management of sport organizations.

THE FINANCIAL EVOLUTION OF SPORT

As previous chapters have demonstrated, sport is now a sophisticated institution with an often complex legal and financial structure. It is in many respects a fusion of business and entertainment where the consumers are the fans and the players, the producers are the clubs, associations and leagues, and the distribution channels are the sport arenas and sport stadiums (Carter 2011; Foster et al. 2006; Gomes et al. 2010; Quinn 2009; Shropshire & Davis 2008; Smit 2007; Stewart 2007). Like all forms of business, sport organizations require a strong system of financial management to ensure their long-term sustainability. However, this has not always been the case, and sport around the world has gone through four phases of commercial and financial development over the last 50 years.

This metamorphosis of sport into a form of business, with its associated financial systems, begins in Phase 1 with sport as a recreational and cultural practice where sport organizations are rudimentary, their revenue streams are small, sport is played mainly for fun, and activities are organized and managed by volunteer officials. This model is often described as a kitchen-table approach to sport management, since the game is administered by a few officials making key decisions from a member's home. It has some strengths, since it not only ensures the involvement of grassroots players and members, and provides a strong local community club focus, but it also nurtures a strong set of values that centre on playing the game for its own sake, and the concomitant ideal of amateurism. At the same time, it perpetuates a simple system of management driven by an administrative committee made up of a few elected members and self-appointed officials. There is the president who is the public face of the club or association, and a secretary who keeps things ticking over by maintaining a member register and organizing others to manage teams, run events, and maintains the clubrooms and playing facilities. There is also a treasurer who looks after the financial affairs of the organization. The treasurer is more often than not unfamiliar with the theory and principles of accounting, but makes up for a lack of expertise with a mind for detail, and a desire to ensure receipts run ahead of expenses.

The second phase is commercialization, where more revenue streams are utilized, and both staff and players are paid for their services. Whereas the kitchen-table model depends on member subscriptions, player registration fees and social activities for their financial viability, the commercialized sport model uses sport's commercial value to attract corporate and other sponsors. In this phase, sports that have the capacity to draw large crowds increasingly understand that these crowds can be used to attract businesses who want to increase product awareness, secure a special and exclusive sales channel, or obtain access to a market segment that will be receptive to their product. Sport is still a recreational and cultural practice, where the sport's overall development is the primary goal, but there is also an emerging or secondary strategy that focuses on elite development and the building of pathways by which players can move to the premier league or competition.

The third phase is bureaucratization, where the structures of sport organizations become more complex, administrative controls are established, and functional specialization increases. This phase is heavily dependent upon its antecedent phase, since an effective bureaucracy requires additional resources. In this phase, club, league and association structures are transformed so as to include a board of directors whose prime responsibility is to set the strategic direction, and ensure compliance with government regulation. This then, establishes an organizational divide between the 'steerers' (the board) and the 'rowers' (the Chief Executive Officer and operational staff) who are expected to implement the board's plans and policies. In addition a business-like set of functions and processes are created, which are built around administrative support, marketing, finance, game development, coaching player development and the like. In this phase less management space is given to the sport-as-recreation-and-cultural-practice model, and more to the sport-as-business model.

The fourth and final phase is corporatization, where sport embraces the business model by valuing brand management as much as it does player and fan relations. Revenue streams are increasingly dominated by sponsorships and broadcast rights fees, merchandise sales are deepened, and managers adopt a more professional outlook where the need to secure a competitive edge overrules the desire to hold on to old traditions. This is the phase in which players become full-time employees, player associations are established to protect their interests, and the sport's governing bodies take on the role of employers. A formal industrial relations system is created that leads to detailed contractual arrangements, collective bargaining agreements and codes of conduct. The marketing process also becomes increasingly sophisticated as the sport club, association or league becomes a brand, members and fans become customers, sponsors become corporate partners, and the brand name and image is used to strengthen its corporate partner arrangements, and build up a merchandising arm.

This phase also features a move toward managerialism, whereby sport becomes more accountable to its stakeholders for its performance and use of resources. This is particularly evident in sport's relationship with government, where government funding becomes increasingly contingent upon sport meeting certain specific and agreed-upon outcomes. This focus on managerialism also leads to greater transparency through an emphasis on performance measurement. Under this framework it is no longer appropriate to only measure player performance, but also things like internal processes and efficiency, financial performance, market performance, employer, and in particular player behaviour, and even social responsibility.

The above forces make sport more complex to operate, and, as a result, sport organizations become generally more regulated. In some instances the regulations are initiated by government-framed legislation. Government controls include venue safety rules, anti-discrimination programs, and crowd control policies. In other instances the regulations are internally imposed. Internal regulation is highly visible within professional sport leagues and competitions, where player recruitment is governed by drafting rules, player behaviour is constrained by a combination of collective agreements and codes of conduct, salaries are set within a total wage ceiling, revenues are redistributed from the most wealthy to the most needy clubs and associations, and games are scheduled to ensure the lowest cost and greatest revenue. While this type of corporate regulation can be problematic because of its heavy emphasis on bureaucratic control and detailed performance measurement, it also ensures a disciplined system of management by creating a common purpose, setting a clear strategic direction and securing strong leadership (Beech & Chadwick 2013; Stewart 2007). A summary of each phase in the sport-as-business evolution is provided in Table 10.1.

TABLE 10.1 Sport as business: Evolutionary phases and features

	Values	Revenue focus	Structural focus	Management focus
STAGE 1 Kitchen table	Amateurism Volunteerism	Member funds Social club income	Management Committee	Sustaining operations
STAGE 2 Commercial	Viability of sport Member service	Gate receipts Sponsorship	Management portfolios	Marketing the club
STAGE 3 Bureaucratic	Efficient use of sport resources Accountability	Corporate income Merchandising	Divisions and departments	Improving club efficiency
STAGE 4 Corporate	Delivering outputs Building the brand	Brand value Broadcast rights	Board policymaking Staff operations	Increasing club value Regulating constituents

FUNDING SOURCES FOR SPORT

It is clear that the new business-based, corporate model of sport involves a significant expansion of income. However, it is important to not throw the baby out with the bath water, and so traditional forms of revenue have been maintained, although in a slightly more sophisticated form. Member fees are still important, as too are fundraising from social activities and gate receipts. However, as was touched upon previously, new and varied revenue streams have opened up over the last 30 years which have transformed sport and the way it operates (Foster et al. 2006; Szymanski & Kuypers 2000). The funding of sport organizations begs a number of questions, the main ones being listed here:

1   Where does the money come from?
2   Where is the money spent?
3   How are the movements of money monitored?

In answering these questions it is important to distinguish between funds that are used to create infrastructure and facilities, and funds for use in managing the day-to-day activities of a sport organization. So, there are two types of basic funding uses. The first is funds for investment in capital development, and the second is funds for recurrent and operating activities.

Capital funding

Capital funding, which is money to finance investment in assets, can come from a number of sources listed here:

1 Government grants which may be federal, state or local. The point to note is that there are differences between sports which reflect not only their scale of operation but also their likelihood of generating international success. Funding may also be subject to certain conditions being met, like adopting certain policy requirements or working within a legislative framework.

2 Loans and borrowing which could be short term (up to a year), or long term (up to 20 years). Loans and borrowings are known as debt finance. The points to note are that it provides ready cash for investment in facilities and income-producing assets. On the other hand, it also incurs an interest burden, and may not always generate an increase in income.

3 New share issue or a public float which is known as equity finance. The points to note are that like borrowings, it provides ready access to cash, but unlike borrowing does not impose the burden of interest payment or repayment of the principle to lenders. However, it does hand over control to shareholders, and there is expectation that a dividend will be delivered.

4 Retained earnings, which is money reinvested in the sport organization. The points to note are there is no interest payment and control is retained over funds used. For nonprofit sport organizations, the retention of earnings is mandatory, since this is a legal requirement.

Recurrent funding

The recurrent funding of sport involves money to fund day-to-day operations, which comes from a variety of sources depending on the type of sport enterprise. The main revenue sources are briefly noted below, together with the strengths and weaknesses of each source:

1 Membership fees which may be full adult, associate, family and similar categories. The points to note here that they are usually upfront and relatively stable and therefore provide an immediate source of cash. Membership also serves a marketing function by establishing a core customer base.

2 Spectator admission charge which includes the categories of full adult, family, special groups and premium. The points to note are that while there is a high degree of flexibility it is subject to significant variation because of changing attendance patterns and differences in the scheduling of games.

3 Corporate facilities including boxes and hospitality. The points to note are that a large investment is required but the strengths are that business connections are made and premium rental can be charged.

4 Player fees and charges include entry fees, facility charge and equipment hire. The points to note here are that revenue is dependent on demand, and the user pays for the experience.

5 Special fundraising efforts are another source of recurrent funding and may include a dinner dance, rage-party, auction night, a trivia night and so on. The points to note here are that the burden is on staff and members to arrange and attend functions. However, these types of events can be profitable through large markups on food and drink.

6 Lotteries and gaming such as raffles, bingo and gaming machines. The points to note here are that permits are often required, margins are low, and there is solid competition from other venues.

7 Merchandising such as memorabilia, scarves, T-shirts, jackets and autographed equipment. The point to note here is that while it can produce a significant short-run increase in revenue, it can plateau out with a fall in on-field success.

8 Sponsorships and endorsement are another good source and may include naming rights, partnerships, signage, product endorsements and contra deals. However, the points to note are that the organization can lose control and become dependent on sponsor income and defer to their partners' demands.

9 Catering may include takeaway or sit-down food or drink. The point to note here is that it is labour intensive, but because it is delivered in a non-competitive environment higher profit margins can be sustained.

10 Broadcasting rights such as television and radio, and more recently internet and mobile phone streaming rights. The points to note are that it focuses on elite sports with a large audience base, and may be irrelevant for most sports associations and clubs. At the same time it provides the single largest revenue source for professional sport leagues.

11 Investment income such as interest earned and share dividends. However, the points to note are that share prices can vary at short notice, and losses can be made which increases the level of risk. In addition, interest rates may be low.

12 Government grants which may be federal, state or local. The points to note are that there are often marked differences between sports, they can vary from year to year, and, like government capital funds, are subject to certain conditions being met.

The expenses incurred in running a sport enterprise are also varied. They include:

1 Wages and salaries such as permanent, contract or casual administration staff and players. The points to note are that it is usually the largest expense item and is subject to inflation and competitive bidding as clubs aim to secure the best playing talent.

2 Staff on-costs, which include insurance, training, leave and superannuation. The points to note here are that they are legally required, ongoing, and linked to the employment contract.

3 Marketing costs include advertising, sales promotion, site visits, trade displays and give-aways. The point to note here is that it is easy to exceed budget estimates since there is always a tacit assumption that too much marketing and promotion is never enough.

4 Office maintenance includes power and light, phone and fax, postage and stationery and printing. The points to note here are that it is ongoing and tight control is required.

5 Venue maintenance includes the playing area, the viewing area and member facilities. The point to note here is that maintenance expenditure is ongoing and frequently absorbs a significant amount of revenue.

6 Player management includes equipment, clothing and footwear, medical services, fitness and conditioning, and travel. The points to note are that while they constitute an essential investment in improved performance, they also require tight budgeting.

7 Asset depreciation includes facilities, buildings, cars and equipment. The point to note here is that assets lose value and must be replaced. Also, depreciation is a non-cash expense, and it is essential that assets be amortized as expenses over their lifetime.

KEY FINANCIAL MANAGEMENT QUESTIONS TO ASK

At the same time, it is important to note that while significant segments of sport are now big businesses, most sport organizations are relatively small, and depend on the support of club members, volunteer officials, community businesses and local government to sustain their operations. While high profile professional sport leagues turn over hundreds of millions of dollars a year, the majority of sport clubs and associations are lucky to secure any more than a million dollars to fund their operations (Dolles & Soderman 2013; Quinn 2009). The majority of sport is really a form of small business. A suburban supermarket turns over more money than most sport clubs and associations.

However, no matter what the scale or size of sport organizations, they all need to be managed in a sound and responsible manner (Shibli & Wilson 2012). Many sport administrators do not feel comfortable handling money, or planning the financial affairs of clubs and associations, which often arises out of poor background knowledge and a lack of experience in managing complex financial issues. In practice, there are many straightforward, but essential financial questions that sport managers need to answer. They include:

1 What do we own?
2 What do we owe?
3 What did we earn?
4 What did we spend?
5 Did we make a profit?
6 Do we have enough cash to pay debts when they fall due?
7 How big is our interest bill?
8 Are we borrowing too much?
9 Did we improve upon last year?
10 How do we compare with other similar sport organizations?

UNDERSTANDING FINANCIAL INFORMATION

There is also the problem of making sense of the vocabulary of accounting. The distinction between assets and liabilities is mostly clear, with assets amounting to all those things we own, and liabilities being all those things we owe to others. However, the distinction between tangible and intangible assets and current and non-current liabilities may often be less clear. The concepts of owner's equity, shareholder's funds and net worth can also cause confusion, while further difficulties can arise when contrasting operating profit with net profit.

Consequently the effective management of any sport organization requires not only a sound knowledge of the principles of financial management, but also the support of a financial recording and reporting system that allows a quick and easy reading of clubs' or associations' financial health (Hart 2006; McCarthy 2007). It is now taken for granted that a professionally managed sport organization will produce three integrated annual financial reports. The first document is a statement of performance, or profit and loss, which reports on the revenues earned for the period, and the expenses incurred. The second document is a statement of position, or balance sheet, which reports on the current level of assets, liabilities and equity. The third document is a statement of cash flows, which identifies the cash movements in and out of the organization. The cash flow statement is divided into activities related to day-to-day operations, activities that involve the sale and purchase of assets, and activities that involve the securing and borrowing of funds and their repayment. The balance sheet, profit and loss statement, and cash flow statement are discussed in more detail below.

THE BALANCE SHEET

The balance sheet measures the wealth of a sport organization. Assets are placed on the left hand side of the balance sheet, while liabilities are placed on the right hand side. Proprietorship (also termed owners' equity, net worth or accumulated funds) is located on the right hand side, and represents the difference between assets and liabilities. The balance sheet gives a clear picture of a sport organization's wealth at a point in time by contrasting its assets (things it owns) with its liabilities (things it owes). The balance sheet also indicates how the assets of the organization have been funded. It can be through equity, (i.e. the capital of the owner/s), or from borrowed funds from some other organization or individual.

It is important to note that not all assets are the same. They can be broken down into a number of categories (Hoggett et al. 2006), as can liabilities. As a result a balanced sheet will be set up to provide a clear picture of the level of both current and non-current assets, and current and non-current liabilities. The level of owner's equity or shareholders' capital (or accumulated funds as it is usually called in nonprofit organization statements) will also be identified in the balance sheet since it is effectively the difference between the two. This is because assets can be accumulated through either the owner's capital, reinvested profits, or borrowed funds.

Assets

As noted above, assets are all those thing owned by an organization. To put it more technically, they constitute resources owned and controlled by an entity from which future benefits are expected to flow. The assets of a balance sheet are not only broken down into their various categories, but they are also listed according to their degree of liquidity, with the most liquid coming first and the less liquid coming later in the statement. The measure of an asset's liquidity is the ease with which it can be converted to cash, and all those assets which can easily converted are listed under the current assets heading. The most frequently cited current assets are cash in bank, accounts payable or debtors (which include those short-term invoices or bills for which payment has not yet been received), investments in the share market (which can be converted to cash through quick sale) and stocks of material and merchandise (which at a pinch can be sold for cash). Items like prepaid expenses (that is, bills paid in advance) can also be included here. The level of current assets is an important indicator of the financial health of a sport organization since it is the means by which bills are paid and creditors' demands for payment are met.

Assets are also listed as fixed or non-current. These assets include everything that cannot be easily and quickly converted to cash. Some stock and materials will be listed here when they do not have high turnover. The main items will be all those tangible or material assets that are essential for generating revenue, but are difficult to sell at an appropriate price in the short term. These items include office furniture and equipment (including all sorts of sports equipment), motor vehicles, buildings and land. Building improvements (e.g. a stadium upgrade) are also examples of fixed assets. The main categories of assets are listed in Table 10.2.

TABLE 10.2 Balance sheet: Asset categories

Asset category	Degree of liquidity	Example
Cash in bank	High (current)	Trading account balance
Accounts receivable	Medium (current)	Monies owed by club members
Prepaid expense	Medium (non current)	Payment of next year's insurance
Company shares	Medium (current)	Ownership of shares
Inventory	Medium (current)	Stock of sports equipment
Office equipment	Low (non-current)	Computer system
Other equipment	Low (non-current)	Office furniture
Motor vehicle	Low (non-current)	Ownership of vehicle
Property	Low (non-current)	Ownership of office building
Building improvements	Low (non-current)	Stadium renewal

The balance sheet of a sporting organization can be complicated by a number of other factors. For example, assets can either increase in value over time (i.e. appreciate) or decrease in value over time (i.e. depreciate). Property, stocks and shares, and various scarce artefacts and memorabilia are particularly prone to increase in value. On the other hand, there are other assets that can lose value quickly, and include those things that incur constant use and wear and tear, or become obsolete, or both. Moreover, there are assets that, while not tangible, clearly add value to the organization, and should be accounted for. Accountants have recognized these financial facts of life for many years, and have consequently devised strategies for managing these phenomena (Atrill et al. 2006).

Depreciation

Depreciation is based on the principle that all non-current assets represent a store of service potential that the organization intends to use over the life of the asset. Assets therefore have a limited life as a result of their ongoing wear and tear and probable obsolescence. Accounting for depreciation is the process whereby the decline in the service potential of an asset, such as a motor vehicle, is progressively brought to account as a periodic charge against revenue. That is, the asset is devalued in response to its purchase price or market value, and offset against income. In order to allocate the cost of the asset to the period in which it is used, an estimate must be made of the asset's useful life. This will usually be less than its physical life. For example, in the case of a motor vehicle, it may be decided that after three years it will not be operating as efficiently and therefore will be worth less after this period, even though it is still running. If an asset has a residual, or resale value, then this amount will be subtracted from the asset cost to establish the actual amount to be depreciated.

The simplest method for depreciating an asset is the straight line or prime cost method. This method allocates an equal amount of depreciation to each full accounting period in the asset's useful life. The amount of depreciation for each period is determined by dividing the cost of the asset minus its residual value by the number of periods in the asset's useful life. Take for example, a computer system that was purchased for $11,000. It is anticipated that the system will have a resale value of $1,000 after five years. Using the straight line method of depreciation the annual depreciation will be $2,000. This figure is obtained by dividing the difference between the purchase price and the residual value ($10,000) by the five years of anticipated useful life. This annual depreciation will then be posted as an expense in the profit and loss statement for the following five years. This process of spreading the cost of an asset over a specific period of time is called amortization. The idea behind this process is that there needs to be a clear way of showing the relationship between spread of benefits from an asset's use and the costs involved in creating those benefits.

Asset valuation

Asset values can also be changed to reflect current conditions and prices. Unless otherwise stated, assets are valued at their purchase price which is known as historical cost. However, many assets, particularly land and buildings, can increase in value over time. Unless this is periodically done, the true values of assets can be seriously understated. This problem can be overcome by a revaluation of the assets by a certified valuer, with a note to this effect accompanying the annual statement of financial operations and standing.

In Practice 10.1 Sport stadium asset management:
The case of Melbourne Cricket Club

Around the world there are many sport stadiums that have made a strategic decision to completely refurbish and redesign their facilities. Of course, we all know that this type of 'grand plan' comes at a cost. We also understand that the stadium owners and managers will be most often required to secure funds from external sources to make it all happen.

Take, for example the internationally famous and iconic Melbourne Cricket Ground (MCG), and its occupant, the Melbourne Cricket Club (MCC). In 2002 it decided to demolish its ageing stand and start again by putting up 'state of the art' facilities. But, to make all this happen it had to borrow a significant amount of money. In fact, its borrowings totalled well over AUS$300 million. In 2006, and just in time for the Commonwealth Games, it had spent all its borrowed money, but what it got in return was a scintillating bundle of world-class facilities. But, as we all know, when you borrow money you not only have to pay back the full amount you borrowed – which is commonly called the 'principal', but you also have to pay an annual interest charge. If we assume the annual interest charge is around 6 per cent, then in the first few years the total interest bill will be something in the order of AUS$204 million. This represents a serious drain on one's cash deposits.

This heavy repayment burden immediately raises the question as to just what benefits are going to accrue from this very big investment, and when it might be clear that the decision to borrow all this money was, in fact, a good one. And there is a risk that the repayment burden may be so severe that the ability to repay may be impossible.

But the MCC/MCG has a strong cushion against any cash flow problems. It is its 'membership'. It has many thousands of members, and is able to maintain a 20-year waiting list with virtually no promotional or marketing effort whatsoever. Moreover, it is Australia's premier sport stadium, and has no difficulty securing tenants, the main ones being the Australian Football League and Cricket Australia. And, to top it off, it regularly attracts 50,000 to 80,000 spectators to games. These strong attendance figures consequently enable it to

1 negotiate big catering and hospitality contracts;
2 hire out expensive corporate suites with no difficulty; and, finally,
3 secure big-brand advertisers to place signage around the ground.

The financial 'moral' to this story is short and sharp. It is that investing in expensive assets is a sound thing to do, but only if you are sure the assets can deliver the best quality services. If this eventuates then you can be confident that these services will generate sufficient additional revenue so that not only will all loans and interest bills be paid off, but that there will be a handsome surplus with which to undertake even further investments. If, on the other hand, the newly created assets are unable to deliver these benefits, the future will look very uncertain indeed. In the case of the MCC/MCG, it took a calculated risk, and reaped the rewards.

Liabilities

Simply put, liabilities are those things that an organization owes others. To be more exact, they are the present obligations of an entity which, when settled, involve the outflow of economic resources (Hoggett et al. 2006). Like assets, liabilities can be categorized into current and non-current. Current liabilities included monies that are owed to people in the immediate future for services and goods they have supplied. For example, a club may have purchased some sporting equipment on credit for which payment is due in 30 to 60 days. This is called accounts payable or debtors. Other current liabilities include short-term borrowings, member income received in advance, and taxes payable in the short term. Income received in advance is an interesting case because it is often intuitively viewed as revenue or asset and not a liability. However, under the accrual accounting model it is clearly not relevant to the current flows of revenue and expenses. But as monies received it has to be accounted for. So, what happens is that it is debited to cash in bank and credited as something we owe to members in the future. That is, it is a liability which is listed as income received in advance. Non-current liabilities include long-term borrowings, mortgage loans, deferred tax liabilities, and long-term provisions for employees like superannuation entitlements.

The accumulation of liabilities is not of itself a problem, so long as the debt is used to build income-earning assets. However, if increasing debt is associated with losses rather than profits, then the gap between assets and liabilities will increase. It is not uncommon in sport for clubs to have liabilities that exceed the value of their assets. As the major case study in this chapter indicates, hundreds of football clubs in Europe make losses, and a sizeable proportion of these loss-making clubs have more liabilities than assets. This situation is replicated in Australia where the net worth of some clubs in rugby and Australian Rules football is negative (that is, they have more liabilities than assets). In the long run these trends are unsustainable.

Balance sheets can say a lot about a sport organization's financial health. However, balance sheets do not tell us much about a sport club's earnings, profits and losses over the course of a month, quarter, or year. For this information we must turn to the profit and loss statement, or as it is often called in the nonprofit sector of sport, the income statement.

PROFIT AND LOSS STATEMENTS

It is not just a matter of examining a sport organization's assets and liabilities at a point in time in order to diagnose its financial health, it is also crucial to shift one's attention to the financial operation of sport clubs and associations over time (Atrill et al. 2006). The first thing to be said about the profit and loss statement is that it can go under a number of names. It can also be called an income statement, which is the nonprofit sector terminology, and is also referred to as a financial statement of performance. The point to remember about most sport organizations is that they do not focus on profits and losses, but rather surpluses and deficits (Anthony & Young 2003). In any case, it does not alter the fact that these statements look at the revenue earned during a period (say three or twelve months) and compare it with the expenses incurred in generating the revenue. Profit and loss statements are straightforward to compile, and moderately easy to understand, but there are some tricky areas that need to be discussed.

The first point to make is that while profit and loss statements contain many cash movements, they do accurately represent the total cash movements in and out of the organization, since they are essentially about earned income and incurred expenses. As a result they will include many transactions that do not include the movement of cash. In other words, revenue can be earned, while the cash may come much later. But it is still a revenue item that needs to be identified in the profit and loss statement. For example, a sport consulting business may have completed a strategic planning exercise for a large national sport association, and invoiced it for $50,000. If, at the end of the accounting period, the invoice has not been paid, it will still be included in the profit and loss statement as income. The adjustment or offset in the accounts will be an equivalent (i.e. $50,000) increase (or debit) in the accounts receivable asset account. If the invoice had been immediately paid, the adjustment would have been made as an increase (or debit) of $50,000 to the cash in bank asset account.

Revenue, or income as it is frequently called, is typically divided into operating and non-operating items. Operating items include all those revenues like member income and merchandise sales that provide the funds to support the day-to-day running of the club or association. Non-operating items include funds that are irregular, or even out of the ordinary. An asset sale, a special government grant or a large donation are examples of non-operating income. As noted in the early part of this chapter, sport organization revenues have expanded dramatically over recent years, but for the non-professional clubs the main sources are member fees, gate receipts, government grants, fundraising activities, and sponsors.

Expenses should also be treated cautiously. The profit and loss statement should include all incurred expenses rather than just paid expenses. Buying something on credit or by cash is an expense. On the other hand, paying for something that will not be used until next year, for example, should not be listed as an expense for the period under consideration. It is an asset (i.e. a prepaid expense). For example, rental or insurance paid in advance involves a movement of cash out of the club or association, but does not constitute an expense incurred for the current period.

Depreciation

Depreciation is another expense issue that has to be dealt with. And, to repeat, depreciation is an estimate of the wear and tear of working assets. In an office setting, computers are quickly depreciated for two reasons. First, they are heavily used, and second, they quickly become out of date and obsolete. Depreciation is therefore recognized as an expense and should be included in a profit and loss statement. Depreciation can be calculated in a number of ways, the most simple being the straight line method. If, for example, a motor vehicle is purchased for $30,000, has an estimated life of five years and no residual value, then the depreciation expense for the following five years will be $6,000 per annum. Some sporting club finance managers make the mistake of listing the full cost of the motor vehicle in year 1 as an expense, but this is clearly misleading. The correct way to treat this transaction is to list it as an asset, and then depreciate (i.e. amortize) it over its estimated lifetime. Interest-paid and interest-earned also appear on profit and loss statements. Interest paid will be classified as an expense while interest received will be classified as revenue.

Operating versus net profits

When analysing profit and loss statements it is also important to distinguish between operating profit (or surplus) and net profit (or surplus). The differences between these two terms comprise abnormal revenue and expenses, and extraordinary revenue and expenses. A transaction will be classified as abnormal if it is a regular occurrence, but in a specific case is significantly higher than normal. In the case of a sporting club an abnormal item might be an accelerated depreciation of office equipment, or a supplementary government grant. A transaction will be classified as extraordinary if it is a significant transaction, and does not regularly occur. A sporting club example includes fines for breaching salary cap regulations. (This happens frequently in the Australian Football League and the National Rugby League) or the sale of an asset (this occurs in the English Premier League where players can be traded under certain conditions).

Operating profit does not include the abnormal and extraordinary items, and is confined to those transactions that are directly related to day-to-day activities that regularly recur over the standard accounting cycle. So, operating profit is the difference between operating income and operating expenses. Net profit is something else again, and will take into account all abnormal and extraordinary items. If the sport club happens to be part of profit making entity, then it may be required to pay tax on its profits. This item will be subtracted from operating profit to get to a net profit figure.

Depreciation is also frequently listed as a non-operating item and can also make a significant difference to the level of profit. An operating profit can be transformed into a net loss by the inclusion of depreciation as a non-operating expense. Sometimes claims are made that depreciation can distort the real profit of a sport organization, but in fact the opposite is the case. Depreciation is a legitimate expense since it takes into account that amount of assets used up to generate revenue. In the context of the above discussion a typical profit and loss or income statement is illustrated in Table 10.3.

TABLE 10.3 Profit and loss statement template

Item	Amount ($)	Total ($)
Operating income		
Member fees	50,000	
Events	10,000	
Grants	30,000	
Total operating income		90,000
Operating expenses		
Administration	50,000	
Events	20,000	
Insurance	10,000	
Total operating expenses		80,000
Operating profit		10,000
Non-operating income		
Special government grant	10,000	
Non-operating expenses		
Depreciation	20,000	
Net profit		0

In Practice 10.2 The International Cricket Council

The international governing bodies for sport, otherwise known as International Sporting Organizations (ISOs), depend for their financial viability on the revenues they can secure from major sport events. One of the most highly credentialed ISOs which recently shifted its headquarters from London to Dubai in the Middle East is the International Cricket Council (ICC).

The ICC, which has 96 member countries, has traditionally run two major competitions, the World Cup and the Champions Trophy, both 50 over per team competitions. The World Cup was last run in 2011 and 2007, while the Champions Trophy was last run in 2009 and 2005. In recent times the ICC has conducted a 20–20 competition. The success of these events is immediately reflected in the sharp subsequent increases in the ICC's operating income. The ICC's financial indicators for 2007 and 2010 are listed in Table 10.4.

TABLE 10.4 Financial indicators for International Cricket Council

	2007	2010
	US$ million	US$ million
Operating income	273	77
Event income	260	75
Operating expenses	15	28
Cricket development	3	6
Total assets	151	190
Cash assets	120	40
Total liabilities	126	161
Current liabilities	125	160

Source: ICC Financial Statements 2007 and 2011

As this table starkly shows, the ICC depends for its financial strength on the revenue from its international tournaments. They generate enormous amounts of cash. This means that its revenues increase sharply just after a major event, but in the seasons between events, falls away appreciably. It is also important to note its surpluses are used to

1 fund the operations of its member nations;
2 promote the game around the world; and
3 assist national governing bodies develop the game locally.

CASH FLOW

We can now move on to the cash flow statement. It should be apparent that profit and loss statements do not give a clear picture of the movement of cash in and out of a sporting club or association. Cash flow statements aim to fill this gap by listing all movements of cash under three main headings. These headings are operating activities, investing activities and financing activities. The aim here is to get a picture of the net inflow and outflow of cash, and the extent to which a club or association is able to meet its cash payment obligations. This is an important issue, since without sufficient cash to pay bills when they fall due, there is the lingering possibility that creditors will take legal action to ensure payment. This may result in insolvency and bankruptcy.

The transactions that are included in the operating activity section include all those day-to-day activities that are required to keep the organization running. They include wages and salaries, (cash out) and payment for supplies (cash out) on one hand, and membership income (cash in) and government grants (cash in) on the other. Good financial management will aim to ensure that the cash coming from operating activities will exceed the cash going out, although a short-term net cash outflow may not be all that serious.

Investing activity transactions include all those things that involve the purchase and sale of assets. The sale of assets will be associated with cash inflow, while the purchase of assets will produce an outflow of cash. The purchase and sale of office equipment and property of various sorts will fall under the investing heading, and so too will the purchase and sale of stocks, shares and debentures. While the sale of assets can generate a quick supply of cash, it will also deplete the organization of income-earning resources, so a balance needs to be struck to ensure that crucial assets are not depleted. On the other hand, the purchase of assets immediately absorbs cash, and it is therefore important to monitor the amount of cash being used for this purpose.

Financing activities involve all those things that involve the procurement of equity and borrowing of funds on one hand, and the withdrawal of funds and repayment of borrowings on the other. An increase in cash holding can come from loans, bonds, mortgages, debentures and other borrowings, while a fall in cash holding will come from the repayment of loans and the redemption of debentures.

A cash flow statement provides a clear and concise picture of how cash is used internally, and where it goes externally. It also signals the level of liquidity and the ease with which cash payments are supported by cash reserves. A chronic net cash outflow on operating activities is cause for concern, since it is likely to lead to asset sales or borrowings being used to finance the cash deficit. And, as was noted previously, this can lead to a fall in club or association net worth, and threaten its long-term viability.

BUDGETING SYSTEMS

Budgeting is a crucial part of the financial management process (Hoggett et al. 2006; Wicker at al. 2010). It is one thing to construct some simple accounts and diagnose the financial health of sport clubs, associations and leagues. It is another thing to make sure resources are available for allocation to the various parts of their operations. No matter how wealthy a sport organization is, its resource base will always be limited, and decisions have to be made as to not only where the resources are allocated (facility maintenance, player salaries, coaching staff, equipment upgrade), but also how much each operational activity will receive. Moreover, budgets are finite, and the constraining factor will always be the amount of available funds.

Budgets are really financial plans that involve the allocation of funds to strategically important operations and activities. Budgets are essential for ensuring that costs and expenses are contained and do not exceed the planned revenue. Good budgets act as a constraint on spending, and also provide a clear picture of the anticipated sources of revenue. Budgets come in different shapes and forms but they all share the desire to control spending patterns and make sure the spending is grounded in an appropriate level of funding and financial backing.

Benefits of budgeting

A good system of budgeting is crucially important for sport clubs and associations. As already noted, the sport world has become increasingly complex, and the need to manage money effectively is stronger than ever. In addition a well-planned budget is the basis for efficient management and ensuring viability over the long term. The benefits of budgeting are many. They can

1 help anticipate the future and thereby assist the strategic planning process;
2 give a clear picture of resource needs and program priorities;
3 signal where there may be revenue shortfalls;
4 allow management to better manage and monitor spending;
5 communicate the club or association's financial plans to key stakeholders; and
6 enable precise measures of financial performance to be made.

Types of budgets

As already noted, budgets indicate the spending limits on different activities over particular periods. On one hand there is the operational budget (which is sometimes called a recurrent budget), and on the other hand there is the capital expenditure budget (which is sometimes called an investment budget). Whereas an operating budget refers to spending on the day-to-day operations of the sport club, association or league, a capital budget refers to spending on buildings, facilities and equipment, and other tangible assets.

Operating budgets

An operating budget is a statement of the anticipated levels of revenue for a period of time, and how the revenue will be spent. The figures are estimates only, since there will always be unforeseen circumstances that will change the financial parameters in which a club or association conducts its affairs. As a result, the financial projections that underpinned the budget figures may not be realized due to changing economic and social conditions. For example, a sponsor may want to renegotiate its agreement, membership income may fall because of poor on-field performance, and coaching and support staff costs may blow out because of an increased demand for skilled specialists.

An operating budget aims to accurately estimate the likely level of revenue that a club or association will have to play with, and the anticipated expenses associated with the earning of that income. For every sport club and association it is crucial to ensure that revenue and expenses will balance, and at best, work toward the generation of a healthy surplus. The following example in Table 10.5 illustrates what an operating budget will look like, and what items might be included.

TABLE 10.5 Sleepy Meadows Table Tennis Club: Operating budget

	First quarter ($)	Second quarter ($)	Third quarter ($)	Fourth quarter ($)	Year ($)
Revenue					
Donations	500			1,000	1,500
Sponsor	6,000				6,000
Member fees	1,400	200	200	200	2,000
Gaming	1,400	1,300	1,100	700	4,500
Total	9,300	1,500	1,300	1,900	14,000
Expenses					
General administration services	2,000	2,000	2,000	2,000	8,000
Coaching					0
Event administration		1,000	1,000		2,000
Travel		500	500	500	1,500
Table Tennis supplies	2,000				2,000
Total	4,000	3,500	3,500	2,500	13,500

The budget in Table 10.5 reveals a number of important things. First it identifies the main items of revenue and spending. Clearly, in this fictitious case, the Sleepy Meadows Table Tennis Club (SMTTC) is heavily dependent on the local sponsor which just so happens to be the main hotel in town. It also shows that the day-to-day administration expenses are significant, although it would be good to have a breakdown of this item, since it might reveal specific activities like marketing or office rental that need to be monitored. Second, it also shows when the revenue is earned and the expenses are being incurred. While this is a not a cash budget it does indicate possible times of cash flow problems. However, this is unlikely to be a problem here since most of the revenue is expected to arrive early in the year. The budget consequently allows the SMTTC to monitor the balance between expense commitments and revenue collections for different parts of the financial planning period.

Operating budgets can be organized in different ways as well. For example an operating budget may be structured as a line item budget which is illustrated above in Table 10.5. This involves breaking down spending and income into specific categories like administration, travel, marketing, and entertainment, and applying overall spending limits to each item. All of the different activities or programs in the organization will work to these limits. The SMTTC budget uses the line-item method in setting its forecast figures. At the same time, operating budgets can be re-jigged as program budgets or performance budgets.

RESHAPING BUDGETS

A budget can also be organized as a program budget. This involves allocating a designated amount of funds to each activity or program. Each program area is then allowed to spend on what they want, up to, but not beyond, the designated limit. For example the SMTTC may allocate funds to each of its junior, regional and veterans' league programs along the following lines of Table 10.6.

	Junior league program ($)	Regional league program ($)	Veterans league program ($)
TABLE 10.6 Sleepy Meadows Table Tennis Club: Program budget			
Budget	4,000	8,000	2,000

Each program manager can then decide how best to distribute the funds to each of its program activities. Program budgets can be converted into performance budgets without too much difficulty. The strength of a performance budget is that it links the budget to the club's or association's strategic plan. It forces the program manager to not only work within the budget parameters, but also ensure that the funds are directed to the achievement of relevant outcomes. In the case of the SMTTC a performance budget could take the following shape as indicated in Table 10.7.

TABLE 10.7 Sleepy Meadows Table Tennis Club: Performance budget

Junior league program	Regional league program	Veterans league program
Goal: to provide activities that attract young children to the club	Goal: to provide activities that attract quality players through access to elite competition	Goal: to provide activities that balance social and competition table tennis
Anticipated outcome: increase in registered juniors	Anticipated outcome: all teams finish in top half of league table	Anticipated outcome: viable competition
Budget ($)	Budget ($)	Budget ($)
4,000	8,000	2,000

In Practice 10.3 Budgeting for mega sport events: London 2012 Olympic Games and the 2010 Delhi Commonwealth Games

In 2005 London won the right to host the 2012 Olympic Games. The bid was impressive, and there is little doubt that the Games, as both a spectacle and as a major sporting event, were a raging success. By all accounts the massive urban renewal program that accompanied the London Games project provides for significant commercial and social benefits. However, it was never clear as to whether it would be a financial success. Like all bids before it, the London Bid Committee created a budget that quickly escalated in size.

In the initial draft bid document of 2003, the costs of staging the London Games were estimated to be just under £2 billion, which by previous Games standards was significant, and certainly in excess of the Sydney Games. In 2006 the budget was re-set at around £3.5 billion. However, in 2007, the Minister for the Olympics, Tessa Jowell, announced an updated budget of £9.3 billion. This was a massive increase, and it raised the questions of

1 just what capital and operating activities the budget would cover;
2 what specific costs had been identified, or not identified; and
3 why they had escalated so much in such a short space of time.

While the then Mayor of London, Ken Livingstone, optimistically confirmed that the Games Organising Committee would aim to make a profit, there was growing concern that the Games budget was spiralling out of control.

As it turned out, the London Games came in just over the adjusted budget of £9.3 billion, but it was still a massively expensive event to organize, facilitate and run. To make the London Games happen, around £1 billion was spent on security, be it civilian or military. Just under £2 billion was spent on preparing the Olympic Park site, while another £1 billion was spent on creating a user-friendly park once the Games had been completed and the Games experience was a distant memory. And, this doesn't even include the facility construction costs or the operating costs.

The escalating costs of running the Olympic Games were starkly revealed soon after Tokyo was awarded the right to host the 2020 Games. Hakubun Shimomura, the Minister for Education, Sports and Finance, proudly announced that the showpiece of the Games would be an 80,000-seat stadium that would double as a major public art-work. But when it was stated that the stadium would cost 130 billion yen, or almost US$1.3 billion, enormous criticism erupted, with local architects claiming the project was indefensible, even if the stadium became an international design masterpiece. Even when the Olympics are involved, there are financial limits to be observed.

The 24th Commonwealth Games, succinctly known as CWG 2010, were held in Delhi, India, in October 2010. It was the first time that the Commonwealth Games were held in India and the second time it was held in Asia, with Kuala Lumpur, Malaysia's capital city, having staged the festival in 1998. Just over 6,000 athletes from 71 nations competed in 21 sports and 272 events. It was big, and in fact was the largest international multi-sport event ever to be staged in India, eclipsing the Asian Games of 1951 and 1982.

While the opening and closing ceremonies were successfully delivered at the Jawaharlal Nehru Stadium, it was generally agreed that there were many organizational teething-troubles during the early stages of the Games. Crowds were also very thin during the first week of the Games. Despite these problems the Games were enjoyed by not only most of the people who attended, but also by the athletes themselves. The television broadcasts were professionally produced, and the events themselves were often quite memorable, with many outstanding individual results.

As is always the case with these types of events, the initial total budget estimates by the Indian Olympic Association in 2003 for hosting the Games were highly optimistic at around US$360 million. This was quite a conservative figure for such a big event – and for some critics, frighteningly low – but it was considered reasonable in view of India's world-renowned capacity to deliver solid results with meagre resources. However, by 2006, the event budget had escalated and projections at the time reached US$1.4 billion, nearly a four-fold increase. A report of the Standing Committee on Human Resource Development provided a revised budget breakdown, and the following figures were published:

- the conduct/operation of the games would now cost US$200 million;
- the Games Village would now cost US$220 million;
- venue infrastructure, but without furnishing, was now set at US$380 million;
- civil infrastructure came in at US$294 million; and
- the Indian contingent's training program would cost US$70 million.

In early 2010 another review found that the Games budget was out of control, and had increased exponentially. Many explanations were given for the blow-out, and included things like

1   there was a bout of steep inflation;
2   all the projects had been delayed;
3   waste and inefficiencies were the rule rather than the exception; and
4   some projects had been mismanaged.

It was also hinted that some additional 'shadowy' practices – that is, bribery – had occurred, but they were largely anecdotal. In a climate of high anxiety the following points were noted:

- The Commonwealth Games Village, which had an initial 2003 budget estimate of US$100 million, was now about US$230 million. In addition capital losses had occurred because many apartments remained unsold, and the Indian Government was forced to buy them off contractors.
- The budget for 11 stadiums was US$280 million in 2003, but in the space of seven years had risen to US$1.2 billion. Construction was also way behind deadline, which was another concern that had to be monitored.
- Work on road flyovers were altered mid-way, and new unplanned additions had to be made. The budget for this item came in at US$380 million.
- Street-scaping was another unplanned expenditure with a budget of US$250 million.
- Security, too – and not surprisingly – had been allocated additional expenditure with a revised budget of US$80 million.
- In the light of frequent delays, event planning also suffered. What was estimated to cost US$240 million in 2003, now had a budget estimate figure of US$550 million.

As the Games approached, the official total budget – which took into account both capital and operating items – accelerated to an estimated US$2.6 billion, a figure which had crucially excluded non-sports-related infrastructure development. The American publication *Business Today* reckoned this was hopelessly conservative, and claimed that the Games actually cost US$13.3 billion, when all the related urban renewal projects had been included. Whatever the precise number was, it was agreed that the 2010 Delhi Commonwealth Games were probably the most expensive ever, and reached a figure that was never envisaged. So why did things go so horribly wrong?

In the first place, the organization of CWG 2010 was beset by delays. In January, 2010, the Indian Olympic Association vice-chairman Raja Randhir Singh expressed concern that Delhi was not up to speed in forming and organizing its Games Committee. And, following a 2009 Indian Government report showing two thirds of venues were behind schedule, the Commonwealth Games Federation president Mike Fennell stated that the slow progress constituted a serious risk to the whole event. Singh also called for a revamp of the Games Organising Committees. A.K. Walia, the Indian Finance Minister also noted that so many things had come at the last moment, and cited the 'street-scaping project as a case in point'. He went on to say that while the Indian Government was looking at international sporting events as a chance to increase their urban infrastructure, it had actually resulted in several projects being approved which had no direct relation to the Games, but which had in fact been included in the budget allocation. In addition, all of this was framed by allegations of long delays, and chronic corruption amongst many of the event planners and organizers. It was a very bad 'gig' indeed!

But, even more to the point, why is there a budget blow-out at nearly every modern-day mega sports festival? Are the people drawing up the budget estimate incompetent, or are they so optimistic that they cannot face the reality of a high cost operation? Or, alternatively, do they decide that escalating costs is part of the essential nature, or, indeed, the embedded character of the mega-sport-event 'beast', and that it just cannot be controlled, whatever is done?

SUMMARY

The above discussion of sport finances demonstrates that sound financial management is essential for the ongoing viability of sport organizations. The importance of having a proper system of financial planning, record keeping, monitoring and evaluation becomes increasingly crucial as sport becomes more commercialized and corporatized. A basic starting point is to identify the different ways in which funds can be raised to underwrite the operation of a sport club, association, event or league. It is also essential that sport managers be able to design detailed budgets that provide transparent information that makes it clear as to not only what an activity, program or event will cost to mount and operate, but also where the money will be coming from. It is equally important for sport managers to be able to understand financial statements, use them to diagnose the financial health of a club association, event or league, and subsequently manage costs and revenues to ensure a regular surplus or profit. It is particularly important to be able to distinguish between the different ways of measuring surpluses and profits, and, in particular, the difference between operating and net profit.

REVIEW QUESTIONS

1 Identify the different commercial stages sport has gone through in the last 50 years, and the implications it has for sport's financial operations.

2 Explain the essential features of corporate sport, and what makes it increasingly challenging to manage it from a structural and financial perspective.

3 Why are budgets so fundamental to the effective management of sport clubs, associations, events and leagues?

4 Distinguish between a capital budget and an operating budget.

5 Balance sheets are important tools for monitoring and measuring the financial health of a sport organization. What comprises a balance sheet, and what does it measure?

6 Identify the main asset categories of a professional sport club, and explain under what circumstances players can be treated as assets.

7 Identify the main liability categories of a professional sport club, and explain under what circumstances long-term borrowings can be seen as either a drain on resources, or alternatively a crucial means of generating revenue and profits.

8 Surpluses and profits are important to the long-term development of sport organizations and clubs since they indicate that not only were all costs covered for the period under consideration, but that there are funds available for reinvestment in the club's or association's future activities and programs. What is required for profits and surpluses to be generated, and under what circumstances can an operating profit end up leading to a net loss.

9 What is the easiest way of distinguishing a wealthy sport organization from a poor sport organization?

10 What must a sport organization do if it aims to increase its wealth and financial health over the long term?

FURTHER READING

The four-phase model of sport's economic and financial development was first developed by Bob Stewart in Stewart, B (ed.) (2007). *The Games are Not the Same: The Political Economy of Football in Australia.* Carlton: Melbourne University Press, pp. 3–22.

For an extensive discussion of the finances of North American professional sport leagues see Howard, D. and Crompton, J. (2004). *Financing Sport.* 2nd edn. Morgantown, WV: Fitness Information Technology. This book provides a chapter-by-chapter breakdown of revenue sources, with special attention to ticket sales and broadcasting rights' fees. See also Foster, G., Greyser, A. and Walsh, B. (2006). *The Business of Sports: Texts and Cases on Strategy and Management.* Mason, OH: Thompson South-Western.

One of the most detailed analyses of English Premier League finances is contained in Szymanski, S. and Kuypers, T. (2000). *Winners and Losers: The Business Strategy of Football.* London: Viking. See also Carter (2011) for a lot of interesting updates on the financial structure of big time commercialized sport.

For a simple introduction to the structure and function of balance sheets and profit and loss statements and cash flow statement see Hart, L. (2006). *Accounting Demystified: A Self Teaching Guide.* New York: McGraw Hill. For a more detailed and technical review of financial statements and what they say, see Hoggett, J., Edwards, L. and Medlin, J. (2006). *Accounting.* 6th edn. Milton: Wiley. See also Atrill, P., McLaney, E., Harvey, D. and Jenner, M. (2006). *Accounting: An Introduction.* Frenchs Forest, NSW: Pearson Education Australia. For a succinct discussion of financial statements of non-profit organizations see Anthony, R. and Young, D. (2003). *Management Control in Non-profit Organizations.* 7th edn. New York: McGraw Hill.

RELEVANT WEBSITES

- For details of Manchester United FC financial position and the general financial operations of the English Premier League, see www.footballeconomy.com/stats2/eng_manutd.htm.
- For more details on the financial operation of the International Cricket Council see www.icc-cricket.com/about/111/publications/overview. Then click on 'annual reports' to secure finance details.
- To secure a detailed evaluation of the London Olympic Games budget see the National Audit Office (NAO) report at www.nao.org.uk/report/the-budget-for-the-london-2012-olympic-and-paralympic-games
- For an alternative assessment of the London Olympic Games budget, with a breakdown of the costs of various venues, see https://uk.eurosport.yahoo.com/news/london-2012-final-cost-london-2012-games-revealed-135956051.html

CASE STUDY 10.1

More rules required! UEFA Financial Fair Play Regulations

UEFA (the Union des Associations Européennes de Football) is the governing body of European football. It was established in 1954, and now represents the interests of 25 national football authorities. According to the EUFA website it has 'grown into the cornerstone of the game on this continent, working with and acting on behalf of Europe's national football associations and other stakeholders in the game to promote football'. It has thus become the 'guardian' of football in Europe, 'protecting and nurturing the well-being of the sport at all levels, from the elite and its stars to the thousands who play the game as a hobby'.

Financial integrity is an especially important image to have since it affects the capacity of sport enterprises to secure funds, maintain sound credit ratings, build public trust, and maintain community goodwill. Financial integrity can be viewed from a number of angles, but first and foremost it is essentially about taking the stance that transparency, openness, public disclosure, and professional scrutiny are good things. The problems that are associated with secrecy and cover-ups has led many of sport's governing bodies – with UEFA being a good example – to apply the idea of 'fair play' to its club-licensing arrangements.

The belief that sporting enterprises must meet some sort of minimum financial reporting standard was confirmed in 2010 when 372 of Europe's of most prominent clubs (which is 65 per cent of the total number of prominent clubs), had made aggregated losses of just over €2 billion (Muller et al. 2012, pp. 119–120). The data also showed that 195 top-flight clubs reported average losses of 20 per cent. That is, for every dollar of income earned, there was a dollar and twenty cents spent on some other item. Additionally, 237 of Europe's top-division clubs had accumulated negative equity, which meant they had more debts than assets. The other cause for concern was that many of the loss-making clubs were also very wealthy. So, while they had lots of assets and huge revenue streams, they also had large debt levels and exponentially increasing expenses.

Italian football had been under additional stress. In 2010 most clubs reported losses over the previous season, with the most serious problems experienced by A.C. Milan (€70 million), Genoa (€17 million) and Fiorentina (€10 million). In addition Inter Milan had accumulated losses of just over €1 billion over the previous 15 years, while Lazio was part way through repaying a €140 million overdue tax bill. Only eight clubs were able to deliver a profit during the 2010–2011 season. Overall, the Italian Serie A League (the premier Italian competition) had incurred a cumulative net loss of €428 million, while incurring negative equity (that is, an excess of liabilities over assets) of €204 million.

According to the Deloitte Finance group, the financial problems in Italian football worsened in 2011 and 2012. Club match-day revenues declined by €6 million (around 3 per cent) to €191 million which was driven in large part by a 7 per cent fall in average league match attendances to 22,000. By European elite football league standards this was critically low. In contrast, the German Bundesliga attracted average crowds of just under 40,000. Italian football clubs were also becoming heavily dependent on television broadcast rights fees, and most Serie A clubs had 50 per cent of their revenue coming from 'TV money'.

These exceedingly poor financial results, especially when they are covered up or selectively released, not only dented the sport's reputation, but also led to a loss of public confidence. In response to these unflattering outcomes UEFA introduced a bundle of Financial Fair Play regulations (FFP). The FFP rules had the overarching goal of protecting the long-term viability and sustainability of European club football. This feeds into two subsidiary goals which are to first, ensure the smooth running and integrity of the competition, and second, protect the participating clubs' creditors, which begins with players and administrative staff as a priority, and then includes other clubs, suppliers, corporate partners, ground managers and the like. The following operating objectives then fall out of these goals:

- Encourage sensible long-term financial planning.
- Limit the amount of debt that is accumulated.
- Encourage clubs to spend no more than they make in income, which means adopting a 'break-even' rule.
- Encourage clubs to settle their debts – especially short-term ones like player and staff benefits – on time.
- Stop excessive transfer fees and salary payments.
- Promote investment in youth development.
- Promote additional investment in infrastructure, especially training grounds and stadiums, and player development programs.
- Ensure clubs are more transparent in their dealings with stakeholders and desist from engaging in financial 'foul play'.

There are signs that clubs are reining in their spending, and reducing debt levels. However, it is too early to tell just how effective the FFP rules are in stabilizing the financial operations of European professional clubs.

CASE STUDY QUESTIONS

1 What is the major financial problem facing many European professional football clubs?
2 What is causing this problem?
3 Is it is a revenue shortfall, or is it over-spending, or is it a combination of both?
4 Is there a problem with Italian football?
5 Is it a debt problem with Italian football, or is it a revenue problem?
6 Is there a debt problem?
7 What is UEFA doing to sort out this problem?
8 Is it working?

CASE STUDY 10.2

No accounting for success: Portsmouth Football Club and the USA Girl Scout Movement.

PREAMBLE

As we have noted throughout this book, large slabs of sport have become complex commercial industries employing thousands of staff and building lucrative partnerships with corporate giants and national television networks. It would therefore be reasonable to expect most professional sport enterprises to 'make ends meet' without too much difficulty. At the same time we should not be surprised to see not-for-profit service organizations struggling to meet the demands of its members, and 'keep afloat' financially speaking. However, as the following cases show, the opposite has occurred. Thus, the obvious question that follows is why can this happen, and how can it be explained?

PORTSMOUTH FOOTBALL CLUB

Portsmouth Football Club (PFC) is a professional football club based in the city of Portsmouth, on the south coast of England. The club was established in 1898, and the inaugural chairman was John Brickwood, owner of the local Brickwoods Brewery. Portsmouth won the first division premiership twice, once was in 1949 and again in 1950. The club has also won the FA Cup on two occasions. The first win was in 1939, while the second win was in 2008. PFC has never been in the elite group of English professional football clubs, but neither has it been a perennial loser.

It therefore came as a surprise that soon after its 2008 FA Cup victory, the club's financial affairs were found to be in disarray. In 2009, it was announced that the club had failed to pay the players for more than two months. There was also a problem with player payments in early 2010, but despite this looming crisis, the club won as many games as it lost. Things came to a head after Manchester United Football Club and the Revenue and Customs Office (HMRC) filed a winding-up petition against Portsmouth in the High Court in London for the non-payment of debts. While the petition was withdrawn, it was revealed that the club had total debts of more than £70 million. Meanwhile HMRC re-submitted its winding-up petition in order to secure at least part of its unpaid taxes.

Portsmouth went into administration, which meant that the club had to be wound up, its assets liquidated, and its creditors paid out in line with the cash available. The major debts it had to service were two-fold. There were the football-related debts on one hand, and commercial debts on the other:

Football debts
- Transfer fees – £17 million
- Players' bonuses – £1 million
- Players' image rights – £1 million
- Employee Benefit Trust – £2 million

Commercial debts
- Trade creditors – £2 million
- Agents and scouting fees – £9 million
- HM Revenue and Customs – £17 million
- Pension arrears – £250,000
- Loans (unsecured) – £36 million

PFC tried its best to get all the cash it needed to pay its debts, but it was not enough. It sold its players, and in one instance it secured £2 million for Kevin-Prince Boateng in a transfer deal with Genoa Football Club, but it only filled a small part of the debt gap.

In 2010 the club's income was just under £22 million, but only £3 million came from ticket sales. Around £7 million came from the sale of players, which is a one-off revenue gain. In addition, expenses exceeded revenue, with player payments, administration expenses, and taxes and charges adding up to £19 million. The whole enterprise was unsustainable.

And, to make matters even worse, the club's asset base had shrunk dramatically as it entered 2011. They were as follows:

- Freehold property – £7 million
- Leasehold properties – £100,000

- Player registrations – £4 million
- Chattels – £500,000
- Stock – £100,000
- Foreign player sales monies – £4 million

The future for PFC is very bleak indeed.

GIRL SCOUTS USA

The Girl Scout movement has a long history, but not quite as long PFC. It was founded in 1912 by Juliette Gordon 'Daisy' Low, who assembled a 'Troop' of 18 local girls in Savannah, Georgia in the USA. She wanted to take girls out of the narrow confines of the home and domesticity, and lead them into the outdoors, and in doing so provide them with a variety of 'enriching experiences'. Her aim was to use these experiences – which included field trips, sports skill-building clinics, community service projects, and environmental stewardships – to make her 'girls' grow into 'courageous and strong' adults.

Today, the Girl Scout mission is to help girls develop their full individual potential; relate to others with increasing understanding, skill, and respect; develop values to guide their actions and provide the foundation for sound decision-making; and contribute to the improvement of society through their abilities, leadership skills, and cooperation with others.

These are very ambitious goals, but there is a lot evidence to say that millions of young girls have, over many years, found their scouting experience to be both highly enjoyable and often transformative. Girl Scouts USA (GSUSA) now has a membership of more than 3 million girls and adults. And, overall, just over 59 million women in the USA today were once Girl Scouts.

While both PFC and GSUSA have physical activity and the outdoors as common features, in other respects they are poles apart. And, surprisingly one of these differences centres on their financial affairs. Unlike PFC, GSUSA has a very healthy balance sheet and generates a very strong flow of annual revenue. A snapshot of its 2012 financial performance is provided below.

Operating revenues – US$129 million, including

- Memberships – US$37 million
- Merchandise sales – US$28 million

Operating expenses – US$128 million, including

- Service delivery – US$33 million
- Program development and training – US$26 million
- Management and administrative support – US$16 million

Non-operating revenue – US$1.5 million, including

- Endowments – US$1 million

Assets – US$186 million, including

- Cash – US$20 million
- Investments –US$126 million
- Property and equipment – US$20 million
- Stock – US$12 million
- Accounts receivable – US$6 million

Liabilities – US$61 million, including

- Staff pensions – US$36 million
- Accounts payable – US$10 million
- Deferred revenues – US$13 million

CASE STUDY QUESTIONS

1 How did PFC get itself into so much financial difficulties?

   What was the fundamental cause of the problem?

2 What could PFC have done to extricate itself from the problem?

3 Why does the PFC problem occur in so many other mid-range professional football clubs?

4 How does GSUSA compare with PFC?

5 How do you explain the financial stability of GSUSA?

6 How do you see the financial future of GSUSA?

7 Which organization has the most promising future, and why?

CHAPTER 11

Sport marketing

OVERVIEW

The principles and tools of sport marketing are essential knowledge for sport managers to be able to position their sport club, player, code or event in the highly competitive sport market. This chapter examines the marketing of sporting organizations, sport leagues and codes, players and athletes, sporting equipment and merchandise, and sporting events. The purpose of this chapter is to overview the key concepts of sport marketing, with special emphasis on the process of sport marketing as outlined in the Sport Marketing Framework provided.

After completing this chapter, the reader should be able to:

- explain the key concepts of sport marketing;
- describe the process of sport marketing using the steps of the Sport Marketing Framework;
- define the role of strategy, positioning and branding in sport marketing; and
- understand how to deploy the sport marketing mix.

DEFINING SPORT MARKETING

Marketing generally refers to the process of planning and implementing activities that are designed to meet the needs or wants of customers with particular attention on the development of a product, its pricing, promotion and distribution. Marketing seeks to create an exchange, where a customer or consumer relinquishes money for a product or service that they believe is of equal or greater value. Sport marketing is focussed on satisfying the needs of sport consumers, or those people who use sport-related goods or services through playing sport, watching or listening to sport, buying merchandise, collecting memorabilia or using sporting goods. There are two dimensions to sport marketing: the marketing *of* sports and marketing *through* sports. The first dimension is the marketing *of* sport products and services directly to consumers such as sporting equipment, professional competitions, sport events and facilities, and recreational clubs.

The second dimension involves the marketing of other, non-sport products and services *through* sport. Some examples include a professional athlete endorsing a food or fashion brand, a corporation sponsoring a sport event, or even a drinks manufacturer arranging to have exclusive rights to provide their products at a sport event.

In order for a sport organization to be successful, it must mean something to sport consumers. In practice, this demands that a consumer is aware of the sport organization, its brand, and the products or services it offers, and has responded to them in a positive way. The process of cultivating such a response is known as branding, and when a sport brand has carved out a firm place in the market and in consumers' minds, then it is said that it is positioned. The consequence of successful branding and the acquisition of strong market positioning is an ongoing relationship between a sport brand and its users.

Sport marketing is therefore best understood as the process of planning how a sport brand is positioned, and how the delivery of its products or services are to be implemented in order to establish a relationship between a sport brand and its consumers. This may be achieved by the marketing *of* a sport brand, or marketing *through* a sport brand.

THE SPORT MARKETING FRAMEWORK

The Sport Marketing Framework puts the sport marketing definition into practice by providing an approach to meeting sport consumers' needs. The Framework outlines a step-by-step process for planning and implementing the key principles of sport marketing. The Sport Marketing Framework involves four stages:

1   identify sport marketing opportunities;
2   develop a sport marketing strategy;
3   plan the marketing mix; and
4   implement and control the strategy.

Stage 1 of the Sport Marketing Framework – identify sport marketing opportunities – involves analysing the conditions of the external marketplace, considering the conditions within the sport industry specifically, and examining the activities of competitors. This stage also involves studying the internal capabilities of a sport organization by identifying its goals and limitations. Finally, in order to identify marketing opportunities, it is necessary to collect information about market circumstances with a particular emphasis on existing customers and other potential consumers. After all of this information has been collected and analysed, Stage 2 of the Framework – develop a sport marketing strategy – may be undertaken. Stage 2 involves determining the direction of the sport marketing program, taking into account what was learned during stage one. It is important at this stage to document the strategy with both objectives and performance measures in order to keep it on track, and ultimately to evaluate whether the strategy was successful. Once the direction is set, the specific tactics of the strategy can be specified revolving around how to distinguish or 'differentiate' the sport organization's brand and products in the market, deciding on to whom the strategy is targeted (segmentation), and what marketing mix (the product offering, pricing strategies, promotional strategies and distribution systems) will be employed. Stage 3 of the Framework involves the precise determination of the sport marketing mix and how they will combine to achieve the strategy set out. Finally, Stage 4 – implement and control the strategy – involves measuring outcomes and taking remedial action so that the plan stays on target. Figure 11.1 provides an illustration of the Sport Marketing Framework.

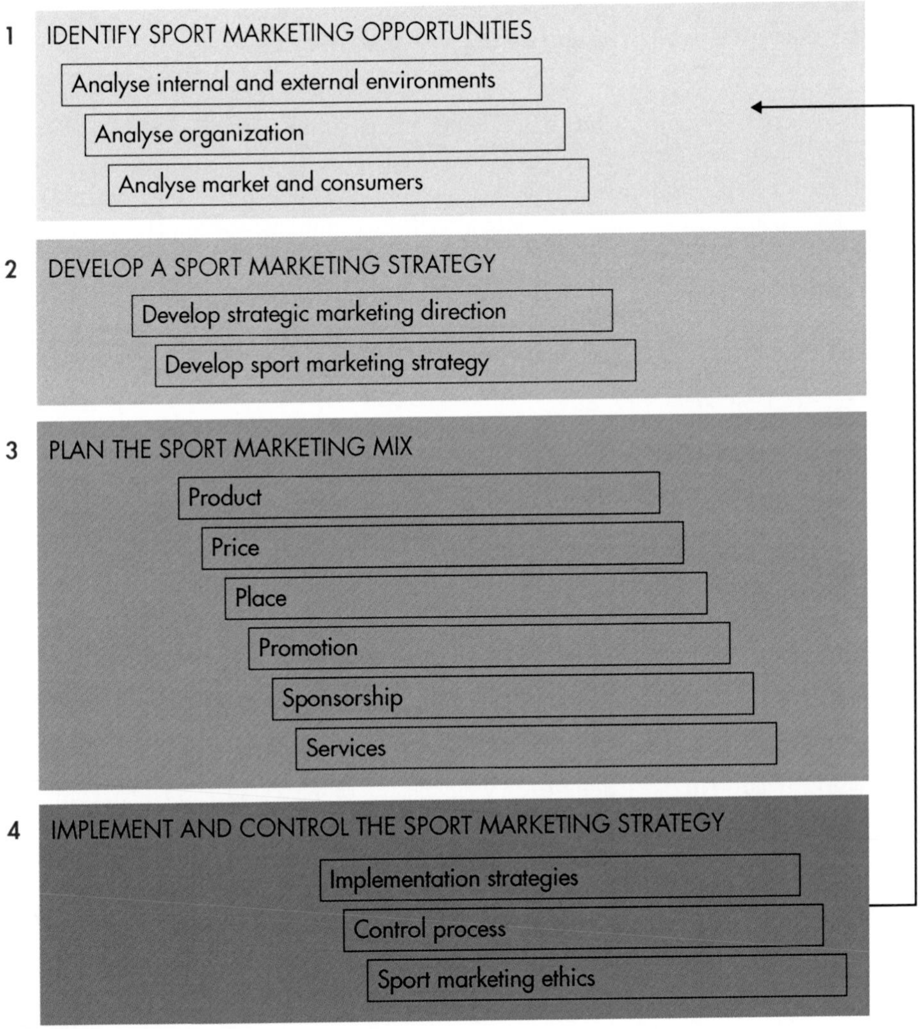

FIGURE 11.1 The Sport Marketing Framework

STAGE 1: IDENTIFY SPORT MARKETING OPPORTUNITIES

This step shows that it is important to collect information and conduct research before introducing sport marketing activities. It is essential to know what opportunities exist in the marketplace, what competitors are doing, what can be delivered, and what consumers actually want. Identifying sport marketing opportunities involves three elements:

1 analysing the internal and external environment;
2 analysing the organization; and
3 analysing the market and consumers.

Analyse the internal and external environment

The first element in identifying sport marketing opportunities involves assessing the internal and external environments of the sport organization. The internal environment refers to the conditions in which a sport organization undertaking the marketing process is placed. The external environment refers to the market in which the sport organization is operating, including the broad national/global environment, the sport industry and the sport organization's competitors. There are five main tools for conducting an internal and external analysis:

1 SWOT analysis;
2 competitor analysis;
3 five forces competitor analysis;
4 organizational analysis; and
5 market and consumer research.

Given that these aspects of internal and external analysis overlap with those conducted for any strategic planning and are covered in more detail in Chapter 5, they will only be mentioned briefly here.

The term SWOT is an acronym for the words strengths, weaknesses, opportunities, threats. The SWOT analysis can be divided into two parts. The first part represents an internal analysis of an organization, which can be summarized by its strengths and weaknesses. Strengths are those things an organization does well and weaknesses are the things an organization finds difficult to do well. The second part of the SWOT technique is concerned with external factors, or opportunities and threats. Opportunities could include environmental situations used to the organizations' advantage. The SWOT analysis influences what a sport organization is capable of achieving in their marketing plan and highlights potential areas in which there might be an opportunity.

A competitor analysis focuses on the external environment by revealing opportunities or threats associated with other organizations in the same marketplace. A competitor analysis should examine several kinds of competitors: *direct* competitors who produce a similar product or service; *secondary* competitors who sell substitute products that meet similar customer needs but in a different way; and *indirect* competitors who sell different products and services altogether that might satisfy consumers' needs. A competitor analysis should consider a wide range of variables, including their strategies, strengths, vulnerabilities and resources, as well as their next likely actions.

In addition to conducting a competitor analysis, it is possible to conduct a five forces analysis that focuses on five forces driving competition in the sport industry. It is used to help work out whether the industry is an attractive one to conduct business in, and whether there is scope for existing or new products to be developed. The five forces are described in detail in Chapter 5.

Analyse the organization

The second component of Stage 1 involves understanding the purpose, aims and goals of the sport organization developing the plan, as well as understanding the needs of its stakeholders. The first three of these elements can be determined by locating (or if necessary developing) the mission statement, vision statement and objectives of the sport organization. More about these can be found in Chapter 5.

Stakeholders are all the people and groups that have an interest in a sport organization, including, for example, its employees, players, members, the league, association or governing body, government, community, facility-owners, sponsors, broadcasters, and fans. A marketing strategy can be strongly influenced by the beliefs, values and expectations of the most powerful stakeholders. As a result, careful analysis of the goals and objectives of each stakeholder must be completed before a strategic direction can be set.

Conduct and examine market and consumer research

The final step in Stage 1 is to conduct and examine market research. Market research means gathering information about the market and the consumers it contains. It is the process of learning about the marketplace and what consumers want, listening to their desires and expectations, and determining how to satisfy them. It is also used to determine whether consumers have reacted to a marketing plan as expected.

In general there are two broad types of market research: quantitative and qualitative. Quantitative research gathers statistical information that is superficial but diverse. The most common method of gathering quantitative information is to conduct a survey or questionnaire. Qualitative research gathers non-numerical information (such as words from an interview of a person). Qualitative information is in-depth, and usually gathered from a narrow and relatively small sample of people. Common types of qualitative research in sport include focus groups, suggestion boxes and complaint analysis. This information is pivotal in deciding what kinds of products and services should be offered to sport consumers.

STAGE 2: DEVELOP A SPORT MARKETING STRATEGY

The second stage of the Sport Marketing Framework involves two components: 1) develop strategic market direction; and 2) develop a sport marketing strategy. With the information-gathering stage completed, the direction of the sport marketing strategy can be determined and documented in the form of objectives and performance measures. These act as a guide through all the coming stages of the Sport Marketing Framework. Next, the actual sport marketing strategy can be decided in the form of a positioning approach that differentiates the sport organization's brand and product offerings from competitors and segments the market into target groups.

Develop strategic marketing direction

A marketing objective is a goal that can realistically be achieved as the result of the marketing strategy. It can be expressed as a sentence expressing what will occur as a result of marketing activities. There are basically four different types of marketing objectives that sport organizations might wish to pursue: higher levels of participation or involvement, on-field performance, promotion of messages about the sport or its benefits, and profit.

For each objective set it is important to add a performance measure. In this case, the term means a way of objectively estimating, calculating or assessing whether the objective has been achieved. It usually involves finding a way to quantify or put a number to the objective.

Develop a sport marketing strategy

Assuming that sport marketing objectives and performance measures have been set, the second part of Stage 2 can be undertaken by developing the actual sport marketing strategy. The process of developing a sport marketing strategy requires four steps. Steps one and two are associated with market segmentation, step three is the choice of market positioning strategy, and step four involves determining the marketing mix.

Market segmentation is a term that describes the process of categorizing groups of consumers together, based on their similar needs or wants. A market is the total group of potential consumers for a product and includes retailers, businesses, government, media and individuals. Market segmentation is a process of breaking this total group down into smaller groups based on a characteristic that the consumers have in common like age, gender, sporting interests or attendance levels. Once a particular segment or segments of the market have been targeted, it is possible to customize the product and marketing strategies to meet their specific needs.

The process of market segmentation involves two steps. First, the market must be divided into sub-groups based on a common feature or features. This can be done with the help of market research. There are six common factors that are often used to divide a market into sub-groups: demographic, socio-economic, lifestyle (psychographic), geographic, product behaviour, and product benefits. After the market is divided into sub-groups, the segments to be targeted must be specified. The segment or segments chosen must be big enough and different enough from the others to justify the effort.

There are three approaches to segmentation: focussed segmentation, multiple segmentation and undifferentiated segmentation. Focussed segmentation occurs when one segment only is chosen and one marketing mix is customized for it. Multiple segmentation involves choosing more than one segment, and then developing one marketing mix for each segment. Finally, undifferentiated segmentation involves no choice at all, where the entire market is considered a legitimate and worthwhile target.

Once decisions have been made about market segmentation, the next step is to choose a market positioning strategy for each segment identified. Market positioning refers to how a sport organization would like consumers to think and feel about their brand and its product offering when compared to competitors. For example, does a sport organization want to be thought of as offering luxury, high quality products, or basic, value-for-money ones? Do they see it as conservative and reliable or exciting and changeable? There are many different positioning strategies that can be selected that may suit the segment that is being targeted. It is important that the positioning strategy reflects a form of differentiation. That is, the positioning strategy must communicate to each target segment that the sport organization's brand and product offerings are special or different in some way from others available. It may be on the basis of the components of the product offerings, the quality of the products or services delivered, the price at which they are offered, or even the method that they are delivered. If Stage 1 has been completed carefully, there should be many possibilities for capitalizing on market opportunities that align strongly with the internal capabilities of the sport organization. Like all strategic decisions, market positioning and differentiation should reflect a match between external opportunities and internal competitive advantages.

The idea of branding is closely linked with positioning. A brand is like an identifying badge (often a name or a logo) that helps consumers recognize a product or an organization. A brand becomes linked with the consumers' opinions and views of the sport organization. Because branding and positioning are linked, it is important to keep branding, segmentation and positioning strategies closely related.

STAGE 3: PLAN THE SPORT MARKETING MIX

The marketing mix is a set of strategies covering product, price, promotions and place (distribution) and is commonly referred to as the 'four Ps'. They are collectively identified as a 'mix' because they should be combined and coordinated together in order to deploy the market positioning strategy. To the traditional four Ps it is necessary to add an additional two elements of the marketing mix: sponsorship and services. Both are already part of the marketing mix; sponsorship is part of 'promotions' and services are considered through 'product'. However, both are of central importance to sport marketing and are therefore given elevated status here.

Product

A product can include:

1   a good (physical item being sold);
2   a service being delivered;
3   an idea; and/or
4   a combination of any of these.

A sport product can be defined as the complete package of benefits that a sport organization presents to sport consumers through offering goods, services and/or ideas. Sport goods are physical items that can be touched. Sport shoes, tennis rackets, memorabilia, golf-balls and skateboards are examples. These goods are all tangible, meaning that they exist as physical objects. Sporting goods usually have a high degree of reliability, meaning that their quality does not change much from one product to the next. They can also be stored after they are made, because they are not perishable. Sport services will be considered independently in a forthcoming section.

A sporting product can be made up of a mixture of both goods and services. One important principle in sport marketing is to try to design products to have a mixture of tangible and intangible elements in order to help it stand out from competitors. To do this sport marketers think of the sport product as having three important variables:

1   the core benefit;
2   the actual product; and
3   the augmented product.

Figure 11.2 shows that the core benefit represents the main advantage that consumers receive from buying the product. The actual product refers to the features of the product itself. As long as consumers want the core benefit of the product, then developing the right features can help to make it fit their needs perfectly. The augmented product refers to any extras or extensions that are added to the features of the product. These may be additional benefits, bonus extras, or even the image of a product and how people see it.

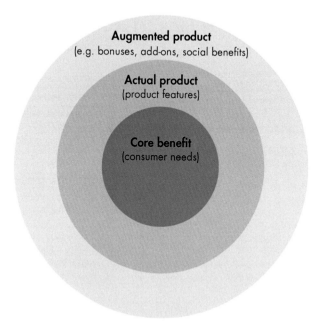

FIGURE 11.2 Sport product features

In Practice 11.1 Tradition: The core benefit for Wimbledon

On the final day of the All England Lawn Tennis and Croquet Club's (AELTC) iconic event, The Championships, Wimbledon, AELTC management and event organizers reflect on the success of their brand and event. Wimbledon is one of four Grand Slam tennis tournaments (the others are the French, US and Australian Opens) staged every year. However, Wimbledon undoubtedly commands the leadership as the longest running and most prestigious event in tennis. The intangible nature of the Wimbledon Grand Slam tennis event leads to a unique product offering. For example, each of the four Grand Slam surfaces, grass, clay, 'plexicushion' and hard court, require different styles of play, the effect producing unpredictable challenges and opportunities resulting in different kinds of tournaments. Understanding the unique dimensions of the sport product forms the basis of all sport marketing strategy.

The Wimbledon Championship was first played in 1877, and has now become an institution on the international tennis calendar. From its origins as an amateur competition to a mega event, Wimbledon has successfully combined tradition and originality in its core product. The first Wimbledon Championship attracted 200 spectators. By 2014 that figure reached around 500,000 with a global broadcast audience of more 370 million viewers across 198 countries. In the past, the strength of Wimbledon's popularity relied on the benefits spectators acquired from being 'at Wimbledon'. Historically the AELTC has steadfastly stuck to many of the traditional elements of tennis and has been less hurried than other Grand Slam tournaments to refashion the game with the use of synthetic surfaces, ball detection technology, and other technologies and commercializations associated with the 'modern game'. More recently, however, the event's marketing success has increasingly focussed on the product's core benefit and its augmentation, rather than on the original product.

By diagnosing the Wimbledon product components we can better understand how the success of the event can be attributed to any or all of its product dimensions. To begin with, the core benefits of status and traditionalism go a long way in marketing Wimbledon. Tradition in particular, represents a unique selling point (USP) differentiating Wimbledon from the other three Grand Slam events. Tennis fans and sport tourists respect the traditions upheld for this esteemed event. They value the allegories of discretion and its eccentricities that are synonymous to Wimbledon. Such benefits compel spectators in either virtual or located space to loyally support the tournament as a bastion of unadulterated sport and a connection with a cherished and probably inflated notion of a past amateur ideal.

Of course, the actual Wimbledon product is simply a game of tennis; the core product is the game itself. Qualities such as strictly enforced conduct and dress codes for participants and spectators, Grand Slam status, and restricted membership, surround the generic product. For example, highly restrictive membership allows only 375 full or life members (this figure represents the number of seats available in the historic Wolpole Road Stand). Past Grand Slam men's champions can only become honorary members and the waiting list for a full membership is over 1,000, with most waiting almost a lifetime to be accepted. Exclusivity represents an immensely valued and appreciated aspect of the Wimbledon consumption experience.

Augmentation amplifies the value of the core product at Wimbledon, especially since few rule changes or other modifications have been added to make the event more palatable to the impatient, contemporary sport consumer. While the atmosphere accompanying the Grand Slam does not reside exclusively with Wimbledon, the event's ability to amplify its traditional experience for the consumer has proven a key strength. One of the more interesting traditions supporting Wimbledon includes the availability of strawberries and cream, and Pimms and lemonade. In addition, the use of idiomatic titles such as 'Miss and Mrs' when referring to female competitors, and 'ladies and gentleman' when referring to match participants, provides a nostalgic flair. Also, when players enter centre court, they are required to acknowledge any members of the British Royal family present.

In the modern era, however, a disenchantment and impatience with some of the Wimbledon traditions has begun to emerge. For example, one of the event's quirks was the lack of telecommunication reception within the grounds. Despite the positive traditional links, inconsistent smart phone connectivity has proven an inconvenience to players, sponsors, spectators, and the media attempting to cover the event. In 2014, the AELTC expanded its electronic and mobile connectivity services due to the increased demand. Furthermore, although sponsorship strategies have always been dealt with discreetly, as commercialization and media opportunities have intensified, maximum brand exposure strategies by sponsoring corporations have challenged the traditional, understated Wimbledon standards. These developments have caused a tension between the event's core benefit emphasizing conformity and tradition, and the commercial realities ensuring that the event will survive into the future. As a result, the Wimbledon Board of Management has worked to balance the tensions without compromising the distinctive flavour of the event. In fact, they recognize a need to focus on the augmented product more closely so as to preserve the one thing that makes it stand apart. For example, the traditional all-white dress code of players has been preserved and reinforced as players in recent years have displayed more subtle uses of colour and branding with clothing, footwear and headgear.

Marketers generally seek augmentations to a core product in order to refresh their brands and match the ever-changing expectations of a demanding sport-weary audience. How can Wimbledon – an event steeped in tradition and dependent on its core product – market its augmentations more effectively to remain relevant? Should the AELTC make changes to its heritage product so that it can sustain its popularity in the future? Understanding the potential of a product in the future would mean exploring opportunities such as technological developments, or making changes to the core product. But, these strategies must add value to the customer if they are to be successful!

SPORT PRODUCT INNOVATION

Sport marketers may consider the possibility of new product development through a process of innovation. Developing a new product can be expensive and risky. Every year there is a proliferation of new sport products introduced to the market, but only a small fraction of these are successful. If a new product is a failure, the sport organization has lost time and money, and perhaps even some of their reputation. But what does it mean to develop a new product? A new product does not have to mean a brand new product. In sport marketing, a new product can take many forms, such as the improved performance of an existing product, new functions added to an existing product, a new way to use an existing product, combining existing products, or a new look or design for a product. Whatever form the new or revised product takes, it arises through a successful process of innovation.

Innovation has come to mean a multiplicity of things from simple creativity to complex manufacturing. For us, from a sport product perspective, innovation refers to the translation of a new idea into a tangible deliverable via a technology, physical product, or process-based service. Unlike an invention or a discovery, an innovation actually takes a place on the real-world stage, either as a novel solution to an existing consumer problem, an improvement to a consumer experience, or even a completely new offering for a consumer to try that they had never contemplated before. Because innovation tends to be synonymous with inspiration, considerable mystery surrounds its cultivation.

In sport, product innovations can be found in several forms. First, mobile technology is changing the way consumers and participants connect with sport. For example, smart devices allow consumers to watch and experience sport from anywhere and at any time. Participants, and especially elite athletes, can collect, store and analyse a vast amount of training and performance data that offer vital clues for subsequent improvement. Second, sport product innovations have made a serious impact on the support systems for sport performance, such as sports medicine, rehabilitation, pharmaceuticals, nutrition and supplements. Also, of course, sport managers and marketers can benefit from new innovations that augment audience size, consumer viewing experiences, broadcasting coverage and quality, media channels, regulation, rule enforcement and officiating, and general spectator safety and comfort.

As a result of these major opportunities arising from the application of innovations, sport marketers would be well advised to become conversant with the processes surrounding innovation. But this does not mean that sport marketers must await the development of new technologies. Instead they can aggressively pursue new product innovations through the application of available ideas and tools in new ways. Many sports, for example, have founded modified versions of their games in order to attract new audiences, including formats specifically designed for children, and those exclusively conceived for maximum entertainment. For our purposes, innovation relates to product outcomes that are more attractive to a targeted audience. An innovation can be incremental in that it shifts the existing product in modest but important ways, or radical, where a product can be completely re-designed or even replaced by something consumers never expected.

This first step in product innovation involves creating and collecting new product possibilities and ideas. While the product innovation process can occur either spontaneously, or evolve almost unnoticed over a long period of incremental improvements, sport marketers can benefit from noting a series of steps typically present in any innovation outcome. Although beginning with a problem to be solved is a conventional and quite obviously sensible approach, innovation does not necessarily need something wrong to get it going. Most product developers and marketers imagine new products and services impelled by thoughts on new opportunities. Opportunities are the engine of innovation. For this reason, product innovation begins with the desire for new value. Step one in the sport product innovation process therefore seeks to cultivate an abundant, diverse and rich platform of potential concepts from which to conceive new value. It is important that the ideas are remain unconstrained from the usual practicalities associated with convention, resources and preconceived assumptions about what sport consumer's want.

The second step in product innovation involves sifting through all the ideas that have been collected and only keeping the ones that fit with the marketing objectives of the sport organisation. It is also helpful to consider how well the new product ideas fit with existing products, and how they relate to current trends. This is not the stage to be concerned about financial realism. However, by the end of this step, new product opportunities should be ranked according to priorities determined by marketing objectives. In short, the lengthy set of ideas from step one need to be reduced to a workable handful. A range of methods can be employed, including voting and weighting systems, predetermined priority areas, expert advice, panels and workshops, and the capability product champions have to quickly develop their ideas into testable prototypes. Subsequently, product and service innovations should be tested as quickly and inexpensively as possible.

Step three of the process involves a more careful assessment of the ideas that were retained following step two. In fact, the highest ranking options should be identified and piloted to determine their potential in the market. This is the time to check feasibility by undertaking cost and financial estimates, and to conduct additional market research, or concept testing. Concept testing involves giving potential customers a description of the new product, and asking them if they would be likely to buy it. It may also mean providing a prototype of the new product for customers to try. One powerful option at this stage involves creating a 'rapid prototype'.

Recently popularized and infused into marketing and business circles, rapid prototyping is a method of quickly testing an idea to see whether it could work before significant resources are expended on creating it for the market. Because rapid prototyping has been appropriated from designers, the process reflects the fluid and iterative methods they use in testing their nascent ideas. A prototype can range from a basic sketch or flowchart to a mock-up product of an unrefined but fully functional technology. The key is not in the finish but rather in the start. Most innovations never make it to the market because they take too long to develop or require too much investment without really knowing whether it will pay off or not. Rapid prototyping attempts to sidestep the development lag that most product innovations face. By quickly converting an idea into something tangible that can be tested – preferably by the same kinds of sport users and consumers who might buy it in the end – and subsequently refined and re-tested, the innovation process can be radically shortened. Often, the result is the choice to abandon the innovation. This is sometimes referred to as 'fast failure' or 'cheap failure', but reflects a positive outcome where resources have been protected from wastage in the light of early trials. In rapid prototyping, experimentation remains central, which leads to better design, faster.

It is important to understand that the rapid prototyping method does not seek to create fully functional products or services. However, they do need to evoke an experience in users that will provide them with a first-hand insight into what it is like to try the new product. For example, a marketer might conceive a new process for sport consumers to purchase tickets to events though a mobile application. Instead of spending months and thousands of dollars on development, the marketer might simply construct some cards or off-line screens reflecting the steps through which a consumer would use the application. By working with users to test the idea, the marketer can quickly ascertain whether their consumers have an appetite for the actual product. A prototype could range from the low fidelity, like a series of sketches on paper, to high fidelity, like a working application with limited functionality. The important issue is that users can be exposed to the kind of experience that the ultimate product seeks to elicit. Better prototypes duplicate the final product experience with greater precision than lesser prototypes. But even a poor prototype can be enough to provide sufficient feedback for a successive, refined version.

Most consumers find it difficult to imagine their responses to product innovations in the absence of any tangible experience in which to base their expectations. Prototypes vastly amplify the productivity of market testing, and have therefore become a pivotal tool in the sport product development arsenal.

With the results of the new product's feasibility and market testing available, it is time to make a final decision about how to proceed. It is possible that the best decision is not to proceed and to choose the next highest ranked new product opportunity to investigate. If the feasibility and testing results are promising, the final product composition should be determined. This involves specifying the core product benefits, actual product features and augmented product composition. The other elements of the marketing mix will also need to be determined to provide the appropriate positioning strategy.

Finally, if a sport product has successfully made it through all these stages, it is ready to be released onto the market. With this decision, an implementation plan will need to be created to support the deployment of all the variables in the marketing mix.

Branding

Branding is one of the key strategies that sport marketers use to augment their products by associating them with certain ideas. The added value that a product has because of its brand name is called brand equity. Branding is much more than choosing a good name, or having a good logo designed; it revolves around building the brand. Once potential consumers are aware of a sport brand, it is important to help them connect certain ideas about what it stands for that reflect an intended positioning strategy. Sport marketers achieve this by manipulating the brand image, which encompasses all of the symbols and ideas that influence the image of a brand such as its name, logo, product features, product quality/performance, packaging, price, advertising, promotion, customer service and distribution channels. The ultimate goal of branding is consumer loyalty. Brand loyalty is improved through high levels of product quality, convenience of distribution, keeping up regular contact with customers, and customer loyalty programs.

Related to the idea of branding is licensing. Licensing occurs when a sport organization allows another organization to use their brand name or logo for a fee. The company who buys the right to use the brand (called the licensee) will then produce a good, service or promotion, and will give a percentage of the money they make back to the real owner of the brand (called the licensor). Licensing is a common product strategy in sport, and each year it generates billions of dollars in sales internationally. It is particularly popular with merchandising (toys, collectible cards, games, school supplies, videos, DVDs and magazines) and apparel. Sport clubs and leagues do not have the resources to make all of these products by themselves. Instead, they may make an agreement with another company to make the merchandise for them, and agree to share a percentage of profits.

Price

The way that a sport product is priced not only influences it financial impact, but also has a powerful effect on the way that consumers perceive it. The price of a sport product represents what a consumer gives up in exchange for using or owning it. Price is usually thought of in financial terms, but may include other things that a customer has to give up in order to obtain the product, such as time (e.g. waiting in a queue), or social costs (e.g. being in an aerobics class with others instead of a one-on-one instruction). A useful way to think about pricing decisions is to consider them in terms of value. In sport marketing, the value of a product is a factor of how its price relates to the benefits that consumers believe they will receive in exchange. The value of a sport product is the relationship between its price and the benefits a consumer believes they will receive from it.

There are six main steps involved in setting the right price for a sport product:

1 setting a pricing goal;
2 determining price sensitivity;
3 conducting a break-even analysis;
4 assessing pricing variables;
5 selecting price tactics; and
6 setting a price point.

First, because different pricing strategies will achieve different things, it is important to determine what outcome is being sought, and should be specified in the form of pricing goals. These may range from those focussed on maximizing profit to those designed to provide the product or service to as many different sport consumers as possible. Second, it is necessary to determine how sensitive consumers are to price changes. Consumers are sensitive to price if they do not buy a product when the price is high, or if they buy more of it when the price is lowered. The more sensitive they are, the more they will change their buying habits when the price changes. Third, a break-even analysis should be conducted to ascertain how many sales are needed in order to recover the costs of producing the product. Fourth, other variables that might affect price should be considered including the pricing strategies of competitors, legal or regulatory limitations that may be relevant, and the impact of the other marketing mix variables.

Fifth, a pricing strategy should be selected that underscores the overall market positioning strategy. There are many different types of pricing strategies that sport organizations might use including those designed to maximize profit: following competitors, setting a low introductory price, adding a flat margin to costs, using market demand as a guide, and pricing according to the segment of consumers being targeted. Sixth, and finally, a price point is selected. It is important to realize that price needs to be reconsidered constantly and should always remain consistent with a market positioning strategy.

Promotion

Promotion is concerned with communicating with consumers, providing them with information about product offerings and trying to persuade them to buy. Ultimately, promotion is pivotal in shaping and cultivating brand image. Sport promotion can be defined as the way that sport marketers communicate with potential consumers to inform, persuade and remind them about their product offerings.

There are four main promotional activities known together as the promotions mix because they are typically used in concert to create an integrated promotional strategy. The promotion mix elements are:

1   advertising;
2   personal selling;
3   sales promotion; and
4   public relations.

Advertising is a form of one-way communication where a sport marketer pays someone else to have their product or company identified. Common examples include television commercials, magazine and newspaper advertisements, radio spots, internet pop-ups, posters, billboards, and advertisements on public transport. Personal selling involves one-to-one communication between a consumer and a salesperson such as talking to a customer on the phone, talking face-to-face, or even telemarketing. Endorsements and sponsorships are two forms of personal selling that are common in the sport industry. Sales promotions are short-term programs that aim to stimulate an increase in sales. They give consumers an incentive (or a bonus) to use the sport product. Common examples include 'two-for-one' offers, prize give-aways, competitions, and free trials or samples. Public relations programs try to build a favourable image for a sport organization, its brand and product offerings in the community. It is not paid for by the sport organization and usually involves publicity in the media in the form of a news item.

Place

Place refers to the location where a sport product or service is delivered or the method of distributing a product. As a result, the terms 'place' and 'distribution' are interchangeable. Both describe how a sport product or service gets from the producer to the final consumer. The process of distribution can be explained through the concept of a sport distribution channel, which comprises a series of organizations or individuals through which a sport product must pass. There are both direct and indirect distribution channels. A direct distribution channel is short where the producer sells the product directly to the consumer. Examples include internet sales of sporting merchandise and sport services like live matches and coaching lessons. An indirect distribution channel is longer where there are a number of organizations or people (called intermediaries) involved along the way. Examples include sporting goods products like athletic shoes and equipment.

Ticket sales are one of the most important sources of revenue for sport organizations that run competitions or events. Ticket distribution is therefore an extremely important issue for sport marketers that relates to the 'place' element of the sport marketing mix. When consumers contact a ticket distributor to buy a ticket for a sport event, they are often looking for more than just a ticket. They want convenience, fast and friendly service, questions answered, and a reasonable price. If a consumer becomes unhappy with the service or price they receive from a ticket distributor, they can feel dissatisfied about the sport event or club as well. It is essential that sport organizations carefully control their contracts with ticket distributors.

The sport facility is perhaps the most important distribution channel in the sport industry. There are numerous features of sport facilities that affect their success as a distribution vehicle for sport products. The important features of a sport facility can be summarized into four main areas:

1   location and accessibility;
2   design and layout;
3   facilities; and
4   customer service.

Table 11.1 summarizes the variables influencing distribution in sport facilities.

Sport marketers do not always have control over the features of sporting facilities and may be able to do little to enact change without substantial resources. For this reason it is important that sport marketers attempt to bolster the distribution of sport by managing a number of other aspects of the venue. First, seating selection influences sport consumers' experience and can be used to enhance their viewing comfort as well as the marketing messages they are exposed to. Second, scoreboards and signage are an essential method of communicating marketing messages irrespective of the size of a venue, and can enhance sport consumers' experience of the event. Third, lighting and sound systems can be used to attract sport consumers at appropriate times and can also improve the atmosphere of a venue and event. Fourth, transport can be used to assist sport consumers in accessing a facility and can be marketed as a special customer service. Fifth, media facilities can encourage broadcasting and general media interest in events that occur in a sport facility. Sixth, the provision of child-care facilities can be important in attracting sport consumers during non-peak periods or to special events. Seventh, selling merchandise in sport facilities is a powerful marketing tool because it provides sport consumers with a convenient way of spending more money on items that emphasize the sport product's brand image. Finally, the supply of food and beverages is amongst the most lucrative of all services that can be offered at a sport facility.

TABLE 11.1 Distribution variables of sport facilities

Location and accessibility	Attractive location Convenient to get to Good signage and directions Enough parking Accessible by public transport Accessible by different forms of public transport Easy to enter and exit facility Disabled access (ramps, lifts, washroom facilities)
Design and layout	Fits in with local area Attractive design (size, colour, shape and light) Ambience and atmosphere Easy to get from one area to another Good direction signs Seating arrangements with good viewing Weather protection Control of noise levels Areas for non-smokers and non-drinkers Lighting of playing area Protection from heat and cold Air circulation Adequate storage Safety issues (emergency procedures, fire detection, stand-by power, emergency communication, exits) Security (surveillance, control room, entrance security) Spectator control (zones, safe barriers, security, police)
Facility infrastructure	Variety of food and drink outlets Overall seating quality Premium seating available Corporate boxes and special services Toilets – number and location for convenient access Child-care facilities Scoreboards and screens Message centres and sound systems Emergency medical services Merchandise areas Broadcasting and media requirements
Customer service	Queuing and waiting times Prominent information stands/booths Efficient, friendly and helpful staff Sufficient security and emergency staff Entrance staff, ushers Services for elderly, disabled and children Telephone enquiry service

In Practice 11.2 From fanzines to ezines in sport marketing

The fanzine concept is older than most people assume. In fact, since the 1930s science fiction fans have supported their contemporaries in publishing their own stories through what became known as fanzines. With fanzines, the space between creator and reader narrows, with fans assuming much of the information dissemination responsibility. Under the fanzine model, fan collectives gather a wide range of audio, print and online materials for circulation to other fans, media or stakeholder groups. Marketing communications through fanzines aims to engage groups of fans with similar preferences by using peer-to-peer interactions. In many ways, fanzines were the first form of 'tribal' and 'viral' marketing used by organizations and interest groups.

In sport, fanzines emerged in the 1970s structured primarily as 'magazines' generated by football fans. Since the 1980s, Premier League and Rugby League fans in the United Kingdom have generated scores of fanzines in support of their clubs. With the widespread availability and low cost of digital technologies, combined with the desire to engage a global fan-base, a new version of the fanzine has proliferated in the form of online fan magazines, or 'ezines'. For example, the Liverpool Football Club has one of the largest selections of fan sites throughout the world and tracking their communications would be a nightmare for any sport marketer. So popular is fan-driven communication that there are even umbrella Football Supporters Federations throughout the world identified as democratic entities representing the rights and views of the football supporter.

Given their low cost and technological ease, fanzines and ezines are no longer exclusive to elite sport competitions, with opportunities for fans of all sports at all levels to get involved. For example, the Brighton Rollers ezine site supports the team's roller derby fan base and has attracted a fierce and dedicated group of contributors, while the Bleed and Blue is an independent online ezine for ice hockey supporters. Each ezine platform provides an alternative means for fans to 'talk shop' with other fans. These peer-to-peer 'hot knowledge' repositories represent credible and highly valuable marketing opportunities. For the sport marketer, tracking ezine engagement can offer a cost efficient way of researching fan attitudes and behaviours.

Ezines have surged in popularity because they engage on the fan's level with the use of fan-centric language and imagery reflecting the sport or club from the committed supporter's perspective. Ostensibly, an ezine community operates like an underground communications network conveying information and opinions about a range of current topics and issues peculiar to a prized sport or team. Responses are immediate and authentic, avoiding any suspicion that savvy sports consumers might hold that their opinions or behaviours are being manipulated by club-directed communication or media-driven propaganda. With ezines, fans appreciate the camaraderie of sharing knowledge with like-minded supporters. Supporters satisfied with club decisions or team results want to express their views right away. And, of course, when they are disappointed or annoyed, they need to vent. Sport marketers can evaluate the information gleaned from ezine activity and respond with improved services or information.

While some sport marketers might feel vulnerable given the lack of content control with ezines, between fans the credibility of information delivery remains high. The growing popularity of ezines suggests that when content falls to supporters, engagement and interaction with the sport enterprise soars, helping to institutionalize loyalty. For sport organizations seeking lifetime value from their fans, providing an ezine platform, and allowing supporters to run it unencumbered, represents a powerful mechanism for developing fan loyalty.

Sponsorship

Although sponsorships and endorsements are part of the promotional mix, they are so important to sport that they deserve special treatment. Sport sponsorship is a business agreement where an organization or individual provides financial or in-kind assistance to a sport property (the sport organization or person being sponsored such as an athlete, team, event, association or competition), in exchange for the right to associate itself with the sport property. Sponsorship is an example of marketing *through* sport. The objectives of sponsorship can vary greatly, depending on the size of the partners, the type of sponsorship, and the type of sport property being supported. Some common objectives for the sponsor are to promote the public image of their organization, to increase customer awareness, to manage their brand image, and to build business relationships. In general, sponsorship helps to generate goodwill amongst consumers. The amount of goodwill generated can vary depending on the kind of sport property being sponsored, the degree of involvement that consumers have in the sport property, the time at which the sponsor becomes involved, and when/how the sponsor ceases the sponsorship.

Sponsorship works through an image transfer from the sport property to the sponsor. This image transfer works best when there is a strong sponsorship affinity, or a good fit or match between the sponsor and the sport property. Two things are particularly important for ensuring a good match: first, an overlap of target markets and, second, an overlap of brand positioning strategies. As a result, sponsorship works best when the two partners are linked to the same group of consumers and have a similar kind of message. Most sponsors support their sport sponsorship programs by leveraging them with additional marketing activities. For a sponsor to make the most of a sponsorship they usually need to undertake other promotional activities drawing attention to it. Sometimes sponsorship leveraging can cost several times the amount that is spent on the sponsorship itself. Sponsors also have to be careful about ambush marketing – where another company (other than an official sponsor, and often a competitor to the official sponsor) creates marketing communications that give the impression that they are associated with the sport property. Whilst evaluating sponsorships can be difficult, it is important that a careful evaluation strategy is implemented. Being able to demonstrate that sponsorship has a positive outcome for corporations is the best way to legitimize it as a marketing technique, and to attract and retain sponsors.

Services

Sport services cannot be seen, felt or tasted; they are intangible because they exist only as an experience, inconsistent in terms of quality, and perishable in that they can only be offered and experienced once at any point in time. Sport services are inseparable because they are consumed at the same time as they are produced. Sport organizations offer services where their staff, team or athletes provide an experience to consumers. For example, services are offered through fitness centres, local participation-based competitions, professional sport matches, and support services like sport physiotherapists.

It is a common view that when it comes to marketing a service there are three additional Ps that should be added to the standard four. These are participants, physical evidence, and process. Participants are those individuals who are involved in delivering and receiving a service. Physical evidence refers to the tangible or visual elements of a service such as a sporting facility. Process is concerned with the steps involved in delivering a service. All three of these new Ps revolve around service quality and customer satisfaction. Sport consumers are more likely to be loyal users of a service if they perceive it to be of high quality with consistent levels of delivery, leading to satisfaction.

Service quality may be seen as the degree to which a service meets the needs and expectations of customers. For example, if a customer expects a level of service that is higher than what they feel they actually receive, they are likely to believe that the service is lower quality, and will tend to be dissatisfied. One key method of focussing on service quality is to work hard on ensuring that five aspects of its delivery are present. These five areas are reliability, assurance, empathy, responsiveness and tangibles. Reliability refers to the ability to offer a service in a consistent and dependable way. Assurance refers to the level of confidence and trust that a customer has in the service. Empathy refers to the ability to get to know customers and their needs, and to deliver a personalized service. Responsiveness refers to a willingness to help customers, and to provide them with the service on time. Tangibles refer to the physical features of the service such as information booklets, equipment, the appearance of staff, facilities, and characteristics of a sport venue. If these aspects of service quality are emphasized, then customer satisfaction is likely to be maximized.

DIGITAL SPORT MARKETING

It is easy enough to understand digital sport marketing as any form of marketing that utilizes technology, which of course means a focus on the internet and all the devices, channels and media that it involves. At the same time, this broad definition no longer helps distinguish digital marketing from other forms in an era when just about every marketing activity involves a digital aspect. Even conventional printed flyers rely on print-on-demand technologies, while even modest sporting events utilize digital ticketing in order to save money. The simple act of watching sport live cannot escape the digital era either. Most surveys suggest that around half of sport fans refer to their smart phones for extra content during events. At the same time as the technologies and tools of the digital era have become entrenched in our marketing expectations, sport marketers must come to terms with a new way of looking at their offerings. In short, sport digital marketing and social media demands a new kind of mindset where the conventional distance between sport properties, their marketing representatives, and fans is completely blurred, and where success means constant adaptation. No longer are digital and social media tools just 'add-ons' to the standard marketing methods. Today, a digital world needs a digital message.

Digital marketing is often described as electronic marketing and is usually associated with the internet, computers, and forms of mobile communications. To phrase this more generally, digital marketing refers to communications that are generated by electronic means or through recent (non-analogue) technological platforms. Digital marketing refers to technologically sophisticated platforms or vehicles for transmitting and communicating information. All of these digital platforms are revolutionizing sport marketing and have justifiably become essential tools in the toolkit. By including the escalation of digital channels, as a secondary goal of this chapter, we also explain how social media must become a central element in a sport organization's digital profile. The term 'social media', like the term 'marketing', can mean different things depending on the context. We take a broad view in referring to social media as any instrument or means of communicating information that relies on the interactions between networked groups of individuals. It is important to take a broad view like this because technology has provided the sport marketer with so many innovative ways of communicating with the general public that they no longer have to rely only on traditional 'media' organizations.

Today, digital content is delivered through many devices such as smart phones, PDAs, tablets and MP3 music players. The information can even be transferred seamlessly from one digital technology to another and from one digital format to another (for example, from a mobile phone to a computer). Another feature of digital media is that data, or information, is accessible in real time. Digital media is especially important in sport marketing because it permeates all aspects of consumers' lives.

Not long ago, digital media, and especially social media, were seen as the latest technological trends, but it has now become indisputable that they have significant and permanent implications for sport marketing. Digital media is more than technology and tools; it requires a different style of marketing where sport marketers can communicate in novel ways with sport consumers. It is also important because it creates additional opportunities in sport, such as new assets and revenues (like website and mobile digital rights, as well as new sales channels), and new possibilities in licensing and merchandising (such as computer games). Although the types of technologies that are available continue to change and develop, the principle remains the same: sport marketers can use advanced technology to communicate with their customers and sell them extra products and services that are associated with sport. Perhaps more importantly, the social media dimension of the digital revolution allows marketers and sport organizations an unprecedented connectivity with their customer and fan base.

The popularity and prevalence of digital and social media technology mean that it provides sport marketers with innovative ways of communicating with consumers. Many of these communication approaches are far more rapid, responsive and interactive than other marketing strategies. For example, compare the one-way content of television with the opportunity to customize a replay directly to a consumer's smart phone. Not only are digital media platforms fast and direct, they are also inexpensive compared with traditional techniques of sport marketing. Even more importantly, digital media enables sport organizations to develop messages that are personalized to key target audiences.

SPORT MARKETING AND SOCIAL MEDIA

You want to know how your team performed. Forget about the TV or the newspaper, and even the online news is a bit slow and cumbersome. Go directly to Twitter for your live sports ticker and, for more information and perhaps a conversation about the results, go directly to the sport fans' hub, Facebook. Hyperlinks to YouTube can offer the footage within moments of the big play. All of this is possible on the run – on your smart phone, iPad, or any other WiFi or mobile device. In fact, most surveys in North America, Western Europe and the Asia Pacific report that between two-thirds and 85 per cent of fans use social media during games, while up to half check scores or watch highlights after the event using smart phones. By the time you read this text, the figures are likely to have climbed even higher. However, as we shall discuss in this section, savvy digital sport marketers know that while data and updates are compelling services for fans, the real power of social media lies in its unprecedented ability to create close, personal engagements between sport properties and their followers. In the end, like all marketing, we aim for better relationships, experiences, feedback and advocacy. One conclusion is absolutely undisputed: the use of social media has become an essential investment rather than an interesting experiment at the periphery of sport marketing.

Few could argue that the contemporary sport consumer has changed radically in just a few, short years. We want sport content at our convenience, which typically means on the run, and often comes with the expectation of updates from our favourite and most trusted sources of social networking insight. In short, we want to know what is going on, and we want to be able to find out '24/7'. In a world rapidly heading towards two billion smart phone owners, the implications for digital sport marketing are enormous. To start with, sport consumers want instant access. Next, that access must be customized, or at least 'customizable', in order to meet the fickle preferences of each fan. Access must also arrive seamlessly. That means both a smooth download as well as an integrated platform where the sport fan needs only engage with a single or a few locations for their updates. Integration plays a central role in effective digital marketing because consumers are using their smart phones and mobile devices for internet browsing almost as much as through computers. In addition, they check email and social networking messages and sites, post photos and comments, listen to voice messages, consult their calendars, check the weather forecast, use apps, and play music and games. Although it varies depending on the region, some studies suggest that consumers within certain demographics pick up their phones more than 100 times a day. No wonder hardware manufacturers and app developers are so focussed on providing an interface that captures the user's demand for intuitive functionality. Because sport consumers are so well educated about sport and technology, they expect more than the garden-variety results. Rather, content must be accompanied by novelty, entertainment and insight. Finally, attending sporting events can be prohibitively expensive leading sport consumers to find alternative ways of engaging with game content as well as looking for new ways of generating the excitement and buzz of the contest. Enter social media.

In Practice 11.3 Is social media a help or a hindrance to sport?

Social media has become the dominant marketing platform for a wide range of organizations. In the world of sport, YouTube has provided a continuous stream of video footage highlighting the excellent, the average, and the extraordinary endeavours that occur on the sporting field of play. In addition, Facebook offers an unprecedented means by which 'friends' congregate in virtual space to share their experiences, passion and knowledge of sport. At the same time for the more impatient sports fan, the instantaneous application of 140 characters of information has made Twitter the hottest news wire around. Social media delivers a cost effective way of communicating to fans and club members, and offers sport enthusiasts a unique opportunity to discuss, debate and dissect current sport events. A well-thought-out social media strategy embracing the likes of Facebook, Twitter and YouTube, among other potential platforms, has surely become a must for sport marketing at all levels from grassroots to international mega events.

As an example of the power of social media tools, FC Barcelona and Portuguese star Christian Ronaldo appear in the top 20 Facebook fan pages. In fact, football (soccer) clubs constitute seven of the top 10 most popular sports teams on Facebook. In terms of Twitter, Ronaldo again commands the strongest following with over 27 million followers. While consumers tend to discuss sport more readily on Facebook, when it comes to game day, Twitter is used 1.5 times more than Facebook, reinforcing its unchallenged value as an instantaneous news and opinion channel.

When National Basketball Association (NBA) clubs and players use social media like Facebook, Instagram and Twitter, their intention is to engage with sport fans in a positive and direct way. For the NBA this approach involves communicating high profile newsworthy stories prior to their release by the mainstream media, thereby demonstrating to followers a privileged access. Associated sponsors to the NBA tap into a ready market, exposing their brands, products and other attention-grabbing information. Players prioritize the opportunity to increase their profiles by sharing feelings, expectations and the personal, behind-the-scenes stories unavailable elsewhere, such as injury recovery updates, or simply insight into the lifestyles of famous sporting celebrities.

In spite of the exciting and cost effective means for communicating about sport brands, sponsors' products and supporters' opinions, social media exposure comes with concerns. First, access to a wider marketplace also means that the audience can express their angst or anger in an anonymous way, sometimes leaping over the line of taste, appropriateness and ethics. For example, the NBA and its constituent clubs are grappling with how to manage negative publicity, remarks and bigotry towards teams and individuals when they do not control the channels of communication, and where the contributors are outside the NBA's influence or remain hidden under a pseudonym. Second, attempting to control information feeds from individual players, coaches or staff from within a club can cause a negative backlash. For example, New York Knicks player J.R. Smith directed an aggressive rant towards an opposition player via Twitter. Of course, since Twitter delivers instant communication and feedback, by the time the club had realized the damage done, it was too late. Furthermore, to delay player Tweets as a result of club censorship will undermine the very advantage the medium offers, not to mention aggravate the players and communicate to fans that the messages all reflect watered-down club rhetoric and propaganda. Third, a corporate sponsor or shareholder can create negative publicity, such as when the owner of the Los Angeles Clippers was captured making racist comments, leading to severe branding repercussions for his club.

In response to managing social media practices, sport organizations like the NBA include a social media policy in their marketing and communication strategies. Part of the policy guidelines detail the content acceptable for posts and communications issued by players, coaches, officials and all others associated the NBA and its teams. In addition, strictly enforced rules have been introduced relating to when and where players can use social media platforms to communicate to their fans. Players are not allowed to tweet information during games for 45 minutes before and after the game. As social media increasingly becomes a preferred means of communication in the sport industry, brand management associated with appropriate use has escalated in importance. While social media guidelines offer one means for managing behaviour, what other strategies can be imposed to harness the positive aspects and lessen the negatives side effects of social media?

STAGE 4: IMPLEMENT AND CONTROL THE SPORT MARKETING STRATEGY

The final stage of the Sport Marketing Framework is to implement and control the sport marketing strategy. Implementing a sport marketing strategy means putting the plans into action. Many sport organizations discover that it is harder to implement a marketing strategy than it sounds. There are, however, two important actions that sport marketers can perform in order to help them to implement a marketing strategy more effectively. These are to use implementation strategies and to use a control process.

A sport marketing plan is more likely to be successful if there is a clear leader or group of leaders who take responsibility for its implementation. In addition, it is important that all members of the sport marketing team have a good understanding of the marketing plan and, where possible, have all made a contribution according to their unique skills and knowledge. This demands a team comprising a combination of staff and volunteers who have the right mix of skills, experience and attitudes in the first place. Whether the implementation of marketing strategy will be successful depends on the individual and team efforts of staff and volunteers. The final part of implementing a marketing strategy is to review and evaluate its outcomes on a regular basis. It is vital to keep track of how well the plan is going, and to make changes if things are not going as intended. A control process provides the structure to this feedback.

The sport marketing control process has five main steps. The first step involves setting performance measures. These should already be in place in accordance with Stage 2 of the Sport Marketing Framework. The second step is to put the performance measure into action by evaluating performance before and after the marketing strategy has been implemented, leading to the third step, a comparison of results to determine gaps, shortfall and performance successes. Considering the data seen in the comparison, the fourth step is to determine whether the variance is favourable or not, and whether intervention needs to occur. The final step is to make remedial changes to the marketing strategy and mix, in order to bring it back in line with the marketing objectives.

While the implementation of a sport marketing plan should align with a sport organization's objectives, it should also fit within the broader boundaries of ethical behaviour. Ethics in sport marketing typically refers to whether the traditional four Ps of the marketing mix are deployed within a moral and professional code. Mostly these include issues associated with unsafe or poor quality products, deceptive or predatory pricing, misleading or dishonest promotions, and exploitative or collusive distribution. In the sporting world, other major marketing issues are concerned with publicizing the private lives of athletes, exploiting passionate fans and children who idolize sport stars through athlete endorsements of commercial products, the use of venues with unsafe facilities, unrealistic promises associated with health, fitness and weight loss products, the use of performance-enhancing drugs, and the over-pricing of high profile matches and special sport events. In short, informed, autonomous consumer decisions based on the faithful representation of the product features and its price lie at the core of responsible and ethical sport marketing.

SUMMARY

This chapter was structured around the Sport Marketing Framework. Stage 1 is to identify sport marketing opportunities which involves undertaking several kinds of assessments: a SWOT analysis, a competitor analysis, a five forces competitor analysis, an organizational analysis, and market and consumer research. All of these analyses allow sport marketers to better understand market circumstances, consumer preferences, the sport industry, competitors' activities, and the internal organization context.

Stage 2 of the Sport Marketing Framework is to develop a sport marketing strategy. This stage begins with decisions about the direction of the marketing program, which is subsequently documented using marketing objectives and performance measures. Stage 2 also involves deciding on the basic theme of the marketing strategy. To that end, it requires the identification of the target market/s (segmentation), the positioning strategy (differentiation), and the composition of the marketing mix to deploy the strategy.

Stage 3 of the Sport Marketing Framework requires planning the sport marketing mix in detail. Here, decisions about the four Ps of marketing, the product, price, promotions and distribution (place) are determined, along with specific approaches to sponsorship and the management of sport services.

Finally, Stage 4 is to implement and control the plan. Plans are put into action, facilitated by implementation strategies. It is also essential to keep the plan on track by using a control process that emphasizes the comparison of the results from marketing activities with the performance indicators and objectives set in Stage 2. Remedial action is then taken to correct the plan where it has been unsuccessful, has strayed off course, or needs supplementation in order to capitalize on some unexpected opportunity.

Sport marketing revolves around the premise of satisfying the needs of sport consumers, in so doing cultivating a relationship with them that leads to a strong brand loyalty. Sport marketing lies at the intersection of strategy, where sport organizations focus on what they are good at, and market opportunities, where sport consumers are offered what they want. The best way of finding this intersection is to use a systematic approach like that outlined in the Sport Marketing Framework.

Most of modern life is spent within close proximity to several screens including the television, computer, pad and smart phone. In fact, most of us take at least one device with us everywhere we go, and sport viewing is no exception irrespective of whether it is live or through a broadcast. Sport marketers have grasped the opportunities that go with constant connectivity to draw fans more deeply into the game, its players, and all the intrigue, excitement and hype that occurs via the seemingly personalized communications that smart phones deliver. A sporting experience no longer means just viewing a game or event. Sport fans have at their fingertips a smorgasbord of information, statistics, live feeds, replays, messages and insider observations with which to engage. Twitter feeds and Facebook posts can integrate with broadcasts. Venues and media channels can provide customized apps with real-time updates to enhance the viewing experience. It has now also become common for major sporting venues to provide enhanced WiFi in stadiums to encourage fan use of social media and content highlights. Numerous stakeholders have an interest including the social media platform, sport properties, advertisers, sponsors and broadcast content-owners.

REVIEW QUESTIONS

1   Explain the difference between the marketing *of* sport, and marketing *through* sport.

2   What are the steps in the Sport Marketing Framework?

3   What is the relationship between sport marketing objectives and performance measures? How are these relevant to controlling the marketing plan?

4   What is the purpose of market positioning?

5   What is the difference between a sport product and a sport service?

6   What effect does pricing have on positioning? Provide an example of how price can influence a consumer's perception of a product.

7   What are the four tools of the promotions mix? Provide an example of each.

8   Provide a good example of a sponsor and sport property relationship that enjoys a high level of affinity.

9   What is the relationship between service quality and customer satisfaction?

FURTHER READING

Dos Santos, M.A. (2014). *Strategies in Sports Marketing: Technologies and Emerging Trends.* Hershey, PA: IGI-Global.

Earnheardt, A.C., Haridakis, P. & Hugenberg, B. (2013). *Sports Fans, Identity, and Socialization Exploring the Fandemonium.* New York: Lexington Books.

Fortunato, J.A. (2013). *Sports Sponsorship: Principles and Practices.* Jefferson, NC: McFarland Publishers.

Lee, J.W. (2010). *Branded: Branding in Sport Business.* Durham, NC: Carolina Academic Press.

Pritchard, M.P. & Stinson, J.L. (eds) (2013). *Leveraging Brands in Sport Business.* London: Routledge.

Simons, E. (2013). *The Secret Life of Sports Fans: The Science of Sports Obsession.* New York: Overlook Press.

Smith, A. & Stewart, B. (2014). *Introduction to Sport Marketing.* 2nd edn. London: Routledge.

RELEVANT WEBSITES

- East Coast Lifestyle at http://eastcoastlifestyle.ca
- Forbes Magazine at http://forbes.com
- Football Supporters Federation at http://fsf.org.uk
- Liverpool Football Club fan sites at www.redandwhitekop.com
- Brighton Rollers fan site at http://brightonbrats.com/tag/fanzine
- Independent online fanzine for Ice Hockey at http://bleedandblue.co.uk
- All England Lawn Tennis and Croquet Club's (AELTC) at http://wimbledon.com
- Bwin online gambling website http://bwin.com

CASE STUDY 11.1

Anchors away: The East Coast Lifestyle branding story

Beginning in the early 1900s, branding began to shift from an agricultural platform as a simple means for labelling cattle, to a manufacturing platform, focussing on health products, cosmetics, foodstuffs and clothing. In the late twentieth and early twenty-first century, branding as a marketing tactic escalated to include services, people, ideas, places, and of course, sport. Initially, consumers attached a preference to branded products and services as a matter of course. The authoritative nature of branding 'telling' consumers what branded products and services they needed worked well with audiences used to being passive, and relatively new to the media channels being employed. However, by the late twentieth century, the 'snake oil' promises made on behalf of promoted brands were failing to charm consumers to the same level. As a result, the notion of brand authenticity arose as an increasingly important marketing variable. Contemporary branding strategies concentrate on cultural and psychological connections in order to reflect a consumer's identity and establish a bond of belonging. However, personalizing a sport brand and tapping into an individual's identity, aspirations and emotions remain a challenging task. Yet, in terms of identification, we see in sport the most powerful brand affiliations ever created, some of them using the traction of sport to assign connections to fashion products and equipment.

Cultivating a sport brand in an already cluttered market comes with risks. Branding creates an identity and a promise. The more it is recognized, the more powerful it becomes. *Forbes* categorizes sports brands into four areas: the athlete, the team or sport organization, sports events, and sports goods manufacturing. Each of these sport brand domains has the capability to tap into an individual's emotional and aspirational needs while simultaneously fulfilling a cultural and personal identity. Notably, some of the most successful branding endeavours have managed to thread together several of these four strands, despite only offering one category. In this case, the East Coast Lifestyle brand demonstrates how the use of athletes, team sports, and sporting events can all be leveraged in order to sell clothing.

Athlete branding occurs when individuals who are successful in their sporting careers generate a mass of support from fans and corporations, who in turn, pay for the privilege to be associated with the athlete. For the consumer, purchasing products or services endorsed by an athlete fulfils desire and identity needs. Here, the athlete possesses tangible commercial value. According to one method, an athlete's brand value can be calculated by subtracting the average endorsement income of the top 10 athletes in a particular sport from what the particular athlete earns from endorsements. The intent is to capture the value premium the athlete's name can yield versus the other top endorsers in the same sport. For example, recently Tiger Woods was named the number one sport personality brand, valued at US$35 million, despite his income from golf declining and the withdrawal of one or two critical sponsors.

Individual athlete branding sits alongside sport team branding. Increasingly, sport clubs and teams are improving their brand identities and values due to better global exposure through more ubiquitous media channels. For example, a few years ago the New York Yankees brand was worth US$328 million (21 per cent of their US$1.6 billion total team value), with English Premier League club Manchester United's brand worth estimated at US$285 million (16 per cent of their US$1.835 billion value). Shortly afterwards, the Yankees enjoyed a merchandising frenzy thanks to a 27th World Series title and a new stadium opening. By 2013, Spanish La Liga giant, Real Madrid FC, had become the world's most valuable sports franchise, worth US$3.3 billion, surpassing former leader Manchester United. Real Madrid, 'Los Blancos', command the highest revenues of any team in sports (approximately US$650 million per season) while revenues have climbed around 62 per cent over the last three years. Madrid's operating income (earnings before interest, taxes, depreciation and amortization, and player trading) of US$134 million is second only to the NFL's Dallas Cowboys among sports teams.

Sports events generate significant media exposure, attendance, tourism and merchandising opportunities. World championships like the FIFA World Cup, the summer and winter Olympics, and the Moto Grand Prix series are so focussed on brand value that they have developed highly regulated corporate branding policies. National level events like the US Super Bowl wield an enormous global presence with a brand value more than US$460 million, mainly as a result of immense media coverage and advertising revenues.

In terms of sporting goods brands, few can compare to Nike's impact as the most valuable sports brand in the world, worth US$15.9 billion (excluding its other autonomous brands like Cole Haan, Converse, Umbro and Hurley). Forbes noted that Nike has continued to grow its brand with an increase of US$1.4 billion, or 9.7 per cent since 2007, despite a tarnished global reputation as a result of perceived human rights improprieties. The Nike name accounts for over one third of the athletic gear maker's market value.

For most sport entities, competing with the top brands seems impossible. However, a branding strategy remains critical to the success of all sport products and services today. Engineering a successful sport brand requires opportunistic flair and resourcefulness. One innovative Canadian university student found a niche in the marketplace in the form of a casual sporting clothing line. East Coast Lifestyle (ECL) clothing was first created to fulfil a university course assessment, but its emotional link to the east coast of Canada through its line of casual clothing depicting a stylized anchor logo, provided an evocative cultural connection to many local consumers.

The brand was first launched through a social media strategy in 2013 via Instagram, Twitter and Facebook. Branding scope was accelerated when images were posted of consumers wearing ECL branded T-shirts and sweatshirts during the northern hemisphere spring break. Potential customers began to associate the brand to the east coast way of living. 'Hot knowledge', or peer-to-peer information sharing, helps establish brands quickly in the marketplace. Once photos were made public, ECL's owner reposted them and asked on-liners to show where they would be proud to wear their ECL look. The social media platform for promotion was so successful that the brand generated over 250,000 sales in one summer. Friends and supporters were keen to self-promote from all parts of the world and the #EastCoastLifestyle tag on Instagram helped to spread the word rapidly and at little expense.

A lean start-up approach like this is a cost efficient way of testing the marketplace and making decisions about whether to continue with production. In this case the brand generated interest rapidly in its first year when sporting identities across North America were seen wearing ECL clothing. East coast Canadian professional hockey players were placing orders, as were renowned musicians from the region.

As the ECL case exemplifies, a branding strategy should consider several key issues. First, the product itself should be a 'must have' item, or at least, generate a must have response. All major sports clubs around the world capitalize on this demand with well-designed merchandise duplicating the team uniform. In fact, team and club jerseys and other apparel demonstrate allegiance publically to a player, team and region. Elite athletes originating from the east coast of Canada, but playing in major North American leagues, approached founder Alex McLean for orders; people were associating East Coast Lifestyle with elite sport.

Second, the branding design must be memorable and visually appealing to the target audience. Too much detail can easily get lost in translation across the various media through which sport is presented. ECL's founder believed that 'East Coasters' were proud of their heritage and would readily support a brand that reflected the region and promised to 'give back' to the east coast community. The simple anchor symbol hit the mark. However, if the symbol is too prosaic or overexposed then its impact is diluted.

Third, branded products need to be accessible through appropriate physical and online distribution channels. Sport teams like Manchester United and the New York Yankees have been able to make their branded products accessible to fans all over the world through licensed agreements and online purchasing facilities. ECL created an awareness and interest in their products via an online social media platform. Applying a push strategy to potential consumers – especially those located around the globe but still fiercely east coast in identification – enabled demand to rapidly intensify, fuelled by its viral social media exposure. For ECL the anchor symbol struck a chord by inspiring images of lazy summer days on the east coast of Canada. Now, ECL has the opportunity to include other seasonal activities or other communities where the east coast lifestyle strikes a similar chord.

Finally, in an environment where brands come and go regularly, refreshing the brand revitalizes and renews interest for heritage customers and stimulates brand awareness and potential purchasing behaviour from new customers. For example, when the National Hockey League concluded successful contract negotiations, ensuring that there would actually be a professional hockey season after a year off, the league decided that it was time to revitalize its brand identity. Since the league had not modified it brand identity since 1918, the move was perhaps overdue! This step was also designed to polish up the tarnished image of the league with fans. Knowing when to launch a brand or rebrand is critical to its success. Timing the launch for pre-season also attracts greater interest and less confusion than if introduced mid-season. McLean's ECL brand was let loose on the market at a time when northern hemisphere students were poised for semester breaks and holiday travel. Friends and peers were interested in their fellow students' exploits and actively followed along online, resulting in further enquiries to ECL and subsequent opportunities to build brand equity.

Linking to experiences beyond the playing field gives a sport brand wider appeal. For example, four-wheel drive car brands such as Subaru appeal to a wider audience than just off-road enthusiasts. The ECL brand reflects a lifestyle as much as a sport. McLean's intention is to peddle his wares at major beach hang-outs and concerts for young people down the east coast of the United States, encouraging them to take 'selfies', post online to their friends, and share the brand motif.

From a brand authenticity viewpoint, savvy consumers understand the difference between what a brand represents and what the owning corporation practices. An authentic brand must also reflect values consistent with its portrayed identity. In this case the ELC creator donated T-shirts to the homeless and supported disabled children through athletics programs. For small organizations, applying a lean start-up business model and delivering through social media platforms enables the brand manager to keep costs down while maximizing exposure to a desired target market. Marketing a sport clothing brand is as much about presenting a holistic brand beyond the target market as it is about making sales.

CASE STUDY QUESTIONS

1   How symbolic is the East Coast Lifestyle brand for a wider audience?

2   Where can the ECL brand go to from here? Does it have global potential?

3   How should the brand be sold in the future: online only presence, licensed through sport retailers, ECL specialist stores or a mixed mode of distribution? Justify your answer.

CASE STUDY 11.2

A sure bet for sport fans: Using bwin to market online gambling though sport

The very nature of sport performance contains elements of risk. Every time a participant enters the sporting arena they take a gamble, as do their fans and supporters. In order to work successfully in sport, managers must come to terms with the kinds of risks that go along with delivering sport to live and broadcast audiences. Despite the outcome uncertainty that accompanies sporting performance, the most significant risk in sport is the same as in any other substantive business: financial loss. Because sport does not always attract conventional business investors, sport managers have to work hard to find the right backing for their products. However, while essential for funding the sport product delivery, attracting and maintaining investors raises its own series of risks. As a result, sport organizations sometimes form partnerships that allow their sport or brand to provide a vehicle for other profit-making enterprises. That is, instead of marketing their sport, a sport organization can market some other product *through* their sport in order to secure an additional source of revenue.

Major international events such as the Olympic Games and FIFA World Cup provide examples of sport products possessing immense global appeal that can be on-sold to corporations wishing to be associated through sponsorships, licensing arrangements or other kinds of deals where a privileged access to the sporting product can enhance profit opportunities. In recent times, however, the commonplace version of marketing through sport – the sponsorship – has been augmented by other business models emerging with the availability and agility of online applications and mobile devices. Sport gaming and gambling sit at the top of the list of lucrative business models that can exploit sport for new sources of profit. Not only do sport consumers enjoy watching sport, they also display a huge appetite for making wagers on various facets of sports events. In fact, gambling and sport have always enjoyed a synonymous relationship, magnified by personal identification and the belonging sport fans associate with their favourite teams. To make matters even more attractive to companies offering sporting wagers, most sport fans over-estimate their sporting expertise, typically assuming that they have a special knowledge about a game's likely outcome. Gambling organizations have always existed, both legally and unlawfully. Now, however, the industry has become fully embedded with sport.

With the increased engagement between the sport fan and information communication technologies, online sports gambling has grown into a global industry. In 2003 the market volume for online betting was estimated at US$7.4 billion. By 2014 it had more than quadrupled its volume to over US$35 billion. Sports betting constitutes the largest category for online gambling activity, now worth around US$15 billion. Of course, all of these figures reflect the legal, registered online gambling agencies. It remains unclear just how much money disappears through illegal sport gambling, but it is probably far more than the amount generated through legal channels. Amongst the most prominent legal online gambling companies are Betfair, Sportingbet, 188bet and bwin. Of these sport betting agencies, Betfair attracts the largest interest with seven million members across 200 countries. Their strength lies with product diversity by offering a wide range of sporting and gambling options across 22 sports products. However, Betfair faces increasing competition as sport betting agencies have proliferated recently. At the same time these agencies must consider marketing strategies that best reach the sport consumer.

'Betandwin', or bwin, offers a good example of an online gambling company that has been successful in marketing through sport. Founded in 1999, bwin fast became a major player in the relatively small Spanish market. Although the Spanish were not avid internet sport gamblers at the time, gambling legislation was non-existent, and the opportunity to establish an online sport gambling market was unconstrained by either competition or regulation. Initially, the primary customers were experienced British online sport gamblers who spent their holiday season in Spain. Unibet and bwin consequently became the dominant legal agencies for sport gambling in the nation.

In the early days, bwin enjoyed relative freedom from regulatory compliance. Online sport gambling legislation did not arrive in Spain until 2008, around the same time as physical betting facilities specifically targeting the Spanish market had become thick in cities like Madrid. With such a surge in gambling, the Spanish authorities implemented new laws to regulate betting, including the lucrative online betting industry. Once legislation took hold, it compelled many organizations that did not want to purchase a Spanish licence, including major player, Unibet, to abandon the Spanish market. The new competitive arena opened up opportunities for bwin to create a solid footing.

Gaming in Spain was becoming widespread with sport being a natural product addition given the passion and interest in professional football. In fact, by 2011, more than 90 per cent of Spaniards between the ages of 18 and 75 years were gambling in some form, whether on the national lottery or on their preferred sport. Demographics of the 'average' gambler had becomes almost identical to those of the La Liga fan: male, aged 25 to 55 years, and of middle class income. Behaviourally, the online gambler and sport fan also displayed similar traits of resilience, emotional engagement, and a detailed knowledge of their pursuit. Furthermore, both gamblers and sports fans had greater access to, and usage of internet, smart phones and tablet technologies in order to extend their involvement with the team beyond match day activity.

In 2007, the World Sponsorship Monitor reported 21 gambling or lottery sport sponsorship deals. By 2014 the figure had nearly quadrupled, revealing a significant connection between the gaming industry and sport. Even during the financial crisis, which impacted Spain severely, when other more mainstream sport sponsors scaled down their involvement with sport, betting companies took up the slack. In 2008, bwin intensified their campaign to attract Spaniards by sponsoring La Liga's powerhouse club, Real Madrid. Real's success is built around a 'galactico' attitude. Securing superstar players from around the world, coupled with on-field success gave the club an unprecedented global exposure. With over 80,000 'socio' members at Real Madrid, and a burgeoning international following, bwin had the ideal platform to market their product on a broader scale.

Bwin had successfully deployed a brand awareness strategy coupled with a concentrated advertising campaign punctuated through a high profile sport sponsorship deal. The company focussed on tradition and success as the key linking concepts between sponsor and sponsee. Its philosophy at the time focussed on 'no sports, no sports betting', directing its marketing towards the Madrid membership along with match day incentives. Reaching the European football market became bwin's primary investment.

The increasing ubiquity of cheap and fast internet in Spain and the growing prominence of the Spanish professional sports sector, helped to augment bwin's marketability, along with some savvy product decisions. Bwin's core product became pre-match and live sports betting. It deliberately exposed sports betting to the Spanish market via key sponsorships of football, supplemented by basketball and motor sport. Despite the popularity of basketball and motor sport, nothing rivals football in Spain. The La Liga stage became pivotal for marketing online gaming through sport.

Real Madrid commands over 35 per cent of the domestic football fan market in Spain, equating to nearly seven million people. As bwin strengthened their position in the sports sector and built additional digital partnerships, their strategy shifted towards social integration in order to enable fans to experience sport through digital media and real-time experiences. For example, bwin used its long-term sponsorship of the Spanish Grand Prix to place branding reminders around the course aimed at spectators and television viewers. Through a smart phone, any race aficionado, irrespective of their location, can bet on the fastest lap, pole position, and a range of head-to-head challenges.

Bwin's 'marketing through sport' strategy focussed on building a long-term partnership with Real Madrid. Theirs was more than just a sponsorship. Even though the more traditional promotional practices of banner advertising, shirt branding and a complementary media campaign were employed, bwin recognized that by creating a trustworthy relationship with Real fans, they would be more likely to capture them in sport betting practices. According to market research, Spanish consumers tend to believe in fate when it comes to gambling. Bwin addressed this social attribute by reinforcing images of destiny and providence through their connection to Real Madrid. Consequently, as the football club built an international following, bwin gained positive global attention. Good fortune in winning corresponded to good fortune in gambling.

The initial strategy for bwin relied on transforming brand awareness and visibility through sport sponsorship of Real Madrid, to more customers using its online sports gambling services. Having worked, bwin's current strategy seeks another type of conversion focussing on digital partnerships. A digital sponsorship approach enabled bwin to create online content and integrate it with technological tools like smart phones and tablets in order to create a direct engagement with their target audience. Today bwin wants to be the leading global brand for online sport betting. Interestingly, masculinity comprises part of bwin's brand identity strategy. They hope to reinforce the perception that sport represents a masculine pursuit, along with the boldness that risk-taking through gambling demands. All of the sports bwin sponsors are traditionally male-dominated.

With over 20 million registered customers, bwin is a world leader in online gambling. Its determination to secure a beachhead in Spain to market its products to the remainder of the world worked magnificently due, in large part, to its Real Madrid partnership. Despite re-emerging from the global recession more slowly than other European nations, Spanish sport fans have embraced online gambling. Online betting operators like bwin seem to be recession-proof. They entered a marketplace when competition was low and built up awareness and acceptance with Spanish fans. Bwin have been able to continually adapt their product to include a variety of gambling opportunities for every sporting event, thus appealing to a broader customer base. The internet has allowed sport fans to access their team and its performances across temporal, geographic and even legal boundaries.

This case exemplifies how marketing a product through a high profile sporting club can generate new business and stimulate new behaviours from existing club members.

CASE STUDY QUESTIONS

1 Identify the various sources of environmental information available in the case and determine the opportunities and threats that exist for bwin in marketing through sport.

2 Who benefits the most from the bwin–Real Madrid relationship?

CHAPTER 12

Media

OVERVIEW

This chapter examines the key features of the relationship between sport and the media with reference to its management. It provides an examination of the ways in which sport and the media interact depending on the three sector model of sport, the commercial foundations of the sport–media relationship, in particular the sale of broadcast rights, and the ways in which governments regulate the sport–media relationship. It concludes with a brief acknowledgement of the role of the sport media manager in the professional sport industry.

After completing this chapter the reader should be able to:

- identify the ways in which the sport–media relationship is dependent on the three sector model of sport;
- understand and explain the various dimensions of the commercial foundations of the sport–media relationship;
- understand and explain the rationale for government to intervene in the sport–media relationship via regulation;
- comment on the development of the role of the sport media manager.

WHAT IS THE MEDIA?

The media is often considered to provide three broad functions in a society: information, education and entertainment. However, in terms of the sport–media relationship, it has become increasingly clear that media organizations and consumers are interested in professional sport in particular because of its entertainment value. The exploits of leagues, teams and athletes are reported throughout the world, across a wide range of print (e.g. newspapers and magazines) and broadcast (e.g. radio, television and the internet) media. Some of this media coverage is provided as 'news', which essentially means that media organizations report on what is happening in sport in much the same way they report on politics or world events. However, a significant component of broadcast coverage is provided through exclusive arrangements in which media organizations purchase the rights to broadcast an event or season(s).

In understanding the management of the sport–media relationship it is important to keep in mind that the word 'media' has a diverse set of meanings. The word 'media' can represent the entire media industry, particularly when we refer to the sport–media relationship, or the way in which the media reports on a particular sport or athlete. The word media can also be used to refer to a form, channel, platform, company, network or station, depending on the context. Television, radio, print and internet can all be considered media forms or distribution channels. These media forms and channels also have individual outlets: television networks or stations such as ESPN (a network) or FUEL TV (a station on the FOX Sports network), specific newspapers (such as *La Gazzetta dello Sport*, the Italian sport newspaper published since 1896); radio stations (such as SEN, a sport radio station in Melbourne, Australia) or internet websites (such as www.si.com, the website of Sports Illustrated, owned by company Time Inc.). These outlets are typically privately owned and employ journalists, writers and commentators to generate content, in order to attract an audience, in the hope of returning a profit. A television network is typically a collection of individual stations that people tune into to watch their favourite sport or catch up on daily news, which is owned by a media company (refer to In Practice 12.1 related to the Walt Disney Company for more information on a specific media company that has multiple media networks, with their own sport and non-sport outlets). More recently, the term platform has been used to describe media such as Facebook or Twitter, where the interactivity and user-driven content is such that they cannot be considered a media outlet in the same way as a single newspaper or television station.

THE SPORT–MEDIA RELATIONSHIP

In the first chapter of this book you were introduced to the three sector model of sport: public, nonprofit and private. In Chapters 2 and 3 the public and nonprofit sectors were examined, while in Chapter 4 the professional sport industry was explored. In order to understand the relationship between sport and the media it is important to acknowledge that all three sectors of sport need the media in order to survive and prosper in contemporary society. However, it is also important to acknowledge that each sector seeks to establish a relationship with the media for different purposes. In order to provide context for the rest of the chapter, and for other chapters within the book, it is important to explore each sector in turn.

In Chapter 2 the role of the state and the reasons for state intervention were explored. When the state seeks to regulate or control sporting activities, for example, it also typically seeks to explain the rationale for its decisions and any subsequent actions it might take. The state may wish to make its citizens aware that it has regulated a particular sporting activity in order to make it safer for children, to reduce the injury toll or ensure that corruption is eliminated. It is very difficult for the state to communicate effectively with its citizens directly – this is most problematic for national governments and least problematic although still difficult for local governments. Instead, the state relies on the media to act as an intermediary between it and its citizens. Governments and government departments also use the media to seek social, political and economic legitimacy, as well as promote their activities and gain status. National sporting institutes are often funded almost entirely by national governments and operate as de facto government departments. Taxes collected from citizens are spent on the selection, training, coaching, accommodation and welfare of elite athletes, in order to secure international sporting success at events such as the Olympic Games and world championships. As such, the success or failure of a nation's elite athletes is invariably a public issue – the Games or events are broadcast on television and widely reported throughout the media. If a nation's athletes perform well then the state and its agencies are likely to claim that they had an important role and that this demonstrates their strategic and managerial abilities. These claims are made through the media and in doing so the approval of a nation's citizens is sought. If a nation's athletes perform poorly and below expectations, then the media is likely to actively question the performance of the elite institute and by association the government and its agencies. In these cases the state is somewhat unwillingly drawn into discussion about its performance that is conducted by and through the media.

In Chapter 3 the role of nonprofit sport organizations was examined and it was noted that nonprofit sport organizations exist at all levels of the sport industry and landscape, which influences the ways in which they interact with the media. For example, the following organizations are all nonprofit: the International Olympic Committee (IOC), which runs the Olympic Games; New Zealand Rugby, the national governing body for rugby union in New Zealand, which is responsible for the development of community rugby as well as the performance of the national team the All Blacks; Netball Queensland, the governing body for the sport of netball in the State of Queensland, Australia; and Hills Ultimate Frisbee, an ultimate frisbee league in the Western suburbs of Sydney, Australia. The relationship with the media is vastly different across each of these nonprofit organizations. The IOC receives almost US$3 billion every four years from media organizations for the right to broadcast the summer and winter Olympics. The media interact with New Zealand Rugby on a number of levels, but perhaps most of all in covering the All Blacks, the most popular and prominent national team in New Zealand, and in paying broadcast rights fees for international and Super Rugby matches. Netball Victoria seeks the support of the regional media outlets in encouraging more people to play the sport of netball, as well as in promoting the Queensland Firebirds, a semi-professional team in the ANZ Championship (an international netball league comprised of teams from Australia and New Zealand). Hills Ultimate Frisbee predominantly seeks the support of local media in promoting the sport of ultimate frisbee in order to attract more people to the sport, which in turn ensures the viability of its leagues and clubs. These examples all illustrate that the nonprofit sector is the most varied of all the sport sectors in terms of the types of organizations as well as the sport–media relationships that are developed and fostered.

In Chapter 4 the role and activities of professional sport organizations were examined. Professional organizations, such as the teams that play in the National Football League (NFL) in the USA, compete in Formula 1 across the world or play in the English Premier League, are considered to be at the apex of the sport industry because of the scope of their operations and because the athletes and staff associated with these organizations are full-time professionals. These organizations have an intimate relationship with the media, to the point that the financial viability of large media organizations and professional sport leagues and teams are inextricably linked. Professional sport organizations receive broadcast rights fees directly from media organizations, leverage the media coverage they receive through these agreements to secure lucrative sponsorship deals, as well as seek to secure as much media coverage as possible through media outlets not governed by exclusive rights agreements. At the same time, media organizations are seeking to cover professional sport organizations in order to increase their audience, which has necessitated sport organizations employ staff in a variety of media, public relations and communication management roles. The proliferation of media channels, particularly online and social, has made these roles more complex and specialized.

In order to understand the management implications of a relationship between sport and media organizations, it is essential that you are aware of the type of media organization and the type of sport organization that is involved. As illustrated by the above discussion of the three sectors of sport, the type of sport organization can significantly alter the type of sport–media relationship that is negotiated or entered into. For a sport organization, the relationship could be predicated on securing a financial return on investment, generating political legitimacy or credibility in the marketplace, or promoting activities and events in order to attract more members or to increase participation. These goals and outcomes will also be influenced by the type of media organizations that are engaged in the relationship. It is important to keep in mind that not all sport–media relationships are the same, and each must be examined in detail in order to reveal the expectations, agreements and benefits.

In Practice 12.1 The Walt Disney Company

The Walt Disney Company started as a cartoon studio in the 1920s and has grown into a global business empire. The Company views itself as an 'international family entertainment and media enterprise', with five business segments: media networks; parks and resorts; studio entertainment; consumer products; and interactive media. The Walt Disney Company is perhaps best known for its theme parks such as Disneyland, which opened in 1955, part of a business segment that now comprises 11 theme parks, 44 resorts and 4 cruise ships. Studio entertainment continues to be a mainstay of the Company's business operations, with feature films released under banners such as Pixar, Marvel Studios, Lucasfilm and Touchstone Pictures. The consumer products segment of the Disney business consists of toys, apparel, books and art, distributed through a retail chain of more than 350 stores worldwide. The interactive media segment of the business is focussed on the development, production and sale of mobile and console games, as well as virtual worlds and websites.

The fifth segment of the Walt Disney Company business is media networks, which is of most relevance to an analysis of the relationship between sport and the media, although it is important to keep in mind that it is one element of a much larger integrated global business. The Company's media networks division consists of broadcast (free-to-air), cable (pay), radio, publishing and digital businesses. These businesses are split across two divisions – the Disney/ABC Television Group and ESPN Inc. Both the ABC Television Group and ESPN have significant interests in the sport industry. According to the Company's 2013 annual financial report and shareholder letter, ESPN is the leader in sport media:

> the brand's groundbreaking WatchESPN service is now available to more than 55 million U.S. homes, allowing fans to stream live sports programming on a variety of devices. And ESPN continues to lead the digital media sports space – in November alone, ESPN reached more than 68 million fans across digital platforms, and sports fans spent more than four billion minutes during that single month connected to ESPN on their smart phones and tablets. Across all platforms, ESPN has been the number one with sports fans since the industry started officially tracking multiplatform usage – leading in audience share, total visits, total minutes, and average audience per minute, among other measures. For sports fans it seems the more devices they have the more ESPN they want.
>
> (p. 2)

In its 2013 annual report the Walt Disney Company reported that ESPN had an estimated 99 million subscribers, and that the network holds the rights for the National Football League (NFL); National Basketball Association (NBA); Major League Baseball (MLB), the Bowl Championship Series; major college football and basketball conferences; NASCAR; the Wimbledon Championships; US Open Tennis; British Open Golf; and the Masters Golf tournament. ESPN3, the broadband service available to more than 85 million subscribers delivers more than 4,800 live events to its audience.

Source: Walt Disney Company website and annual reports at http://thewaltdisneycompany.com

COMMERCIAL DIMENSIONS OF THE SPORT–MEDIA RELATIONSHIP

The way in which the commercial dimensions of the sport–media relationship operate can be divided into five interrelated components, which are represented in Figure 12.1. First, media organizations pay for the right to broadcast a sport event, season or series of games. These broadcast rights are typically limited to free-to-air television, pay television, radio and the internet, and of these four the two television forms are by far the biggest players. In Figure 12.1 this is demonstrated by the sport organization providing the official broadcaster with content and in return the broadcaster pays a rights fee. In contrast to most forms of electronic media, however, the print media typically reports on sport in a heavily competitive environment in a news or public interest capacity, rather than a promotional capacity via an exclusive contract or arrangement, and as such are not charged a fee by sport organizations.

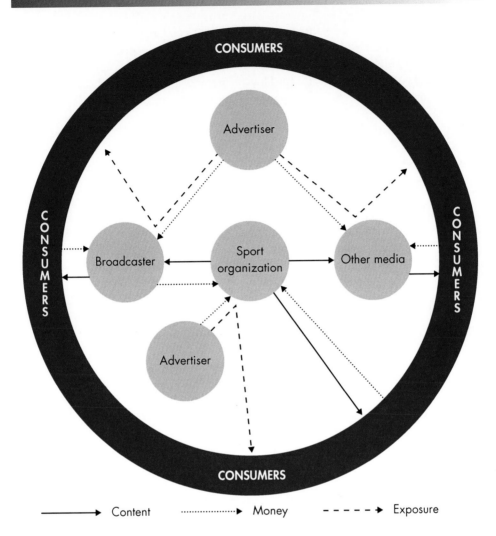

FIGURE 12.1 Sport and media relationships

Source: Adapted from Nicholson (2007)

Second, media organizations that purchase the rights to broadcast a sport event, season or series of games seek to secure a return on investment. On free-to-air television this is primarily achieved through the sale of advertising space and time, which in Figure 12.1 is represented by the advertiser acquiring exposure to consumers via the broadcaster. The number of people, as well as the type of people, watching the sport is directly proportional to advertising revenue and to broadcast rights fees. On pay television a return on investment is achieved by the sale of advertising space and by attracting subscribers who, in general terms, are prepared to pay for a generic service, dedicated sport channels or pay-per-view events. In Figure 12.1 this relationship is represented by the consumer paying the broadcaster for content which has previously been purchased by the broadcaster from the sport organization. In the case of pay television, the number of people watching sport and more specifically those who are prepared to pay, is directly proportional to the broadcast rights fees. The popularity and appeal of sport also means that acquiring the rights to broadcast sport events and games can increase the broadcaster's brand awareness, which in turn might increase the demand for other non-sport-related content (Hoehn & Lancefield 2003). This phenomenon is likely to be greater if a broadcaster has held the rights for an extended period of time and consumer loyalty to both the sport and media products has been established.

Third, media organizations that do not have the exclusive broadcast rights will also seek to attract advertising revenue through coverage of sport. For example, a sport magazine or newspaper will invest in the coverage of sport in a non-exclusive and typically a non-official capacity, which will in turn attract consumers. This is represented in Figure 12.1 where consumers pay other media providers for sport related content. Based on the size and demographics of the readership, advertisers will pay the magazine or newspaper to access consumers.

Fourth, sport organizations seek to attract sponsorship revenue based on the sport's popularity, which in turn is proportional to the amount of media coverage achieved. In this way, sport organizations secure additional revenue via the broadcaster, as well as via the media coverage provided by other media outside the exclusive rights agreement. The consumer might pay for the content by purchasing a newspaper or magazine, or may receive the content for free through an internet or radio news program. These relationships are represented in Figure 12.1, whereby the sponsor receives exposure to consumers via the broadcaster and other media, and the sport organization receives a direct financial benefit. Thus, sport organizations must not only maximize media coverage that results from exclusive broadcast rights agreements, but must also seek to maximize general media coverage, thereby increasing exposure, awareness, interest and audience share.

Finally, sport organizations are able to provide mediated sport content directly to consumers. In Figure 12.1 this is represented by consumers paying the sport organization for the product or content. With the rapid advancement of technology, over the last ten years in particular, organizations have been able to provide content direct to fans and consumers (this is illustrated by the In Practice contained within this chapter that relates to FEI TV). Large sporting teams in popular national leagues now have their own 'television' channels, which are typically broadcast through the internet, either free or as a special addition to subscription and membership packages. Whether the product or content is free or has been purchased, the popularity of sport organization created content is such that companies beyond the traditional suite of sponsors are now prepared to pay to get access to the consumers of this media. In Figure 12.1 this is represented by advertisers paying sport organizations directly, in order to get access to the consumers and fans of the sport organization. The amount that advertisers are prepared to pay is directly proportional to the size and type of the audience. Prior to the development of technologies that have enabled sport teams, leagues and federations to become their own broadcasters, these type of advertising relationships were rare and commercial relationships were limited to key sponsors. While it is still true that sponsors are the dominant advertisers within this setting, the value of being able to access a distinct and measurable consumer market is now also becoming evident to non-sponsor advertisers.

The example of the Australian Football League illustrates the importance of the media to the commercial success of contemporary sport organizations. The Australian

Football League is the governing body for Australian football and manages the national competition, the AFL, as well as being responsible for game development throughout the nation. The AFL competition consists of 18 teams and is the most popular sport in Australia in terms of live attendance, television ratings and the size of its television broadcast rights. The AFL is also one of the world's most popular sports using the criteria of average game/match attendance. In 2013 the AFL's revenue was AUS$450 million, of which 'broadcasting and AFL media' accounted for AUS$234 million. In addition, commercial operations accounted for AUS$168 million, a significant proportion of which was received from sponsors. These sponsors, as demonstrated by the above discussion of the commercial foundations of the sport–media relationship, are prepared to invest in the sport on the basis of increased exposure, awareness and sales, which are generated most significantly through the sport's media coverage. It is clear that the financial stability of the AFL, like almost all national sporting leagues throughout the world, is dependent on the media.

In Practice 12.2 FEI TV

Formed in 1921, the *Fédération Equestre Internationale* (FEI) is the international governing body for equestrian sports across its seven recognized disciplines: dressage, jumping, eventing, driving, endurance, vaulting and reining. Like other international governing bodies, the FEI has an important role in establishing the regulations and rules that govern its various disciplines, approving and organizing major national and international championship events, and developing equestrian sports throughout the world. The FEI has 132 member federations and is one of the few sports in the world in which men and women compete together in 3,500 annual events held throughout the world. The FEI is the property rights holder for a series of major events and series including the FEI World Equestrian Games, the FEI Nations Cup, the FEI World Cup and World Championships across its constituent disciplines. Like the Olympic Games and the FIFA World Cup, the FEI World Equestrian Games are held every four years, with eight world championships held simultaneously, the show-piece of the sport globally. The FEI World Equestrian Games typically attract 500,000 spectators and a significant global television audience, particularly in Europe, North America and the Middle East.

Part of the FEI's role is the promotion of equestrian sport, including broadcasting, which is managed by the FEI commercial department. The vast majority of the FEI's annual broadcasting product is the FEI World Cup, the FEI Nations Cup and the FEI Classics. In the main these events are held in Europe, the location of the majority of the equestrian sport's fan-base. For example, the 37th edition of the premier international indoor showjumping series, the Longines FEI World Cup, was held in the following locations in 2014/2015: Oslo; Helsinki; Lyon; Verona; Stuttgart; Madrid; London; Mechelen; Leipzig; Zurich; Bordeaux and Gothenburg. The competition culminated in a final held in Las Vegas, USA. IMG Media, a division of IMG Worldwide, is charged with global distribution of the FEI's major events and broadcast products.

Many of the FEI's annual events and competitions receive significant television coverage, particularly in Europe where the equestrian disciplines of dressage, jumping and eventing are popular. The sport is also popular outside Europe, but television coverage is often sporadic and limited to pay or cable television highlights packages. The global fan-base and relatively limited television exposure has facilitated the development of FEI TV, an online subscription broadcast product provided directly to consumers via the FEI website. This model is not unique to the FEI, but is a useful example of how niche sports are able to monetize the media coverage of their sport beyond traditional broadcast rights agreements. Three subscription options are available through FEI TV: 24 hour access for US$18.99; monthly access for US$44.99 initially and then US$14.99 per month thereafter; or yearly access for US$79.99. It is clear that pricing options are designed to encourage equestrian fans to pay for a yearly subscription, rather than to make ad hoc payments for individual events throughout the year. The annual subscription allows equestrian fans to access up to 80 live events throughout the year – including the prestigious events and championships, which do not come at an extra cost – on-demand coverage and video archive, exclusive interviews and features, and behind the scenes access.

Source: FEI website at www.fei.org

BROADCAST RIGHTS

The importance of sport is such that major national and international broadcasters almost always bid for the rights to high profile sports (Hoehn & Lancefield 2003). In fact, the rights to 'premium' sports have become such an important commercial property that not having them can adversely impact a company's financial bottom line or, in extreme cases, lead to the demise of media organizations (which in some jurisdictions has led to the regulation of exclusive rights agreements with a single broadcaster). Sport and sport broadcasting rights have special features that are not exhibited by other media products, making them extremely valuable national and global commodities. Sport events and games are an ephemeral product or perishable good, which means that they endure or last for a very brief period of time (Tonazzi 2003; Sandy et al. 2004). Consider the difference between sport programs and drama programs broadcast on television. Sport programs almost always exist for the duration that they are live – the unpredictability of sport attracts people to a spectacle that appears to unfold or develop as the audience is experiencing it. Great sporting events and contests contain enough stories, intrigue and emotion that they prompt commentators and fans alike to wonder whether a script writer could have written it any better. This is particularly true when games are won in the last seconds, when heroic deeds are performed at personal expense and when sport transcends political, racial and geographic barriers and stereotypes. Drama programs, by contrast, have a significant 'shelf-life'. Popular television drama programs are watched again and again by fans, often in large quantities as part of 'binge consumption'. Even though consumers know the plot, characters and ending after a first viewing, second and third viewings are still pleasurable. Except for the diehard fan, this is almost never the case with sport, perhaps in part because there are new games and matches being played continuously around the world. Individual instances of sporting consumption are fleeting, but the institution itself is enduring, which in turn makes it extremely attractive to broadcasters.

The value of sport broadcast rights is also increased by the fact that it is also very difficult for consumers of sport to satisfactorily substitute one product for another (Tonazzi 2003). In other words, a viewer who wants to watch televised games of a football league has little option but to consume the product offered by the broadcaster who has secured the rights. It is unlikely that the viewer will consider watching tennis or golf on another network a viable substitute. By contrast, a viewer interested in watching a criminal or legal drama is likely to be able to substitute a variety of products on a variety of networks and stations. In essence, each sport is a relatively unique product, which means that it is of more value than a product with multiple variants or imitations. Finally, unlike the multitude of news and drama that is available to television networks in particular, the amount of professional sport is finite (Tonazzi 2003). Moreover, premium sport leagues and events are even more limited, which means that competition to acquire the rights is greater.

The limit of substitutable products and the desire of consumers to view matches or events 'as they happen' make sport a highly valued and sought after commodity for media organizations. Media organizations that bid for the rights to sport often view these rights as an opportunity to capture a specific demographic or new markets (see the In Practice that relates to pay-per-view in this chapter, which refers specifically to the demographic of the UFC). Premium sport content can in the best cases draw consumers to a television network, increase advertising revenue and make non-sport network programming more popular and viable through association and cross promotion. The fact that sport is viewed as a key driver of direct and indirect revenues for media organizations has a significant impact on the size of broadcast rights, the competition to secure them, the ability of sport organizations to maximize their revenue through sponsorship, and the service that media organizations demand from their sport partners.

In Practice 12.3 Pay-Per-View pain

As discussed in this chapter, most sporting leagues and events sell the rights to broadcast their games, matches and tournaments to television networks or stations for a set fee or price. These broadcasters are typically categorized as either free-to-air or pay (or cable). Free-to-air broadcasters usually ensure a return on investment via the sale of advertising, while pay or cable broadcasters sell subscriptions to channels or packages. So, in short, audiences either watch sport for free but have to watch advertisements, or pay a monthly or annual fee to watch additional coverage or games, or sports that are only available on a pay or cable network. There are, however, some sports and sport organizations that utilize a different model, in which viewers are asked to pay an additional fee to watch premium content. This model only works in certain sports, in which regular 'standard' programming builds the excitement and interest in what can be considered 'ultra-premium' programming that is scheduled or staged sporadically throughout the year. The sports and organizations that have utilized this pay-per-view model most effectively are combat sports.

The World Wrestling Entertainment (WWE), although not technically a sport and perhaps more like a soap opera, has successfully been using the pay-per-view model of broadcasting for decades. The WWE has several weekly broadcasts across a range of television stations and channels. These weekly television programs are used to develop characters and storylines, as individual wrestlers compete in order to work their way up the WWE 'rankings'. Like in other sports, these weekly broadcasts are based on live action in arenas and stadiums in front of a live audience and feature the 'superstars' of the 'sport'. The weekly broadcasts also build tension and plotlines that are resolved in pay-per-view events, the most famous being 'WrestleMania', the thirtieth instalment of which was held in 2014. Most pay-per-view events, of which one is held almost every month, cost US$44.95 to watch, while WrestleMania costs US$59.95.

The pay-per-view broadcasting/financial model has been so successful for the WWE and sports such as boxing has also been adopted by The Ultimate Fighting Championship (UFC), one of the fastest growing sports in America, with an international profile and brand. The UFC started in 1993 and is now the world's leading mixed martial arts organization, with headquarters in Las Vegas and offices in London, Toronto and Beijing. According to the UFC itself, the organization produces more than 40 live events each year and is the largest pay-per-view provider in the world. UFC events are broadcast in almost 150 countries in 30 different languages. After slowly developing its profile and popularity, the UFC broke into the mainstream commercial and media markets in 2011 via a seven-year broadcasting agreement with FOX Sports Media Group. Through this agreement FOX channels FX and FUEL TV broadcast approximately 30 live fight events and The Ultimate Fighter, a sport reality show. At the time of signing the agreement, FOX chairman David Hill noted that the deal was important because of the UFC's ability to attract male viewers aged 18–34 years of age, a demographic essential for television networks and advertisers. The programming aired on the FOX channels serves to increase interest in the UFC, which is then monetized via pay-per-view events. These pay-per-view events are priced according to the strength of the fights being broadcast. For example, for UFC 168 the UFC raised the price by US$5 to US$49.95 for standard definition and US$59.95 for high definition.

The pay-per-view model works well for sports such as UFC and boxing, where sport fans are prepared to pay for 'event television'. In 2013 ESPN reported that the middleweight boxing match between Floyd Mayweather Jr and Saul 'Canelo' Alvarez, broadcast on Showtime, generated a record US$150 million from 2.2 million pay-per-view buys. This fight broke the record previous held by another Mayweather fight in 2007 against Oscar De La Hoya, which generated US$136 million from 2.48 million pay-per-view buys. These two fights are the only occasions that pay-per-view events have exceeded two million buys. By way of comparison, the UFC's largest pay-per-view buy was reported to be 1.6 million, and UFC drawcard events typically attract one million pay-per-view buys.

Sources: WWE website at www.wwe.com; UFC website at www.ufc.com; ESPN website at http://espn.go.com

REGULATING THE SPORT–MEDIA RELATIONSHIP

The interdependence of the sport and media industries, and in particular the overtly commercial relationship between sport and television, has presented a series of challenges for governments all over the world. These challenges have included ensuring that its citizens have reasonable access to sport broadcasting on television and that media and sport organizations do not engage in practices or behaviour that is anti-competitive. The regulation of sport broadcasting by government (the state) attempts to ameliorate the problems that result from often divergent interests of audiences, broadcasters, sport organizations and governing bodies. Hoehn and Lancefield noted that the

> pre-eminent position of sports programming in a channel's offering and as a key driver of a TV delivery/distribution platform has forced governments to intervene in media merger proposals, sports-rights contract negotiations, and disputes among TV distribution systems over access to content.
>
> (2003, p. 566)

This government intervention has had a significant impact on the way in which sport is broadcast, the amount of sport that audiences have access to via free-to-air (network) television, the ways in which sport organizations are able to sell broadcast rights and in some celebrated cases the ownership of sport teams.

The media industry's ever-changing complexity and diversity is such that governments often find it difficult to apply regulatory frameworks that adequately meet their policy objectives and allow the market to function as efficiently as possible. The sport media landscape is also often regarded as a separate component of the much broader media landscape because of its special features: significant audience appeal; vigorous competition between broadcasters; relatively cheap production costs; and a mutually reinforcing web of promotion between different types of media (modes and relationship to the sport). The importance of sport to both the modern media industry and consumers has resulted in government seeking to regulate the relationship between sport and broadcast media in four major areas. First, government regulation attempts to prevent the broadcast rights to sport events migrating exclusively from free-to-air television to pay or subscription television. Second, governments have developed regulatory policy aimed at ensuring that sport and media organizations do not engage in anti-competitive behaviour in the buying and selling of these broadcast rights. Such behaviour can lead to monopolies being created that will necessarily restrict supply, which in turn will raise price to a level that will exploit consumers (New & LeGrand 1999). Third, governments regulate to prohibit certain types of advertising being associated with sports broadcasting, such as tobacco advertising. Finally, government regulation attempts to limit or prevent any negative consequences of the vertical integration of the sport and media industries, such as the purchase of a sport team or league by a media organization.

Preventing the migration of premium sport content from free-to-air (network) television to pay (cable) television has been the area of most significant government regulation. Prior to the introduction of subscription and pay-per-view television, the general public were able to access sport via commercial free-to-air broadcasters and, in some instances, via public broadcasters funded by the state. Advocates for the continuation of this system, in which consumers have free access to major sporting competitions and events, have argued that sport has cultural and social significance that needs to be protected and that the migration of sports to pay or cable television will result in less people having access to the product because the cost imposed on the consumer will be too great. The responses by governments have varied depending on national and regional contexts. In the USA, relatively little government regulation has been required for major sports such as the NFL, because no single company or network can afford the exclusive rights and segmenting the rights across free-to-air, pay and satellite providers is financially beneficial for the league (for more information on the NFL and its broadcast rights, see the Case Study within this chapter). The European Commission has argued that events such as the FIFA World Cup, the European Football Championship and the Olympic Games are of major importance to society and as such has regulated to prevent instances where these events are broadcast exclusively on pay television. In smaller nations such as Australia, where the number of commercial free-to-air television networks was small and the perceived threat from pay television providers was considered high, the national government regulated in favour of the commercial free-to-air networks. Ensuring that free-to-air broadcasters essentially had first access to the rights to major sports and events, the government placed pay television operators at a commercial disadvantage in order to protect the interest of its citizens. This was particularly problematic for pay television providers as sport is one of the major drivers of pay television's market penetration.

A ROLE OF GROWING IMPORTANCE: THE SPORT MEDIA MANAGER

In 1919, Notre Dame Football Coach Knute Rockne forever altered the relationship between sport and the media. Dissatisfied with the way in which his college football program was being reported in the local newspaper, Rockne appointed sportswriter Archie Ward as a 'press agent', whose role was to be an 'official correspondent' for Rockne's football program. Ward was able to set the agenda for what was reported in the press, which in the contemporary sport and media landscape seems entirely reasonable but in the early part of the twentieth century was a revolutionary response to managing the media. As such, Ward is considered to be the first public relations practitioner in sport (Stoldt 2013). Professional leagues in the USA soon adopted the Rockne model of media management and control by employing staff in 'press offices'. The role of the sport organization based sport media practitioner or manager developed slowly during the middle part of the twentieth century, but by the latter part of the century, once sport had commercialized in the 1970s and 1980s, media relations and media management were entrenched divisions within the largest sporting leagues and teams throughout the world. By the start of the twenty-first century, staff within sport organizations in media management, media relations or sport communications were being employed to make it as easy as possible for the media to cover their sport, essentially by facilitating access to athletes, coaches and administrators via interviews and press conferences, and by supplying media releases, media guides and assorted information to help sport journalists and commentators do their job.

The advent of the internet, the rise of social media and the desire of sport organizations to take a more strategic approach to setting and shaping the sport media news agenda has changed the role of media and communications managers within sport organizations. This change has been particularly evident in large professional sport leagues and clubs. These organizations were previously concerned with facilitating as much media coverage as possible, in as many and varied media outlets as were prepared to cover them. The rise of social media platforms like Facebook and Twitter has meant that 'citizen journalism' is much more prevalent, where a person only needs access to a smart phone and the internet and they can become an individual 'broadcaster'. This has meant that sport organizations no longer have as much control as they once did, for 'official' media outlets now comprise a small proportion of the total overall coverage. This is compounded by the fact that athletes are using social media to enhance their profile and sponsorship potential. As a result, the role of the sport media manager is becoming increasingly complex and important as sport organizations seek to protect their image, brand and status.

SUMMARY

This chapter has provided an outline of the relationship between sport and the media. It has explored the media and the various sport–media relationships prevalent within the three sector model of sport. Importantly, this chapter examined the commercial foundations, particularly with professional sport, that underpin the sport–media relationship. The chapter also examined broadcast rights, the most significant way in which sport and the media interact in the contemporary professional sport landscape. The chapter explored the reasons why governments seek to intervene in the sport–media relationship through regulation, particularly in order to protect the interests of consumers via preventing the migration of premium sport content to pay or cable television. The chapter concluded with a brief introduction to the role of the sport media manager.

REVIEW QUESTIONS

1   Examine some of the largest media companies in your nation. Do many of these large media companies have an interest in sport and sport organizations via broadcast rights or the ownership of sport teams? Are sport broadcast rights held by one or two media companies or by most of the companies?

2   Explore the operations of a sport within the public sector from a media perspective. What is the relationship of this organization to the media, and how does it use the media to further its interests?

3   Explore the operations of a sport within the nonprofit sector from a media perspective. What is the relationship of this organization to the media, and how does it use the media to further its interests?

4   Explore the operations of a sport within the private sector from a media perspective. What is the relationship of this organization to the media, and how does it use the media to further its interests?

5   Using the three examples above, which organization interacts with the most diverse media? Why do you think this is so? Which organization do you think is most dependent on the media and why? What does this tell you about the interaction between sport and the media across the various sectors of sport?

6   What are the media regulations governing the broadcasting of sport in your nation or region? Are there regulations that ensure free-to-air access of particular sports? Do you think there is a political advantage in governments instituting regulation of this type? Why?

7   Examine a prominent sporting league in your nation or region, perhaps by reading their annual report or accessing publicly available documents related to the finances of the organization. What proportion of revenue is derived directly or indirectly from the media?

8   Which media form or platform is most dependent on sport and why?

9   What are the major reasons the role of a sport media manager in a professional sport organization is more complex now than it was prior to 1990, prior to 2000 and prior to now?

FURTHER READING

Billings, A. & Hardin, M. (eds) (2014). *Routledge Handbook of Sport and New Media*. London: Routledge.

Boyle, R. & Haynes, R. (2009). *Power Play: Sport, the Media and Popular Culture*. Edinburgh: Edinburgh University Press.

Hutchins, B. & Rowe, D. (2012). *Sport Beyond Television: The Internet, Digital Media and the Rise of Networked Media Sport*. London: Routledge.

Nicholson, M. (2007). *Sport and the Media: Managing the Nexus*. London: Elsevier Butterworth-Heinemann.

Pederson, P. (2013). *Routledge Handbook of Sport Communication*. London: Routledge.

Raney, A. & Bryant, J. (eds) (2006). *Handbook of Sports and Media*. London: Lawrence Erlbaum Associates.

RELEVANT WEBSITES

*   ESPN at http://espn.go.com
*   Fox Sports at www.foxsports.com
*   Sports Illustrated at www.si.com
*   Twitter at https://twitter.com

CASE STUDY 12.1

The Australian Open's global reach

There are four Grand Slam tennis tournaments held in the world each year – Wimbledon, Roland Garros (the French Open), the US Open and the Australian Open. Also known as the Grand Slam of the Asia-Pacific, the Australian Open is the first major tournament held each year, typically in mid to late-January, and is the premier major event in Melbourne's annual sporting calendar, in a city known as one of the great sporting capitals of the world. Established in 1905, the Australian Open has been played at the purpose-built tennis complex known as Melbourne Park since 1988. In 1988, a total of 266,436 spectators attended the event, which by 2014 had grown to 643,280, a year in which 80,219 attended the middle Saturday, the busiest day of the tournament, almost a third of the entire 1988 attendance. By contrast, 491,084 spectators attended Wimbledon in 2014, 713,026 spectators attended the 2013 US Open and 428,751 spectators attended the French Open in 2013. The US Open and Australian Open attendance figures are comparable when it is considered that the Arthur Ashe Stadium, the main court for the US Open, has a capacity of more than 22,000 compared with Rod Laver Arena, the main court for the Australian Open, which has a capacity of slightly less than 15,000. Live attendances are only one, albeit important, part of the Australian Open, for the tournament has also become a leader in providing tennis fans around the world with access to a multimedia experience. This mediated experience has only been made available to fans in the last decade through the relatively recent development of technology and applications. The Australian Open provides content all year via a specialized team of staff, working to create their own media and engaging content that inspires tennis fans around the globe. The Australian Open 'story' is told across multiple media platforms, as illustrated in the following sections.

The scale of the Australian Open's media operations is staggering compared to 10 or even five years ago. In 2014 the Australian Open covered over 20,000 points of play on more than 20 tennis courts over the two-and-a-half week duration of the tournament. In 2014 there were 1,500 on-site broadcast media at the Australian Open, and more than 700 journalists including 295 international media representatives from 41 countries. More than 14,000 hours of Australian Open vision was broadcast to more than 200 countries worldwide. In Australia the exclusive broadcast partner is Channel 7, one of the three major commercial free-to-air television networks. In mid-2013 it was announced that Channel 7 had secured the broadcast rights for an additional five years to 2019, extending the partnership between the event and the broadcaster to 46 years (from 1973). The new agreement between the Australian Open and Channel 7 included more than 330 hours of free-to-air coverage of the Australian Open and AO Series events (which include the Brisbane International, Apia International Sydney and AAMI

Kooyong Classic), a commitment to broadcast on two free-to-air channels, which would increase the total volume of free-to-air tennis coverage, and a commitment to the live streaming of all Australian Open and AO Series broadcast courts online and via mobiles and tablets. Internationally the Australian Open has broadcast rights agreements with ESPN in North America (until 2021), ESPN in Central and South America (until 2016) and throughout Europe via Eurosport (until 2016). In 2014 there were 342 million cumulative television viewers across the world, of which China accounted for 107.5 million, in large part due to the popularity of Chinese tennis player Li Na, who won the women's singles title. The 342 million cumulative global television viewers represented an almost 13 per cent increase on 2013.

As sport organizations around the world become less reliant on traditional broadcast media such as television and radio, their websites in particular have become increasingly more important, as they seek to control their messaging and image, as well as provide more ways for fans to interact and engage with digital content. The Australian Open is no different and its website (www.ausopen.com) is one of the most important ways that the tournament interacts with fans around the world. In 2014, the website had 17 million unique visitors (an increase of 12 per cent on 2013), 62.5 million visits (21 per cent increase on 2013) and 467 million page views (31 per cent increase on 2013). The site visits and page views have increased at a substantially greater rate than the total unique visitors, which suggests that the fans who are being attracted to the site, a significant number compared to the live attendance, are finding more content that appeals to them across a broader range of options. This is due in part to the Australian Open investing in teams of staff that have the ability, expertise and creativity to produce new and innovative digital content.

Online and social media are the platforms with the most significant growth for the Australian Open, similar to other major sporting events and leagues. In 2014 the Australian Open YouTube site had 7.55 million views, while the AOTV platform had 15.3 million views, an increase of 187 per cent on the 2013 figure, which was in turn a 154 per cent increase on 2012, a clear indication that more people are accessing more customized content outside the parameters of traditional broadcast television, and that there is a rapidly increasing requirement for sport events to satisfy a global online fan-base. The most popular AOTV segment in 2014 was the highlights of 'Murray v Federer', which attracted 323,000 views. On the Australian Open YouTube channel the most popular item was 'Ball Kid gets hit in the face', which was viewed by 1.7 million people. The Australian Open delivers video content to fans in order to meet audience consumption patterns: snack form (5–10 seconds); short form (under three minutes); and long form (over three minutes). This video content includes live streaming, highlights, press conferences, feature stories and interviews.

Social media platforms Facebook, Twitter and Instagram are also used by the Australian Open to engage with fans. At the time of the 2014 tournament, the Australian Open Facebook site had 1.158 million Likes, of which 115,908 came during the 2014 tournament. The audience reach of the Facebook site is 12.5 million with 5.6 million engaged fans, who predominantly come from Australia, USA, India, Philippines and the UK. The Australian Open's Twitter feed had 440,567 followers on Twitter, of which 68,297 joined during the 2014 tournament. There were 3.88 million related tweets, a 20 per cent increase on 2013, with 760,000 using the #ausopen hashtag, a 36 per cent increase on the previous year and 343,000 mentions of @australianopen during the tournament, a 79 per cent increase from 2013. Like many professional sporting events and leagues the Australian Open allows fans to track to the most popular players on Twitter. Developed in partnership with IBM, the 'Australian Open Social Leaderboard' tracks daily leaders as well as overall event leaders, providing fans with an analysis not only of total tweets, but also a sentiment rating that categorizes the tweets as positive or negative. Rafael Nadal was the tournament leader in 2014 with 1.687 million tweets, 79 per cent of which were positive. The greatest percentage of negative tweets about Nadal was during the final of the tournament, as he was losing to eventual winner Stanislas Wawrinka. In 2014 there were also 62,876 followers on Instagram, of whom 25,054 joined during the 2014 tournament. Over 1.4 million Likes were received on AO Instagram photos, while over 100,000 photos used the hashtags #ausopen or #australianopen, which suggests that social media platforms such as Instagram will become increasingly important as sport organizations seek to harness the promotional power and reach of its fans.

The Australian Open App, available for iPhone and iPad via the App Store and for Android via Google Play, is becoming increasingly popular year on year, as fans access Australian Open multimedia content via mobile and tablet devices. The AO App enables fans to access: latest AO news; live scores; draws; the daily schedule; Australian Open radio; photos and video on demand. In 2014 there were 1.23 million downloads of the AO App, spread fairly evenly across Apple and Android devices. The mobile website (m.ausopen.com) had 36.6 million views in 2014, a 92 per cent increase on 2013, while the combined App and mobile views in 2014 totalled almost 257 million, an increase of 37 per cent on 2013.

CASE STUDY QUESTIONS

1   What does the case of the Australian Open suggest about the relative importance of domestic and international audiences for annual major sport events in a hyper-mediated world?

2   Broadcast television rights are still the most important way for sport events to 'monetize' the size of the audience. Is this likely to change in the short- to medium-term future and why?

3   What does the fact that a short video clip of a ball kid being hit in the face was the most popular Australian Open YouTube clip in 2014 suggest about the types of content fans are attracted to and what do sport organizations need to consider when planning their digital and social media engagement?

4   As online content and social media become more popular ways for fans to access sport content, which forms of Australian Open content are most likely to be used: snack form (5–10 seconds); short form (under three minutes); or long form (over three minutes)? Why do you think this will be the case?

Sources: Australian Open website at www.ausopen.com; Tennis Australia website at www.tennis.com.au; Wimbledon website at www.wimbledon.com; Roland Garros website at www.rolandgarros.com; US Open website at www.usopen.org. Thanks also to Tennis Australia for providing additional information used to prepare this case.

CASE STUDY 12.2

Broadcast rights in the National Football League

The National Football League (NFL) is the premier professional football league in North America and one of the most prominent global sporting brands. The NFL consists of 32 teams that are allocated to the National Football Conference (NFC) or the American Football Conference (AFC). Many of these teams are among the most valuable in the world. According to *Forbes* magazine, in 2014 there were four NFL teams in the top ten most valuable sporting team in the world: the Dallas Cowboys were the fifth most valuable sporting teams in the world in 2014 (US$2.3 billion estimated value), the New England Patriots eighth (US$1.8 billion), the Washington Redskins ninth (US$1.7 billion) and the New York Giants tenth (US$1.55 billion). A further 19 NFL teams were estimated to have a value of at least US$1 billion, while 30 of the top 50 teams were from the NFL. The other 20 teams were predominantly from European football (soccer) leagues, Major League Baseball (MLB) and the National Basketball Association (NBA). That 30 of the 32 teams in the NFL are rated in the world's most valuable 50 and the average worth of an NFL team is approximately US$1.2 billion means that the NFL is undisputedly the richest sporting league in the world, and the most lucrative for owners and players in particular.

The financial success of the NFL is underpinned by the world's largest television broadcast rights deals with FOX, NBC, CBS, ESPN and DirecTV. In late 2011 the NFL signed record television rights deals with FOX, NBC and CBS for US$28 billion over nine years, which took effect after the 2013 NFL season. On average the deal was worth US$3.1 billion a year, a substantial increase on the US$1.9 billion a year paid by these networks for the previous agreement. At the same time the NFL signed a $1.9 billion a year deal with ESPN, also a substantial increase on the US$1.1 billion for the previous agreement. In addition, the NFL also has a rights agreement with DirecTV worth US$1 billion annually. In total, television broadcast agreements deliver the NFL approximately US$6 billion per year.

The NFL's revenue from television rights increased significantly in the later part of the twentieth century in particular (Vrooman 2012). In the 1970s the NFL signed a series of four-year agreements with ABC, CBS and NBC worth US$188 million, US$218 million and US$646 million. In the 1980s the NFL signed agreements with the same broadcasters worth US$2,100 million (5 years) and US$1,428 million (3 years), but it was in the 1990s, as cable television providers ESPN and TBS became more significant players, in addition to free-to-air networks ABC, CBS, NBC and newcomer FOX, that broadcast rights began to increase exponentially. Broadcast rights revenues were US$3,600 million from 1990–1993, US$4,388 from 1994–1997 and US$19,600 from 1998 to 2005; this last deal included US$600 million per year from ESPN, US$550 million per year from ABC and FOX, US$500 million per year from CBS and US$400 million per year from satellite television provider DirecTV. Annual television rights revenue for the NFL increased from US$47 million in 1970 to US$4,065 million in 2012, an 86-fold increase over a 40-year period.

The NFL's ability to secure such large broadcast rights agreements is due to a number of important non-sport factors. First, the USA is the world's largest economy, with a gross domestic product that is almost twice the size of China, the world's second largest economy, and almost as large as the entire European Union. Second (and related to the first), the USA has a very high household and per-capita income. According to Gallup, using data from 2006 to 2012, the median household income in the USA was calculated to be US$43,585, fifth of all countries (with at least 2,000 responses) behind Luxembourg, Norway, Sweden and Australia and the median per-capita income was US$15,480, sixth of all countries, with four Scandinavian countries in the top five. These high household and per-capita income levels means there is more capacity for discretionary spending in the USA, relative to other countries in the world, for commercial products related to and through sport and the media. Third, the USA is one of the world's largest countries by population and size. The USA has more than 300 million residents, third behind giants China and India, which combined with its size means there are many significant population and commercial centres throughout the nation.

There are also a range of sport related factors that have enabled the NFL to continue to improve the value of its broadcast rights in an increasingly competitive domestic and international professional sport market. The most important among these is that the NFL has been able to segment its media product, which has occurred in part by design and good management and in part because no single broadcaster can afford to purchase the entire suite of NFL rights. The NFL season consists of a regular season of 17 weeks, in which each teams plays 16 games. Games are typically played on Sunday, where the game that is available on local television will depend on where the viewer is located and due to time differences games start at 1:00pm or between 4:00pm and 4:30pm. In addition to the Sunday 'regional' games, a series of nationally televised games are broadcast each Thursday night, Sunday night and Monday night. For these games there is no competition and the game is broadcast throughout the USA on a free-to-air or cable network depending on the day of the week.

For example, for the first week of the 2014 season, the Green Bay Packers played the Seattle Seahawks on Thursday night at 8:30pm Eastern Time. This game was broadcast on NBC, one of the free-to-air networks. On Sunday, 10 games were played at 1:00pm Eastern Time, four of which were broadcast by FOX and six of which were broadcast by CBS. An additional two Sunday afternoon games were played at 4:25pm, both of which were broadcast by FOX. The Indianapolis Colts played the Denver Broncos in the only game broadcast on Sunday night at 8:30pm Eastern Time; this game, like the Thursday night game, was broadcast exclusively by NBC. On 'Monday Night Football', an American broadcasting institution, two games were played, the first between the New York Giants and Detroit Lions at 7:10pm Eastern Time and the second between the San Diego Chargers and the St Louis Cardinals at 10:20pm Eastern Time. Both these Monday night games were broadcast on cable television provider ESPN. In most weeks of the season, only one Monday night game is played. Depending on how teams are performing, the NFL retains the right in conjunction with the broadcasters to move one of the Sunday afternoon games into the Sunday night slot in the second half of the season. In addition to the arrangements with NBC, CBS and ESPN, the NFL also has an agreement with satellite broadcast company DirecTV, which offers a subscription package 'NFL Sunday Ticket', which allows all the regional Sunday afternoon games to be watched, not just the games broadcast in the viewers' local area.

CASE STUDY QUESTIONS

1 Do any other major sporting leagues around the world segment their broadcast rights packages in a similar way to the NFL? Which leagues do this and why? Are some leagues within some countries more or less able to do this? Why might this be so?

2 What additional rules and regulations have the NFL put in place to protect live attendances and media audiences? Is this to maximize revenue for teams or for broadcasters, or both?

3 The NFL also has agreements with media organizations beyond free-to-air and cable television providers. Investigate these agreements and suggest whether these are in competition to the television broadcast rights, are complementary or are catering to a completely different market.

4 Which of the demographic factors referred to in the case are most important for the size of broadcast rights outside the USA and why?

Sources: National Football League website at www.nfl.com; *Forbes* website at www.forbes. com, Gallup website at www.gallup.com, World Bank website at www.worldbank.org; Vrooman, J. (2012) The economic structure of the NFL. In Quinn, K. (ed.) *The Economics of the National Football League: The State of the Art.* New York: Springer.

CHAPTER 13

Sport governance

OVERVIEW

This chapter reviews the core concepts of organizational governance, explores the unique features of how sport organizations are governed, and summarizes the key research findings on the governance of sport organizations. The chapter also provides a summary of principles for governance within community, state, national and professional sport organizations.

After completing this chapter the reader should be able to:

- identify the unique characteristics of organizational governance for corporate and nonprofit sport organizations;
- differentiate between the various models and theories of governance relevant to sport organizations;
- understand and explain the role of boards, staff, volunteers, members and stakeholder groups in governing sport organizations;
- understand some of the challenges facing managers and volunteers involved in the governance of sport organizations; and
- identify and understand the drivers of change in governance systems within sport organizations.

WHAT IS GOVERNANCE?

Organizational governance is concerned with the exercise of power within organizations and provides the system by which the elements of organizations are controlled and directed. Governance is necessary for all groups – nation states, corporate entities, societies, associations and sport organizations – to function properly and effectively. An organizational governance system not only provides a framework within which the business of organizations are directed and controlled but also 'helps to provide a degree of confidence that is necessary for the proper functioning of a market economy' (OECD 2004, p. 11). Governance deals with issues of policy and direction for the enhancement of organizational performance rather than day-to-day operational management decision-making.

The importance of governance and its implied influence on organizational performance was highlighted by Tricker (1984) when he noted 'if management is about running business, governance is about seeing that it is run properly' (p. 7). The Australian Sports Commission (ASC) defines governance as 'the structures and processes used by an organization to develop its strategic goals and direction, monitor its performance against these goals and ensure that its board acts in the best interests of the members' (ASC 2004). Good organizational governance should ensure that the board and management seek to deliver outcomes for the benefit of the organization and its members and that the means used to attain these outcomes are effectively monitored.

A 1997 report to the Australian Standing Committee on Recreation and Sport (SCORS) identified a major concern amongst the sporting community, which was the 'perceived lack of effectiveness at board and council level in national and state sporting organizations' (SCORS Working Party on Management Improvement 1997, p. 10). Major sport agencies in the UK, New Zealand and Canada have also identified improving governance of sport organizations as a strategic priority. Failures in the governance of national sport organizations such as the Australian Soccer Association (2003), Athletics Australia (2004), Basketball Australia (2007) and Cricket Australia (2011), together with reviews of professional sport governance such as those conducted by the Football Governance Research Centre at the University of London, continue to highlight the importance of developing, implementing and regulating sound governance practices in both amateur and professional sport organizations.

CORPORATE AND NONPROFIT GOVERNANCE

The literature on organizational governance can be divided into two broad areas: (1) corporate governance that deals with the governance of profit seeking companies and corporations that focus on protecting and enhancing shareholder value, and (2) non-profit governance that is concerned with the governance of voluntary based organizations that seek to provide a community service or facilitate the involvement of individuals in social, artistic or sporting activities.

Studies of corporate governance have covered 'concepts, theories and practices of boards and their directors, and the relationships between boards and shareholders, top management, regulators and auditors, and other stakeholders' (Tricker 1993, p. 2). The literature in this field focuses on the two primary roles of the board in first, ensuring conformance by management, and second, enhancing organizational performance. Conformance deals with the processes of supervision and monitoring of the work of managers by the board and ensuring that adequate accountability measures are in place to protect the interests of shareholders. Enhancing organizational performance focuses on the development of strategy and policy to create the direction and context within which managers will work.

The unique characteristics of nonprofit organizations demand a governance framework different to that of the corporate firm. Nonprofit organizations exist for different reasons than do profit seeking entities, and generally involve a greater number of stakeholders in their decision-making structures and processes. The relationships between decision-makers – the governance framework – will therefore be different to that found in the corporate world. The management processes employed to carry out the tasks of the organizations might well be similar, but a fundamental difference between nonprofit and corporate organizations is found in their governance frameworks.

While many sports organizations such as major sporting goods manufacturers, athlete management companies, retail companies and venues can be classed as profit seeking, the majority of sport organizations that provide participation and competition opportunities are nonprofit. These organizations include large clubs, regional associations or leagues, state or provincial governing bodies and national sport organizations.

IS THERE A THEORY OF SPORT GOVERNANCE?

Clarke (2004) provides a unique overview of the development of theories of corporate governance. Some of the important theories applied to the study of organizational governance include agency theory, stewardship theory, institutional theory, resource dependence theory, network theory and stakeholder theory. In this section we shall examine each of them in turn and assess how relevant they are to understanding the governance of sport organizations.

Agency theory proposes that shareholders' interests should prevail in decisions concerning the operation of an organization. Managers (agents) who have been appointed to run the organization should be subject to extensive checks and balances to reduce the potential for mismanagement or misconduct that threatens shareholders' interests. This has been the predominant theoretical approach to the study of corporate governance and has focussed on exploring the best ways to maximize corporate control of managerial actions, information for shareholders and labour in order to provide some assurance that managers will seek outcomes that maximize shareholder wealth and reduce risk. In relation to corporations operating in the sport industry that have individual, institutional and government shareholders, this theory helps explain how governance systems work. For the majority of nonprofit sport organizations, which have diverse stakeholders who do not have a financial share in the organization (aside from annual membership fees), agency theory has limited application.

Stewardship theory takes the opposite view to agency theory and proposes that rather than assume managers seek to act as individual agents to maximize their own interests over those of shareholders, managers are motivated by other concepts such as a need for achievement, responsibility, recognition and respect for authority. Thus, stewardship theory argues that managers' and shareholders' interests are actually aligned and that managers (agents) will act in the best interests of shareholders. This theoretical view can also be applied to sport corporations such as Nike, Fox Sports or a listed professional football club franchise. The application of either agency or stewardship theory is dependent on the actions of the managers (who choose to act as agents or stewards) and the view of shareholders (who create either an agent or stewardship relationship through their conscious choice of governance framework). Stewardship theory is arguably more applicable than agency theory to the study of nonprofit sport organizations where managers may have a connection to the sport as a former player, coach or club official and therefore have a deeper sense of commitment to the organization and are more likely to act as stewards.

Agency and stewardship theories focus on the internal monitoring issues of governance. Three theories that seek to explain how organizations relate to external organizations and acquire scarce resources are institutional theory, resource dependence theory and network theory. Institutional theory argues that the governance frameworks adopted by organizations are the result of adhering to external pressures of what is deemed acceptable business practice, including legal requirements for incorporation. Such pressures reflect wider societal concerns for proper governance systems to be employed. Further, if all organizations of a similar type and size seek to conform to these pressures they are likely to adopt very similar governance frameworks, a situation know as institutional isomorphism. Evidence of this is apparent throughout club based sporting systems such as in Canada, Australia, New Zealand and the UK where most national and state or provincial sporting organizations operate under remarkably similar governance frameworks.

Resource dependence theory proposes that in order to understand the behaviour of organizations, we must understand how organizations relate to their environment. Organizations paradoxically seek stability and certainty in their resource exchanges by entering into interorganizational arrangements which require some loss of flexibility and autonomy in exchange for gaining control over other organizations. These interorganizational arrangements take the form of mergers, joint ventures, co-optation (the inclusion of outsiders in the leadership and decision-making processes of an organization), growth, political involvement, or restricting the distribution of information (Pfeffer & Salancik 1978). Such arrangements have an impact on the governance structure adopted, the degree to which stakeholders are involved in decision-making, and the transparency of decision-making.

A final theory that attempts to explain elements of governance based on how organizations relate to external organizations is network theory. Network theory posits that organizations enter into socially binding contracts to deliver services in addition to purely legal contracts. Such arrangements create a degree of interdependency between organizations, and facilitate the development of informal communication and the flow of resources between organizations. This is particularly true of sport organizations that, for example, rely on personal contacts to facilitate the success of major events by securing support from high profile athletes, using volunteers in large numbers from other sports organizations, and depending on government support for stadium development or event bidding. Network theory can help explain how governance structures and processes, particularly concerning the board of sports organizations, evolve to facilitate such informal arrangements.

These three theories emphasize the need to examine governance in terms of the external pressures that organizations face, and the strategies, structures and processes they put in place to manage them. Such an approach offers a more realistic view of how and why organizations have a particular governance framework than agency and stewardship theories.

Stakeholder theory provides another perspective for examining the relationship between organizations and their stakeholders. It argues for conceptualizing a corporation as a series of relationships and responsibilities which the governance framework must account for. This has important implications for corporations acting as good corporate citizens and particularly for sport organizations that need to manage a myriad of relationships with sponsors, funding agencies, members, affiliated organizations, staff, board members, venues, government agencies and suppliers.

Much of the writing and research on organizational governance has been based on corporations rather than nonprofit entities. Applying a particular theory to the study of sport organizations must be done with regard to the type and industry context of the sport organization being studied. Sport organizations and their governance frameworks have diverse elements that prevent the development of an overarching theory of sport governance. The value of the theories presented here is that each of them can be used to illuminate the governance assumptions, processes, structures and outcomes for sport organizations.

GOVERNANCE STRUCTURAL ELEMENTS

The governance elements of a corporate or profit seeking sport organization are the same for any general business operation. These elements can include paid staff, including a CEO who may or may not have voting rights on a board, a board of directors representing the interests of many shareholders (in the case of publicly listed company), or directors who are direct partners in the business. The real differences in governance elements can be found in volunteer sport organizations.

A simple governance structure of a VSO is depicted in Figure 13.1 and comprises five elements: members, volunteers, salaried staff, a council and a board. Normally, members meet as a council (usually once per year at an annual general meeting) to elect or appoint individuals to a board. If the organization is large enough, the board may choose to employ an executive and other paid staff to carry out the tasks of the organization. Together with a pool of volunteers, these employees deliver services to organizational members. The board acts as the main decision-making body for the organization and therefore the quality of its activities is vital to the success of the organization.

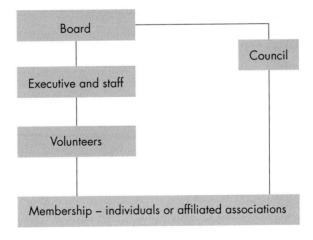

FIGURE 13.1 Typical governance structure of a voluntary sport organization

Members of a VSO can be individual players or athletes, or in some cases, members are classified as other affiliated organizations such as a club that competes in a league provided by a regional sports association. Members can also be commercial facility providers such as basketball, squash or indoor soccer stadiums. The membership council comprises those people or organizations that are registered members and who may be allocated voting rights according to membership status. The board comprises individuals who have been elected, appointed or invited to represent the interests of various membership categories, geographic regions or sporting disciplines in decision-making. The senior paid staff member, often designated the CEO, is employed by and reports directly to the board. Other paid staff are appointed by the CEO to assist in performing various organizational tasks. These staff must work with a variety of volunteers in sport to deliver essential services such as coaching, player and official development, marketing, sport development and event delivery. Finally, a wide range of stakeholders such as sponsors, funding agencies, members, affiliated organizations, staff, board members, venues, government agencies and suppliers must be consulted and managed in order for the organization to operate optimally.

The majority of national and state or provincial sport organizations that provide participation and competition opportunities in club based sporting systems are governed voluntarily by elected office bearers, who fill positions on either committees or boards. Most of these VSOs operate under a federated delegate system with club representatives forming regional boards, regional representatives forming state or provincial boards and state or provincial representatives forming national boards.

This traditional governance structure has been criticized for being unwieldy and cumbersome, slow to react to changes in market conditions, subject to potentially damaging politics or power plays between delegates, and imposing significant constraints on organizations wishing to change. On the other hand, the majority of sports organizations still use this model today and value its ability to ensure members have a say in decision-making, the transparency of decisions and the autonomy granted to organizations at every level of the system. In Practice 13.1 explains a typical governance structure of a large national sport governing organization.

In Practice 13.1 Hockey Canada

2014 will see Hockey Canada, the sole governing body for amateur hockey in Canada, celebrate its 100-year anniversary, a year in which it won both men's and women's gold medals at the Winter Olympics. More than 4.5 million Canadians are associated with Hockey Canada as players, coaches, officials, trainers, administrators or volunteers. More than 550,000 registered players and another 1.5 million casual or unregistered participants play hockey at more than 3,000 arenas throughout Canada. Hockey Canada employs over 75 staff and has offices in most Canadian provinces. The organizations that affiliate with Hockey Canada include 13 Branch associations, the Canadian Hockey League and Canadian Inter-University Sport. In conjunction with these member organizations, Hockey Canada facilitates participation in amateur hockey leagues, teams and games through player, coach and referee development, grading of competitions and establishing appropriate rules and regulations for amateur hockey across Canada.

Hockey Canada exists to:

- foster and encourage the sport of amateur hockey throughout Canada;
- foster and encourage leadership programs in all areas related to the development of hockey in Canada;
- recognize and sanction the establishment of governing bodies in Canada in accordance with the principles, philosophy and practices of the Association;
- support and encourage Branches and other members in the development of amateur hockey within their jurisdictions and areas of responsibility;
- establish and maintain uniform playing rules for amateur hockey;
- maintain national insurance programs;
- affiliate with and cooperate with other national or international amateur hockey organizations;
- conduct Inter-Branch and international contests of amateur hockey;
- provide representation for international open hockey competition.

An important element of the structure of Hockey Canada is the large size of the Board of Directors which comprises Officers (eight), Branch Presidents (13), Council Representatives and Directors (eight) and Special Advisory Council Members (five). Each of these positions represents a specific constituent group within Hockey Canada. In addition, the Board of Directors receives reports from a Hockey Development Council of 24 members, again made up of individuals representing the specific interests of regional affiliates, or membership types (i.e. coaches, officials). The Board of Directors has a number of policy sub-committees (five) that deal with areas such as elite competitions, women's programs, policy development, programs of excellence and junior development. Finally, there are 10 standing sub-committees that report to the Board on issues such as insurance, marketing, finance, management and other areas of activity. This appears to be a very cumbersome way to manage the affairs of a relatively simple activity like facilitating games of ice hockey, but the sheer scale and geographic spread of its constituents requires Hockey Canada to maintain a comprehensive governance structure that facilitates decision-making and communication amongst its 4.5 million participants.

The most recent annual report from Hockey Canada highlights the reach of this organization through its web page and social media platforms. In the 2013/14 season there were 22 million page views on the Hockey Canada website, 2.2 billion interactions across Twitter and Facebook accounts associated with Hockey Canada, including 232,000 mentions on Twitter and 12 million engaged users on Facebook. Hockey Canada has almost a quarter of a million Twitter followers and over half a million Facebook fans. Hockey is clearly the national sport of a nation obsessed with hockey; having a good governance system for this sport is not only required but demanded by Canadians.

Sources: Hockey Canada at www.hockeycanada.ca; Hockey Canada (2014). *Annual Report 2014*. Calgary, CA: Hockey Canada.

GOVERNANCE MODELS

There are three generic governance models that can be applied to nonprofit sport organizations: the traditional model outlined by Houle (1960, 1997); the Carver policy governance model (1997); and the Executive led model (after Block 1998; Drucker 1990; Herman & Heimovics 1990, 1994). A governance model can be defined as a set of policies and practices that outline the responsibilities of the various governance elements, and the processes used to carry out the governance function. All of the following models relate to organizations that are governed by boards that employ a paid executive and staff as opposed to more informal organizations that maintain a collective and informal structure. The models are more relevant to these organizations because boards that carry out the 'hands on' work of the organization, such as a small community club, are 'usually so strongly influenced by personalities and special circumstances that few generalizations can be made about their general nature or how they may be improved' (Houle 1997, p. 3).

Traditional model

Houle (1960, 1997) outlined a 'traditional model' for governance of nonprofit organizations that is based on five elements. The first of these is the human potential of the board where the board ensures a systematic recruitment process is in place accompanied with ongoing board member development. Second, the work of the board is structured according to a set of by-laws, policies are clearly defined, and minutes of the board and committee meetings are consistently reported. Third, the roles of and relationships between the board, executive and staff should be well defined and developed, enabling clear decision-making to occur. Fourth, the operation of the board should be undertaken in a positive group culture and based on an annual work plan, regular meetings with well-managed agendas and ongoing evaluation of the board and its work. Finally, the board has a focus on maintaining external relationships through formal and informal representation of the organization to the community. The model advocates that 'the work is done by the staff, the administration by management and the policy making by the board; in this traditional model, the board is truly in charge of the organization' (Fletcher 1999, p. 435).

This model has been widely used amongst nonprofit organizations and is probably the most widely used by nonprofit sport organizations. It clearly separates the tasks of staff and volunteers, and highlights volunteer board members as being accountable for the organization. The model has been criticized for the idealistic view that the board alone has ultimate responsibility for the organization (Heimovics & Herman 1990), and the rather simplistic notion of the board making policy while the staff do the work (Herman & Heimovics 1990), which does not reflect the reality of the working relationships that occur in most nonprofit organizations.

Policy governance model

Carver (1997) outlines five elements of a 'policy governance' model for the effective governing board. The first of these is determining the mission and strategic direction of the organization, with a focus on the desired outcomes, rather than becoming immersed in the detail of the means to achieve them. Second, setting executive limitations or constraints for the work practices and the means that staff employ to achieve the mission set by the board. Third, establishing clear board and executive roles and relationships. Fourth, ensuring governance processes are clearly defined in areas such as board member selection and succession, the reporting of activities of the board and staff, and ensuring the board focuses on the policies of the organization rather than cases or specific issues. Finally, the board's role should be more than simply ensuring conformance to financial procedures and ethical management practice; it should also develop clear performance measures related to strategic outcomes.

Like the traditional model, Carver's model has been criticized for its 'idealized view of the board, operating above the messiness of the board-executive relationship as it really exists in nonprofit organizations' (Fletcher 1999, p. 436). The model also does not address the important role of the board in managing external relationships and it 'clearly subordinates the CEO to the board and expects the board alone to set the parameters of the relationship' (Fletcher 1999, p. 436).

Executive led model

The executive led model, in contrast to the previous models, advocates the executive as central to the success of nonprofit organizations. Drucker (1990) argued that the ultimate responsibility for the performance of a nonprofit organization, including its governance, should rest with the executive. His views were supported by Herman and Heimovics' (1990) research that found that the reality of most boards was that they depended on their executive for information almost exclusively and looked to them to provide leadership. Hoye and Cuskelly (2003) also found this was the case in VSOs. Block (1998) argued that because the executive is working in an organization much more than the average board member, they have better access to information and therefore they must also 'be at the core of leadership and decision-making activities' (p. 107).

BOARD–STAFF RELATIONSHIPS

The gradual introduction of professional staff into VSOs over the last 20 years has created the need for volunteers and paid staff to work together at all levels, including the board table. This has led to some degree of uncertainty about what roles should be performed by each group and the extent to which staff and volunteers should be involved in strategic planning, policy development, performance evaluation and resource acquisition. The potential for tension between these groups as they negotiate their respective roles has been well established, as has the ongoing desire of volunteers to maintain a degree of involvement in decision-making while at the same time utilizing the expertise of paid staff to assist them in running their organizations. This then is the crux of board–staff relationships: What areas do volunteers maintain control over and which do paid staff control?

Hoye and Cuskelly (2003) found that VSO boards perform better if a degree of trust exists between the board and staff and that board leadership was shared amongst a dominant coalition of the board chair, executive and a small group of senior board members. As mentioned earlier, the executive controls the flow of information to board members and so the quality, frequency and accuracy of this information are vital to their ability to make decisions. Ensuring the board and executive work together effectively enhances this information flow and therefore the performance of the board.

PRINCIPLES OF GOOD ORGANIZATIONAL GOVERNANCE

The notion of good organizational governance extends beyond the ideas of monitoring to ensure conformance and developing to improve performance, discussed earlier in this chapter. Henry and Lee (2004) provide a list of seven key principles for good organizational governance in sport organizations:

1   Transparency: Ensuring the organization has clear procedures for resource allocation, reporting and decision-making.
2   Accountability: Sports organizations need to be accountable to all their stakeholders.
3   Democracy: All stakeholder groups should be able to be represented in the governance structure.
4   Responsibility: The board has to be responsible for the organization and demonstrate ethical stewardship in carrying out that responsibility.
5   Equity: All stakeholder groups should be treated equitably.
6   Efficiency: Process improvements should be undertaken to ensure the organization is making the best use of its resources.
7   Effectiveness: The board should establish and monitor measures of performance in a strategic manner.

This list of principles is not exhaustive but it does give us a clear indication of the philosophical approach organizations should adopt in designing and implementing an appropriate governance framework. It may be somewhat surprising to find that even some of the more high profile sport organisations in the world struggle to implement good governance standards.

Corporate governance of English Premier League football clubs has come under increasing scrutiny in recent years, due in part to the annual reviews of corporate governance undertaken by the former Football Governance Research Centre (FGRC) based at Birkbeck in the University of London. The Premier League (PL) is the flagship of the game's governing body in England, the Football Association (FA), which was explored in the Chapter 6 Case Study. The FA is in turn under the control of a European governing body, the Union of European Football Associations (UEFA), which in turn is a member of the world's governing body, the Federation of International Football Associations (FIFA).

The regulatory system for Premier League clubs comprises four elements:

1 regulation by the football authorities;
2 regulation through the legal system in terms of company law, consumer law, labour law and competition law;
3 regulation by a code of corporate governance developed by the Premier League; and
4 shareholder activism and stakeholder participation.

The football authorities (namely FA and UEFA) have developed criteria such as a 'fit and proper person' test aimed at improving the quality of individuals appointed or elected to govern Premier League clubs, and the development of a code of corporate governance that provides guidelines for good governance. These actions are largely designed to ameliorate the effects of poor financial management within the Premier League clubs (since 1992, 50 per cent of PL clubs have been in hands of administrators or insolvent) and to improve the sustainability of clubs that are promoted or relegated between the FA leagues. The FGRC noted that the PL clubs that regularly compete in the UEFA Champions League hold a distinct financial advantage over other PL clubs. As a consequence the governing body of the PL must be cognizant of the more powerful clubs and their potential to influence decision-making at the board table.

The English legal system requires PL clubs to fulfil a number of obligations for communicating with shareholders, consultation with fans, the use of customer charters, and dialogue with supporters' trusts. The FGRC noted that while the majority of PL clubs do an adequate job in this area, there was room for improvement. In addition, PL clubs that are listed public companies must follow a Combined Code that sets out principles for the activities of directors, director's remuneration, accountability and audit requirements, relations with shareholders, and institutional shareholders. The FGRC found that while PL clubs are moving towards having more independent directors, they fall short compared to other listed companies.

There are now more than 70 supporters' trusts for clubs in the FA, and about 60 per cent of PL clubs have a supporters' trust. The trusts fulfil an important governance role, with 25 per cent of PL clubs having a trust representative on their board. This representation means that committed fans have the chance to participate in decision-making at the highest level in regard to the future of their club, and in return support the club in sport development, marketing and fundraising activities.

While there are signs that PL clubs have generally accepted good governance practices and abide with the majority of codes of conduct and principles for good governance, they do fall down in certain areas of governance practice. These include the lack of performance evaluation of individual directors or the overall board in a small number of clubs, and a significant portion of clubs failing to adopt standard strategic planning practices. While the English PL enjoys enormous global profile as a leading football competition, the governance of the member clubs does not reach such exalted heights.

These failures in football governance are also evident in other countries; Hamil et al. (2010) documented the failings in governance that have plagued Italian football in recent years, noting

> there is a clear and transparent system of regulatory oversight for the Italian football industry{…}[and a licensing system that]{…}suggests a high standard of club governance should exist{…}[but]{…}there is a very serious gap between theory

and practice, a gap which has had significant consequences for the health of the Italian football industry.

(Hamil et al. 2010, p. 379).

They argue that inappropriate ownership and governance structures among football clubs have led to a series of problems that have dogged Italian soccer over the last three decades including betting scandals, doping, false passports, bribery and match-fixing, and violence. They cite the problems of clubs being controlled by familial networks with little separation of ownership and control (one of the central tenets of effective governance) as being a central cause of these problems. Hamil et al. (2010, p. 388) also noted that 'what emerges in football are networks consisting of powerful individuals connected with clubs, governing bodies, political parties and the media, which are in prominent positions to influence decision-making within football and the business of football'. The legacy of a lack of competitive balance in the Italian league and the growing disparity of resources that exists between mid-tier clubs and those few large clubs that play in the lucrative UEFA Champions League also compound the problem. They concluded that Italian football should adopt 'modern regulation – including sanctions for misdemeanours – and clear guidelines for strong governance' (Hamil et al. 2010, p. 404). The importance of good governance for a sport is highlighted in In Practice 13.2.

In Practice 13.2 Amateur Swimming Association

The Amateur Swimming Association (ASA) was the first governing body of swimming to be established in the world (1869) and has evolved to become the English national governing body for swimming, diving, water polo, open water, and synchronized swimming. The ASA supports over 1,200 affiliated swimming clubs through a National/Regional/and sub-regional structure. It endeavours to ensure every athlete – whatever their age or level of experience – belongs to a club that provides the best possible support and environment through schemes such as swim21, the ASA's 'Quality Mark' for clubs (similar to the Sport England CLUBMARK program discussed in Chapter 3). It organizes competitions throughout England, from grassroots to elite level, including the highly successful Age Group and Youth Championships that attract more than 1,600 young swimmers aged 11–17, and the ASA Nationals.

The ASA website (www.swimming.org/asa) states that the English talent program is a world-leading, seamless pathway that puts in place performance opportunities for swimmers to develop their skills and potential. The ASA operates a Learn to Swim award scheme based on the National Plan for Teaching Swimming. Over 2 million certificates and badges are issued to children all over the world under this scheme. Swimming is the number one participation sport, with over 20 million people swimming every year, and the ASA is dedicated to giving more people, more opportunities to swim for health and for fun.

It should be noted that the ASA is not a provider of swimming facilities, therefore it acts as a catalyst and facilitator to ensure suitable facilities, with appropriate access and programs, are provided to meet the needs of the community and aquatic clubs. The ASA operates comprehensive certification and education programs for teachers, coaches and officials. It has pioneered work on the UK Coaching Framework and is developing e-learning programs, all of which are helping to drive up quality and 'raise the bar' to ensure the ASA has an appropriately skilled workforce for the whole swimming industry.

The ASA's Strategy for 2013–2017 sets out six strategic objectives:

1   To increase the number of schools providing quality swimming in line with ASA guidelines as part of a local learn to swim network.
2   To maximize the effective use of available water space in England in order to attract, retain and grow the number of people taking part in regular aquatic activities.
3   To build, develop and maintain a quality sustainable club infrastructure and network that meets the needs of the community it serves.
4   To increase the size and success of the English talent pool.
5   To improve the skills and technical capabilities of the aquatics workforce and its ability to innovate.
6   To enhance the ASA's leadership of the swimming industry.

The ASA's success is dependent on many people across the organization, both staff and volunteers, working together to deliver services at the right standard. Good governance is essential in monitoring and supporting the performance of individuals and member clubs and associations in that endeavour.

Source: The ASA website at www.swimming.org/asa

BOARD PERFORMANCE

Board performance has been found to be related to the use of appropriate structures, processes and strategic planning, the role of the paid executive, whether the board undertakes training or development work, personal motivations of board members and the influence of a cyclical pattern in the life cycle of boards. How to measure board performance, however, is a subject of ongoing debate. Herman and Renz (1997, 1998, 2000) support the use of a social constructionist approach to measure board performance based on the work of Berger and Luckmann (1967). Their view is that the collective judgements of those individuals directly involved with the board can provide the best idea of its performance. A widely used scale, the Self Assessment for Nonprofit Governing Boards Scale (Slesinger 1991), uses this approach and provides sporting and other nonprofit organizations with an effective way to gauge board performance.

Aspects of board activity that are evaluated using a scale of this type include: the working relationship between board and CEO, working relationships between board and staff, CEO selection and review processes, financial management, conduct of board and committee meetings, board mission statement and review of the mission, strategic planning, matching operational programs to the mission and monitoring program performance, risk management, new board member selection and training, and marketing and public relations. The performance of the board in undertaking these activities is then rated by board members, executives and the chair of the board. While this approach is open to accusations of self-reporting bias, the fact that the whole group makes judgements on performance and then compares perceptions is an aid to board development and improvement.

The evaluation of individual board member performance is more problematic. Research into the human resource management practices related to board members shows that smaller sports organizations may struggle to find board members, while larger sports have an element of prestige attached to them so the problem is the opposite – how to engage in succession planning within a democratic electoral process. Very few board members are inducted, trained, provided with professional development opportunities, and evaluated at all in regards to their role and the role of the board, a potentially serious problem for nonprofit sport organizations given the significant responsibilities with which board members and board chairs are charged.

DRIVERS OF CHANGE IN GOVERNANCE

VSOs are increasingly under pressure from funding agencies to improve the delivery of their core programs and services. Funding agencies recognize that sports' capacity for this delivery depends to a large extent on sport organizations being appropriately governed and as a result have implemented a range of measures to improve the governance of VSOs. For example, the Australian Sports Commission has a dedicated program of management improvement for NSOs that provides advice on governance issues, funding to undertake reviews of governance structures, and provides information on governance principles and processes. Sport England has negotiated detailed strategic plans with NSOs to improve the delivery and coordination between regional sport organizations.

The threat of litigation against sport organizations, their members or board members has forced sport organizations to address issues such as risk management, fiduciary compliance, incorporation, directors' liability insurance, and board training and evaluation. The heightened awareness of the implications of governance failure due to several much publicized corporate cases of impropriety worldwide has also forced sport organizations to improve their governance systems. Legislative changes to address issues of equity and diversity are additional pressures sports organizations must face and their governance systems, particularly membership criteria, voting rights, and provision of information must change accordingly.

The threat of competition in the marketplace also has forced sports organizations to become more commercial and business focussed, primarily through employing paid staff. Large clubs and regional sports associations that in the mid-1990s were exclusively run by volunteers are increasingly investing in paid staff to manage the increased compliance demands from government and their members and customers. As discussed earlier, the employment of paid staff changes the governance structures, the decision-making processes and the level of control exerted by volunteers. Maintaining governance structures devised decades ago creates many problems for sports organizations. In Practice 13.3 highlights some of the problems that result from poor governance and how one organization has been forced to change.

In Practice 13.3 The trouble with Scottish football

In the executive summary of Henry McLeish's exhaustive report of his 2010 *Review of Scottish Football* he said:

> The Governance of the game may have been appropriate and effective in another era but is totally inappropriate for the modern era. The representative and participative structure of the Scottish Football Association (SFA), the traditions, procedures and decision-making and the inherently defensive and insular approach of the organisation all present a serious obstacle to the modernisation of football in Scotland. Modernising the governance of the game is the central challenge of this review.

In other words, the governance system could not have been worse. The failure of the national team to qualify for any major international tournament since the 1996 European Championships and the 1998 World Cup, the inconsistent performance of the top Scottish clubs in European competitions, and the lack of sustainable growth in both the quantity and quality of players emerging from the Scottish football system were the catalysts for the review. McLeish went on to detail a litany of problems with the governance of football in Scotland:

> The governance is inappropriate for the current and future context of football:

- There is a lack of effective formal consultation between the major stakeholders in the game and a serious lack of respect, confidence and trust.
- The game is very fragmented and at times lacks any overall sense of purpose.
- There is a great deal of insularity, exclusiveness and isolationism.
- Decision making is slow and delivery does not match the urgency and complexity of the issues involved.
- There is a great deal of sectional and vested interest at work at the expense of the health and well being of the overall game. Openness, transparency and accountability are lacking.
- The game overall generates a great deal of indiscipline and a lack of respect for the rules and regulations of the game.
- Roles and responsibilities are confused and unproductive with the elected officials too involved in what is essentially the work of the Chief Executive and his management team.

- *The committee structure may function for the benefit of the existing representatives but is ill-equipped and outdated and is not able to deal with the modern world of football and the speed with which events and issues emerge and have to be dealt with.*
- *There is no sense of modernisation and while there is some excellent work taking place within the SFA it is hard to see the current organisational structure allowing this to flourish.*
- *There seems little concept of public value or return on investment permeating the SFA and once again the failure to reform decision making, policy and planning procedures and structure means that the full potential of the organisation is not being realised and incentives to change are simply not there.*
- *There is no performance culture within the SFA and for all intents and purposes the work is isolated in silos. It is constantly worth repeating that much of the weakness of the SFA is based on legacy and history and a traditional mind-set that surrounds the work of the institution.*
- *The shape and structure of the organisation has largely remained intact despite the changes in personnel and the passing of time.*
- *There is also a lack of outside involvement in the work and deliberations of the SFA.*
- *Non-football people are thin on the ground and, with the exception of some committees, independent experts and informed outsiders are currently excluded from the different parts of the structure.*

Having said that, McLeish did identify that most people involved in Scottish football wanted things to improve:

There is little dispute as to the importance of the SFA and what, it should strive to achieve as a governing body:

- *Governance with integrity.*
- *Performance of Scotland's national teams.*
- *Effective working relationships with the two other bodies, the SPL and the SFL and the myriad of organisations that make up the game.*
- *Effective oversight of the implementation of the laws of football.*
- *Promotion of participation, standards, and financial well-being of the game.*
- *Fostering of development at all levels.*
- *Constructive dialogue with government and other sports.*
- *Effective representation of the game in Scotland and internationally.*

However, the governance system in the SFA was preventing these very things being achieved.

The work of the SFA has become progressively less suitable and less effective in the light of these limited objectives to carry out its role in the modern game especially at a time when the scale of economic, social and life style change continues to dominate and have such a direct impact on football and the conditions in which it operates. The review has also pinpointed a number of challenging but less tangible issues to address including:

- *The lack of trust, respect and confidence in the governance of football.*
- *The lack of a coherent and comprehensive narrative for the future of the game overcoming the informality of the workings of the structures.*
- *The game is not served well by the general perception of many outside Hampden that the SFA is defensive and where narrow sectional or constituency interests often seem more important that the national interest and the national game.*

This example highlights the impact that poor governance can have on a sport organization. According to the Scottish FA website, since the review McLeish has stated there has been 'significant progress' in implementing 95 per cent of his 103 recommendations from the two-part *Review of Scottish Football* inside the first six months. He is quoted as stating 'The progress made so far has been a major step forward for a game experiencing major challenges [and] there has been significant progress and it is clear that the Scottish FA realized something significant and substantial had to be done.'

Among the changes enacted since June 2011, the Scottish FA has reduced its main board from 12 to seven and made several important appointments of key people in key roles. Their website highlights the appointment of Mark Wotte, the first-ever Performance Director, as signifying the Scottish FA's commitment to elite player development and has resulted in the creation of seven Regional Performance Schools. They also state that Football Development has also been challenged to double the number of participants from 65,000 to 130,000 by 2015, by way of The Big Count. The Scottish FA has also committed to a facilities strategy, headed up by Cameron Watt, and has published a new Equity Policy in line with good corporate governance.

This case highlights the fact that poor governance can occur at the highest level in sport, that when it is so poor it can be most debilitating, but it also shows that governance reforms can be undertaken and that when they are, they can have a very positive effect on a sport.

Source: Scottish FA website at www.scottishfa.co.uk and McLeish, H. (2010). *Review of Scottish Football, Part 2 Governance, Leadership, Structures.* Edinburgh: Scottish Football Association.

SUMMARY

Organizational governance has been described as the exercise of power within organizations and provides the system by which the elements of organizations are controlled and directed. Good organizational governance should ensure that the board and management seek to deliver outcomes for the benefit of the organization and its members and that the means used to attain these outcomes are effectively monitored.

A distinction is made between corporate governance that deals with the governance of profit seeking companies and corporations that focus on protecting and enhancing shareholder value, and nonprofit governance that is concerned with the governance of voluntary based organizations that seek to provide a community service or facilitate the involvement of individuals in social, artistic or sporting activities.

Sport organizations and their governance frameworks have diverse elements that prevent the development of an overarching theory of sport governance. A number of theoretical perspectives, namely agency theory, stewardship theory, institutional theory, resource dependence theory, network theory and stakeholder theory can be used to illuminate parts of the governance assumptions, processes, structures and outcomes for sport organizations.

The traditional governance structure for VSOs outlined earlier has been criticized for being unwieldy and cumbersome, slow to react to changes in market conditions, subject to potentially damaging politics or power plays between delegates, and imposing significant constraints on organizations wishing to change. On the other hand, the majority of sports organizations still use this model today and value its ability to ensure members have a say in decision-making, the transparency of decisions and the autonomy granted to organizations at every level of the system.

A number of models for sport governance exist, each emphasizing different levels of responsibility for the chair of the board and paid executive. VSO boards perform better if a degree of trust exists between the board and staff and that board leadership is shared amongst a dominant coalition of the board chair, executive and a small group of senior board members. While evaluation systems for board performance are still relatively simplistic, they do cover a wide range of board activities. Evaluation of individual board member performance is more problematic and is the subject of ongoing research.

Finally, VSOs are increasingly under pressure from funding agencies to improve the delivery of their core programs and services. The threat of litigation against sport organizations, their members or board members, has forced sport organizations to address issues such as risk management, fiduciary compliance, incorporation, directors' liability insurance, and board training and evaluation. The heightened awareness of the implications of governance failure due to high profile corporate cases worldwide has also forced sport organizations to improve their governance systems.

REVIEW QUESTIONS

1 Explain the difference between corporate and nonprofit governance.

2 What theory would you apply to the study of negligence on the part of a board of directors of a sport organization?

3 Explain the role played by boards, staff, volunteers, members and stakeholder groups in governing sport organizations.

4 What criteria would you apply to gauge the performance of a nonprofit VSO? How would these criteria differ for a professional sport club?

5 What are the important elements in developing good relationships between boards and paid staff in VSOs?

6 Compare the governance structures of a multi-disciplinary sport (e.g. gymnastics, canoeing, athletics) with a single discipline sport (e.g. field hockey, netball, rugby league). How do they differ? What impact does this have on volunteers involved in governance roles?

7 Review the governance performance of a VSO of your choice using Henry and Lee's (2004) seven principles of governance presented in this chapter.

8 What issues does a potential amalgamation present for a VSO?

9 How are board performance and organizational performance linked?

10 Interview the CEO and the Board Chair of small VSO. Who do they perceive to be the leader of the organization?

FURTHER READING

Carver, J. (1997). *Boards that Make a Difference: A New Design for Leadership in Non-profit and Public Organizations*. 2nd edn. San Francisco: Jossey-Bass.

Clarke, T. (ed.) (2004). *Theories of Corporate Governance*. Oxon, UK: Routledge.

Football Governance Research Centre (2004). *The State of the Game: The Corporate Governance of Football Clubs 2004*, Research paper 2004 No. 3, Football Governance Research Centre, Birkbeck, University of London.

Grix, J. (2009). The impact of UK sport policy on the governance of athletics. *International Journal of Sport Policy, 1*, 31–49.

Hamil, S., Morrow, S., Idle, C., Rossi, G. & Faccendini, S. (2010). The governance and regulation of Italian football. *Soccer & Society, 11*, 373–413.

Henry, I. & Lee, P.C. (2004). Governance and ethics in sport. In J. Beech & S. Chadwick (eds.) *The Business of Sport Management*. England: Prentice Hall.

Houle, C.O. (1997). *Governing Boards: Their Nature and Nurture*. San Francisco: Jossey-Bass.

Hoye, R. & Cuskelly, G. (2007). *Sport Governance*. Oxford: Elsevier Butterworth-Heinemann.

Hoye, R. & Doherty, A. (2011). Nonprofit sport board performance: A review and directions for future research. *Journal of Sport Management, 25*(3), 272–285.

Organisation for Economic Co-operation and Development (2004). *Principles of Corporate Governance*. Paris: OECD.

RELEVANT WEBSITES

The following websites are useful starting points for further information on the governance of sport organizations:

- Australian Sports Commission at www.ausport.gov.au
- Sport Canada at www.pch.gc.ca/progs/sc/index_e.cfm
- Sport England at www.sportengland.org
- Sport Scotland at www.sportscotland.org.uk

CASE STUDY 13.1

Governance reform in Australian Football: A perennial challenge?

In August 2002, the then Australian Federal Minister for the Arts and Sport, Senator Rod Kemp, announced that Soccer Australia (SA) had agreed to a major structural review of soccer in Australia to be managed by the Australian Sports Commission. The review was undertaken after almost two decades of crises in the sport with the result that in mid-2002, SA was AUS$2.6 million in debt, had reduced staffing levels at the national office, was racked by political infighting, had a lack of strategic direction and had enjoyed mixed results in the international arena. The review examined the structure, governance and management of soccer at all levels across Australia.

During the course of the review it was found that many of the constituent bodies at state and regional levels suffered from similar financial difficulties, political infighting and inappropriate governance systems. These created problems of mistrust and disharmony, a lack of strategic direction, inappropriate behaviour, and factionalism that hampered national decision-making. While the sport enjoyed a large grassroots participation base, a good talent pool for national teams, good training programs, strong growth in female participation, and passionate public support, its governance system was preventing it capitalizing on these strengths.

The review found that the governance system needed to change in four key areas:

1 Ensure independence of the governing bodies.
2 Separate governance from day-to-day management.
3 Change the membership and voting structures for the national and state organizations.
4 The relationship between SA and the National Soccer League.

In all, the review made 53 recommendations aimed at improving the structure, governance and management of SA. The first three recommendations in the report illustrate the parlous state of affairs that existed in the organization in 2002. The review recommended that:

1 the membership of SA be changed to recognize key interest groups and reduce the power of larger states and the NSL;

2   a new constitution be developed; and
3   each state affiliate adopt a model constitution and membership agreements.

These recommendations alone represent wholesale change in the governance system, but the review went on to recommend a further 50 changes to governance processes and structures throughout the sport.

The sweeping changes made to the governance systems of Soccer Australia as a result of the review, and the subsequent appointment as Chief Executive Officer of John O'Neil (ex-CEO of the Australian Rugby Union who has subsequently returned to the ARU) ushered in a new era for the sport. On 1 January 2005, Soccer Australia changed its name to Football Federation Australia as part of the ongoing process of repositioning the sport. These changes in governance enabled the sport to:

- successfully relaunch a national league – the Hyundai A-League with 8 new teams (now 10) and a lucrative Pay TV rights deal that has enabled it to attract some of the top European-based Australians back to play in Australia, including Harry Kewell and Brett Emerton;
- have the financial capacity to employ a super coach in Guss Hiddink who managed to get the Socceroos to the second round of the 2006 World Cup before being cruelly beaten by the eventual champions Italy; and
- be in a position to bid for the future rights to host the World Cup.

Despite these reforms, football in Australia was still subject to some systemic failures. First, after the dramatic ride to secure entry to the 2006 World Cup, Australia secured a place to the 2010 World Cup after it managed to move from the Oceania to the Asian Federation which had more team slots allocated for the final 32 World Cup teams. Alas, under new coach Pim Verbeek, Australia was bundled out after the first round – the hopes of a nation dashed once again. Second, after 5 years, the new A-League suffered its first casualty with the North Queensland Fury club having its licence withdrawn for its inability to meet its licence obligations with FFA. Third, and most importantly, Australia's bid to win the right to host the 2022 World Cup failed to secure more than a single vote – the AUS$50 million investment by the federal government to support the FFA-led bid amounted to nothing.

After the dust had settled, the federal government announced a second review in eight years into the governance, management and structure of football in Australia, this time to be conducted by the chairman of the Australian Sports Commission. The Press Release from FFA in April 2011 stated:

Former Federal Sports Minister and current Chairman of the Australian Sports Commission, the Hon. Warwick Smith, AM, has been appointed to head a review of football in Australia in partnership with Football Federation

Australia (FFA). The Federal Sports Minister, Senator the Hon. Mark Arbib, announced the joint review as a first step towards ensuring Australian football is in a position to deliver the best possible AFC Asian Cup in Australia in 2015.

The AFC Asian Cup is Asia's premier sporting event and will draw an expected television audience of more than one billion. Over the course of the 23 day tournament in January 2015, up to 500,000 fans are expected to attend the 32 matches, which will be played in New South Wales, Victoria, Queensland and the Australian Capital Territory.

FFA CEO Ben Buckley confirmed that while the Smith Review would primarily focus on the AFC Asian Cup 2015, it would also examine the structures and resources required to continue football's development in Australia. 'Football in Australia has many needs, from the kids playing at the community level through to the Qantas Socceroos on the international stage and now the responsibility of hosting Asia's biggest football event,' said Ben Buckley. 'FFA welcomes the collaborative approach from the Federal Government and their continuing support to ensure the game is positioned to reach its enormous potential across the nation.{...}The review provides the opportunity to look at the efficiencies in our current structure and how the various levels of the game can better work together. We all want to make football the best it can be.'

FFA is well advanced in setting strategic priorities for the next World Cup cycle. There are three pillars around which our strategy is built:

1   Continuing national team excellence, in particular with qualification of the Qantas Socceroos for the 2014 FIFA World Cup.
2   Growth and sustainability of the Hyundai A-League model.
3   Connecting with the 1.7 million Australians who make up the football community to create greater engagement and productive partnerships.

'In this context, the Smith Review is a timely and positive step towards ensuring FFA can implement its strategic plans and make the most of the exciting opportunities ahead,' concluded Buckley.

The review report, handed down in December 2011, concluded that governance reform had been largely achieved. It highlighted the growth in participation from 1.1 to 1.7 million between 2001 and 2009 and the achievements of Australian teams, in particular the Matildas winning the Asian Cup in 2010, as indicators of improved governance. However, the report pointed to the high costs of running the A-League, the disconnect between A-League teams and grassroots participants, and broadcasting as key priorities for improvement. In the context of this chapter on sport governance, the review recommended changes to increase A-League clubs involvement in League decisions and limitations on A-League expansion plans.

CASE STUDY QUESTIONS

1   Why did the Australian federal government initiate the 2003 Review into the governance of football in Australia?

2   What were some of the reasons the FFA was subject to a further review in 2011?

3   Compare the Crawford Review of 2003 with the 2011 report into the review of the Scottish Football Association. What similarities and differences are there in the governance and structural issues of these two football governing bodies?

4   Why do governing bodies of sport seem to be in a perpetual state of review, in particular in the areas of governance and structure?

Source: Australian Sports Commission (2003). *Independent Soccer Review: Report of the Independent Soccer Review Committee into the Structure, Governance and Management of Soccer in Australia*, Canberra: Australian Sports Commission. Football Federation Australia (2011). AFC Asian Cup Focus of Football Review, news release 27 April 2011. Sydney: Football Federation Australia.

CASE STUDY 13.2

Squash Australia

A case that illustrates the difficulty in achieving governance reform is that of Squash Australia (SA), the NGB for squash in Australia that has been in existence since 1934. Like most NGBs or NOs, Squash Australia is focussed on the development of the game across Australia, including:

- the coordination of national teams and programs;
- the conduct of national championships;
- the oversight of national accreditation of coaches and referees;
- membership and representation in the world squash and Australian sporting communities; and
- implementing policies and procedures associated with anti-doping, member protection and governance.

The organization has a federated structure and its members are the State Squash Associations. At the 2011 Annual General Meeting, these members voted to have an independent review undertaken into the governance of SA, to focus specifically on:

- governance procedures;
- structural provisions;
- benchmarking against other relevant sporting organizations;
- operational capacity/performance;
- a governance review model/template be established for utilization by member organizations as appropriate; and
- external funding opportunities to assist SA and member organizations to undertake governance and structural reviews.

The Australian Sports Commission provided funding for the review and in conjunction with SA developed some terms of reference for the review:

1 investigate the relationship between the Board and the State and Territory Members of Squash Australia;
2 review the incumbent Board's strengths and weaknesses, and make recommendations on issues such as election and appointment processes, term duration, and conflicts of interest;
3 assess of the existing role and responsibilities of Board members;
4 investigate and compare the standard of corporate governance of Squash Australia against other comparable models;
5 provide advice on available external funding sources to assist with the conduct of similar reviews as they might be of relevance to members; and
6 provide general comment on any risks confronting the Squash Australia Board and Squash Australia as an organization.

The report from the consulting firm engaged to undertake the review highlights a set of issues that are common to many federated sport organizations:

> SA competes in a very congested market for the hearts and minds of Australians looking to participate in a variety of sports that are on offer to a very sports-minded community. As a consequence of SA's Vision, Mission and Goals, articulated above, SA is undertaking this review as an initial step in adopting best practice in all aspects of its business with a view placing SA in a position where its aspirations as expressed in the Goals can be achieved. It should be noted that SA has a registered player membership of 14,000 while ERASS [the now ceased national sport participation data collection service] tells us that approximately 200,000 people play squash. Additionally Squash Court Finder identifies 400 centres and part of challenge for SA is to better engage these providers into the SA family. SA has also developed a new participation product OzSquash to better engage juniors and schools. Squash Australia has also identified the opportunity to develop a National League which will provide a truly national competition and enhanced profile for the sport. These sort of new initiatives need to be reflected in a revised strategic plan.

It should be recognised that as a consequence of the federated system there is a conflict in the overall business conducted by SA and the Members. Quite rightly SA's business has a focus on High Performance, national and international competition and the development of players through a pathway to the various national teams. While SA seeks to develop policies around the community game the Members are primarily responsible for the delivery of the game at community level. The tension between the respective sides of the sport involves the allocation of limited resources and the inherent conflict between the requirements of SA to run its programs and the Members abilities to conduct the community game that grows the base of the sport. This is exacerbated by the concentration of revenue to SA from external sources for the development of the High Performance aspect of the business.

The conflict between the national and State/Territory bodies is not unique to Squash and indeed is generally replicated wherever there is a federated system which has limited resources and which in-turn relies on its National team to give the sport the public exposure (through its heroes) that assists in drawing participants to the game at the community level.

While not the panacea to solve all problems, a constitution that adopts best practice, places the sport in the best position where, through the strategies adopted by the Board, it can react to business opportunity in the development of the sport. The ongoing success of Squash in Australia however is dependent on SA and the Members adopting a 'Unity of Purpose' in their respective businesses. This for example would facilitate a coordinated approach to high performance through a network of state coaches understanding their role in the pathway, as well as delivery of national participation programs at the other end of the spectrum.

Initially in seeking to identify best practice that could then be incorporated into SA's constitution comparison was made between the current Squash Australia memorandum and Articles ('the Constitution') and the ASC's Sports Governance Principles re-released in 2012. In addition, comment was sought from Members and identified persons who would add value to the review process. While SA may want to move to a hybrid governance model over time it is important to immediately strengthen the current federated model and adopt the behaviours that come with that option in order to build a sound foundation for future structural changes.

As noted above, operationally SA is serviced by 5 full time and 3 part time staff in the areas of administration, finance, coaching and development. The gaps appear to be in the areas of marketing and communication, commercial development and the specific participation development officers identified in delivering the new OzSquash program.

While the focus of this review is very much on the future, it must be acknowledged that the consultation process revealed an underlying culture of disconnectedness, mistrust and poor communication between Squash

Australia and the members. Much of the criticism revolved around decision making on implementation of national projects and policies with what appears to have been little stakeholder consultation or alignment with the strategic plan. There is also a strong desire for a structured appeals process and grievance policy to be able to question decisions or seek more information.

Other criticism from stakeholders focussed on what appears to be a lack of transparency in some senior appointments and decisions related to the direction of national programs such as high performance. Conversely it must also be said that some SA board members and senior staff expressed frustration at perceived roadblocks in trying to deliver national initiatives.

(exSport 2012, pp. 8–10)

The review report goes on to provide 14 recommendations for changes to the national board structure and composition, leadership, strategy and communication. The Squash Australia website in 2014 had a process overview summary that listed the key milestones in this governance review process. This is reproduced in part here to illustrate the time involved in enacting change of this scale, even within a relatively small organization like SA.

2011
• Squash Australia committed to a Governance Review through its 2011 Annual General Meeting. With the financial and organizational support of the Australian Sports Commission a review process was established and a reviewer engaged.

2012
• Submissions called from the Squash and wider community in September 2012.
• The appointed reviewers (exSport) produced and submitted their report *Strengthening Squash Australia* to the Squash Australia Board late in 2012.

2013
• The Squash Australia Board accepts the Report and endorses all fourteen recommendations to the Members for their consideration in early 2013 at a National Governance Workshop.
• The Workshop outcomes based on the review recommendations were considered for progression by the Board and the Members, with priority given to a number of changes to the existing Squash Australia Articles and the drafting of a Squash Australia Constitution to replace the existing Squash Australia Articles & Memorandum of Association.
• The Squash Australia Articles were amended at a General Meeting August 2013 where a working group was formed to develop the Squash Australia Constitution.

- The Squash Australia Board resolved several Committee Terms of Reference and approved the Squash Australia Governance Policies Procedures document at its October 2013 Board meeting.
- Parameters on the draft Constitution were to be discussed at a November 2013 President's Council, which did not progress due to only four members being able to attend.

2014
- The first draft Squash Australia Constitution was brought to the Members for discussion at a National Workshop and General Meeting in February 2014.
- With member input both at and following the February 2014 National Workshop and General Meeting subsequent drafts 2 and 3 were produced. Draft 3 was put to the members but fell short of the required 75 per cent majority to approve at a Squash Australia General Meeting May 2014.

At the time of writing this case study, the review process has yet to conclude, almost three years after the decision to commence the review in late 2011. This case has not been provided to be critical of SA or any people associated with SA during this period, but to highlight the sort of challenges faced by all nonprofit sport organizations in undertaking governance reform where there are a lot of volunteers involved in both service delivery and decision-making, organized within many separate organizational units.

CASE STUDY QUESTIONS

1   Why is it important for organizations such as SA to engage an independent reviewer for any governance reform process? What are the possible negatives and positives of such a process?

2   Why is it so difficult for national boards within federated structures to vote for changes to board composition or voting procedures?

3   Why might state level organizations be critical of national level organizations within such federated models?

4   A major focus of similar reform processes is to align the strategic plans of state and national level organizations. What are the challenges of getting this done and why is governance reform important in aiding this outcome?

Source: Squash Australia website at www.squash.org.au/sqaus/about_us/governance_review. htm and the report titled *Strengthening Squash Australia* (2012) produced by exSport, an external consulting firm, also available on the Squash Australia website.

CHAPTER 14

Performance management

OVERVIEW

This chapter examines the ways in which sport organizations monitor their operations and evaluate their performance. Particular attention is given to the special features of sport organizations, and how these features create the need for sport-specific models of performance management. The importance of using a multi-dimensional model of performance management is highlighted, together with the need to not only accommodate the conflicting demands of multiple stakeholders, but also manage the risk. Cases and incidents are used to illustrate the concepts and principles that underpin effective performance in sport organizations.

After completing this chapter the reader should be able to:

- explain the concept of performance management in sport organizations;
- describe how the special features of sport necessitate the formulation of sport-specific models of performance management;
- identify stakeholders that need to be taken into account when building a performance management model for sport organizations;
- explain why risk management is essential to ensuring high level performance in sport organizations;
- conceptualize the universal importance of financial sustainability as a measure of performance;
- understand the importance of social responsibility as a performance indicator;
- construct multi-dimensional models of performance management that use sport's special features, stakeholder analysis, risk assessment, financial factors, and social responsibility; and
- apply the model to a variety of sport situations and contexts.

SPORT AND PERFORMANCE

From a management perspective, sport is an interesting institution to study since it is both similar to and different from traditional business organizations (Smith & Stewart 1999, 2010). Its similarities have arisen out of its relentless drive over the last 30 years to become more professionally structured and managed. Large segments of sport have consequently copied the values and practices of the business world, and as a result players and administrators are paid employees, and strategic plans are designed. In addition, games and activities become branded sport products, fans become customers to be satisfied and surveyed, and alliances with corporate supporters are developed (Carter 2011; Slack 1997).

At the same time, sport is also different from business (Smith & Stewart 2013). First, it has a symbolic significance and emotional intensity that is rarely found in an insurance company, bank or even a betting shop. While businesses seek employee compliance and attachment, their primary concern is efficiency, productivity and responding to changing market conditions. Sport, on the other hand, is consumed by strong emotional attachments that are linked to the past through nostalgia and tradition. Romantic visions, emotion and passion can override commercial logic and economic rationality (Foster et al. 2006; Quinn 2009). Second, predictability and certainty, which are goals to be aimed for in the commercial world, particularly with respect to product quality, are not always valued in the sporting world. Sport fans are attracted to games where the outcome is uncertain and chaos is just around the corner (Fort 2011; Sandy et al. 2004; Szymanski 2009; Zimbalist 2006). Third, sport is not driven by the need to optimize profit in the ways that large commercial businesses are. In practice, sport organizations face two conflicting models of organizational behaviour when deciding upon their underlying mission and goals. The first is the profit maximization model, which assumes that a club is simply a firm in a perfectly competitive product market and that profit is the single driving motivational force. The second is the utility maximization model, which emphasizes the rivalry between clubs, and their desire to win as many matches as possible (Downward & Dawson 2000; Fort 2011). The utility view assumes that sporting organizations are by nature highly competitive and that the single most important performance yardstick is competitive success. These differences therefore beg the question of where to begin when setting up a performance management system for sport organizations.

WHERE TO BEGIN?

In many respects sport is always subject to intense scrutiny. For example, in elite competitive sport, players and teams are rated and ranked continuously. In cricket, for example, an ever-expanding array of statistics is used to calculate not only batter-scoring rates and bowling-strike rates, but also patterns of scoring and fielding efficiency. Moreover, everyone has an opinion on the performance of coaches in various professional sport leagues which range from win-loss ratios to how the game strategies impact on scoring efficiency and player movements.

At the same time, many sporting clubs do not take the time to undertake a comprehensive evaluation of their off-field performance. This is surprising in view of the fact that, like other organizations that aim to be around for a while, sport clubs and associations must also make sure they can deliver growing memberships and balanced budgets. As a result, it is always better to use a performance evaluation model that covers a range of performance dimensions, and embraces a variety of measures.

A systematic approach to performance management is thus an essential tool for identifying strengths and weaknesses, and revealing the ways in which overall organizational performance can be improved. It is also important for deciding where scarce resources should be allocated in order to achieve the best possible outcome. It can also give a picture of how one organization, club or league is doing in relation to other organizations, clubs or leagues. This performance snapshot can be used to identify weaknesses and design strategies than improve critical result areas in the next season or annual sporting cycle. In short, the use of some sort of performance management model is crucial to the long-term success of sport organizations. However, the question remains as to how best to go about implementing an appropriate model of performance management, and where to begin?

A good starting point is to look at performance management from a strategic perspective. That is, we should initially focus our attention on what the organization wants to achieve. In other words, a performance management system should be linked to an organization's vision, goals and objectives (Hums & MacLean 2009; Robbins & Barnwell 2002). These objectives can be used to identify what it needs to do well to improve its performance. It is at this point that the primary goals of sport organizations become quite different from those of business organizations. While commercial leisure centres and most American professional sport teams are focussed on maximizing profits, most other sports clubs, even with a large revenue base, are more concerned with priorities like winning more games than their rivals, and servicing the needs of members. However, it is not always clear just what the primary goal of a sport organization is, or what is the best measure for deciding how well the organization has performed. In commercial terms the most successful association football (or soccer) club is Manchester United, closely followed by Real Madrid and Barcelona, whose capacity to secure revenue is unrivalled in European football. However, Manchester United did not make it to the Champions League final in 2014, although it was won by Real Madrid. Overall, the wealthiest teams dominate the Champions League, which suggests that commercial and on-field success are, in fact, related.

On balance it has to be said that there is a close correlation between revenue and success in most professional sport leagues. In other words, clubs that have a large resource base and the capacity to secure the best facilities, the best coaches and the best players, will on balance have the best win-loss ratio.

But this also begs the question as to whether there may be other ways of measuring performance, and estimating the success and failures of a sport organization. In some instances it may be important to consider what are called process factors, which includes items like staff retention, player development, and overall level of morale and job satisfaction. However, despite these additional complexities and anomalies, it is clear that any performance management system must take into account, and indeed, should reflect, the primary goals of the relevant club, team, facility, event or league.

BUILDING A PERFORMANCE MANAGEMENT MODEL FROM A STAKEHOLDER PERSPECTIVE

Performance management should also be linked to an organization's key stakeholders (Atkinson et al. 1997; Bryson 2004; Carter 2011). If stakeholders are satisfied with the organization's performance, then it is doing well. In a publicly owned sports retail business for example, a large profit and dividend will be good for management and shareholders alike. However, in a member-based sport club, success will be more about on-field performance and member services than massive profits. On the other hand, for a sport's governing body the interests of its registered players may take the highest priority. In other words, different types of sport organizations will have their own unique goals and priorities, which will in turn reflect the ways in which they rank their stakeholders (Friedman et al. 2004).

Stakeholders may also have conflicting needs. Sponsors may want maximum media exposure and access to players, but the clubs have a primary interest in improving player

TABLE 14.1 Stakeholder expectations of sport organizations

Stakeholder type	Expectations of sport organization
Players	• On-field success • Appropriate pay and benefits • Low injury rates
Employees	• Appropriate pay and benefits • Job security • Professional development
Equipment suppliers	• Reliability of demand • Player endorsement • Brand awareness
Members	• Services and benefits • Overall satisfaction
Owners/shareholders	• Return on investment • Public recognition of club or association
Sponsors	• Positive reputation of club or association • Brand awareness and recognition
Player agents	• High player morale • Payment of market rates
Fans	• Game quality and excitement • High win-loss ratio
Community/society	• Civic pride • Provides role models for young adults
Media	• Mass market • High level of public interest

performance, which may mean less, not more player involvement in sponsor activities. In the case of a national sporting body, the national government may want international success to justify its investment in elite training and coaching programs, whereas the rank-and-file players who make up the bulk of the membership may want more local facilities. Sport organizations are therefore required to balance the often-conflicting needs and 'contradictory interests' of the various stakeholders (Chappelet & Bayle 2005, p. 43). The major sport organization stakeholders and their expectations are summarized in Table 14.1.

The key point to note here is that a sport organization will have multiple stakeholders, and their interests need to be integrated into its evaluation processes.

AN INPUT-OUTPUT APPROACH TO PERFORMANCE MANAGEMENT

In developing a model for evaluating a sport organization's performance, a number of additional principles should be utilized. A second approach is to focus on inputs and outputs. This involves looking at things like quality, quantity, efficiency, cost-benefit ratios, and employee productivity (Anthony & Young 2003; Bouckaert 1995). This approach provides a checklist of essential performance dimensions that need to be addressed. It ensures that no one measure is dominant, and also provides for measures that not only focus on internal processes, but also looks at the organization's relationships with key suppliers and customers. A summary of the ways in which input-output analysis can be applied to sport organizations is illustrated in Table 14.2

TABLE 14.2 An input-output approach to performance management in sport

Dimension	Measure
Output: Quantity	• Premierships • Attendance • Membership • Participation
Output: Quality	• Standard of play • Features of venue/facility • Standard of service • Overall customer experience
Output: Cost/benefit	• Operating profit • Costs of operation • Net economic benefit • Social benefit
Input: Efficiency	• Cost of providing service • Administrative support cost • Waiting time
Input: Staff performance	• Customer/member/fan satisfaction ratings • Staff skills and experience • Staff achievements

A BALANCED SCORECARD APPROACH TO PERFORMANCE MANAGEMENT

A third approach is to avoid the often obsessive emphasis that shareholders place on financial measures by balancing it against the benefits that might accrue to customers, suppliers and employees (Harvard Business Review 1998). This approach is exemplified in the Balanced Scorecard (BSC) model designed by Kaplan and Norton (1992, 1996). The BSC has four dimensions which are reviewed below.

One of the first things Kaplan and Norton note is that a good performance measurement tool should not be a 'controlling system' solely concerned with keeping 'individuals, and organizational units in compliance with a pre-established plan' (p. 25). Rather it should be primarily a 'learning system' concerned with 'communication and informing' (p. 25). To this end Kaplan and Norton aimed to design a performance measurement system that balanced external and easily quantifiable measures like market share and return on investment against internal and more ephemeral factors like administrative processes and staff development.

Kaplan and Norton's first dimension is Financial Perspective. Although they argue that too much emphasis has traditionally been given to the so-called bottom-line result, financial measures are nevertheless a fundamental starting point for evaluating the economic sustainability of an organization. They can range from total sales, operating income and net cash flow, to return on assets, debt to equity ratio and net profit. This dimension answers the question 'how do we look to shareholders'?

The second dimension is Customer Perspective. In this instance the emphasis is on identifying the 'customer and market segments in which the business will compete', and to develop measures that will indicate how well the organization competes in these segments (p. 26). These measures will include total sales in each segment, market share, customer acquisition, customer retention, and customer satisfaction. Kaplan and Norton also suggest that for this performance dimension attention should be given to the factors like short lead times and on-time delivery that actually underpin the levels of customer satisfaction and retention. This dimension addresses the question 'how do customers see us?'

The third dimension is the Internal-Business-Process Perspective. This perspective requires management to identify the 'critical internal processes in which the organization must excel' in order to secure a competitive advantage (p. 26). Kaplan and Norton note that it is not just a matter of ensuring that current value-adding processes are efficient and streamlined, but that there are also systems in place to improve and re-engineer existing processes and products. This dimension addresses the question 'what must we excel at?'

The fourth dimension is the Learning and Growth Perspective. Kaplan and Norton see this perspective as crucial to the long-term success of organizations. In a turbulent business environment there is an ever-increasing likelihood that the technologies and processes required to sustain a market advantage and competitive edge may race ahead of the technical and managerial skills of the staff who are responsible for managing those technologies and processes. In order to close this gap organizations will 'have to invest in re-skilling employees, enhancing information technology and systems, and aligning organizational procedures and routines' (p. 27). This dimension addresses the question 'can we continue to improve and create value?'

Finally, Kaplan and Norton suggest that each of the above perspectives should be linked to a common overarching objective that ensures consistency and mutually reinforcing conduct. In other words, the BSC is more than a 'dashboard' of 'critical indicators or key success factors' (p. 29). In order to be effective it must reflect the organization's mission and goals.

The BSC provides a solid framework for undertaking an analysis of a sports enterprise, sport even, or sports league. Moreover, it is just as applicable to a small community club as it is to a major professional sports team. The following case can also be neatly understood by taking a BSC approach. This is because it allows the analyst to immediately take four different perspectives:

1   financial;
2   customer;
3   internal-processes; and
4   learning and growth.

In Practice 14.1 Women's National Basketball Association

In the United States of America, the Women's National Basketball Association (WNBA) is seen to be a great success story since it is one of the few female sports that has carved out a highly valued and sustainable space for its own professional sports competition. It ticks off many sport performance boxes. It has a national broadcast agreement in place, it has attracted multi-level national brand sponsors, it has recruited the world's best players, and it continues to draw solid crowds to its games. However, if we dig a little deeper we find that things are not as rosy as they seem.

The inaugural WNBA season commenced in the summer of 1997. In the early part of the league's development there were few problems and many successes. First, it was backed by the NBA, and, second, it had a unique organizational and legal structure, since every team was effectively owned by the league. In this 'single entity' competition, clubs were not franchises, but rather operating divisions of the league. This meant the central body had control over wage levels and recruitment, and therefore substantial control over costs, which in the first instance seemed a very good thing.

The league quickly captured the imagination of television viewers, and more than 50 million viewers per week were watching WNBA games as the season progressed. The WNBA also delivered a unique audience profile for an elite sporting competition. In the case of at-arena attendance, the gender breakdown was about 70 per cent female and 30 per cent male. The TV audience was around 50 per cent female and 50 per cent male, with a stronger percentage of non-adult viewers than is normally not the case. In short, a lot of young, mostly middle-class women supported the league.

Following on from the successful inaugural season, the WNBA expanded from eight teams to 16. The Detroit Shock and Washington Mystics joined the league in 1998, the Minnesota Lynx and Orlando Miracle in 1999, and the Indiana Fever, Miami Sol, Portland Fire and Seattle Storm in 2000. The 2002 season was highly successful, and signalled to the sports-going public that a professional sport league for women was not only viable, but also destined to become an integral part of the North American sporting landscape. There were 176 women playing professional basketball in 256 regular-season WNBA games. In the inaugural 1997 season only 28 games were played. The future of the league looked assured.

However, the gloss faded, and the optimism was blunted over the following ten years. The WNBA went through difficult times, and by 2013 – the 17th year of the competition – there were only 12 teams in the league. So what went wrong, both strategically and financially? Strategically, it appears that the league may have expanded too rapidly, and exposed itself to a build-up of costs. Financially, the evidence now indicates that despite its initial progress, and despite the committed support from millions of women who desperately wanted the competition to succeed, it was never going to be financially viable. Looking back it becomes clear that operating revenues rarely covered operating costs, and most clubs were running losses.

As one commentator claimed, the WNBA had, over the course of its first 17 years 'never made a dime', which in accounting parlance means it could never deliver an operating profit for its owners, the NBA. In other words, the WNBA has survived – from a financial perspective – only because of the subsidies provided by the NBA. This may be a harsh and even an unfair thing to say, and additionally play into the hands of sporting traditionalists who see real professional sports as a 'men's only' affair. But it may be also the only reasonable conclusion to be drawn from the facts. But, what are the so-called facts, and who do we believe anyway? To assist in the analysis of this case, the following points are noted:

- The WNBA started out with eight teams, and grew to 16 before several franchises folded. It now fields 12 teams. Six teams – Indiana, New York, Minnesota, Phoenix, San Antonio and Washington – are owned by NBA franchises. The WNBA teams share training facilities and arenas.
- Just how bad, then, are the WNBA's finances? Apparently the league's first-ever 'cash flow positive' team was the Connecticut Sun in 2010. NBA commissioner David Stern regularly conceded that the NBA has subsidized the WNBA in recent years by up to US$4 million a season.
- Sponsorships have been an important revenue stream for the league, boosted by the league's successful marketing campaign geared towards branding the league showcase for healthy values. Team sponsorship revenue has increased by around 10 per cent from 2005 to 2010. The WNBA also secured a strong commercial relationship with Boost Mobile (BM), and the BM logo was placed on 11 of the league's 12 shirts. The league recently added Anheuser-Busch as a major sponsor.

- Average attendance over recent years has fallen by more than 4 per cent. Average game attendance for the league is now around 7,700.
- In 2011 The WNBA signed new partnerships with Jamba Juice, Coca-Cola and Pirate's Booty snack food.
- The WNBA often averages a 0.2 cable rating (around 263,000) on ESPN2. By any measure this is minuscule audience for a nationally telecast American television program.

The above information provides some insight into the structural and financial problems facing the WNBA, but does not provide any significant financial data that can illuminate the overall problem, or identify or expose the key cost burdens and revenue shortfalls. According to the league's collective bargaining agreement (CBA), the 2012 team salary cap was just under US$900,000. When allocated over the player roster it comes in at around US$70,000 per player per season. This, by any professional sports league measure, is meagre. In contrast, the salary cap for the men's league is US$25 million. Most male basketball players claim an annual salary of US$3–4 million. The gap is obscene from a gender equality perspective, but this is the reality of professional sport. It is all about capacity to pay, which suggests that the revenue base of the WNBA has been frighteningly low for the entirety of its existence. This a serious problem, and it appears that unless there are dramatic changes ahead, the league may not be around, at least in its present form, in 2020. If sustainability is the ultimate performance measure, then the WNBA has a very low rating indeed.

COSTS AND BENEFITS OF A PERFORMANCE MANAGEMENT SYSTEM

Planning and implementing a performance management system can be costly, since it involves much time-intensive analysis of an organization's processes and activities. It can also become a bureaucratic nightmare since it can produce hundreds of microscopic statements about the ways thing should be done, and how they must be measured. It should be remembered that the concept of performance management arose out of the mechanistic time-and-motion studies of Frederick Winslow Taylor in the early part of the twentieth century. According to Taylor the key to increasing productivity was to systematically analyse work practices in order to identify the most efficient process, which could then become a best-practice template (Stewart 1989). Taylorism also underpinned the development of Management by Objectives (MBO) and Total Quality Management (TQM) which were later refined into a broader model of performance management (Bouckaert & van Doren 2003). As a result, a rigidly structured performance management system can stifle initiative and creativity by setting narrowly defined work standards and strict standards of workplace behaviour.

At the same time, a well-thought-out performance management system can provide a number of long-term benefits (Anthony & Young, 2003; Williams 1998). First, it makes sure that the core activities of an organization are directly linked to its primary aims and goals. Second, it can motivate employees by setting targets which are rewarded when they are attained. Third, it ensures greater accountability by clearly identifying not only what is to be achieved, but also who is responsible for making it happen. Fourth, it completes the management cycle by making sure processes are monitored, and outcomes are measured against some sort of minimum performance standard. Finally it forces management to come up with a quantifiable measure of its key outputs, and eliminate ambiguous aims and nebulous objectives.

In Practice 14.2 Football leagues: An Australian perspective

The rapid commercialization of sport during the 1980s and 1990s produced many additional sport leagues around the world. This was especially true in Australia, where four football codes had vied for supremacy for most of the twentieth century with varying degrees of success. These codes were Australian Rules football, rugby league, rugby union and soccer.

Things came to a head in 2006 when a revitalized national soccer competition was established comprising eight new professionally run teams. It was completely re-badged, clubs were stripped of their ethnic origins, and the A-League was launched. By 2014 it had become a highly successful spectator sport, and some matches claimed a 40,000 attendance figure. However, most teams found it difficult to scratch out a balanced operating budget.

The National Rugby League competition (NRL) is equally robust, with all players on a full-time professional roster. Although the competition was fractured by the establishment of a rival Super League in 1995, it is solidly entrenched in New South Wales and Queensland, and to a lesser extent Victoria. However, the competition no longer has teams in either South Australia or Western Australia, although this structural problem is slightly compensated for by having a team playing out of Auckland in New Zealand.

Rugby union is an equally interesting, but more brittle case. Like League, it has only moderate support in Australia's southern states, but is a major code in New South Wales and Queensland. Union's Super-12 competition initially comprised five New Zealand teams, three Australian teams, and four South African teams. However, in 2007 another two teams were added to the competition, namely Perth in Western Australia, and a fifth South African team, thereby making it a Super-14 competition. A Melbourne and Perth team was admitted for the 2011 season, and now there are 16 teams in the competition which has been divided into a New Zealand division, an Australian division and a South African division.

Finally, there is the Australian Football League (AFL), which is Australia's most popular indigenous sport, and the nation's most popular sporting competition. Having been a 16-team competition in 1986, in 2011 it became a 17-team competition, having admitted a team from the Queensland Gold Coast. A second New South Wales team was admitted in 2012, making it an 18-team competition with a minimum of two teams in every mainland state. The AFL has thus made significant inroads in the so-called 'hostile' rugby territory of New South Wales and Queensland.

Each of the above football codes has their own unique history and culture, but it is also the case that they are serious rivals in a highly competitive sporting marketplace. There are many arguments about the relative strengths of each code, and which national competition is the most successful (Stewart 2007). In performance management terms, this is an interesting issue to address, but it is not immediately clear as to how one should best go about doing a comparative evaluation of the performance of the leagues. This is because there are many different ways of undertaking the performance management task.

The first point to note is that the management of each national competition is sensitive to developments in the rival leagues. They are also eager to trumpet and promote their successes, particularly if it means they have secured some strategic advantage over their competitors. At the same time, there are a number of critical success factors that are commonly used to rank the performance of the national leagues. These factors are first, total season attendance, second, total club membership, third, aggregate league revenue, fourth, income from television broadcast rights, and, finally, weekly television audiences.

These five somewhat crude measures give a very good indication of just how well each league performs. However, over recent times some additional measures have been incorporated into their performance management models. First, there is the issue of the viability of teams, and the ability to balance their budgets. Second, there is the competitive balance of the league, and the extent to which it can guarantee fans a close and exciting contest. Third, there is the reputation of the league and the extent to which it is seen as a responsible sporting citizen. To this end the leagues are eager to promote equal opportunity for players and administrators, put in place anti-harassment rules, and have a strong anti-doping policy. In general the leagues are sensitive to criticism about player misconduct, particularly when it involves illicit drug use, racist abuse, homophobia, or some sort of sexual assault. A sample of key indicators for measuring the performance of Australian national football leagues is listed in Table 14.3.

TABLE 14.3 Performance measures for Australian national sport leagues

Item	Descriptor/measure	Examples
Financial stability	• League turnover • Net assets	Australian Football League (AFL) turnover is more than $360 million. National Rugby League (NRL) turnover is around $200 million
Corporate support	• Sponsorship income • Stadium suites	AFL supported by more national brands (e.g. Vodafone, Air Emirates, Toyota) than NRL
Broadcasting rights fees	• Fees from TV stations • Fees from radio stations	AFL TV rights fee currently $150 million p.a.; NRL TV rights fee currently around $900 million p.a.

Item	Descriptor/measure	Examples
Media exposure	• Television rating • Print media coverage	AFL grand final draws 2.9 million TV audience; NRL grand final draws 2.3 million TV audience.
Public interest	• Brand awareness • Match attendance	AFL average match attendance 38,000; NRL average match attendance 18,000.
Spread/coverage	• Media coverage • Spread of teams and venues	AFL teams spread around five of six states; NRL teams spread around three of six states plus New Zealand.
Competitive balance	• Win-loss ratios for each team • Premierships won by each team	NRL teams have slightly more closely aligned win-loss ratios (i.e. smaller standard deviation).
Game development	• Junior development programs • Regional development programs	AFL spends $40 million a year on community development; NRL spends $18 million on community development.

Source: AFL (2012) Annual Report 2011 Season, AFL, Melbourne; Stewart, B. (ed.) (2007) *The Games Are Not the Same: The Political Economy of Football In Australia*, Melbourne University Press (Chapter 8).

A MULTI-DIMENSIONAL PERFORMANCE MANAGEMENT MODEL FOR SPORT

The BSC has many strengths, but it also requires significant adjustment to make it better fit the special requirements of sport organizations. One approach is to maintain the four basic dimensions that underpin the BSC, and use it to design a customized performance model that reflects the special features of sport organizations. To this end the following '9 point' model of performance management has been designed.

The first performance dimension focuses on *wins, awards and successes*. This dimension recognizes the fact that most sport associations and clubs want to be seen to be doing well and producing winning players and teams. In other words, faced with the choice of winning a championship, or increasing profits, most clubs would prefer the winner's pennant or medal.

However, like all organizations, sport leagues, associations and clubs need ongoing funding to ensure their long-term viability, to pay their debts when they fall due, and cover their operating costs from year to year. Therefore the second dimension is concerned with *financial sustainability*. In this respect, measures of revenue growth will not be enough, and more specific measures of profit, liquidity, long-term indebtedness, return on investment, and net asset growth are all useful indicators.

The third dimension is *market distribution*, or the extent to which a sport league, association or club is able to facilitate the consumption of its particular sporting practice. If its major concern is with participation, then it needs to be aware of how many facilities it provides, their location and spread, and the experiential quality they offer. If the major concern is the potential audience that can be attracted, then it needs to be aware of the number of spectator seats it can provide, the radio exposure it will receive, and the scale and breadth of any television broadcast.

The fourth dimension is *market size and share*. It is one thing to have a broad range and spread of facilities and venues, and a large number of television-broadcast hours, but it is another thing to attract a consistently large number of participants, spectators and viewers. It is also important to compare the numbers for these indicators with the numbers for other related sports that are seen to be competitors.

The fifth dimension is *customer satisfaction*, which is really a measure of how strongly participants, fans and members approve of the performance of the league, association or club. Sport organizations usually engender very passionate connections with their customer and member base, but there are also many instances when they attend games or activities less frequently, or more seriously downgrade their involvement. Surveys of participants, members and fans can reveal early signs of dissatisfaction, or alternatively indicate what is sustaining the relationship.

The sixth dimension is *internal procedures and processes*. Like Kaplan and Norton's similarly labelled dimension, it aims to highlight the key links in the value-chain and how each stage is performing relative to the others. For sporting organizations it often begins with how well players are recruited, their numbers, and overall quality. The recruitment and retention of members is also an important consideration, and the question often arises as to the capacity of members to contribute time, expertise, and money to the association and the club's activities. The ability of players to improve their skill and overall performance is also a function of the support system, and in particular the skill and abilities of the coaching staff. This leads to the capacity of the organization to ensure a safe environment where the management of risk is taken seriously, and the incidence of litigation is slight. All the above processes are of course linked to *administrative functions* that can either enhance the player and member experience or not, as poor training or sloppy systems can make the experience both unpleasant and costly. Many of the above factors can be difficult to quantify, but they nevertheless need serious consideration.

The seventh dimension is *product improvement*. In this respect sport is no different from business in that it operates in a very competitive marketplace, and constant innovation and product improvement is essential to attract new customers and retain the old. Some sports have been very successful in modifying their games to suit the needs of special groups, while others have been unable to move beyond their traditional practices. In some spectator sports there have been very slow improvements in venue quality, while in others there has been a virtual revolution in terms of stadium design and spectator comfort. Progressive changes in the design of sporting equipment have also improved product quality. In tennis, for example, the use of carbon fibre racket frames and the creation of larger 'sweet-spots' have enabled average club-players to improve their standard of play and overall skill levels.

The eighth dimension is *staff development and learning*. Sport is a very person centred, time-absorbing activity, and therefore requires staff who have highly refined people-management skills, and the capacity to create an organizational culture that retains players and members. The growing technical sophistication of sport also means that traditional administrative, officiating and coaching skills are no longer adequate, and therefore large-scale re-training and education are necessary to ensure a proper fit between the staff competencies and the new technologies and infrastructure that underpin contemporary sport.

The ninth dimension covers the *economic, social and environmental impact* that a sport league, association or club has on its surrounding community. Increasingly the level of support a government will provide a sport organization is contingent upon the organization's ability to produce a positive economic, social or environmental impact. This trend has been exaggerated by the growing popularity of the triple-bottom-line accounting concept, which highlights the importance of going beyond profitability and wealth creation as the sole measure of an organization's contribution to society to include environmental and social impacts (Hums & Maclean 2009; Norman & MacDonald 2004). In this case sport organizations also have a responsibility to carefully manage and sustain its environment, and establish an organizational culture that values things like diversity, equal opportunity, and the fair treatment of gays, lesbians and religious minorities.

This performance management model has the advantage of being broad and inclusive, and geared to the needs of sport in general. But, it needs to be customized to fit different sporting organizations. As we indicated before, an organization's strategic intent, and stakeholder interests, will shape the design of a performance evaluation model (Anthony & Young 2003; Atkinson et al. 1997; Robbins et al. 2002; Williams 1998). For example, the evaluation model for a national sporting body should be different from the model used to evaluate a professional sport club. The national sporting body will be more interested in participation rates, club development, and the provision of quality local facilities. On the other hand, a professional sport club will be more concerned with its win-loss ratio, sponsor income, television ratings, and membership levels.

In Practice 14.3 Formula 1 Grand Prix

Ever since the first motor cars rolled of the assembly plants in the USA in the early part of the twentieth century, people around the world have had an ongoing fascination with them. The idea that cars could be used to create a new form of sport was quickly converted into practice, and by the 1930s many types of race meeting were established, where stock-standard touring cars were competing with customized race-cars for the hearts and minds of car-racing enthusiasts.

An international governing body for motor sports was also established at this time, and having been headquartered in Paris, was given the name of *The Fédération Internationale de l'Automobile*, or FIA for short (Hums & Maclean 2009). It was, and still is, a nonprofit association that now brings together more than 200 national motoring and sporting organizations from just over 130 countries on five continents.

FIA has a multi-faceted role. First, it represents the rights of motoring organizations and motor car users throughout the world. It has campaigned on such things as such as safety, mobility, the environment, and consumer law. The FIA also promotes the interests of motorists at the United Nations, within the European Union, and through other international bodies. The FIA is also the governing body for motor sport worldwide. It administers the rules and regulations for all international four-wheel motor sport including the FIA Formula One World Championship, FIA World Rally Championship and FIA World Touring Car Championship (www.fia.com).

However, plans for an elite level, high performance 'Formula One' drivers' championship were not formulated until the late 1930s. The plans were shelved with the onset of World War 2, but in 1946 the idea was rekindled, races were held, and the following year a decision was made to launch a drivers' championship (Hums & Maclean 2009). The first FIA endorsed world championship race was held at Silverstone in England, in 1950, and while only seven of the 20 Formula One races that season counted towards the title, the championship was nevertheless up and running (Hums & MacLean 2009) .

There was no shortage of so-called 'privateers', who were drivers who operated on their own, and bought and raced their own cars. Nevertheless, the Formula was very quickly dominated by major pre-war manufacturers such as Alfa Romeo, Ferrari, Maserati and Mercedes Benz. Although Giuseppe ('Nino') Farina won the inaugural title in 1950, the dominant driver over the decade was Juan Manuel Fangio from Argentina, who won five drivers' championships. The 1960s was a also a period of growth, with Stirling Moss, an Englishman, and Jack Brabham, an Australian, being the best known racers.

In the early 1970s, Bernie Ecclestone, the English motor sports entrepreneur, rearranged the management of Formula One's commercial rights, and turned the sport into a billion dollar, global business. In 1971 he bought the Brabham team and subsequently gained a seat on the Council of the Formula One Constructors' Association (FOCA). In 1978 he became its president. Before the Ecclestone era, FIA and circuit owners controlled many aspects of the sport, but Ecclestone changed all this when he convinced the teams that their net worth would be enhanced by by-passing FIA and negotiating directly with manufacturers and circuit managers as a coordinated unit. In 1979, FIA not surprisingly clashed with FOCA over revenues and regulations, and matters deteriorated to such an extent that FOCA threatened to boycott races and even form a breakaway global circuit. But, in the end it was understood that FOCA and FIA had to work together to achieve the best outcome for the sport, with Ecclestone front-and-centre.

Further tensions arose in the early 2000s when manufacturer-owned teams – which included Renault, BMW, Toyota, Honda and Ferrari – dominated the championship. They also used the commercial muscle of their Grand Prix Manufacturers Association (GPMA) to negotiate not only a larger share of Formula One's rapidly increasing revenues, but also to have a greater say in the sport's planning and management processes.

Under the ever-opportunistic eye of Eccelestone, the global expansion of Formula One continued, with new races located in lucrative markets in East Asia and the Middle East. Whereas the inaugural 1950 world championship season comprised only seven races, the schedule expanded rapidly over the following 60 years. The number of races plateaued between 16 and 17 during the 1980s and 1990s, but has recently risen to 20.

The current global circuit arrangements for Formula One are impressive, and take in every continent except Africa. But Formula One has also been surrounded by controversies, and allegations of greedy, anti-social, and sometime even corrupt behaviour, which, according to the sport's critics, have taken the following forms:

- It assaults the environment by occupying public space, making an enormous amount of noise.
- It has an embedded dependence on fossil fuel products which makes it at odds with current global government policies aimed at controlling greenhouse gasses by reducing carbon emissions and consequently softening so-called carbon footprints.
- There are regular governance and management battles between FOCA, FIA and GPMA.
- Teams often seem to be on the verge of breaking away from F1 and creating rival circuits.
- There are frequent accusations of race result manipulation. These allegations were confirmed in 2009 when it was revealed that Nelson Piquet Jr had been ordered to crash his car at the 2008 Singapore Grand Prix for the benefit of his team-mate. Renault boss, Flavio Briatore, was subsequently banned from the sport.
- In some cities, and in Melbourne in particular, there is growing concern that the costs of mounting the race are increasing at such a rate that the costs of conducting an event will eventually outweigh the benefits. The Melbourne event, for example, is suffering from a fall in live attendance, and has had extreme difficulty securing sufficient heavyweight sponsors. There is also resentment over the management fee that has to be paid to Ecclestone to retain the event. At the last count it was more than US$25 million, an amount which led some critics to suggest that there was no longer any point in conducting the race in Melbourne, since it was nothing more than a burden on local taxpayers.

Controversies aside, Formula One motor racing is a highly profitable enterprise, and it has enormous global reach through its international circuit, its high profile global sponsors, and its lucrative television broadcast contact arrangements. Its total viewing figure is now in excess of 350 million, and it regularly attracts 100,000–150,000 fans to its race meets (Hums & MacLean 2009). It is the archetypal hyper-commercial, hyper-modern sporting enterprise. According to an analysis undertaken by Deloitte International, one of the world's largest accounting firms, Formula One now boasts the world's highest revenue-generating annual sporting events. Each of its top eight Grand Prix events in 2008 had an average revenue of just under US$220 million. This compares favourably with the per-game/event values of US$25 million in the American National Football league (NFL), US$8 million in the English FA Premier League, and US$2 million in the American Major League Baseball (MLB) (Carter 2011; Zimbalist 2006).

The Formula One's 2008 global revenues of just over US$4 billion make it the third most commercialized sport competition in the world. Only the NFL (US$7 billion) and MLB (US$6 billion) earn more revenue, but they do it by running substantially more so-called events. The Premier League clubs' combined revenue was just under US$4 billion for the same period. The US$4 billion is comprised of 1) central revenues, which come from broadcasting rights fees, race sponsorship, and corporate hospitality, 2) team revenues which include sponsorship and contributions from commercial partners and owners, and 3) circuit revenues which come from ticketing and additional sponsorships (Carter 2011; Hums & MacLean 2009; Zimbalist 2006).

However, when compared with many other major sports, Formula 1 attracts a much lower proportion of its revenues from event day attendees. Ticket receipts and other attendee secondary spending currently represent only around 10 per cent of total revenue, and this is a weakness that organizers are hoping to address in the near future.

So, how should we go about measuring the performance of the Formula One Grand Prix Circuit? Well, the short answer is 'with great difficulty'. The fundamental problem is to actually sort out what it is we aim to measure. In a global enterprise of this type there are not just the financial performance issues to consider, but also its economic, social cultural and environmental impacts. One approach is to build a model of performance evaluation that takes into account all of these factors to some extent or other. A multi-factorial approach is gaining more credence as governments around the world are trying to secure the best outcomes from these mega sport events. The fact of the matter is that commercial businesses are often criticized for thinking only of the profits they make, and ignoring the social consequences of their strategic decisions and the outputs they deliver. This dilemma is particularly striking in the case of tobacco companies, which have always had close commercial links to motor racing. On one hand there are profits to be made, but on the other hand there is evidence that links smoking cigarettes to lung cancer and heart disease. Sport, and motor racing in particular, has for many years had a close relationship with tobacco producers, who have provided millions of dollars of sponsor funds to both community and professional sport (www.thelancet.com).

There is now growing pressure from both government and the public in general for businesses to move beyond the bottom line and take into account the effect their decisions have on the wider community. This idea has given rise to the concept of triple bottom line accounting, which gets businesses to consider their contribution to not just economic prosperity, but also social justice and environmental quality. While the measurement of social justice and environmental quality is fraught with danger, the overall aim is to see that profits and net worth are just one measure of the performance of an organization. Triple bottom line accounting consequently provides for three measures of how a business contributes to society, with each measure being geared around the value-added concept. These measures – which are summarized in Table 14.4 – are Economic value-added, Social value-added, and Environmental value-added.

TABLE 14.4 GRI performance indicators

Performance category	Performance measures
Direct economic impacts	Sales to satisfied customers Purchases from suppliers Employees hired Taxes paid Dividend and interest paid
Product responsibility	Safety and durability Truth in advertising and product labelling
Work practices	Health, safety and security Training, education and consultation Appropriate wages and conditions
Social practices	No bribery and corruption Transparent lobbying Free from collusion and coercion
Human rights	Non-discriminatory hiring practices Free from forced labour
Environmental impacts	Efficient energy use Appropriate water recycling Controlled carbon and other emissions Waste management Maintenance of biodiversity

This way of measuring performance presents many challenges for sport organizations. It has already been noted that sport organizations are motivated by more than money. For a national sporting body the growth of the sport may be equally important, and for a professional sports club the dominant goal may be on-field success. However, despite the primacy of these goals, sport organizations can equally make decisions and produce outputs that have negative consequences for society in general. The heavy use of tobacco companies as sponsors may have secured a valuable source of funds, but the subsequent association of tobacco products with glamorous sport stars was instrumental in convincing young people that smoking was socially desirable, even if it might kill them in the long run. In some sports heavy drinking of alcohol products is part of the club culture, and in these cases no success is seen as complete without a long binge-drinking session. Similarly, in professional sport leagues, where neo-tribalism is strong, groups of rival supporters will often resolve their antagonism with a wild brawl. Football hooliganism in Britain is the archetypal model in this respect. All of these outputs have negative social consequences, and it therefore makes sense to encourage sport clubs, associations and leagues to measure their overall performance in terms of their social and environmental impact as well as their participation impact, win-loss impact, or revenue raising impact.

Recently a number of global businesses with the support of the United Nations developed a corporate social responsibility (CSR) program called the Global Reporting Initiative (GRI). The mission of GRI is to design and promulgate sustainability reporting guidelines for each of the economic, social and environmental outputs identified above. Organizations that sign up to GRI are expected to enact reporting systems that are transparent and accessible, provide quality and reliable information, and include information that is relevant and complete. GRI has also compiled a list of factors under each of the economic, social and environmental headings that indicate specific issues that require addressing.

While the GRI model of performance management is complex, it will encourage sport organizations to be more systematic in the way they build their stakeholder relations. It will also enable them to go beyond revenue growth and on-field success and evaluate the contribution they are making to the wider society, and monitor their impact on the physical environment. This can only be a 'good thing'. But when applied to the Formula One Grand Prix, it is also a 'hard thing'. But it is not impossible, and there are great advantages in taking a more holistic approach to measuring its performance.

Overall, this in-practice example confirms that performance measurement covers many and varied issues. It is thus important to be careful about what will be measured, and what will not. It is important to be clear about 1) the mission of the sport enterprise, 2) what it aims to achieve, and 3) what it values in the broader social sense.

RISK, UNCERTAINTY AND PERFORMANCE

The dimensional performance management models referred to above have breadth, which is a strength. However, sometimes breadth can come at the expense of connectivity, and this can be problematic. One way of securing a stronger sense of integration is to view the model through the operational lens of risk and uncertainty. Risk and uncertainty are pivotal components of any performance management model since they can seriously undermine performance levels if left unattended.

But, but what exactly is risk? At its most succinct, risk is the likelihood that a chosen action, initiative, or activity – or alternatively, a choice to not act, take no initiative, or remain inactive – will deliver some type of harm, lead to a loss, or produce a sub-optimal, or wholly undesirable outcome. This, of course, implies that the chosen action, initiative, or activity will, in fact, have some influence over the anticipated performance outcome.

For the technically minded, and those readers who like to think in short 'grabs', risk can be defined in terms of the following equation:

$$\text{Risk} = \text{Probability} \times \text{Consequences}$$

That is, risk is the probability of a 'bad' or 'harmful' thing happening multiplied by the consequences that will occur if the 'bad' or 'harmful' things do, in fact, happen. Take, for example, the curator of a sports field, who finds that he has not been able to create the expected smooth and well-grassed playing surface, and indeed, has failed to fill some serious potholes, and forgot to remove large bits of broken glass from an expanse of the playing surface. In this case risk is exceedingly high, since the probability of something nasty happening to players will be high, and if something unpleasant does happen, the consequences – including overall levels of performance – will be very serious indeed.

So, we can go on to say that risk management is all about being aware of what may happen as you go about your business and taking steps to mitigate the chances of something going wrong, or deciding that you accept that something may occur and that you are prepared for the consequences. Risk management therefore aims to be proactive rather than reactive, and thus provide the conditions for creating safer physical environments, safer operational procedures, safer playing spaces, and finally, higher levels of performance.

When examining the delivery of a sporting experience, risks can be viewed from a number of perspectives, with each perspective carrying its own mix of clarity and fuzziness. The first perspective is *strategic*. In this case the risks are associated with the high-level longer-term goals, objectives, or strategies of the organization, club, association, or league. The second perspective is *operational*. In this case the risks are associated with the daily functions of the organization such as finance, decision-making, marketing and promotion, and the administrative areas of clubs, associations and leagues. The third perspective is related to a *project or event*. In this case the risks are linked to specific stages of the operational outcome. They include 1) the initiation and concept phase, 2) the planning phase, 3) the execution and implementation phase, and 4) the performance evaluation phase. It is one thing to note the influence risk can have on conduct and performance, but it is another thing to assess the scale and scope of the risk for different phases of an activity, program or event.

Risk assessment involves analysing the likelihood and consequences of each identified risk using whatever measures might be provided. When multiplied out, the overall level of risk can be calculated. The purpose here is to separate high risks from low risks, and to prioritize those areas where resources should be allocated to ensure continuity, predictability and safety.

At this point the two key terms to address are *likelihood* and *consequence*. Likelihood is a qualitative description of probability and frequency. For anything even slightly unpredictable or uncertain it is always useful to ask: what is the likelihood of the risk occurring? Consequence is the outcome of an event or situation expressed qualitatively or quantitatively, being a loss, injury, disadvantage, harm, benefit, or gain. In this instance it is always useful to ask the question what is the consequence if the risk does indeed occur?

In summary, high levels of risk may, in a few lucky instances, lead to a miraculous performance, but in most cases they will deliver obstacles, excessive anxiety and a high probability that things will go wrong. From a performance management perspective this is the worst possible environment to create.

PERFORMANCE MEASURES: LONGITUDINAL OR COMPARATIVE?

Once a performance management model is in place, it is then crucial to design performance measures. These measures should be able to precisely identify and quantify specific indicators of success or failure. Sometimes it is difficult to 'put a number' on a measure. Customer and fan 'satisfaction' readily comes to mind in this respect, but there are often ways of converting a subjective opinion into a measurable indicator.

It is one thing to identify some key performance indicators, and to collect some data under each heading. However, it is another thing to make sense of the data. It is therefore important to develop some sort of benchmark or standard by which to measure the performance of a sport organization. There are two ways of doing this.

The first is to undertake a *longitudinal study* that examines the progress of a sport organization over time. Take, for example, the performance of Athletics Australia (AA), the national governing body for athletics in Australia. A 10-year analysis of its financial performance would show it was often unable to balance its books. In 2003 it had accumulated a seriously worrying level of debt which brought on an organizational crisis. The crisis was addressed, and over the following eight years it expanded its revenue base substantially, and in preparing for the London 2012 Olympics, was relatively resource-rich. At the same time it was still reliant on government funds to balance its books. By any financial measure, AA's performance had improved dramatically over this period, although it was starting off from a low base. The same sort of longitudinal analysis could be applied to its participation levels and elite international performance. In each case the data indicated small but significant improvement.

Another way of looking at AA's performance would be to compare it with other national sport bodies to see how it ranks. That is, it will also be important to undertake a comparative study by which the performance of AA is stacked up against a number of other national sport organizations. There are two ways of doing this. The first way would be compare it with similarly funded Australian national sport bodies like Swimming Australia or Rowing Australia. In this case, AA has not performed well, since both swimming and rowing have achieved regular gold medal winning performances at both World Championships and Olympic Games over the last 10 years. The second way is to compare AA's performance with an equivalent national athletic association from another country. An appropriate point of comparison here might be the Canadian Athletics Federation, since both countries have similar populations and the national athletic associations have a similar resource base. In this case the comparison would yield an elite performance outcome inferior to Swimming Australia, which by international standards performs just below the level of the USA national swim governing body, which makes it number two in the world.

PERFORMANCE MEASUREMENT: FROM GLOBAL TO LOCAL

As noted above, performance measurement has many variants, especially when applied to sport. It could be directed to the impact a mega event has on a local economy, or the operating profit of an international field hockey tournament. It can focus on player achievements in a professional basketball club, it can also revolve around changes in a club's levels of debts, or it can be concerned with the growth in the number of registered players in a local tennis association. It can be global, but it can also be local. It can involve a profit making gym, or a nonprofit fitness centre.

SUMMARY

The above discussion suggests that while the introduction of performance management systems into sport organizations may seem costly, and possibly creates an administrative straightjacket for its staff, officials, volunteers and members, it can also bring substantial benefits. In fact, a sport organization that does not provide a systematic evaluation of its performance would be derelict in its duty to stakeholders. The question is really one of what form and shape the performance management system should take. At this point it is important to say that there is no one best performance management system. It all depends on the particular sport organization being studied, its strategic goals, and the environment in which it operates. A good starting point is to use Kaplan and Norton's BSC as the foundation, and customize it to fit the sport organization's specific needs. The 9-point model described above gives a number of possibilities, but at all times the measures should be quantifiable, linked to the sport organization's primary goals, and consistent with stakeholder expectations.

REVIEW QUESTIONS

1   What does a performance management system aim to do?

2   What are the origins of performance management, and what do these origins tell us about its possible strengths and weaknesses?

3   What might prevent a sport organization from implementing a system of performance management?

4   What are the benefits that will follow from the implementation of a performance management system?

5   What are the key components of Kaplan and Norton's BSC?

6   How might you go about modifying the BSC to make it better fit the special features of sport organizations?

7   What specific measures can best reveal the financial performance of a sport organization?

8   How can the intrinsically vague concept of customer satisfaction be 'hardened-up' to provide a quantitative, concrete measure of the service quality in a community leisure centre?

9   What would you advise a sport club or association to do in order to ensure it was delivering its sport services in a fair, equitable, and environmentally friendly way?

FURTHER READING

To get a more detailed picture of the fundamentals of performance management, and how it has been used in both private and public sectors, see Anthony and Young (2003); Bouckaert et al. (2003); Bryson (2004) and Williams (1978). In order to obtain a fuller appreciation of the theoretical foundations of performance management, its relation to organizational effectiveness, and problems of implementation, refer to Chapter 3 of Robbins et al. (2002), and Bouckaert (1995).

To secure more details on what makes sport both similar to and different from the world of business go to Smith and Stewart (2012).

For a detailed account of how to set up performance management systems for Olympic sport organizations see Chappelet and Bayle (2005), pp. 39–110.

A comprehensive comparative evaluation of the four professional football leagues operating in Australia can be found in Chapter 8 of Stewart (2007).

RELEVANT WEBSITES

- For an update on the balanced scorecard approach to performance management, go to www.balancedscorecard.org
- Japan's professional soccer (i.e. association football) league, the J-League is one of Japan's most popular sport competitions. To obtain a general picture of its overall level of performance, go to www.j-league.or.jp/eng
- In Australia, the Australian Football League is highly profitable, but paradoxically some of its member clubs have had to fight severe financial turbulence over many years. The Institute of Chartered Accountants undertakes an annual survey of club finances. For further details search for the *Enhancing Not-for-Profit Annual and Financial Reporting* report on the www.icaa.org.au site.
- For a detailed discussion of the Global Reporting Initiative (GRI) and related indicators go to www.globalreporting.org
- Nike has developed a strong corporate social responsibility program in recent years. For a detailed discussion of their sustainable business program go to www.nikeresponsibility.com/report

CASE STUDY 14.1

The 2011 Kimberley Ultramarathon

In early September 2011, a 100km ultramarathon event was conducted in the remote, but picturesque Kimberley region of Western Australia, which is in the north-west part of the state. It involved a predominantly off-road course starting from the Emma Gorge airstrip at El Questro and finishing in the town of Kununurra.

The event was titled the 2011 Kimberley Ultramarathon, and was organized by a Hong Kong-based events management business called Racing The Planet Events Limited, or RacingThePlanet, its abbreviated title. It had attracted a sponsorship commitment from EVENTSCORP, the Western Australian Government's events agency and an operating division within Tourism WA, for around US$105,000 with an option for a further two years. It was a significant event. It had captured a lot of media interest, and it attracted competitors from around the world.

The RacingThePlanet business was also very experienced in conducting these sorts of events, and had staged more than 33 footraces in eight countries over the preceding 10 years. This was the second event that RacingThePlanet had staged in the Kimberley region. In April 2010 RacingThePlanet had successfully organized and run a 250km seven-day event in the same area.

The 2011 event secured massive publicity, but for all the wrong reasons. During the event, at least 13 competitors were directly confronted by a large bushfire. Five competitors – Turia Pitt, Kate Sanderson, Martin Van Der Merwe, Michael Hull, and Mary Gadams – were unable to escape the flames and suffered burns of varying degrees of severity. The injuries suffered by Ms Pitt and Ms Sanderson were life-threatening, and left them with permanent scarring, disfigurement and disability. Overall, the event turned out to be a catastrophe.

In response to a public outcry over what appeared to be management incompetence, the WA Legislative Assembly directed its Economics and Industry Standing Committee to investigate the incident. The Committee was asked to examine the actions of the organizer, and the roles and actions of a range of government agencies in respect of the event. The Committee was also asked to consider whether RacingThePlanet had taken all reasonable steps to identify and reduce risks and maintain the safety of competitors, employees, contractors, spectators and volunteers in 1) planning for the event, 2) running of the event and 3) responding to the fire and the injuries, including access to medical support and evacuations.

Having taken thousands of pages of written submissions and oral evidence, the Committee found that RacingThePlanet did not take all reasonable steps to identify risks associated with the 2011 Kimberley Ultramarathon. Nor did the Committee believe that RacingThePlanet had taken all reasonable steps to reduce risks to the safety of competitors, employees, contractors, spectators and volunteers.

The Committee also identified a series of factors which demonstrated that RacingThePlanet did not take all reasonable steps to maintain the safety of the above parties. In the first place, the Committee concluded that RacingThePlanet, in its planning processes leading up to the 2011 Kimberley Ultramarathon, did not involve people who had an appropriate knowledge in identifying risk. Second, the level of communication and consultation with relevant agencies and individuals regarding the event's Management and Risk Assessment Plan was seen to be inadequate, both in terms of its timeliness and its approach. Third, and as a result of the previous two failings, RacingThePlanet deprived itself of the opportunity to identify risks that it may not have contemplated and to establish relationships with key agencies that may have been able to provide ongoing assistance with risk identification and mitigation.

The Committee found that, most crucially, RacingThePlanet did not communicate properly before the event with the local fire authority. It did not link into their fire monitoring expertise and advice prior the race. This would have been highly valuable to RacingThePlanet in terms of whether the race needed to be re-routed – with fires in the vicinity of the course – or possibly cancelled. Similarly, the Committee found that during the race, when a message of fire approaching a checkpoint was relayed to RacingThePlanet staff, proper counsel with the local fire authority regarding the appropriate response could have improved the decision-making capacity of the organizer. The Committee also believed that RacingThePlanet was aware of fires on, and in the vicinity of the course, prior to and on the day of the event. It also found that it was advised to contact the fire authority, but did not do so. In short, RacingThePlanet did not have a plan to monitor fire on the course other than by direct observation.

According to the Committee, another critical shortcoming in the pre-event consultation process was the planning for an emergency helicopter. Despite knowing for some time that a helicopter was the only means of evacuation from the Tier Gorge section of the course, RacingThePlanet only sought to make arrangements for the use of a helicopter in the event of an emergency the day before the race. RacingThePlanet decided not to put a helicopter on stand-by, and instead made informal and inadequate arrangements for the use of the helicopter hired separately by a media company filming the event. The Committee also noted that this helicopter was not appropriately equipped for a range of emergency and evacuation scenarios. Moreover, as the event unfolded on the day, RacingThePlanet's plan for using this helicopter in the event of an emergency was not enacted correctly, was not well understood, and suffered from only having been determined the day before the event.

CASE STUDY QUESTIONS

1   What went wrong?

2   Given what went wrong, how did you rate the overall performance of this event?

3   From your reading of the above case, what were the key risks associated with the event. Categorize them in terms of 1) initiation and concept, 2) planning and 3) execution and implementation.

4   What could have been done better?

5   What risk management strategy would you have put in place for the event?

6   What should be done differently next time?

CASE STUDY 14.2

From local to global: Facility and staff appraisal

As we indicated in the early part of this chapter, performance management systems have infiltrated their way into every nook and cranny of the business environment and public sector (Robbins & Barnwell 2002; Bouckaert et al. 2003). Moreover, they are not only applied to corporate performance, but also to many of the so-called micro activities that comprise the day-to-day operations of business enterprises. Community leisure centres in particular lend themselves to micro-measurement. In the first place, they provide an array of person-centred activities that are subject to strong user responses and perceptions. Second, their services are not only rated on the scale, range and quality of its tangible facilities, but also on the quality of the service provided by the staff. Third, many community leisure centres are funded and subsidized through local government rates and taxes, and therefore need to ensure that scarce community resources are utilized as efficiently as possible (Graaff 1996).

It is useful to examine the performance of community leisure centres from two perspectives. The first perspective focuses on the efficient use of funds, staff and space. To get some idea of how funds are being used it is always good to start with some idea of the relationship between operating costs and income. This will generate an operating profit indicator, and an expense recovery rate. And where more detail is needed, something like fees (admission charges) per visit or fees per unit of space can be calculated. It is also very important to identify not only the gross subsidy that may apply, but also the subsidy per visit. There are also a number of sales and marketing related measures that can be used to indicate how well funds are being used in attracting visitors. They include things like total visits per space used, and promotion costs per visitor. It is also important to measure facility usage. In this instance, measures include visits per metre of space, maintenance cost per unit of centre expenditure, and energy cost per metre of space. Finally, there are a number of measures that provide an indication of how well staff are being utilized. They include staff costs as a percentage of total income, staff costs as a percentage of total centre expenditure, and the ratio of desk staff to programming staff. A sample of performance indicators for community leisure centres is listed in Table 14.5.

The second perspective focuses on the level of service quality. In this instance it is a matter of finding out what visitors think of their experiences in the centre (Beech & Chadwick 2004). Their experiences are usually divided into five categories. They are, first, the quality of the tangible product or service itself; second, the reliability and dependability of the service; third, the responsiveness of staff and their willingness to assist; fourth, an assurance that staff will be trustworthy and courteous; and finally, the degree to which staff are empathetic and provide individual attention. There are many models to choose from, and

TABLE 14.5 Sample of efficiency indicators for a community leisure centre

Indicator	Description	Examples
Expense recovery rate	Ratio of total centre income to total centre expenses	Income of $5 million, expenses of $4.5 million, Expense recovery rate is 1:11
Admission fees per visit	Total fees divided by number of visits	1,000 visits per week, $6,000 in fees, admission fee per visit is $6.
Visits per space available	Visits divided by amount of space	1,000 visits per week, 50 square metres of space, visit per metre-space is 200.
Promotion costs per visitor	Promotion costs divided by number of visitors	1,000 visits per week, $1,000 of promotion per week, promotion cost per visit is $1.
Maintenance costs rate	Ratio of total centre maintenance costs to total centre income	Maintenance cost are $1.5 million, centre income is $5 million, maintenance cost rate is 0.30 or 30%.
Staff costs per unit of space	Staff costs divided by space	Staff costs are $3 million, space is 50 square metres, staff cost per unit of space is $6,000.

many rating tools. Some of the more sophisticated tools aim to calculate a service delivery gap, which is nothing more than the difference between what customers expected, and what they experienced (Graaff 1996). In the end, all they are doing is providing a customer rating of the facilities and personal service provided. Typically this will be done by a survey or questionnaire that asks visitors to score the specific services on a rating scale of 1–5. Ratings of 1 usually indicate low levels of satisfaction, while ratings of 5 will indicate high levels of satisfaction.

RATING SPORT COACH PERFORMANCE

Another example of a localized performance management activity might involve the assessment of a coach's job over the course of season. At first glance, the problem of working out how best to judge the performance of a sport coach appears quite simple. The intuitive response to any question about coaching performance is to examine the sport team's performance by referring to its win-loss ratio. It would follow then, that a team with a win-loss ratio of 0.80 or 80 per cent has outperformed a team whose win-loss ratio was 0.60 or 60 per cent.

Alternatively, a current season win-loss ratio of 0.70 or 70 per cent, when contrasted with a previous season win-loss ratio of 0.50 or 50 per cent, would also suggest an improved level of performance. Not only would the coach be happy with this sort of result, but so too would the club officials and the fans. It is fair to say that coaches are responsible for securing the best outcomes from their team. However, it is also reasonable to propose that coaches can only work within the limits set by the resources and playing talent at their disposal. There is a theory of strategic management called the resource based view (RBV), which says that the key to getting a competitive edge is all to do with the quality of resources at your disposal (Stewart 2007). This competitive edge can be best secured by assembling resources that are 1) valuable, and can consequently generate greater efficiencies, 2) scarce, which means they are difficult to secure, and 3) inimitable, and therefore not easy to replicate. In short, superior performance will result from a strong endowment of resources that cannot be matched by competitors.

This model brings into question the idea that a coach's performance can be measured solely against a series of win-loss ratios. Under the assumptions of the RBV model, team performance has as much to do with playing talent and support service quality as it has to do with the leadership style and technical capacities of the coach. In other words, any rating of coaching performance should take into account the quality and scale of resources that the coaches have at their disposal.

CASE STUDY QUESTIONS

1   Is performance evaluation only good for mega events and corporate sport?
2   What performance indicators do you look for in the operation of leisure centres?
3   What are the differences between efficiency indicators and service quality indicators?
4   What are some examples of service quality indicators?
5   How would you go about assessing the performance of a community club sport coach?
6   If success and wins are not the most appropriate measure, then what are?
7   Would it make sense to use an off-field measure of coaching performance, and if so, then what might it involve?

Bibliography

Allison, M. (2002). *Sports Clubs in Scotland Summary: Research Digest no. 59.* Edinburgh, Scotland: Sports Scotland.

Amar, A.D., Hentrich, C. and Hlupic, V. (2009). To be a better leader, give up authority. *Harvard Business Review,* 87(12): 22–24.

American Marketing Association (2004). *Code of Ethics.* revised edition. Chicago, IL: American Marketing Association.

Amis, J. and Cornwell, T.B. (2005). *Global Sport Sponsorship.* Oxford: Berg.

Amis, J. and Slack, T. (1996). The size-structure relationship in voluntary sport organizations. *Journal of Sport Management,* 10: 76–86.

Anthony, R. and Young, D. (2003). *Management Control in Nonprofit Organizations.* 7th edn. New York: McGraw Hill.

Atkinson, A., Waterhouse, J.H. and Wells, R. (1997). A stakeholder approach to strategic performance measurement. *Sloan Management Review,* Spring: 25–37.

Atrill, P., McLaney, E., Harvey, D. and Jenner, M. (2006). *Accounting: An Introduction.* Frenchs Forest, NSW: Pearson Education Australia.

Australian Bureau of Statistics (2005). *Involvement in Organised Sport and Physical Activity, Australia, Cat. No. 6285.0.* Canberra, Australia: Australian Bureau of Statistics.

Australian Sports Commission (2000). *Committee Management, Active Australia Club/Association Management Program.* Canberra: Australian Sports Commission.

Australian Sports Commission (2003). *Independent Soccer Review: Report of the Independent Soccer Review Committee into the Structure, Governance and Management of Soccer in Australia.* Canberra: Australian Sports Commission.

Australian Sports Commission (2004). *Sport Innovation and Best Practice – Governance* at www.ausport.gov.au/ibp/governance.asp. Canberra: Australian Sports Commission.

Australian Sports Commission (2007). *Report of the Steering Committee into the Structure and Governance Review of Basketball in Australia.* Canberra: Australian Sports Commission.

Australian Sports Commission (2008). *Review of High Performance Pathways in Australian Basketball.* Canberra: Australian Sports Commission.

Baldwin, R. and Cave, M. (1999). *Understanding Regulation: Theory, Strategy and Practice.* Oxford: Oxford University Press.

Baldwin, R., Cave, M. and Lodge, M. (2012). *Understanding Regulation: Theory, Strategy and Practice.* 2nd edn. Oxford: Oxford University Press.

Bass, B.M. (1985). *Leadership and Performance Beyond Expectations.* New York: The Free Press.

Bass, B.M. (1990). *Bass and Stogdill's Handbook of Leadership: Theory, Research, and Managerial Applications.* 3rd edn. New York: Free Press.

Bass, B.M. and Avolio, B.J. (1994). *Improving Organisational Effectiveness through Transformational Leadership*. London: Sage Publications.

Beech, J. and Chadwick, S. (eds) (2004). *The Business of Sport Management*. Harlow, UK: Prentice Hall.

Beech, J. and Chadwick, S. (2013). The commercialization of sport, in J. Beech and S. Chadwick (eds). *The Business of Sport Management*. 2nd edn. Sydney: Pearson, pp. 3–23.

Bellamy, R. (1998). The evolving television sports marketplace, in L. Wenner (ed.). *MediaSport*. London: Routledge, pp. 73–87.

Berger, P. and Luckmann, T. (1967). *The Social Construction of Reality: A Treatise on the Sociology of Knowledge*. London: Penguin.

Bettinger, C. (1989). Use corporate culture to trigger high performance. *Journal of Business Strategy*, 10(2): 38–42.

Block, S.R. (1998). *Perfect Nonprofit Boards: Myths, Paradoxes and Paradigms*. Needham Heights, MA: Simon & Schuster.

Bloomfield, J. (2003). *Australia's Sporting Success: The Inside Story*. Sydney: University of New South Wales Press.

Bouckaert, G. (1995). Improving performance management, in A. Halachmi and G. Bouckaert (eds). *The Enduring Challenges in Public Management*. San Francisco: Jossey-Bass.

Bouckaert, G. and van Doren, W. (2003). Performance measurement and management in public sector organisations, in T. Bovaird and E. Lofler (eds). *Public Management and Governance*. London: Routledge.

Boyle, R. and Haynes, R. (2000). *Power Play: Sport, the Media and Popular Culture*. Sydney: Longman.

Braithwaite, J. (2008). *Regulatory Capitalism: How it Works, Ideas for Making it Work Better*. Cheltenham, UK: Edward Elgar.

Braithwaite, J. and Drahos, P. (2000). *Global Business Regulation*. Cambridge, UK: Cambridge University Press.

Brohm, J. (1978). *Sport: A Prison of Measured Time*. London: Ink Links.

Brown, A. and Walsh, A. (1999). *Not For Sale: Manchester United, Murdoch and the Defeat of BskyB*. Edinburgh: Mainstream.

Bryson, J. (2004). *Strategic Planning for Public and Nonprofit Organisations: A Guide to Strengthening and Sustaining Organizational Achievement*. San Francisco: Jossey-Bass/Wiley.

Carter, D. (2011). *Money Games: Profiting from the Convergence of Sport and Entertainment*. Princeton, NJ: Princeton University, Press.

Carver, J. (1997). *Boards that Make a Difference: A New Design for Leadership in Non-profit and Public Organizations*. 2nd edn. San Francisco: Jossey-Bass.

Cashman, R. (1995). *Paradise of Sport*. Melbourne: Oxford University Press.

Chalip, L., Johnson, A. and Stachura, L. (eds) (1996). *National Sports Policies: An International Handbook*. Westport: Greenwood Press.

Chappelet, J. and Bayle, E. (2005). *Strategic and Performance Management of Olympic Sport Organisations*. Champaign, IL: Human Kinetics.

Chelladurai, P. (2006). *Human Resource Management in Sport and Recreation*. Champaign, IL: Human Kinetics.

Clarke, T. (ed.) (2004). *Theories of Corporate Governance*. Oxon, UK: Routledge.

Coakley, J., Hallinan, C. and McDonald, B. (2011). *Sports in Society: Sociological Issues and Controversies*. 2nd edn. North Ryde: McGraw Hill.

Colyer, S. (2000). Organizational culture in selected Western Australian sport organizations. *Journal of Sport Management*, 14: 321–341.

Cook, R.A. and Szumal, J.L. (1993). Measuring normative beliefs and shared behavioral expectations in organizations: The reliability and validity of the organizational culture inventory. *Psychological Reports*, 72: 1290–1330.

Cousens, L. and Slack, T. (2005). Field-level change: The case of North American major league professional sport. *Journal of Sport Management*, 19(1): 13–42.

Cuskelly, G. (2004). Volunteer retention in community sport organisations. *European Sport Management Quarterly*, 4: 59–76.

Cuskelly, G., Hoye, R. and Auld, C. (2006). *Working with Volunteers in Sport: Theory and Practice*. London: Routledge.

DaCosta, L. and Miragaya, A. (2002). Sport for all worldwide: A cross national and comparative research, in L. DaCosta and A. Miragaya (eds). *Worldwide Experiences and Trends in Sport For All*. Oxford: Meyer and Meyer.

Dejonghe, T. (2001). *Sport in de wereld: Ontstaan, evolutie en verspreiding*. Gent: Academia Press.

Deming, W. (1993). *The New Economics for Industry, Government, Education*. Cambridge, MA: MIT.

Denison, D. and Mishra, A. (1995). Toward a theory of organizational culture and effectiveness. *Organizational Science*, 6: 204–224.

Dess, G. and Lumpkin, G. (2003). *Strategic Management: Creating Competitive Advantages*. Boston: McGraw-Hill Irwin.

Dheensaw. C. (1994) *The Commonwealth Games: The First 60 Years, 1930–1990*. Sydney: ABC/Orca Publishing.

Doherty, A. (1998). Managing our human resources: A review of organizational behaviour in sport. *Journal of Sport Management*, 12(1): 1–24.

Dolles, H. and Soderman S. (2013). The network of value captures in football club management, in S. Soderman and H. Dolles (eds). *Handbook of Research on Sport and Business*. Cheltenham, UK: Edward Elgar, pp. 367–395.

Downward, P. and Dawson, A. (2000). *The Economics of Professional Team Sports*. London: Routledge.

Dressler, G. (2003). *Human Resource Management*. New Jersey: Prentice Hall.

Drucker, P.F. (1990). Lessons for successful nonprofit governance. *Nonprofit Management and Leadership*, 1: 7–14.

England Netball, (2007a). *Student Pack*. Hertfordshire, UK: England Netball.

England Netball, (2007b). *Annual Report 2006–2007*. Hertfordshire, UK: England Netball.

Euchner, C. (1993). *Playing the Field: Why Sports Teams Move and Cities Fight to Keep Them*. Baltimore: John Hopkins University Press.

Ferkins, L., Shilbury, D. and McDonald, G. (2009). Board involvement in strategy: Advancing the governance of sport organizations. *Journal of Sport Management*, 23: 245–277.

Ferrand, A. and Stotlar, D. (2010). Introduction: New perspectives in sport event marketing, *International Journal of Sport Management and Marketing*, 7(3–4): 145–155.

Fiedler, F. E. (1967). *A Theory of Leadership Effectiveness*. New York: McGraw-Hill

Fielding, L., Miller, L. and Brown, J. (1999). Harlem Globetrotters International, Inc. *Journal of Sport Management*, 13(1): 45–77.

Fletcher, K. (1999). Four books on nonprofit boards and governance. *Nonprofit Management and Leadership*, 9: 435–441.

Football Association (FA). (2008). *The FA's Vision 2008–2012*. London: FA

Football Governance Research Centre (2004). *The State of the Game: The Corporate Governance of Football Clubs 2004*, Research paper 2004 No. 3. Birkbeck, University of London: Football Governance Research Centre.

Fort, R. (2011). *Sport Economics*. 3rd edn. Upper Saddle River, NJ: Prentice Hall/Pearson.

Foster, G., Greyser, A. and Walsh, B. (2006). *The Business of Sports: Text and Cases on Strategy and Management*. Mason, OH: Thompson South-Western.

Friedman, M., Parent, M. and Mason, D. (2004). Building a framework for issues management in sport through stakeholder theory. *European Sport Management Quarterly*, 3: 170–190.

Frisby, W. (1986). The organizational structure and effectiveness of voluntary organizations: The case of Canadian national sport governing bodies. *Journal of Park and Recreation Administration*, 4: 61–74.

Frontiera, J. (2010). Leadership and organizational culture transformation in professional sport. *Journal of Leadership and Organizational Studies*, 17: 171–186.

Frosdick, S. and Walley, L. (eds) (1997). *Sport and Safety Management*. Oxford: Butterworth Heinemann.

Gardiner, S., Parrish, R. and Siekman, R. (2009). *EU, Sport, Law and Policy*. The Hague: Asser Press.

Goffee, R. and Jones, G. (1996). What holds the modern company together? *Harvard Business Review*, 74(6): 133–149.

Goldman , R. and Papson, S. (1998). *Nike Culture*. London: Sage.

Gomes. S., Kase, K. and Urrutia, I. (2010). *Value Creation and Sport Management*. Cambridge, UK: Cambridge University Press.

Graaff, A. (1996). Service quality and sport centres. *European Journal for Sport Management, xx/2*.

Grange, P. (2013). *The Bluestone Review: A Review of Culture and Leadership in Australian Olympic Swimming*. Melbourne, Australia: Bluestone Edge.

Gratton, C. and Taylor, P. (1991). *Government and the Economics of Sport*. London: Longman.

Gratton, C. and Taylor, P. (2000). *Economics of Sport and Recreation*. Milton Park, UK: Taylor and Francis.

Green, M. and Houlihan, B. (2005). *Elite Sport Development*. London: Routledge.

Green, M. (2006). From 'sport for all' to not about 'sport' at all: Interrogating sport policy interventions in the United Kingdom. *European Sport Management Quarterly*, 6(3): 217–238.

Greenfield, S. and Osborn, G. (2001). *Regulating Football; Commodification, Consumption and the Law*. London: Pluto Press.

Grix, J. (2009). The impact of UK sport policy on the governance of athletics. *International Journal of Sport Policy*, 1: 31–49.

Grix, J. and Dennis, M. (2012) *Sport Under Communism: The East German Experience*. Global Culture and Sport Series. Basingstoke, UK: Palgrave.

Halpern, D. (2005). *Social Capital*. Cambridge, UK: Polity Press.

Hamil, S., Morrow, S., Idle, C., Rossi, G. and Faccendini, S. (2010). The governance and regulation of Italian football. *Soccer & Society*, 11: 373–413

Hanlon, C. and Cuskelly, G. (2002). Pulsating major sport event organizations: A framework for inducting managerial personnel. *Event Management: An International Journal*, 7(4): 231–243.

Hart, L. (2006). *Accounting Demystified: A Self Teaching Guide*. New York: McGraw Hill.

Harvard Business Review (1998). *On Measuring Corporate Performance*. Boston: Harvard Business Review Press.

Heimovics, R.D. and Herman, R.D. (1990). Responsibility for critical events in nonprofit organizations. *Nonprofit and Voluntary Sector Quarterly*, 19: 59–72.

Henry, I. and Lee, P.C. (2004). Governance and ethics in sport, in J. Beech and S. Chadwick (eds). *The Business of Sport Management*. England: Prentice Hall.

Henry, I. and Uchium, K. (2001). Political ideology, modernity, and sport policy: A comparative analysis of sport policy in Britain and Japan. *Hitotsubashi Journal of Social Studies*, 33(2)1: 161–185.

Herman, R.D. and Heimovics, R. (1990). The effective nonprofit executive: Leader of the board. *Nonprofit Management and Leadership* 1: 167–180.

Herman, R.D. and Heimovics, R. (1994). Executive leadership, in R.D. Herman and Associates (eds). *The Jossey-Bass Handbook of Nonprofit Leadership and Management* (pp. 137–153). San Francisco: Jossey-Bass.

Herman, R.D. and Renz, D.O. (1997). Multiple constituencies and the social construction of nonprofit organizational effectiveness. *Nonprofit and Voluntary Sector Quarterly*, 26: 185–206.

Herman, R.D. and Renz, D.O. (1998). Nonprofit organizational effectiveness: Contrasts between especially effective and less effective organizations. *Nonprofit Management and Leadership*, 9: 23–38.

Herman, R.D. and Renz, D.O. (2000). Board practices of especially effective and less effective local nonprofit organizations. *American Review of Public Administration*, 30: 146–160.

Hersey, P. and Blanchard, K. (1977). *Management of Organizational Behaviour: Utilizing Human Resources*. Englewood Cliffs, NJ: Prentice-Hall.

Hess, R. Nicholson, M., Stewart, B. and de Moore, G. (2008). *A National Game: The History of Australian Rules Football*. Melbourne: Viking/Penguin.

Hess, R. and Stewart, R. (eds) (1998). *More than a Game: An Unauthorised History of Australian Football*. Melbourne: Melbourne University Press.

Hill, L.A. (2008). 'Where will we find tomorrow's leaders?' *Harvard Business Review*, 86(1): 123–129.

Hillary Commission (2000). *The Growing Business of Sport and Leisure: The Impact of the Physical Leisure Industry in New Zealand*. Wellington, New Zealand: Hillary Commission.

Hilton, K. and Bramham, P. (2008). *Sports Development: Policy, Processes and Practice*. Routledge, London.

Hindley, D. (2003). *Resource Guide in Governance and Sport*, Learning and teaching support network in Hospitality, Leisure, Sport and Tourism at www.hlst.ltsn.ac.uk/resources/governance.html

Hockey Canada (2007). *Annual Report 2007*. Calgary, CA: Hockey Canada.

Hoehn, T. and Lancefield, D. (2003). Broadcasting and sport. *Oxford Review of Economic Policy*, 19(4): 552–568.

Hofstede, G. (1991). *Cultures and Organizations: Software of the Mind*. McGraw Hill, London.

Hofstede, G. (2001). *Culture's Consequences: Comparing Values, Behaviors, Institutions and Organizations Across Nations*. Thousand Oaks, CA: Sage.

Hofstede, G., Neuijen, B., Ohayv, D. and Sanders, G. (1990). Measuring organizational cultures: A qualitative and quantitative study across twenty cases. *Administrative Science Quarterly*, 35: 286–316.

Hoggett, J., Edwards, L. and Medlin, J. (2006). *Accounting*. 6th edn. Milton: Wiley.

Hong, F. (1997). Commercialism and sport in China. *Journal of Sport Management*, (11): 343–354.

Horne, D. (1964). *The Lucky Country: Australia in the 1960s*. Ringwood: Penguin Books.

Houle, C.O. (1960). *The Effective Board*. New York: Association Press.

Houle, C.O. (1997). *Governing Boards: Their Nature and Nurture*. San Francisco: Jossey-Bass.

Houlihan, B. (1997). *Sport Policy and Politics: A Comparative Analysis*. London: Routledge.

Houlihan, B. and Green, M. (2007). *Comparative Elite Sport Development. Systems, Structures and Public Policy*. London: Elsevier.

Houlihan, B. and White, A. (2002). *The Politics of Sport Development: Development of Sport or Development through Sport?* London: Routledge.

House, R.J. (1971). A path-goal theory of leader effectiveness. *Administrative Science Quarterly*, 16: 321–338

House, R.J. and Mitchell, T.R. (1974). Path-goal theory of leadership. *Contemporary Business*, 3(Fall): 81–91.

Howard, D. and Crompton, J. (2004). *Financing Sport*. 2nd edn. Morgantown, WV: Fitness Information Technology.

Howard, L. (1998). Validating the competing values model as a representation of organizational cultures. *International Journal of Organizational Analysis*, 6(3): 231–251.

Hoye, R. and Cuskelly, G. (2003). Board-executive relationships within voluntary sport organisations. *Sport Management Review*, 6(1): 53–73.

Hoye, R. and Inglis, S. (2003). Governance of nonprofit leisure organisations, *Society and Leisure*. 26(2): 369–387.

Hoye, R. and Cuskelly, G. (2007). *Sport Governance*. Oxford: Elsevier Butterworth-Heinemann.

Hoye, R., Nicholson, M. and Houlihan, B. (2010). *Sport and Policy: Issues and Analysis*. Oxford, UK: Elsevier/Butterworth Heinemann.

Hoye, R., Nicholson, M. and Smith, A. (2008). Unique aspects of managing sport organizations, in C. Wankel (ed.). *21st Century Management: A Reference Handbook*. Thousand Oaks, CA: Sage, 499–507.

Hughes, H. (1981). *News and the Human Interest Story*. London: Transaction Books [reprint of the 1940 University of Chicago Press edition].

Hums, M. and Maclean, J. (2009). *Governance and Policy in Sport Organizations*. 2nd edn. Scottsdale, Arizona: Holcomb Hathaway.

Hylton, K. and Bramham, P. (eds) (2007). *Sports Development: Policy, Process and Practice*. 2nd edn. London: Routledge.

Hylton, K., Bramham, P., Jackson, D. and Nesti, M. (eds) (2001). *Sport Development*. London: Routledge.

Institute for Volunteering Research (2008). *Management Matters: A National Survey of Volunteer Management Capacity*. London, UK: Institute for Volunteering Research

Institute for Volunteering Research and Volunteering England (2008). *A Winning Team? The Impacts of Volunteers in Sport*. London, UK: Institute for Volunteering Research.

International Monetary Fund (2000–2005). *Globalization: Threat or Opportunity?* Retrieved 1 March 2005 from: www.imf.org/external/np/exr/ib/2000/041200.htm

Jaggard, E. (2006). *Between the Flags: One Hundred Summers of Australian Surf Lifesaving*. Sydney: UNSW Press.

Jarzabkowski, P. and Spee, P.A. (2009). Strategy-as-practice: A review and future directions for the field. *International Journal of Management Reviews*, 11: 69–95.

Jensen, R. (1999). *The Dream Society*. New York: McGraw-Hill.

John, G. and Sheard, R. (1997). *Stadia: A Design and Development Guide*. Oxford, UK: Architectural Press.

Johnson, G. and Scholes, K. (2002). *Exploring Corporate Strategy*. 6th edn. London: Prentice-Hall.

Johnson, G., Langley, A., Melin, L. and Whittington, R. (2007). *Strategy as Practice: Research Directions and Resources*. New York: Cambridge University Press.

Johnson, G., Scholes, K. and Whittington, R. (2008). *Exploring Corporate Strategy*. 8th edn. London: Prentice-Hall.

Johnson, G., Whittington, R., Scholes, K., Angwin, D. and Regner, P. (2014). *Exploring Corporate Strategy*. 10th edn. London: Prentice-Hall.

Jung, T., Scott, T., Davies, H.T.O., Bower, P., Whalley, D., McNally, R. and Russell, M. (2009). Instruments for exploring organizational culture: A review of the literature. *Public Administration Review*, 69(6): 1087–1096.

Kahle, L. and Close, A. (eds) (2011). *Consumer Behavior Knowledge for Effective Sports and Event Marketing*. New York: Taylor & Francis.

Kaplan, R. and Norton, D. (1992). The balanced scorecard: Measures that drive performance. *Harvard Business Review* (January–February): 71–79.

Kaplan, R. and Norton, D. (1996). *The Balanced Scorecard*. Boston: Harvard University Press.

Kikulis, L.M., Slack, T., Hinings, B. and Zimmermann, A. (1989). A structural taxonomy of amateur sport organizations. *Journal of Sport Management*, 3: 129–150.

Kikulis, L.M., Slack, T. and Hinings, B. (1992). Institutionally specific design archetypes: A framework for understanding change in national sport organizations. *International Review for the Sociology of Sport*, 27: 343–367.

Kikulis, L.M., Slack, T. and Hinings, B. (1995). Toward an understanding of the role of agency and choice in the changing structure of Canada's national sport organizations. *Journal of Sport Management*, 9: 135–152.

King, N. (2009). *Sport Policy and Governance: Local Perspectives*. Jordon Hill, UK; Elsevier/Butterworth Heinemann.

Kotter, J.P. (1990). *A Force for Change: How Leadership Differs from Management.* New York: The Free Press.

Kouzes, J.M. and Posner, B.Z. (2006). *A Leader's Legacy.* Hoboken: Jossey-Bass.

Leisure Industries Research Centre (2003). *Sports Volunteering in England 2002: A Report for Sport England.* Sheffield, UK: Author.

Lewis, G. (1993). Concepts in strategic management, in G. Lewis, A. Morkel and G. Hubbard (eds). *Australian Strategic Management: Concepts, Context and Cases.* Sydney: Prentice-Hall, pp. 5–38.

Li, M., Hofacre, S. and Mahony, D. (2001). *Economics of Sport.* Morgantown, USA: Fitness Information Technology.

Locke, E.A. (1991). *The Essence of Leadership: The Four Keys to Leading Successfully.* New York: Lexington Books.

Lyons, M. (2001). *Third Sector: The Contribution of Nonprofit and Cooperative Enterprises in Australia.* Crows Nest, NSW, Australia: Allen and Unwin.

MacLean, J. (2001). *Performance Appraisal for Sport and Recreation Managers.* Champaign, IL: Human Kinetics.

MacLean, J. (2009). Auditing performance management practices: A comparison of Canadian sport organisations. *International Journal of Sport Management and Marketing,* 5(3): 295–309.

Mannell, R. and Kleiber, D. (2013) Psychology of leisure, in T. Blackshaw (ed.). *Routledge Handbook of Leisure Studies.* London: Routledge.

Mason, D., Andrews, D. and Silk, M. (eds) (2005). *Qualitative Methods for Sports Studies.* Oxford: Berg.

McCarthy, J. (2007). The ingredients of financial transparency. *Nonprofit & Voluntary Sector Quarterly,* 36(1): 156–164.

McDonald, I. (2011). High performance sport policy in the UK, in B. Houlihan and M. Green. *Routledge Handbook of Sport Development.* London: Routledge.

Mechikoff, R. and Estes, S. (1993). *A History and Philosophy of Sport and Physical Education.* Madison: Brown and Benchmark.

Miles, R.E. (1975). *Theories of Management: Implications for Organizational Behaviour and Development.* New York, McGraw-Hill.

Miller, T., Lawrence, G., McKay, J. and Rowe, D. (2001). *Globalisation and Sport.* London: Sage.

Muller, C., Lammert, J. and Hovemann, G. (2012). The financial fair play regulations of EUFA: An adequate concept to ensure the long term viability and sustainability of European club football. *International Journal of Sport Finance,* 7: 117–140.

National Intelligence Council (2000). *Global Trends 2015: A Dialogue about the Future with Non Government Experts.* Washington DC: National Foreign Intelligence Board.

New, B. and LeGrand, J. (1999). Monopoly in sports broadcasting. *Policy Studies,* 20(1): 23–36.

Nicholson, M. (2007). *Sport and the Media: Managing the Nexus.* London: Elsevier Butterworth-Heinemann.

Norman, W. and MacDonald, C. (2004). Getting to the bottom of 'triple bottom-line accounting'. *Business Ethics Quarterly,* 14(2): 243–262.

Northouse, P.G. (2010). *Leadership: Theory and Practice,* 5th edn. Thousand Oaks: Sage Publications.

O'Brien, D. and Slack, T. (2003) An analysis of change in an organizational field: The professionalization of English Rugby Union. *Journal of Sport Management,* 17(4): 417–448.

Ogbonna, E. and Harris, L.C. (2002). Organizational culture: A ten year, two-phase study of change in the UK food retailing sector. *Journal of Management Studies,* 39: 673–706.

Organisation for Economic Co-operation and Development (2004). *Principles of Corporate Governance.* Paris: OECD.

Oriard, M. (1993). *Reading Football.* Chapel Hill: University of North Carolina Press.

Parent, M., O'Brien, D. and Slack, T. (2003). Strategic management in the context of sport, in L. Trenberth (ed.). *Managing the Business of Sport* (pp. 101–122). Palmerston North, New Zealand: Dunmore Press.

Pattavino, P. and Pye, G. (1994). *Sport in Cuba: The Diamond in the Rough.* Pittsburgh, PA: University of Pittsburgh Press.

Perryman, M. (ed.) (2001). *Hooligan Wars: Causes and Effects of Football Violence.* Edinburgh: Mainstream Publishing.

Pettigrew, A.M. (1979). On studying organizational cultures. *Administrative Science Quarterly,* 24: 570–581.

Pfeffer, J. and Salancik, G. (1978). *The External Control of Organizations: A Resource Dependence Perspective.* New York: Harper & Row.

Pitt, L., Parent, M., Berthon, P. and Steyn, P. (2010). Event sponsorship and ambush marketing: Lessons from the Beijing Olympics, *Business Horizons,* 53: 281–290.

Porter, M. (1980). *Competitive Strategy.* New York: The Free Press.

Porter, M. (1985). *Competitive Strategy: Creating and Sustaining Superior Performance*: Simon & Schuster, New York.

Porter, M. (1996). What is strategy? *Harvard Business Review,* November–December: 61–78.

Productivity Commission (2003). *Social Capital: Reviewing the Concept and its Policy Implications.* Canberra: Commonwealth of Australia.

Productivity Commission (2010). *Contribution of the Not-for-Profit Sector.* Canberra: Commonwealth of Australia.

Putnam, R. (2000). *Bowling Alone: The Collapse and Revival of American Community.* New York: Simon and Schuster.

Quinn, K. (2009). *Sports and their Fans: The History, Economics and Culture of the Relationship between Spectator and Sport.* Jefferson, NC: McFarland and Co.

Quinn, R. and Rohrbaugh, J. (1983). A spatial model of effectiveness criteria: Towards a competing values approach to organizational analysis. *Management Science,* 29: 363–377.

Quirk, J. and Fort, R. (1992). *Pay Dirt: The Business of Professional Team Sports.* Princeton: Princeton University Press.

Rein, I., Kotler, P. and Shields, B. (2006). *The Elusive Fan: Reinventing Sports in a Crowded Marketplace.* New York: McGraw-Hill.

Rigauer, B. (1981). *Sport and Work.* Columbia: Columbia University Press.

Riordan, J. (1977). *Sport in Soviet Society.* Cambridge: Cambridge University Press.

Riordan, J. (ed.) (1978). *Sport Under Communism: The U.S.S.R., Czechoslovakia, The G.D.R., China, Cuba.* Canberra: Australian National University Press.

Robbins, S. (1990). *Organization Theory: Structure Design & Applications.* New Jersey: Prentice Hall.

Robbins, S. and Barnwell, N. (2002). *Organisation Theory.* Frenchs Forest: Pearson Education Australia.

Robbins, S.P., Bergman, R., Stagg, I. and Coulter, M. (2004). *Management.* 3rd edn. Sydney, Australia: Pearson Education.

Robbins, S.P., Judge, T., Millett, B. and Boyle, M. (2010). *Organizational Behaviour.* 6th edn. Sydney, Australia: Pearson Education.

Robinson, L. (2004). Human resource management. In L. Robinson, *Managing Public Sport and Leisure Services.* London: Routledge.

Rowe, D. (1999). *Sport, Culture and the Media: The Unruly Trinity.* Buckingham, Philadelphia: Open University Press.

Rowe, D. and Callum, G. (2010). Sport, media, and consumption in Asia: A merchandised milieu, *American Behavioral Scientist,* 53(10): 1530–1548.

Sandy, R., Sloane, P.J. and Rosentraub, M. (2004). *The Economics of Sport: An International Perspective.* Basingstoke: Palgrave Macmillan.

Sashkin, M. (1996). *Organizational Beliefs Questionnaire: Pillars of Excellence.* Amherst, MA: Human Resource Development Press.

Schein, E. (1984). *Coming to a New Awareness of Organizational Culture*. San Francisco: Jossey-Bass.

Schein, E. (1985). How culture forms, develops and changes, in R.H. Kilman, M.J. Saxton, R. Serpa and Associates (eds). *Gaining Control of the Corporate Culture* (pp. 17–43). San Francisco, CA: Jossey-Bass.

Schein, E. (2004). *Organizational Culture and Leadership*. 3rd edn. San Francisco: Jossey-Bass.

Schein, E. (2010). *Organizational Culture and Leadership*. 4th edn. San Francisco: Jossey-Bass.

Schermerhorn, J.R., Hunt, J.G. and Osborne, R.N. (1994). *Managing Organizational Behaviour*. 5th edn. Brisbane: John Wiley & Sons, Inc.

Schroeder, P.J. (2010). Changing team culture: The perspectives of ten successful head coaches. *Journal of Sport Behavior*, 33(1): 63–88.

Schudson, M. (1978) *Discovering The News: A Social History of American Newspapers*. New York: Basic Books.

Senge, P. (1990). *The Fifth Discipline*. New York: Currency Doubleday.

Shibli, S. and Wilson, R. (2012). Budgeting and budgetary control in sport, in L. Trenberth and D. Hassan (eds). *Managing Sport Business: An Introduction*. London: Routledge, pp. 185–208.

Shilbury, D., Quick, S. and Westerbeek, H. (2003) *Strategic Sport Marketing*, 2nd edn. New South Wales, Australia: Allen & Unwin.

Shilbury, D., Westerbeek, H., Quick, S. and Funk, D. (2009). *Strategic Sport Marketing*. 3rd edn. Sydney: Allen & Unwin.

Shropshire, K. (1995). *The Sports Franchise Game*. Philadelphia: University of Pennsylvania Press.

Shropshire, K. and Davis, T. (2008). *The Business of Sports Agents*. 2nd edn. Philadelphia, PA: University of Pennsylvania Press.

Slack, T. (1997). *Understanding sport organizations: The application of organization theory*. Champaign, IL: Human Kinetics.

Slack, T. and Parent, M. (2006). *Understanding Sport Organizations: The Application of Organization Theory*. 2nd edn. Champaign, IL: Human Kinetics.

Slesinger, L.H. (1991). *Self-assessment for Nonprofit Governing Boards*. Washington, DC: National Centre for Nonprofit Boards.

Smit, B. (2007). *Pitch Invasion: Adidas, Puma, and the Making of Modern Sport*. London: Penguin Books.

Smith, A. (2008). *Introduction to Sport Marketing*. Oxford: Elsevier Butterworth-Heinemann.

Smith, A. and Shilbury, D. (2004). Mapping cultural dimensions in Australian sporting organizations. *Sport Management Review*, 7(2): 133–165.

Smith, A. and Stewart, B. (1999). *Sports Management: A Guide to Professional Practice*. Sydney: Allen & Unwin.

Smith, A. and Stewart, B. (2010). The special features of sport revisited. *Sport Management Review*, 10(1): 1–11.

Smith A. and Stewart, R. (2013). The special features of sport: a critical revisit, in S. Soderman and H. Dolles (eds). *Handbook of Research on Sport and Business*. Cheltenham, UK: Edward Elgar, 526–547.

Smith, A., Stewart, B. and Haimes, G. (2011). *The Performance Identity: Building High-Performance Organizational Cultures in Sport*. New York: Nova Science Publishers.

Soares, J. and Correia, A. (2009). Factors and focuses in the strategic decisions of sporting organisations: Empirical evidence in sports associations, *International Journal of Sport Management and Marketing*, 5(3): 338–354.

Sport England (2011a). *Clubmark factsheet*. London, UK: Sport England.

Sport England (2011b). *Sport Makers factsheet*. London, UK: Sport England.

Standing Committee on Recreation and Sport Working Party on Management Improvement (1997). *Report to the Standing Committee on Recreation and Sport July 1997*. Canberra, Australia: Author.

Statistics Canada (2004). *Cornerstones of Community: Highlights of the National Survey of Nonprofit and Voluntary Organizations*. Ottowa, Canada: Author.

Statistics Canada (2008). *Sports Participation in Canada, 2005*. Ottowa, Canada: Author.

Stebbins, R. (2007). *Serious Leisure*. New Jersey: Transaction Publishers.

Stensholt, J. and Thomson, J. (2005). Kicking goals. *Business Review Weekly*, 10–16 March: 38–42.

Stevens, J. (2006). The Canadian Hockey Association merger and the emergence of the Amateur Sport Enterprise. *Journal of Sport Management*, 20: 74–101.

Stewart, B. (2007a). *Sport Funding and Finance*. Oxford: Elsevier Butterworth-Heinemann.

Stewart, B. (ed.) (2007b). *The Games Are Not the Same: The Political Economy of Football in Australia*. Melbourne: Melbourne University Press.

Stewart, R. (1989). The nature of sport under capitalism and its relationship to the capitalist labour process. *Sporting Traditions*, 6(1): 43–61.

Stewart, R. and Smith, A. (1999). The special features of sport. *Annals of Leisure Research*, 2: 87–99.

Stewart, R., Nicholson, M., Smith, A. and Westerbeek, H. (2004). *Australian Sport: Better by Design? The Evolution of Australian Sport Policy*. London: Routledge.

Stoldt, C. (2013). 'College Athletics Communications', in P. Pedersen (ed.). *Routledge Handbook of Sport Communication*. London: Routledge.

Surf Life Saving Australia (SLSA) (2010). Annual Report: 2009–2010. Sydney: SLSA.

Szymanksi, S. (2009). *Playbooks and Chequebooks: An Introduction to the Economics of Modern Sport*. Princeton, NJ: Princeton University Press.

Szymanski, S. and Kuypers, T. (2000). *Winners and Losers: The Business Strategy of Football*. London: Viking.

Taylor, T., Doherty, A. and McGraw, P. (2008). *Managing People in Sport Organizations: A Strategic Human Resource Management Perspective*. London: Elsevier Butterworth-Heinemann.

Theodoraki, E.I. and Henry, I.P. (1994). Organizational structures and contexts in British national governing bodies of sport. *International Review for the Sociology of Sport*, 29: 243–263.

Thibault, L., Slack, T. and Hinings, B. (1991). Professionalism, structures and systems: The impact of professional staff on voluntary sport organizations. *International Review for the Sociology of Sport*, 26: 83–97.

Thomas, R.J. (2008). *Crucibles of Leadership*. Boston: Harvard Business School Publishing Corporation.

Tonazzi, A. (2003). Competition policy and the commercialization of sport broadcasting rights: The decision of the Italian competition authority. *International Journal of the Economics of Business*, 10(1): 17–34.

Tricker, R.I. (1984). *Corporate Governance*. London: Gower.

Tricker, R.I. (1993). Corporate governance – the new focus of interest. *Corporate Governance*, 1(1): 1–3.

UEFA (2007). Financial Report 2006–2007. Nyon, Switzerland: UEFA.

Van der Post, W. and de Coning, T. (1997). An instrument to measure organizational culture. *South African Journal of Business Management*, 28(4): 147–169.

Viljoen, J. and Dann, S. (2003). *Strategic Management*. 4th edn. Frenchs Forest, NSW, Australia: Prentice Hall.

Volunteering Australia (2004). *Snapshot 2004: Volunteering Report Card*. Melbourne, Australia: Volunteering Australia.

Vrooman, J. (2012) The economic structure of the NFL, in K. Quinn (ed.). *The Economics of the National Football League: The State of the Art*. New York: Springer.

Ward, T. (2010). *Sport in Australian National Identity*. London: Taylor & Francis.

Westerbeek, H.M. and Smith, A.C.T. (2003). *Sport Business in the Global Marketplace*. London: Palgrave Macmillan.

Westerbeek, H. and Smith, A. (2005). *Business Leadership and the Lessons from Sport*. London: Palgrave Macmillan.

Wexley, K.N. and Yukl, G.A. (1984). *Organizational Behaviour and Personnel Psychology.* Revised edn. Homewood, Illinois: Richard D. Irwin, Inc.

Whitson, D. (1998). Circuits of promotion: Media, marketing and the globalization of sport, in L. Wenner (ed.). *MediaSport.* London: Routledge, pp. 57–72.

Wicker P., Breuer, C. and Pawlowski, T. (2010). Are sports club members big spenders? Findings from sport-specific analysis in Germany. *International Journal of Sport Finance,* 6: 155–169.

Williams, R. (1998). *Performance Management: Perspectives on Employee Performance.* London: Thomson Business Press.

Zimbalist, A. (2006). *The Bottom Line: Observations and Arguments in the Sports Business.* Philadelphia, PA: Temple University Press.

Index

Please note that page references to Figures or Tables are in *italics*.